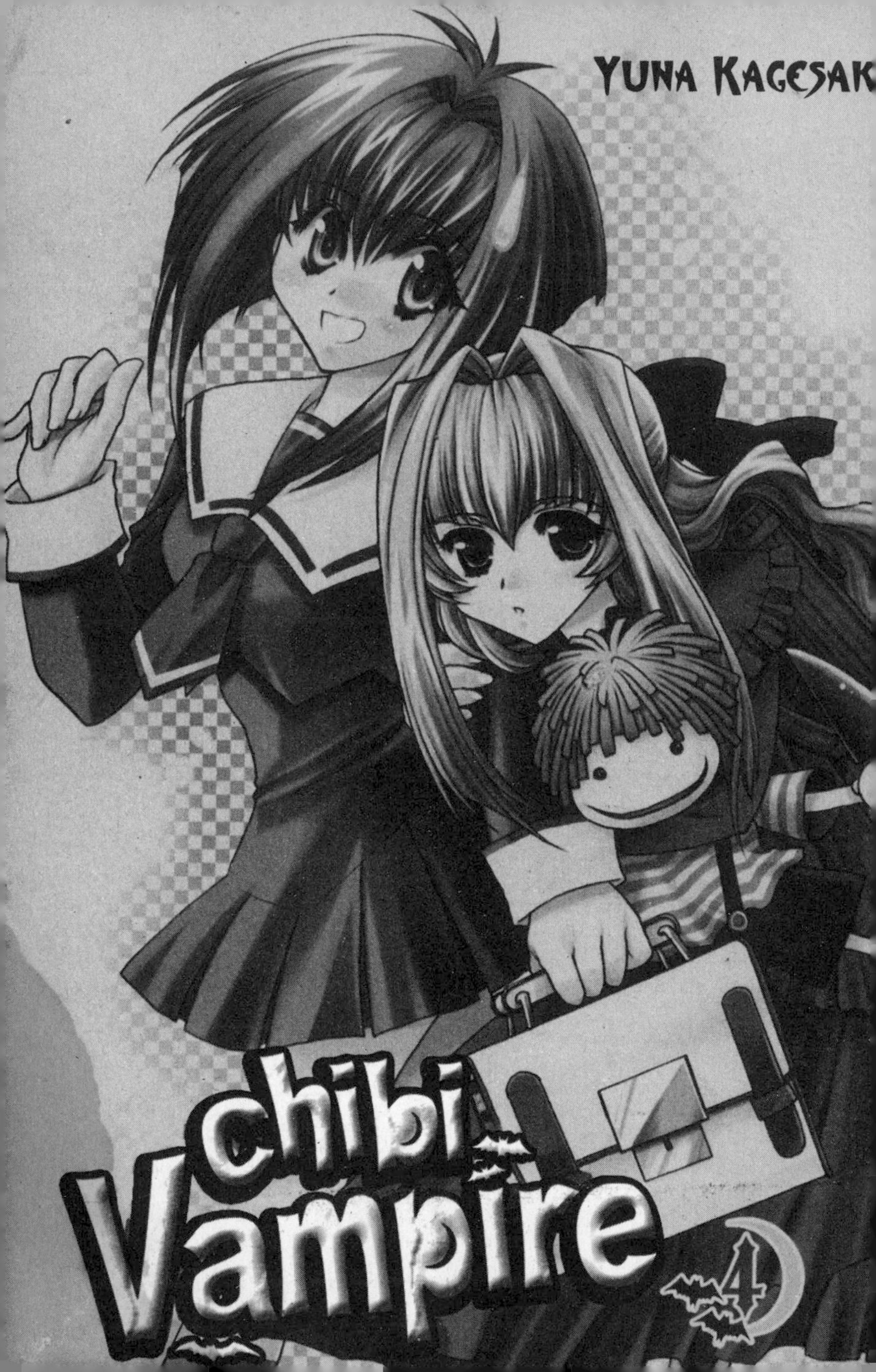
YUNA KAGESAK
chibi Vampire
4

## *Chibi Vampire Vol. 4*
## Created by Yuna Kagesaki

Translation - Alexis Kirsch
English Adaptation - Christine Boylan
Retouch and Lettering - Star Print Brokers
Production Artist - Courtney Geter
Graphic Designer - Fawn Lau

Editor - Tim Beedle
Digital Imaging Manager - Chris Buford
Pre-Production Supervisor - Erika Terriquez
Art Director - Anne Marie Horne
Production Manager - Elisabeth Brizzi
Managing Editor - Vy Nguyen
VP of Production - Ron Klamert
Editor-in-Chief - Rob Tokar
Publisher - Mike Kiley
President and C.O.O. - John Parker
C.E.O. and Chief Creative Officer - Stuart Levy

A 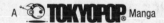 Manga

TOKYOPOP and 🐸 are trademarks or registered trademarks of TOKYOPOP Inc.

TOKYOPOP Inc.
5900 Wilshire Blvd. Suite 2000
Los Angeles, CA 90036

E-mail: info@TOKYOPOP.com
Come visit us online at www.TOKYOPOP.com

KARIN Volume 4© YUNA KAGESAKI 2004 First published in Japan in 2004 by KADOKAWA SHOTEN PUBLISHING CO., LTD., Tokyo. English translation rights arranged with KADOKAWA SHOTEN PUBLISHING CO., LTD., Tokyo through TUTTLE–MORI AGENCY, INC., Tokyo. English text copyright © 2007 TOKYOPOP Inc.

ISBN: 978-1-59816-325-4

First TOKYOPOP printing: April 2007
10 9 8 7
Printed in the USA

# Chibi Vampire

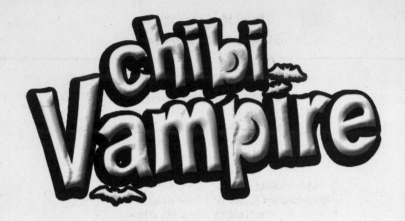

## Volume 4

Created by

Yuna Kagesaki

TOKYOPOP®

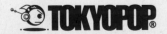

HAMBURG // LONDON // LOS ANGELES // TOKYO

# OUR STORY SO FAR...

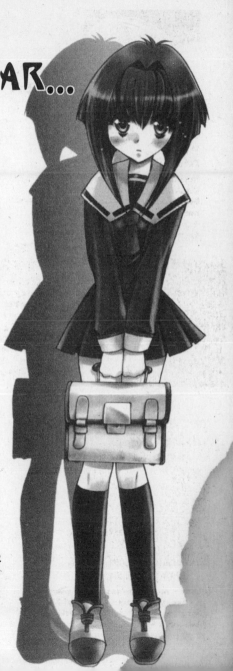

KARIN MAAKA ISN'T LIKE OTHER GIRLS. ONCE A MONTH, SHE EXPERIENCES PAIN, FATIGUE, HUNGER, IRRITABILITY—AND THEN SHE BLEEDS. FROM HER NOSE. KARIN IS A VAMPIRE, FROM A FAMILY OF VAMPIRES, BUT INSTEAD OF NEEDING TO DRINK BLOOD, SHE HAS AN EXCESS OF BLOOD THAT SHE MUST GIVE TO HER VICTIMS. IF DONE RIGHT, GIVING THIS BLOOD TO HER VICTIM CAN BE AN EXTREMELY POSITIVE THING. THE PROBLEM WITH THIS IS THAT KARIN NEVER SEEMS TO DO THINGS RIGHT...

KARIN IS HAVING A BIT OF BOY TROUBLE. KENTA USUI—THE HANDSOME NEW STUDENT AT HER SCHOOL AND WORK—IS A NICE ENOUGH GUY, BUT HE EXACERBATES KARIN'S PROBLEM. KARIN, YOU SEE, IS DRAWN TO PEOPLE WHO HAVE SUFFERED MISFORTUNE, AND KENTA HAS SUFFERED PLENTY OF IT. KARIN DISCOVERED THIS WHEN SHE BIT KENTA'S MOTHER, AN INCIDENT THAT WAS UNFORTUNATELY WITNESSED BY KENTA. NOW, KARIN'S CONVINCED THAT SHE CAN KEEP HER NOSEBLEEDS UNDER CONTROL AS LONG AS SHE KEEPS KENTA HAPPY, AND KENTA HAS PROMISED KARIN'S PARENTS THAT HE'D HELP HER OUT DURING THE DAYTIME. A SIMPLE ENOUGH PLAN, BUT IT'S ABOUT TO BECOME A LOT MORE COMPLICATED. REN, KARIN'S OLDER BROTHER, IS DRAWN TO WOMEN WHO ARE STRESSED, AND IT NOW SEEMS THAT HE'S SET HIS SIGHTS ON KENTA'S MOTHER. WILL THE SIBLING RIVALRY BETWEEN THESE TWO VAMPS BECOME BLOODY?

# THE MAAKA FAMILY

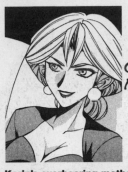

## CALERA MARKER

**Karin's overbearing mother. While Calera resents that Karin wasn't born a normal vampire, she does love her daughter in her own obnoxious way. Calera has chosen to keep her European last name.**

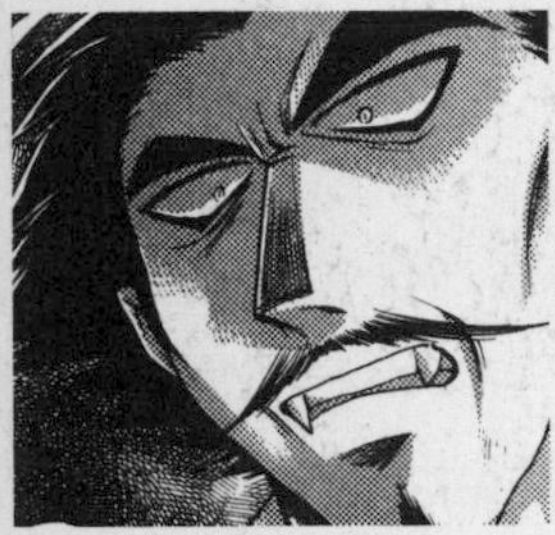

## HENRY MARKER

**Karin's father. In general, Henry treats Karin a lot better than she's treated by her mother, but the pants in this particular family are worn by Calera. Henry has also chosen to keep his European last name.**

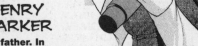

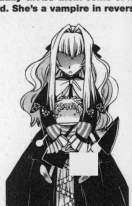

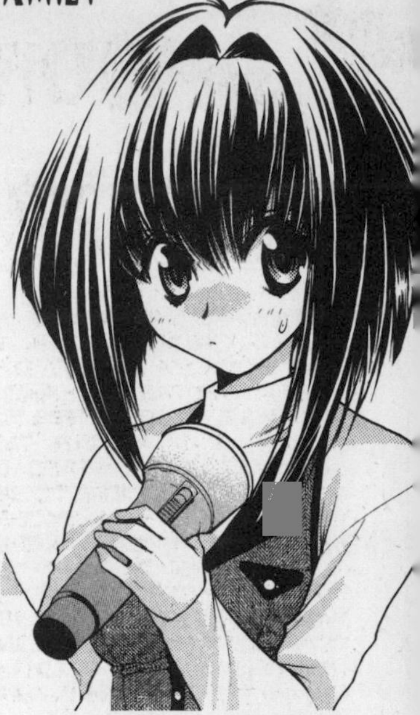

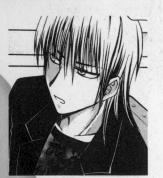

## REN MAAKA

**Karin's older brother. Ren milks the "sexy creature of the night" thing for all it's worth, and spends his nights in the arms (and beds) of attractive young women.**

## KARIN MAAKA

**Our little heroine. Karin is a vampir living in Japan, but instead o sucking blood from her victims, sh actually GIVES them some of he blood. She's a vampire in revers**

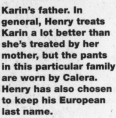

## ANJU MAAKA

**Karin's little sister. Anju has no yet awoken as a full vampire, bu she can control bats and is usuall the one who cleans up after Karin' messes. Rarely seen without he "talking" doll, Boogie**

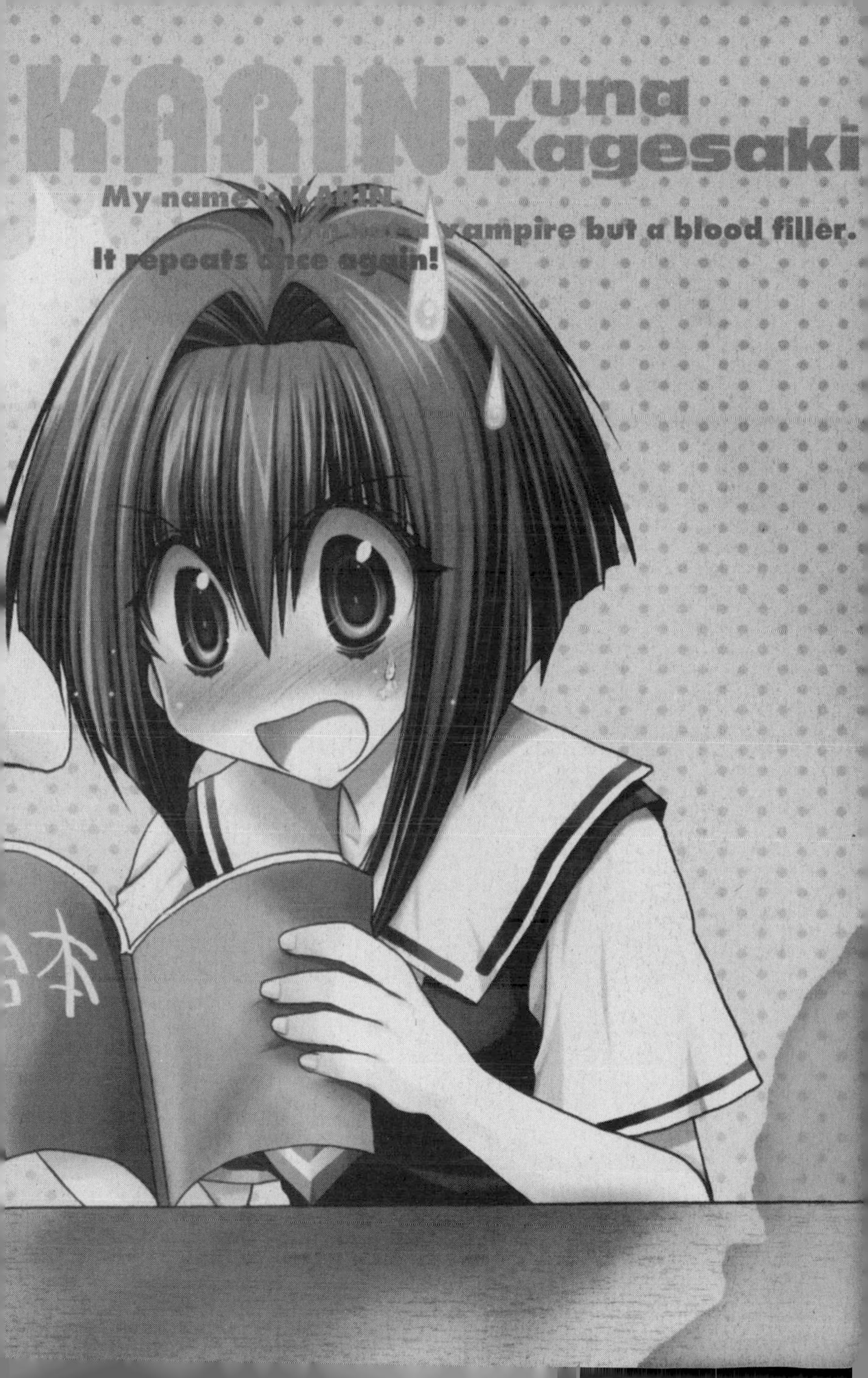
KARIN
Yuna Kagesaki
My name is KARIN.
vampire but a blood filler.
It repeats once again!

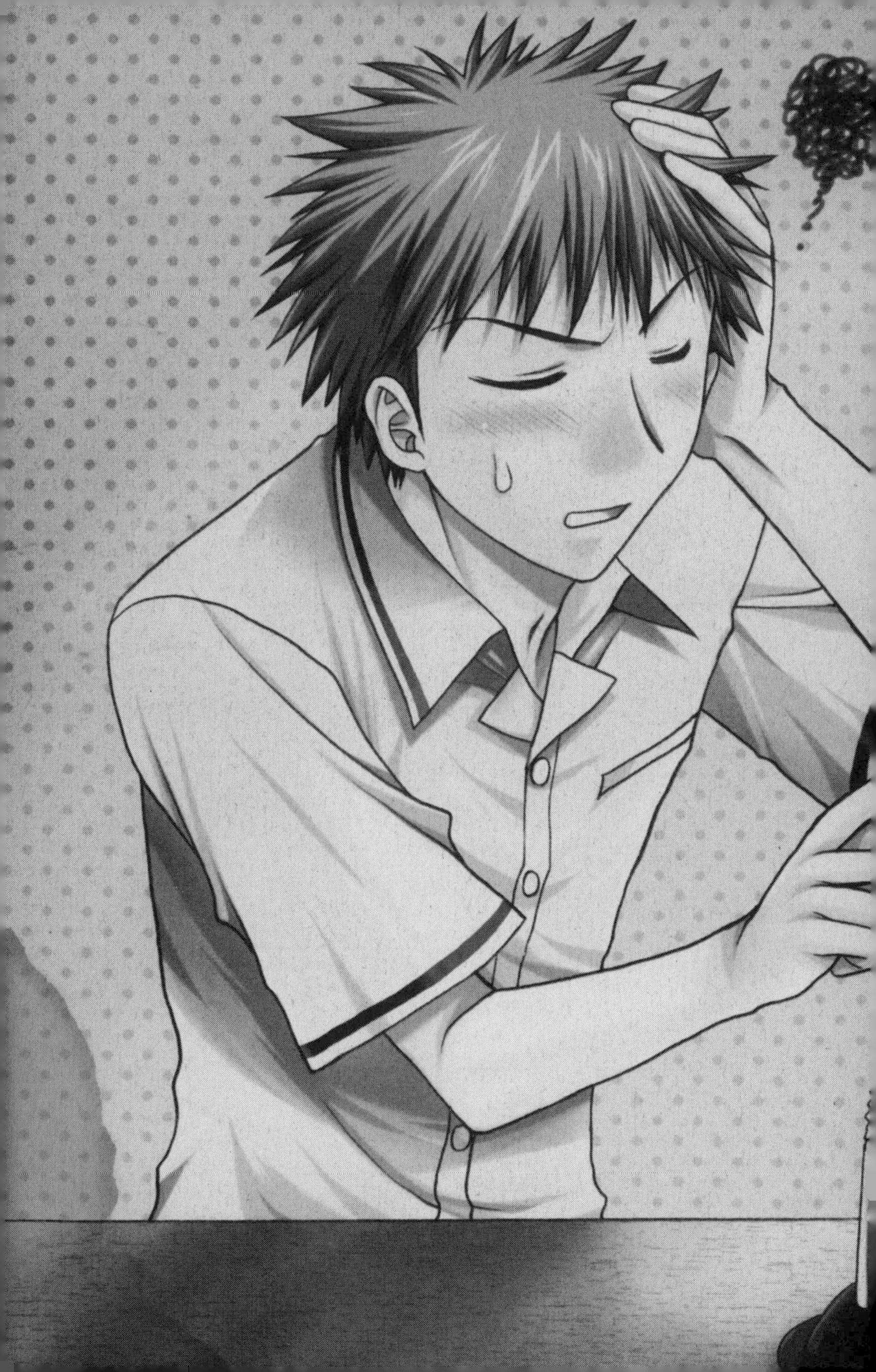

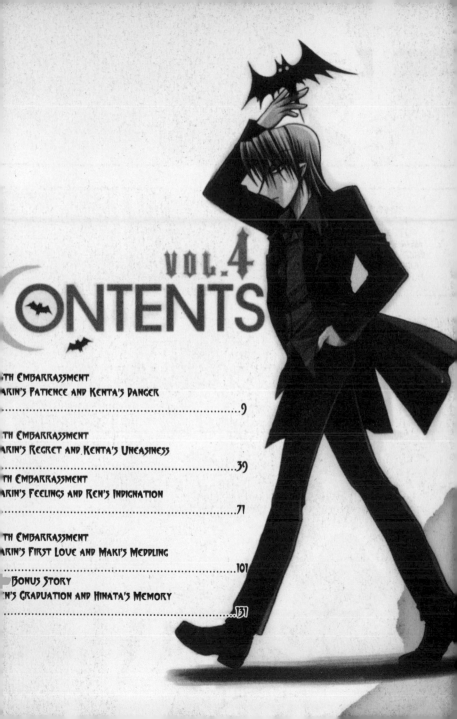

# VOL.4

# CONTENTS

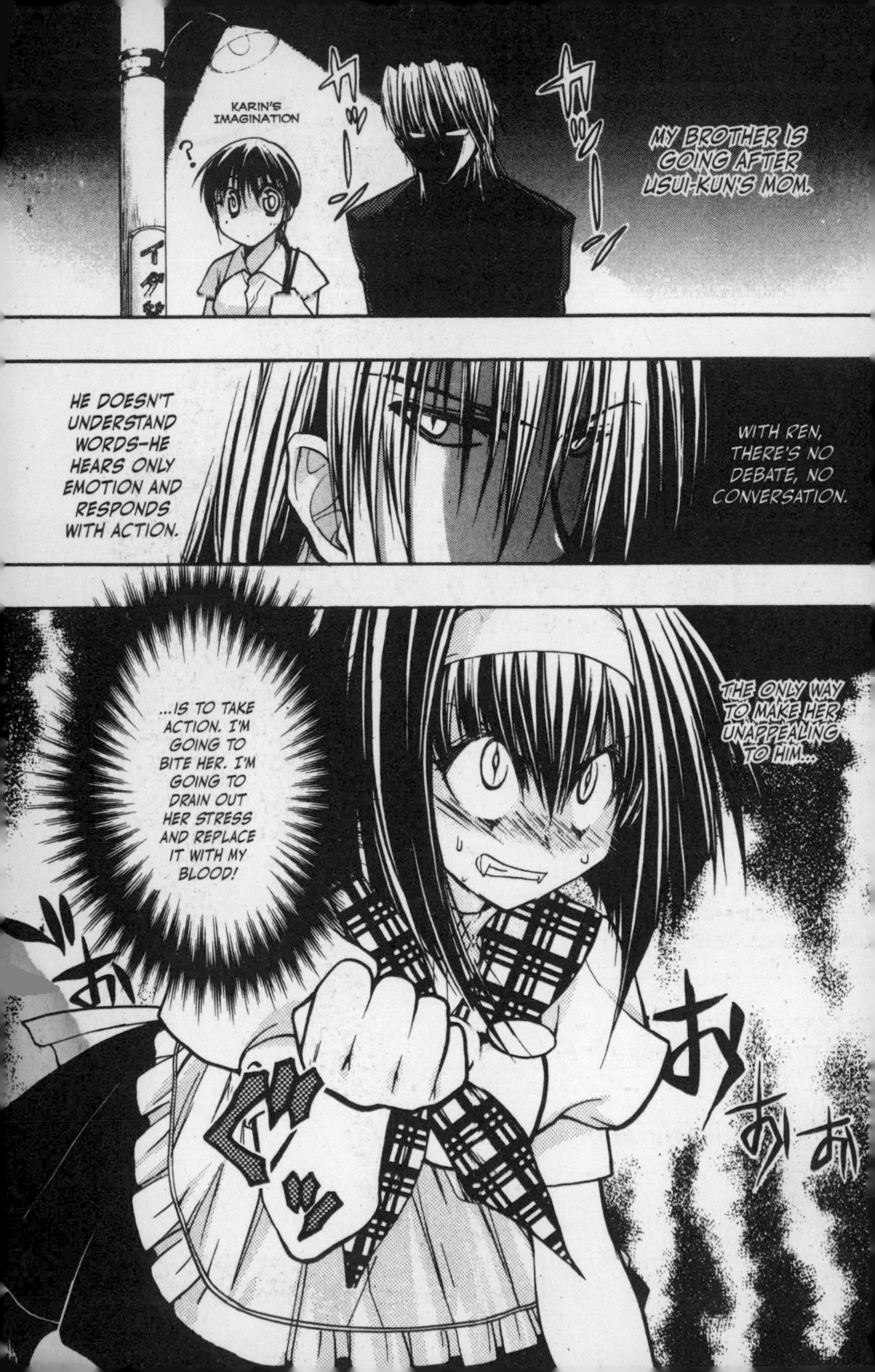
MY BROTHER IS GOING AFTER USUI-KUN'S MOM.
KARIN'S IMAGINATION
WITH REN, THERE'S NO DEBATE, NO CONVERSATION.
HE DOESN'T UNDERSTAND WORDS—HE HEARS ONLY EMOTION AND RESPONDS WITH ACTION.
THE ONLY WAY TO MAKE HER UNAPPEALING TO HIM...
...IS TO TAKE ACTION. I'M GOING TO BITE HER. I'M GOING TO DRAIN OUT HER STRESS AND REPLACE IT WITH MY BLOOD!

# 15th Embarrassment ) Karin's Patience and Kenta's Danger

~Patience~

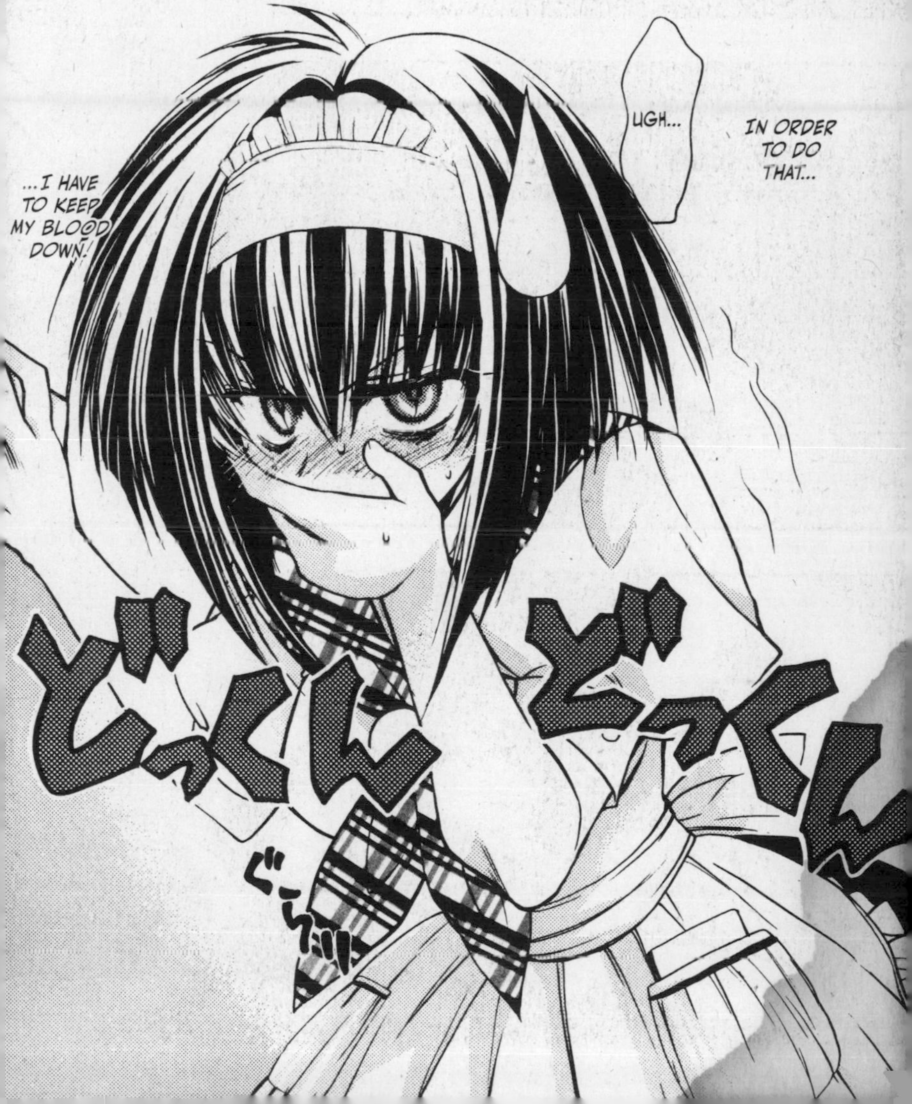
IN ORDER TO DO THAT...
UGH...
...I HAVE TO KEEP MY BLOOD DOWN!
どくん どくん

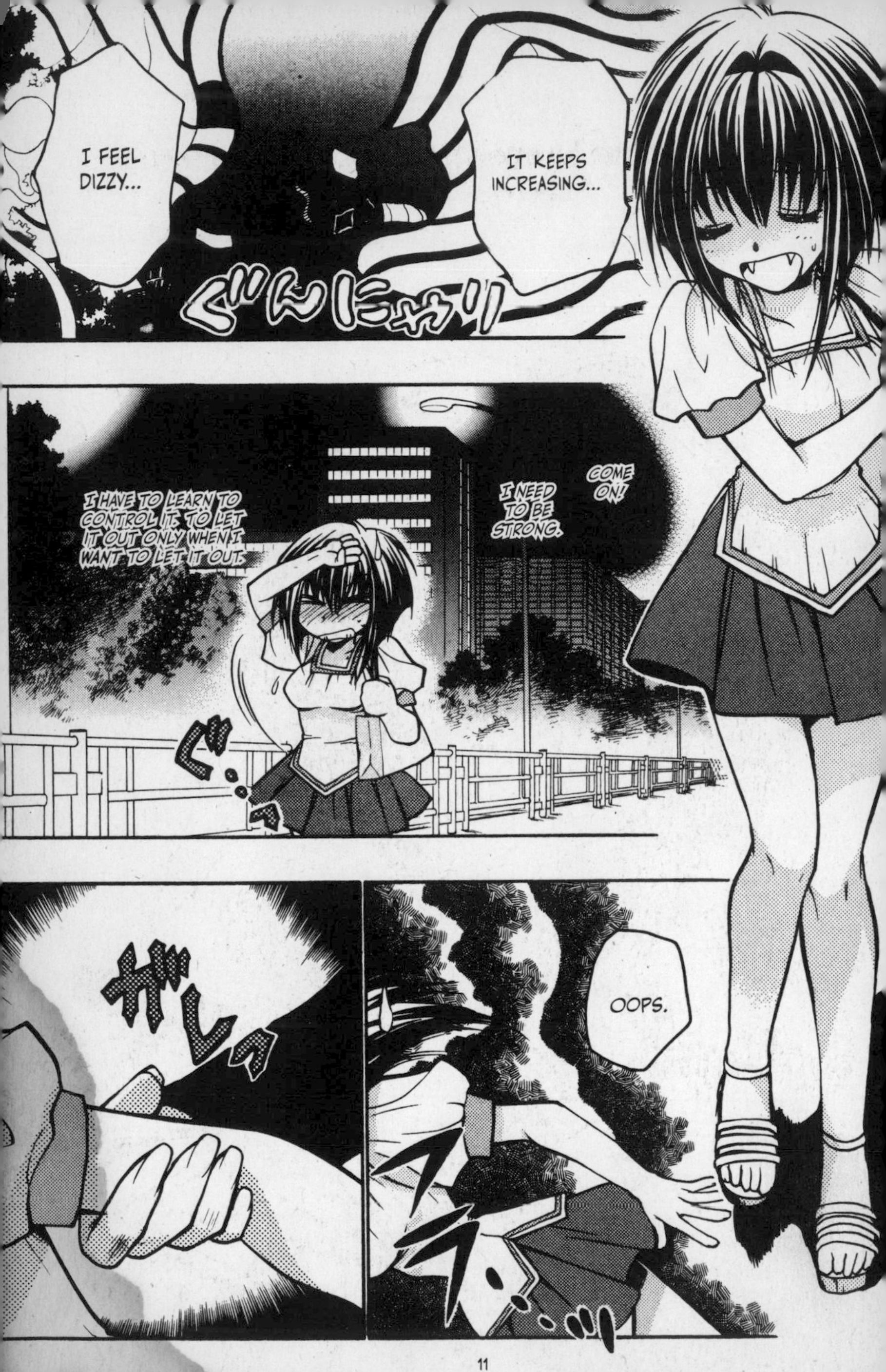
IT KEEPS INCREASING...
I FEEL DIZZY...
COME ON!
I NEED TO BE STRONG.
I HAVE TO LEARN TO CONTROL IT. TO LET IT OUT ONLY WHEN I WANT TO LET IT OUT.
OOPS.

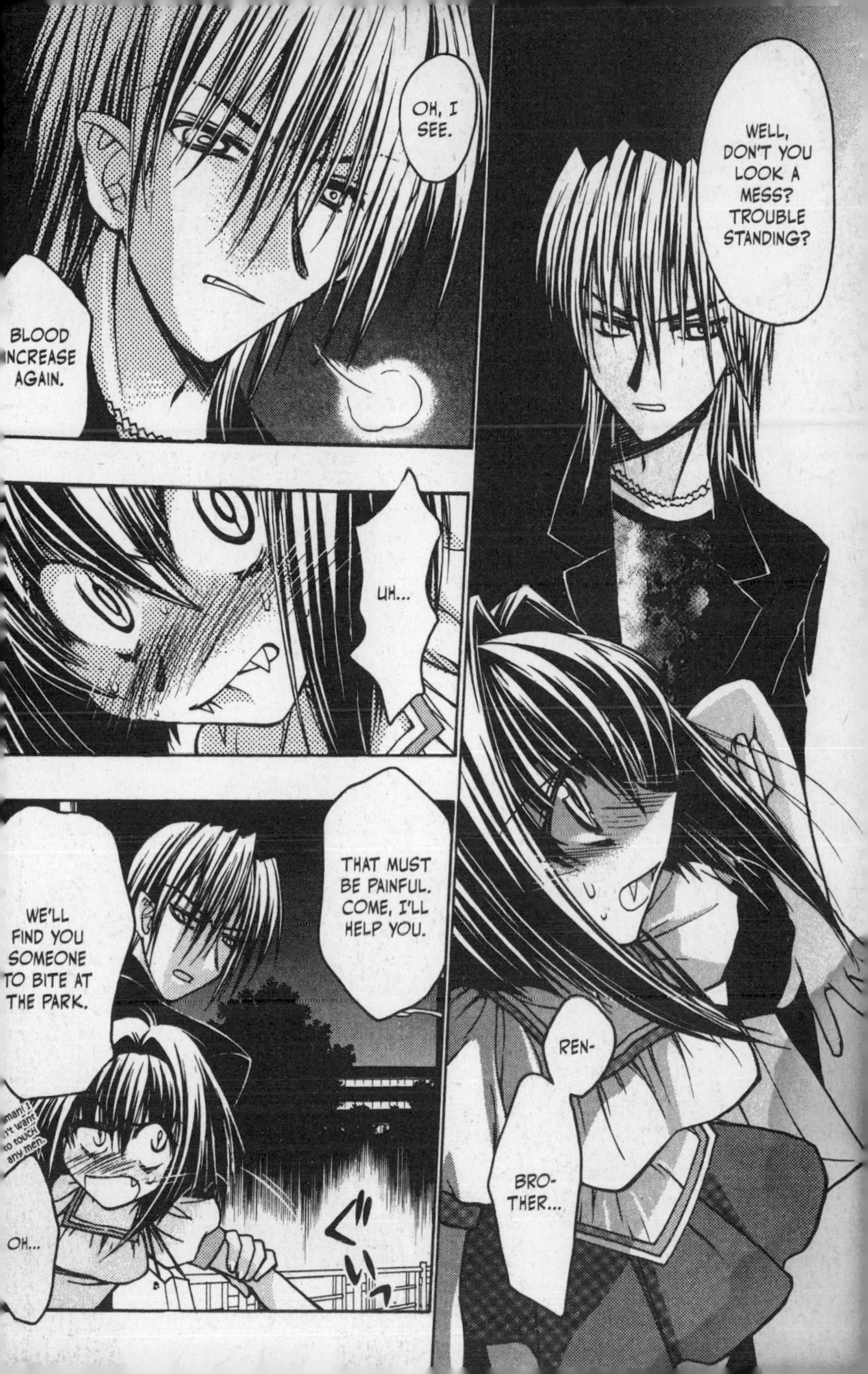
WELL, DON'T YOU LOOK A MESS? TROUBLE STANDING?
REN-
BROTHER...
OH, I SEE.
BLOOD INCREASE AGAIN.
UH...
THAT MUST BE PAINFUL. COME, I'LL HELP YOU.
WE'LL FIND YOU SOMEONE TO BITE AT THE PARK.
OH...
ぐいっ

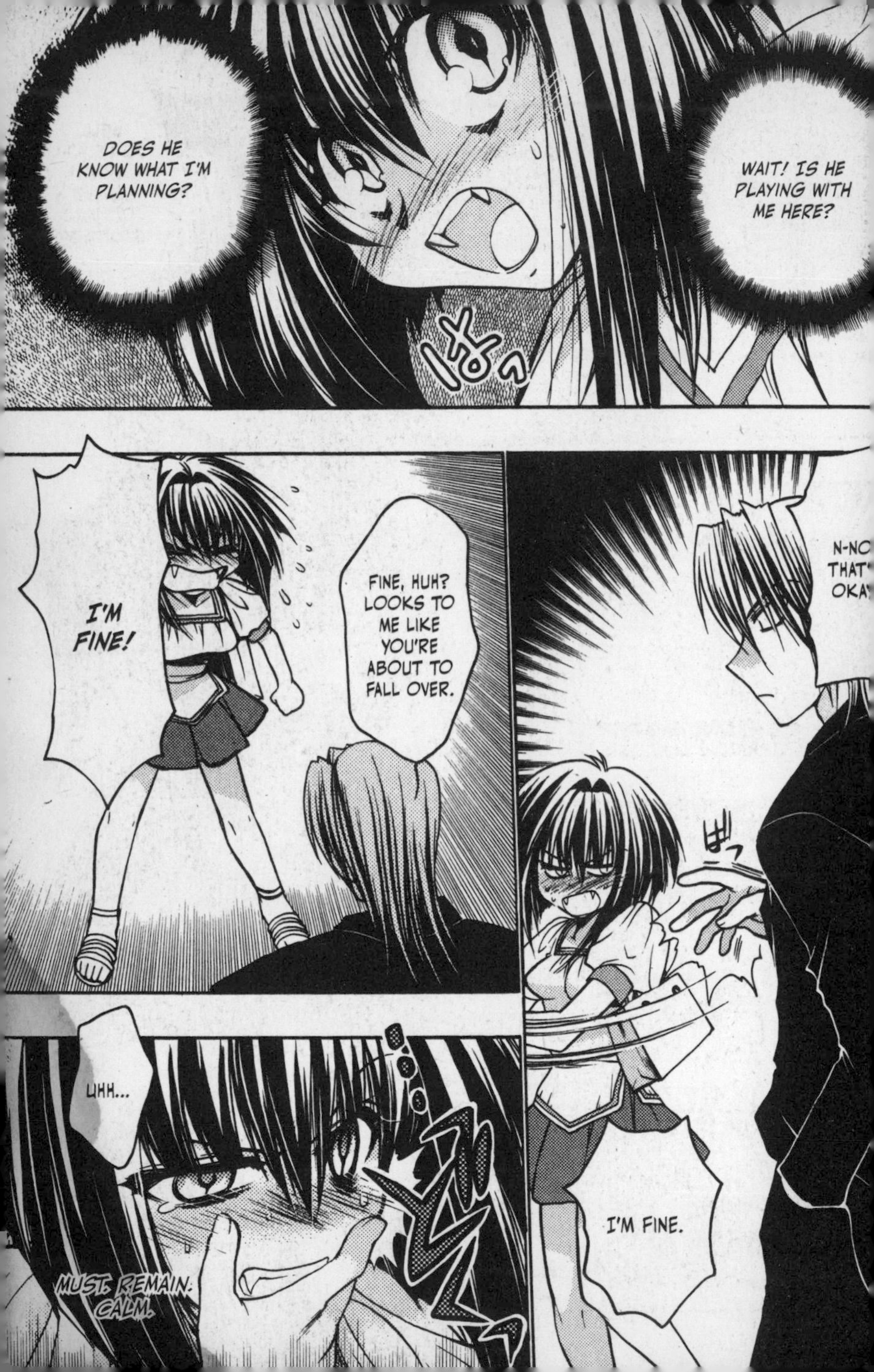
WAIT! IS HE PLAYING WITH ME HERE?
DOES HE KNOW WHAT I'M PLANNING?
はっ
N-NO THAT' OKA
ばっ
I'M FINE.
FINE, HUH? LOOKS TO ME LIKE YOU'RE ABOUT TO FALL OVER.
I'M FINE!
UHH...
MUST. REMAIN. CALM.

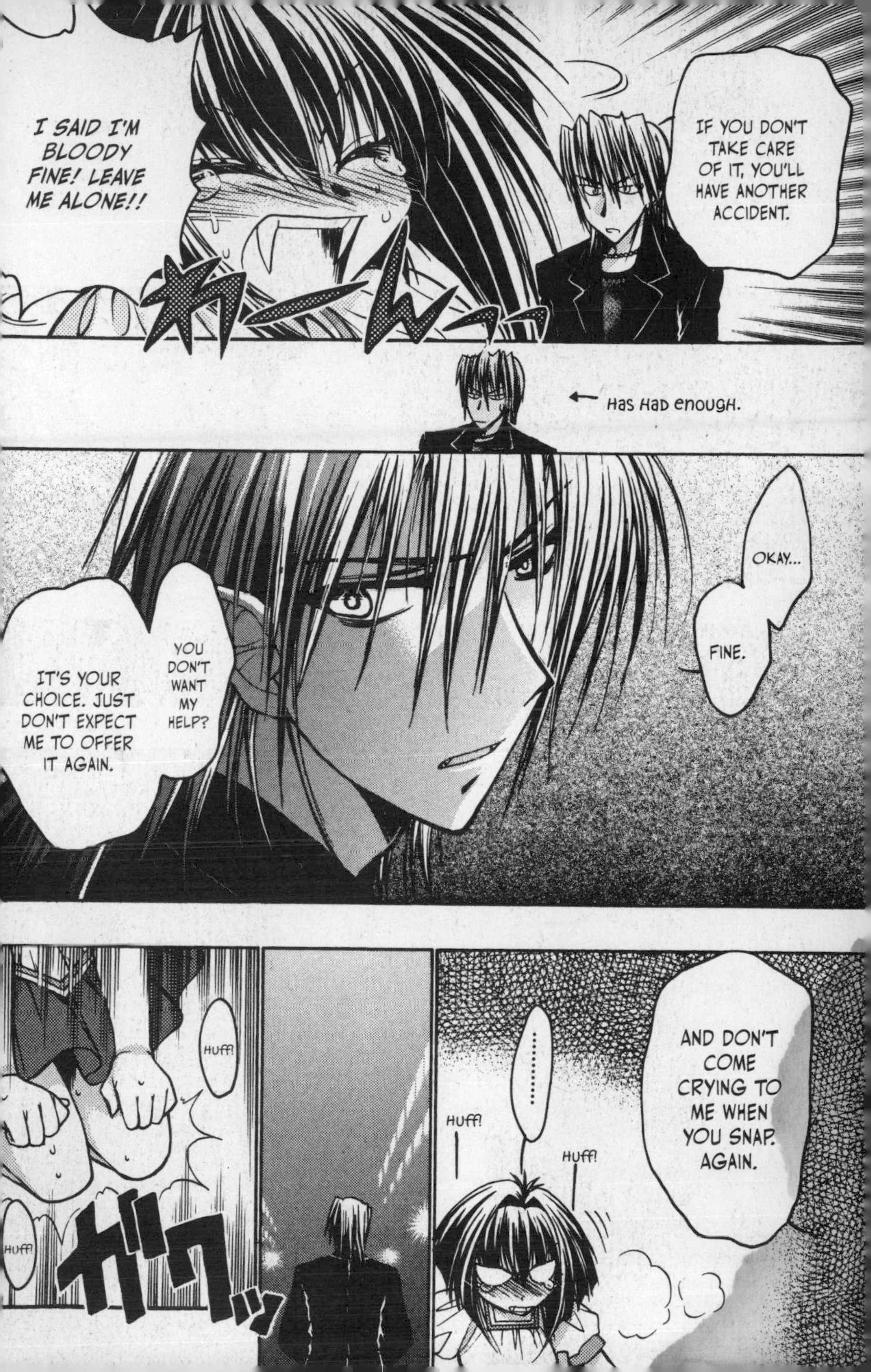
IF YOU DON'T TAKE CARE OF IT, YOU'LL HAVE ANOTHER ACCIDENT.
I SAID I'M BLOODY FINE! LEAVE ME ALONE!!
← Has had enough.
OKAY... FINE.
YOU DON'T WANT MY HELP?
IT'S YOUR CHOICE. JUST DON'T EXPECT ME TO OFFER IT AGAIN.
AND DON'T COME CRYING TO ME WHEN YOU SNAP. AGAIN.
HUFF!
........
HUFF!
HUFF!
HUFF!

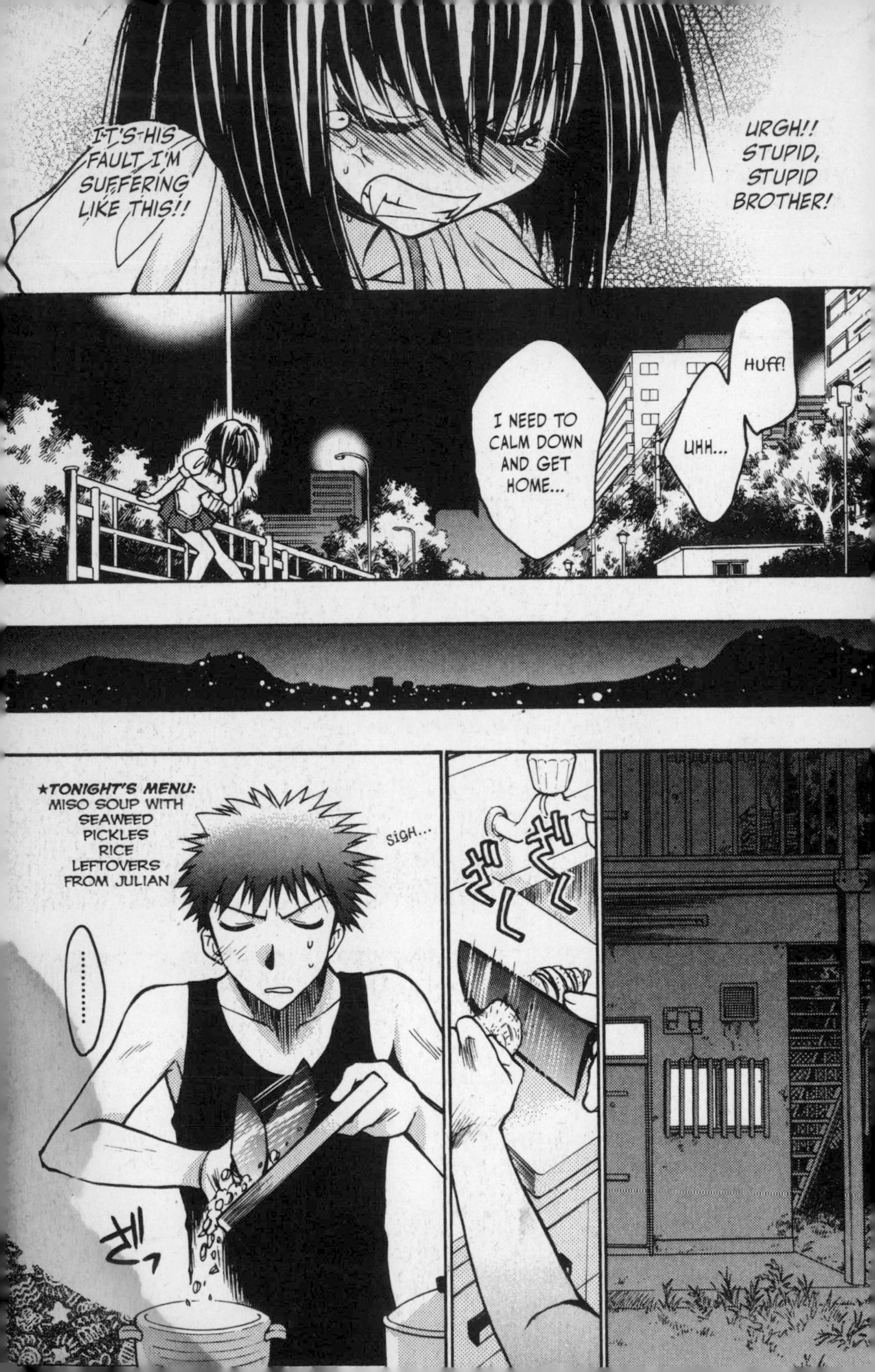
URGH!! STUPID, STUPID BROTHER!
IT'S HIS FAULT I'M SUFFERING LIKE THIS!!
HUFF!
UHH...
I NEED TO CALM DOWN AND GET HOME...
SIGH...
★TONIGHT'S MENU: MISO SOUP WITH SEAWEED PICKLES RICE LEFTOVERS FROM JULIAN
........

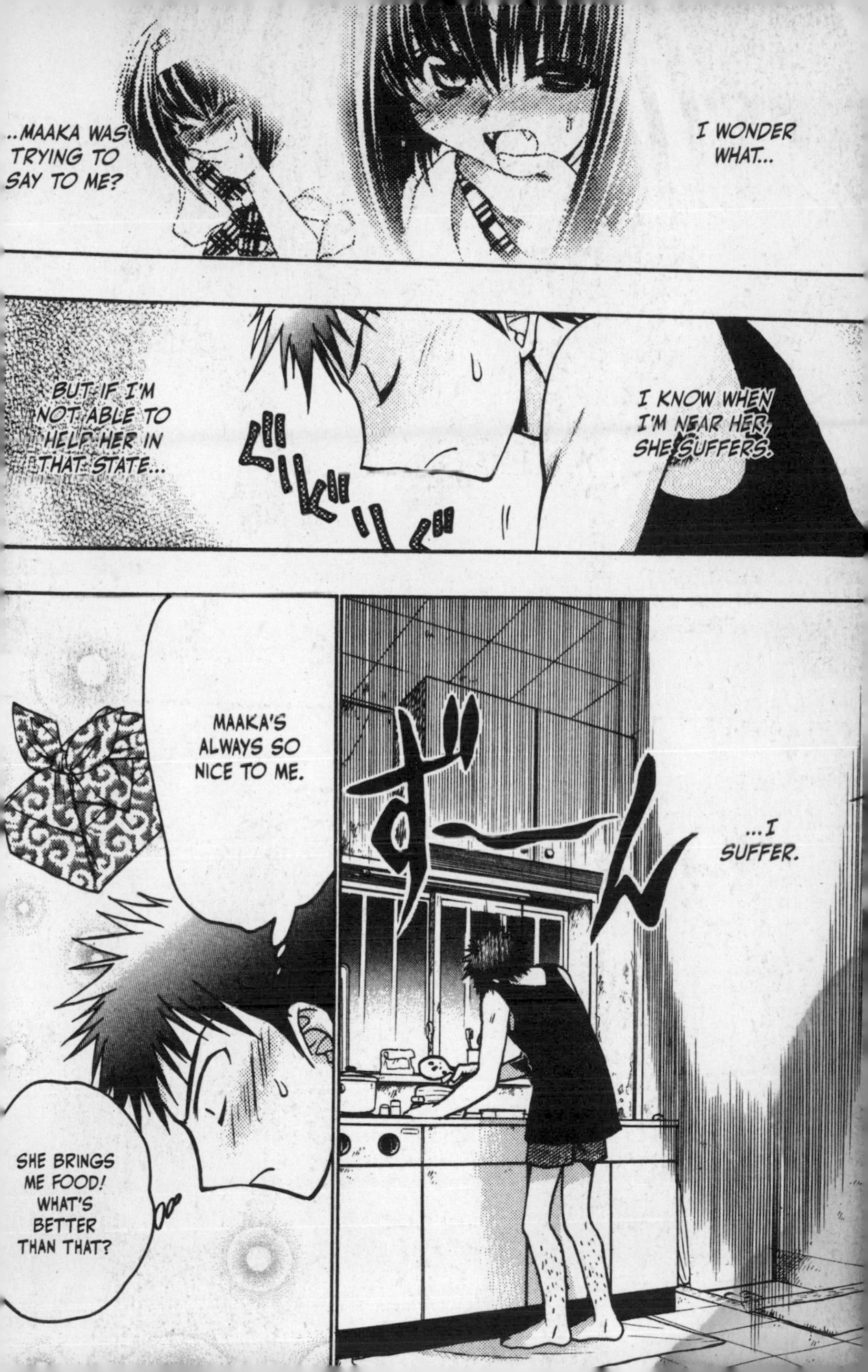
I WONDER WHAT...
...MAAKA WAS TRYING TO SAY TO ME?
I KNOW WHEN I'M NEAR HER, SHE SUFFERS.
BUT IF I'M NOT ABLE TO HELP HER IN THAT STATE...
ずーん
...I SUFFER.
MAAKA'S ALWAYS SO NICE TO ME.
SHE BRINGS ME FOOD! WHAT'S BETTER THAN THAT?

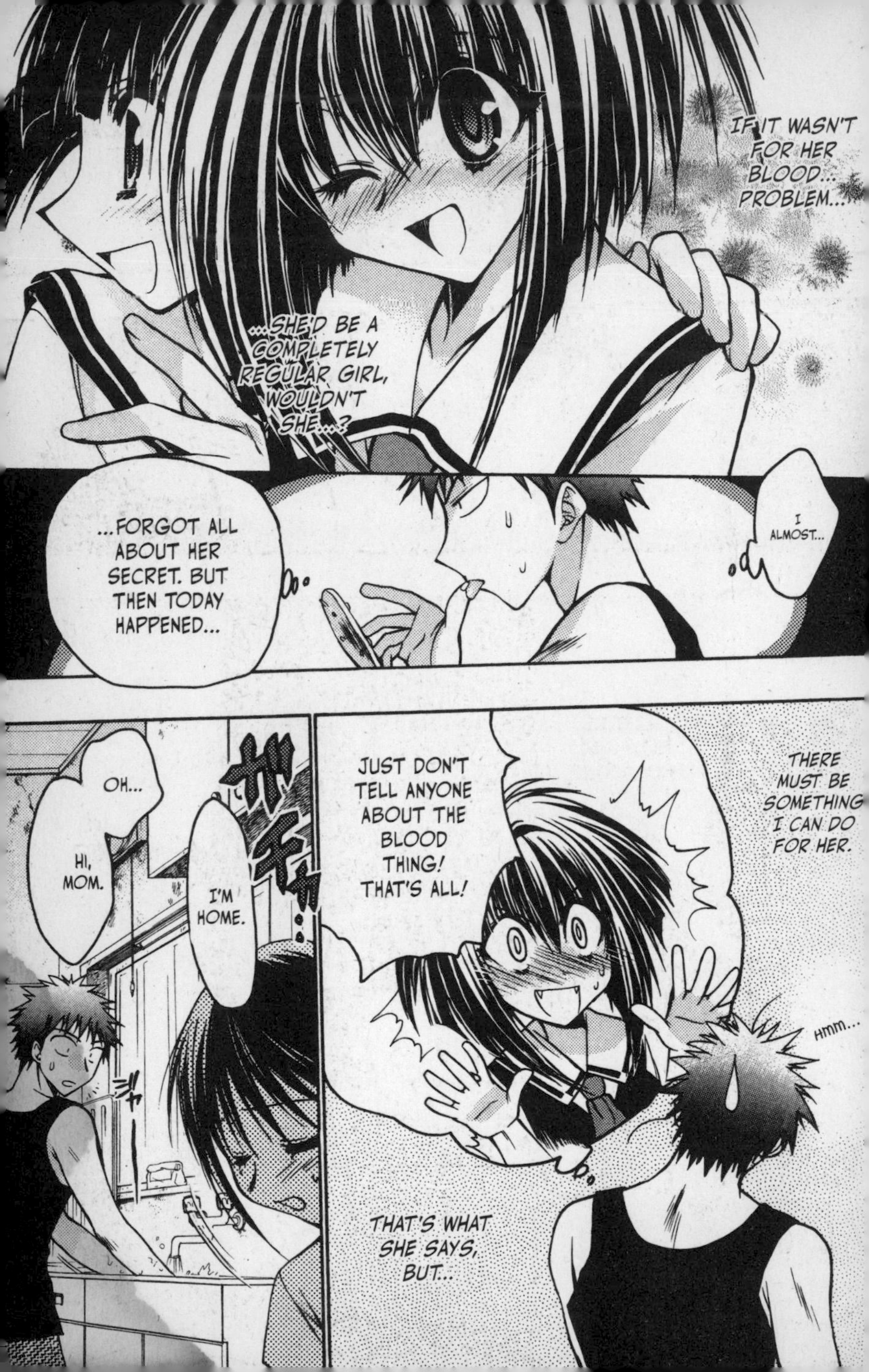
IF IT WASN'T FOR HER BLOOD... PROBLEM...
...SHE'D BE A COMPLETELY REGULAR GIRL, WOULDN'T SHE...?
I ALMOST...
...FORGOT ALL ABOUT HER SECRET. BUT THEN TODAY HAPPENED...
THERE MUST BE SOMETHING I CAN DO FOR HER.
JUST DON'T TELL ANYONE ABOUT THE BLOOD THING! THAT'S ALL!
HMM...
THAT'S WHAT SHE SAYS, BUT...
I'M HOME.
OH...
HI, MOM.

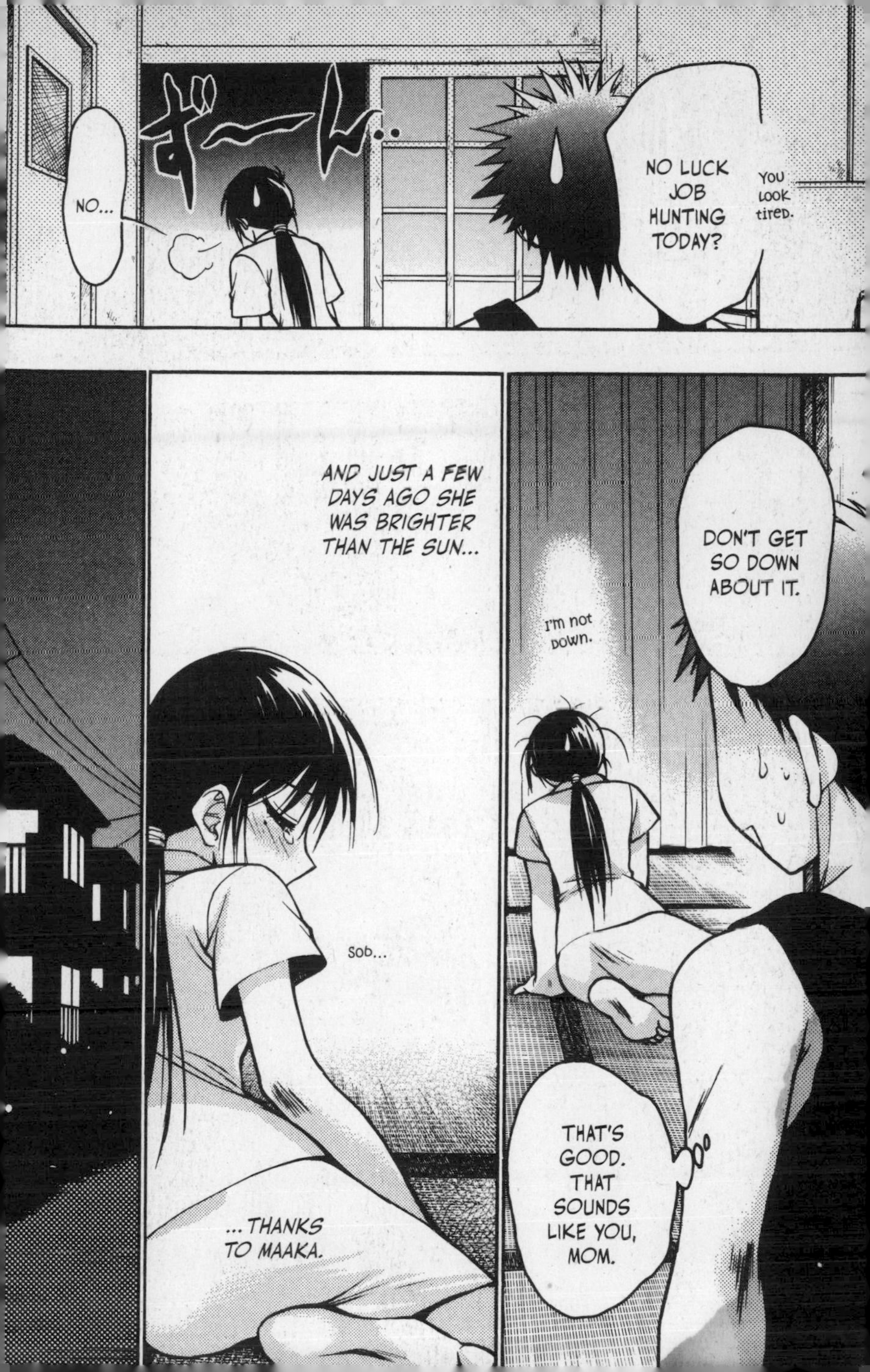
NO LUCK JOB HUNTING TODAY?
You look tired.
ず〜ん..
NO...
DON'T GET SO DOWN ABOUT IT.
I'm not down.
THAT'S GOOD. THAT SOUNDS LIKE YOU, MOM.
AND JUST A FEW DAYS AGO SHE WAS BRIGHTER THAN THE SUN...
Sob...
...THANKS TO MAAKA.

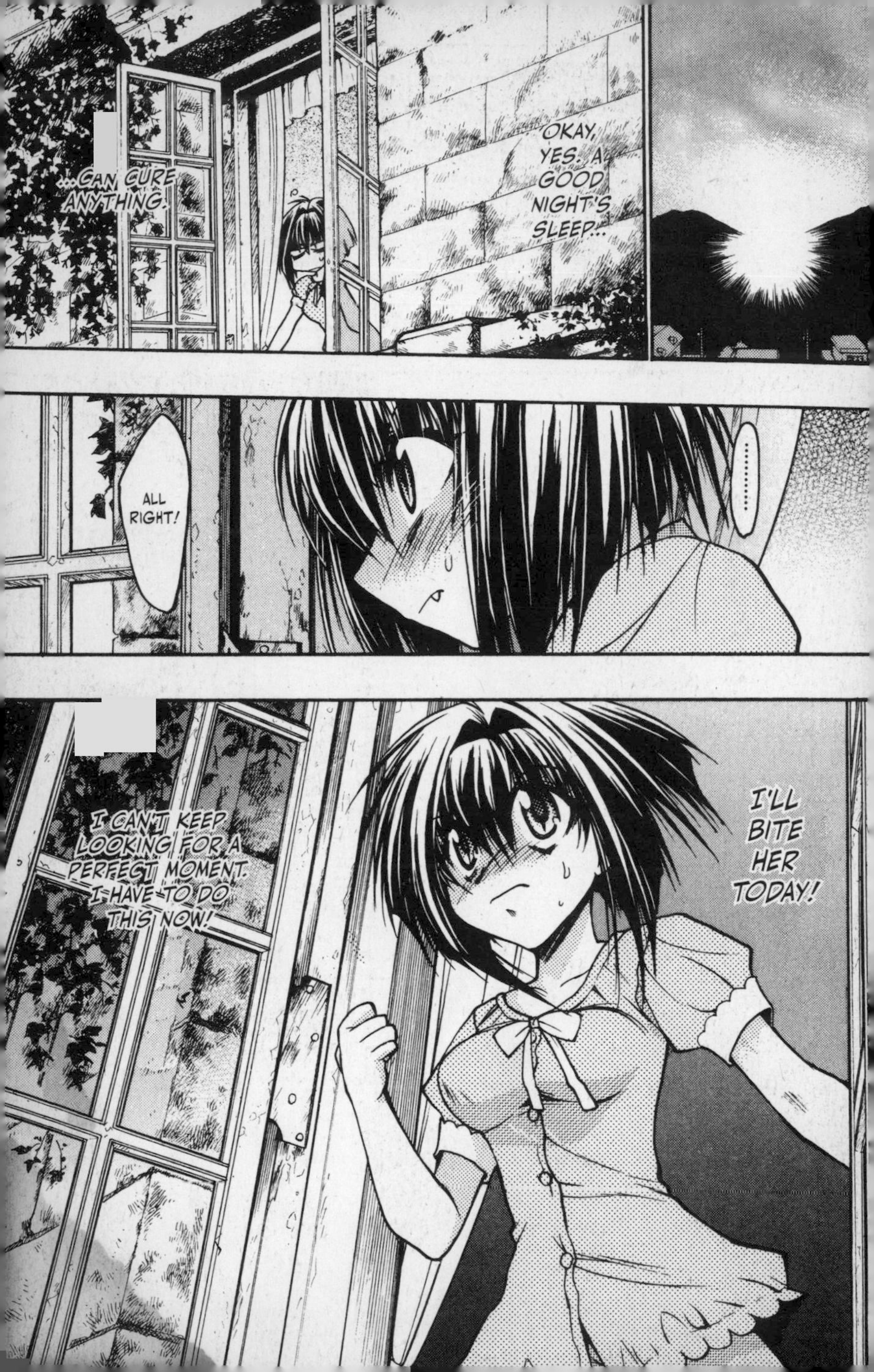
OKAY, YES. A GOOD NIGHT'S SLEEP...
...CAN CURE ANYTHING.
......
ALL RIGHT!
I'LL BITE HER TODAY!
I CAN'T KEEP LOOKING FOR A PERFECT MOMENT. I HAVE TO DO THIS NOW!

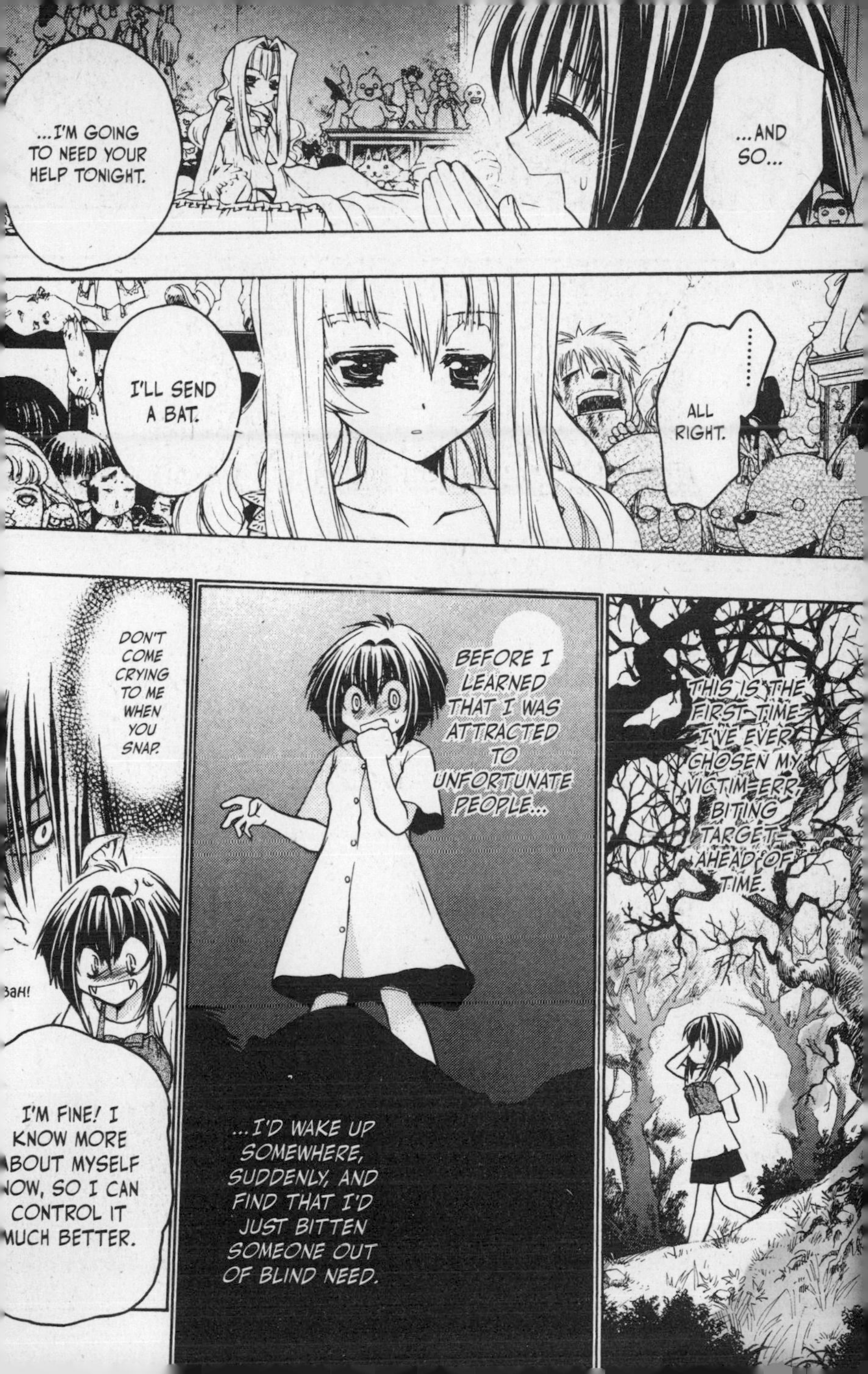
...AND SO...
...I'M GOING TO NEED YOUR HELP TONIGHT.
...... ALL RIGHT.
I'LL SEND A BAT.
THIS IS THE FIRST TIME I'VE EVER CHOSEN MY VICTIM—ERR, BITING TARGET—AHEAD OF TIME.
BEFORE I LEARNED THAT I WAS ATTRACTED TO UNFORTUNATE PEOPLE...
...I'D WAKE UP SOMEWHERE, SUDDENLY, AND FIND THAT I'D JUST BITTEN SOMEONE OUT OF BLIND NEED.
DON'T COME CRYING TO ME WHEN YOU SNAP.
BaH!
I'M FINE! I KNOW MORE BOUT MYSELF OW, SO I CAN CONTROL IT MUCH BETTER.

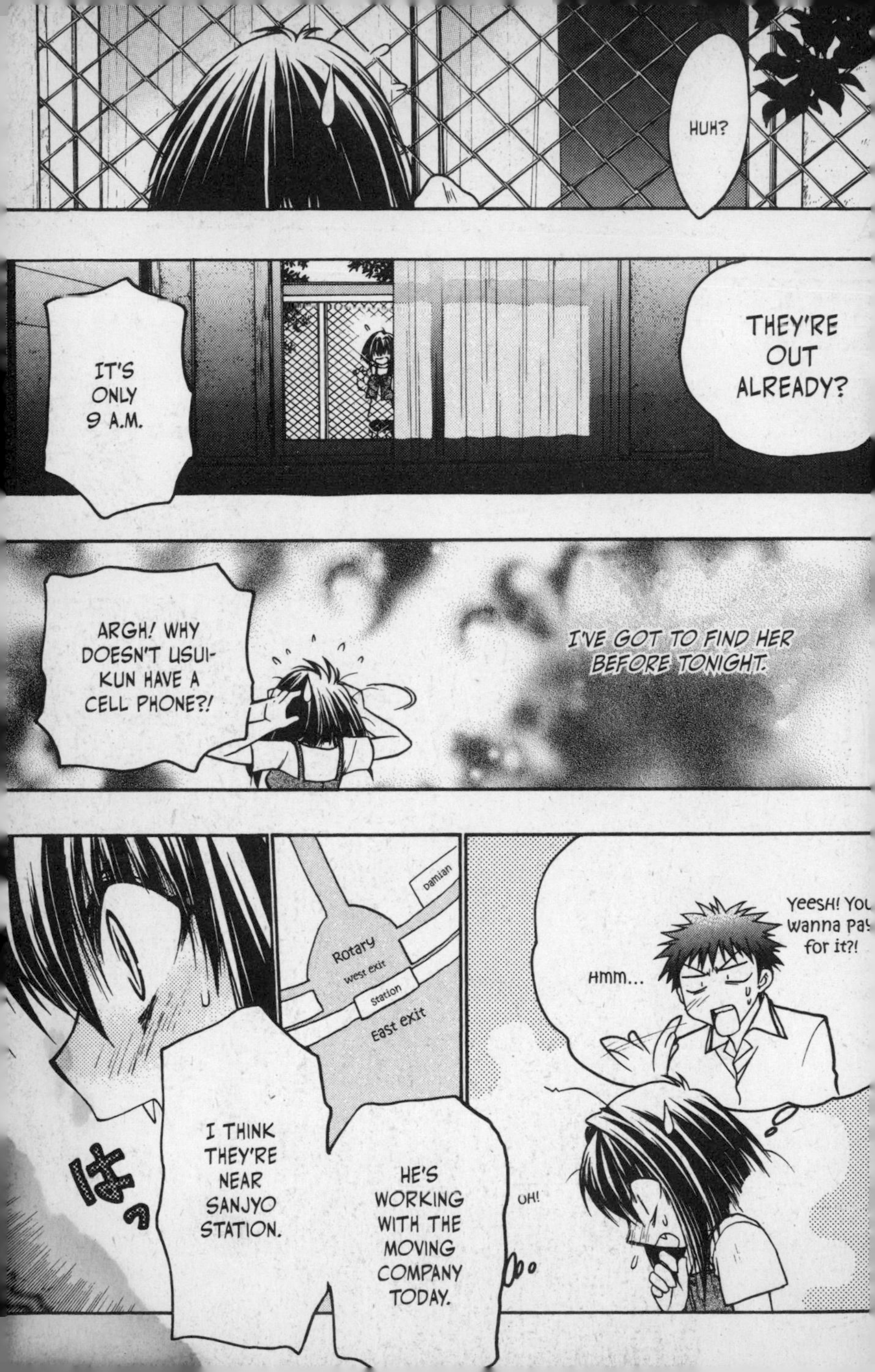

HUH?
THEY'RE OUT ALREADY?
IT'S ONLY 9 A.M.
I'VE GOT TO FIND HER BEFORE TONIGHT.
ARGH! WHY DOESN'T USUI-KUN HAVE A CELL PHONE?!
YeesH! You wanna pay for it?!
Hmm...
OH!
Damian
Rotary
West exit
Station
East exit
HE'S WORKING WITH THE MOVING COMPANY TODAY.
I THINK THEY'RE NEAR SANJYO STATION.
はっ

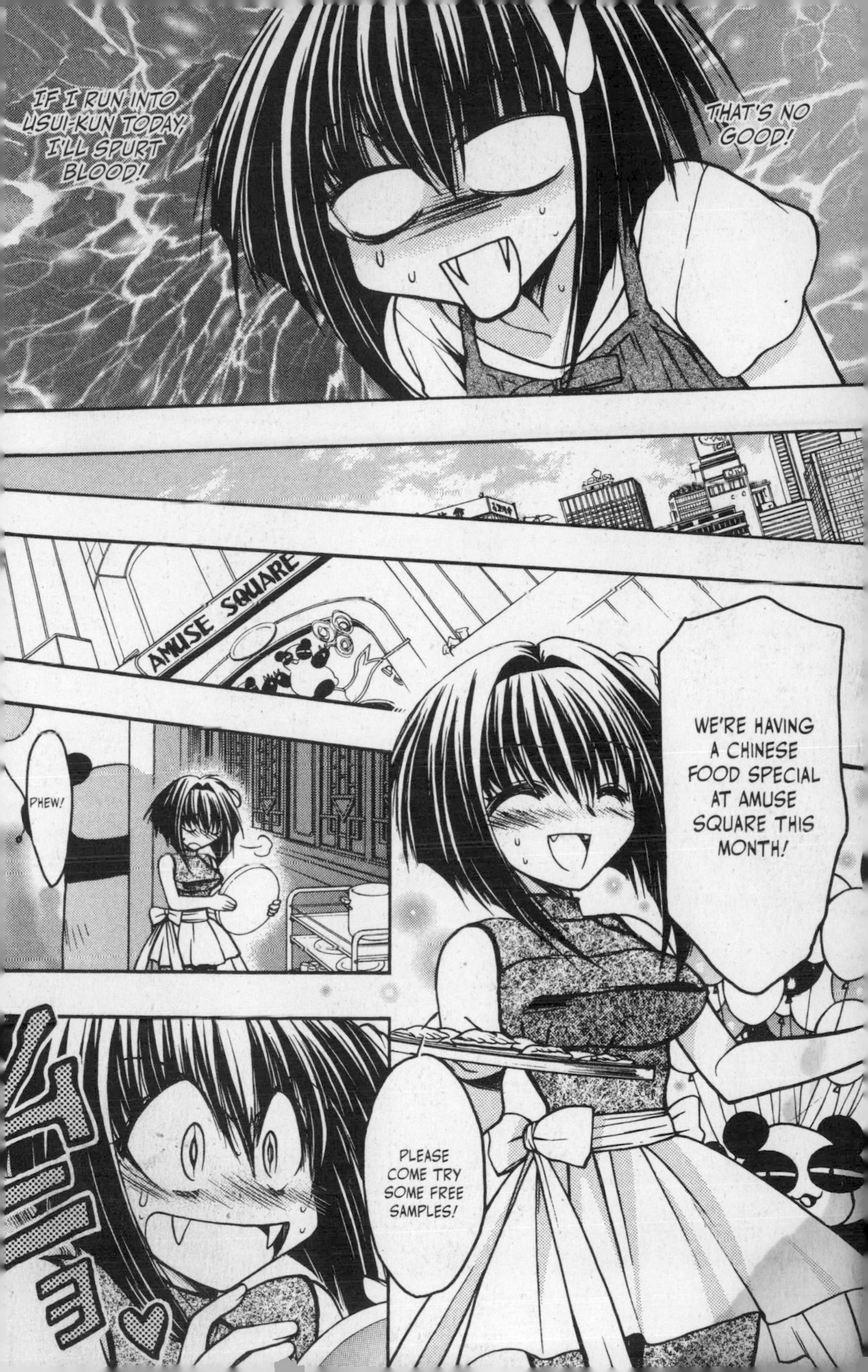
THAT'S NO GOOD!
IF I RUN INTO USUI-KUN TODAY, I'LL SPURT BLOOD!
AMUSE SQUARE
WE'RE HAVING A CHINESE FOOD SPECIAL AT AMUSE SQUARE THIS MONTH!
PLEASE COME TRY SOME FREE SAMPLES!
PHEW!

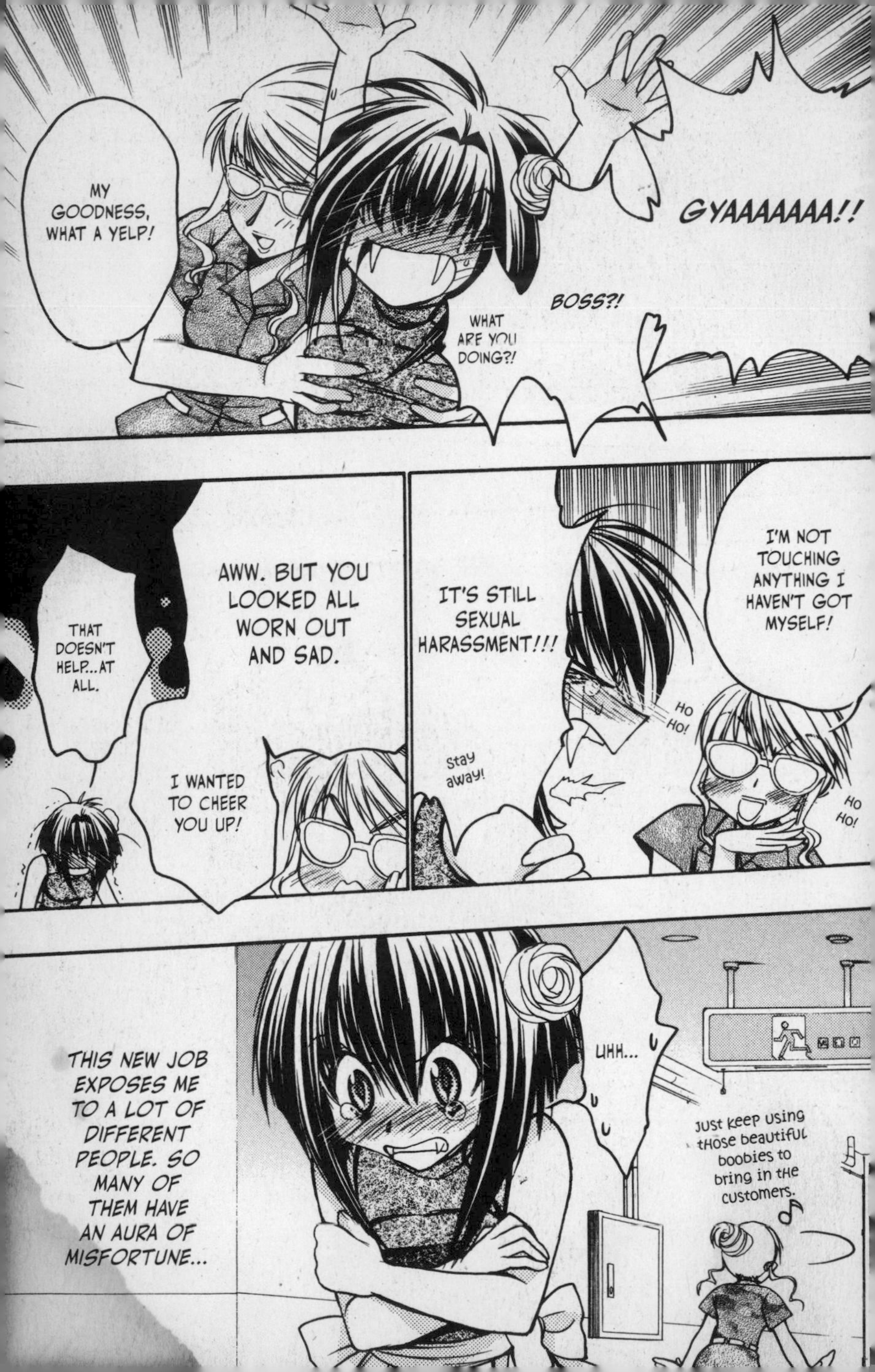
GYAAAAAAA!!
BOSS?!
WHAT ARE YOU DOING?!
MY GOODNESS, WHAT A YELP!
I'M NOT TOUCHING ANYTHING I HAVEN'T GOT MYSELF!
HO HO!
IT'S STILL SEXUAL HARASSMENT!!!
HO HO!
Stay away!
AWW. BUT YOU LOOKED ALL WORN OUT AND SAD.
I WANTED TO CHEER YOU UP!
THAT DOESN'T HELP...AT ALL.
Just keep using those beautiful boobies to bring in the customers.
UHH...
THIS NEW JOB EXPOSES ME TO A LOT OF DIFFERENT PEOPLE. SO MANY OF THEM HAVE AN AURA OF MISFORTUNE...

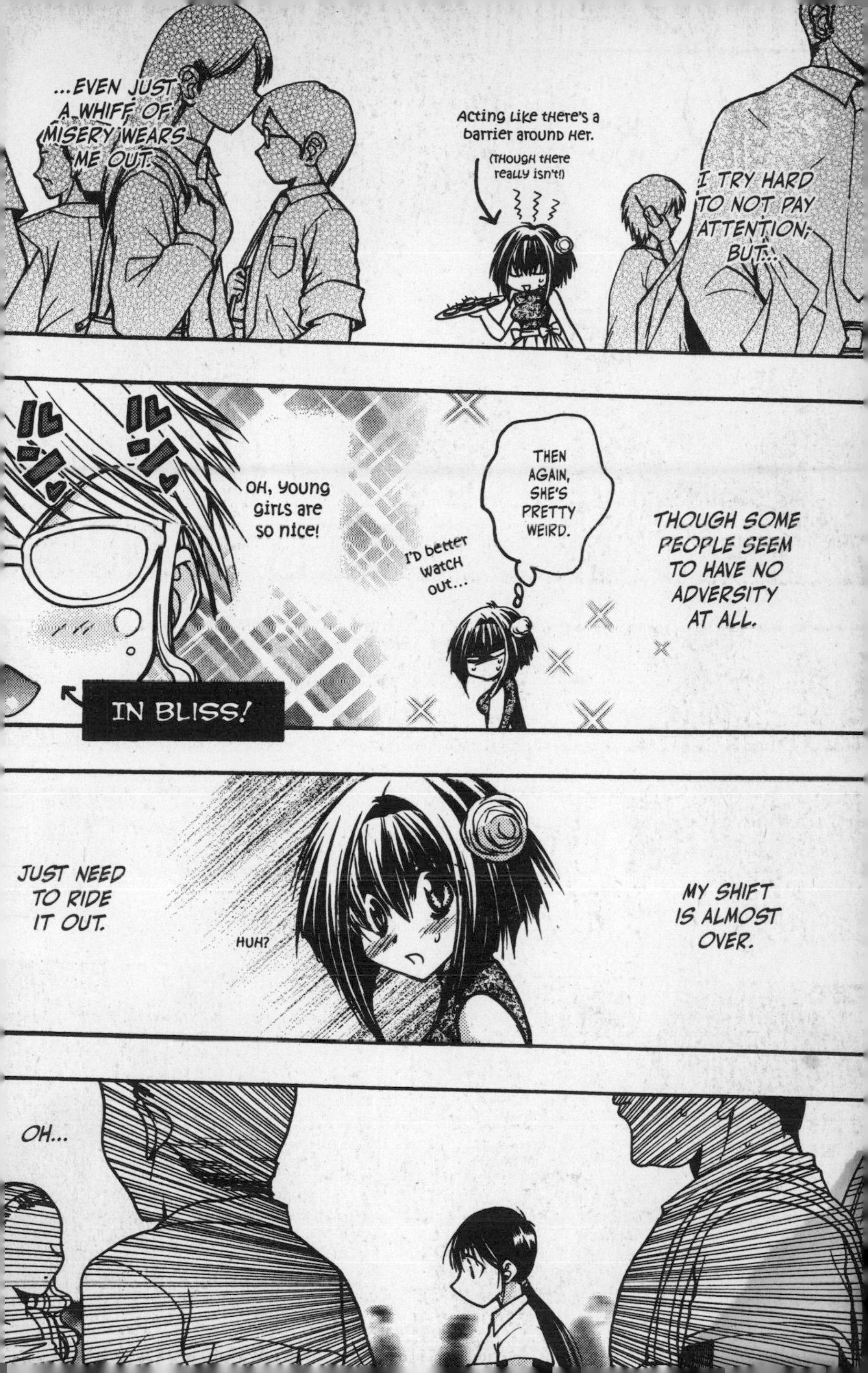
I TRY HARD TO NOT PAY ATTENTION, BUT...
Acting like there's a barrier around her.
(Though there really isn't!)
...EVEN JUST A WHIFF OF MISERY WEARS ME OUT.
THOUGH SOME PEOPLE SEEM TO HAVE NO ADVERSITY AT ALL.
THEN AGAIN, SHE'S PRETTY WEIRD.
I'd better watch out...
OH, young girls are so nice!
IN BLISS!
MY SHIFT IS ALMOST OVER.
HUH?
JUST NEED TO RIDE IT OUT.
OH...

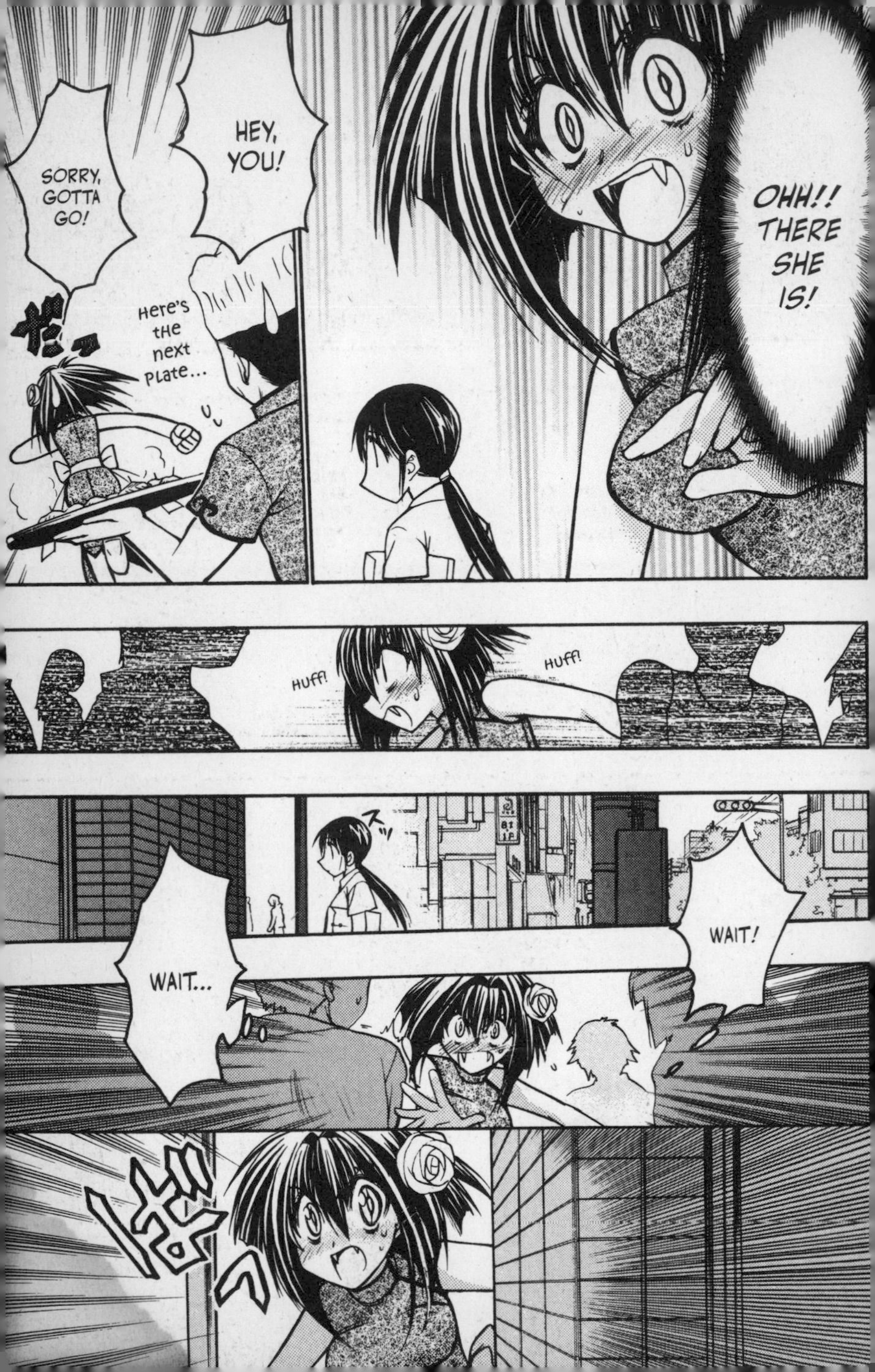
OHH!! THERE SHE IS!
HEY, YOU!
Here's the next plate...
SORRY, GOTTA GO!
HUFF!
HUFF!
WAIT!
WAIT...

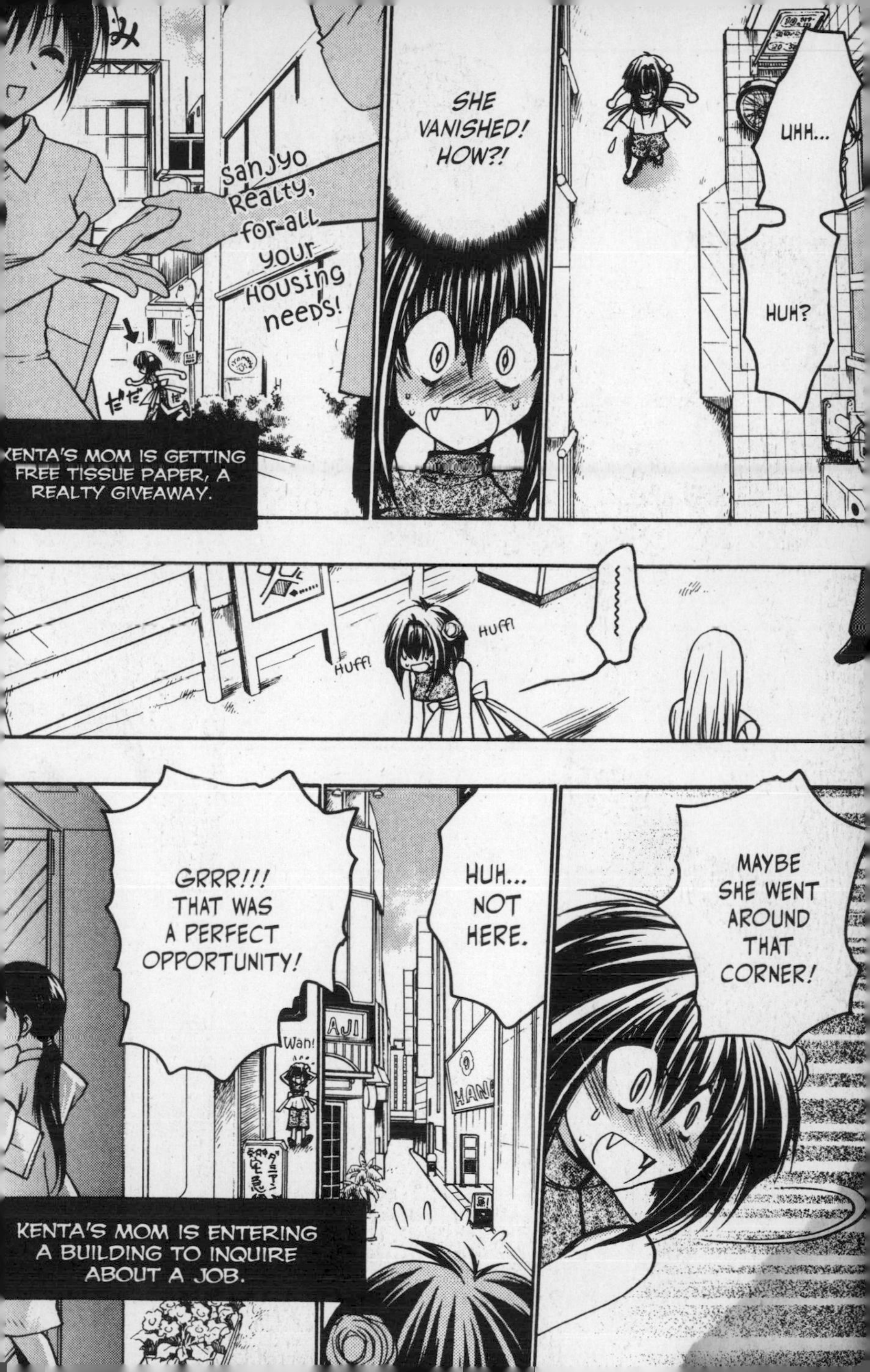

UHH...
HUH?
SHE VANISHED! HOW?!
Sanjyo Realty, for all your Housing needs!
KENTA'S MOM IS GETTING FREE TISSUE PAPER, A REALTY GIVEAWAY.
Huff!
Huff!
MAYBE SHE WENT AROUND THAT CORNER!
HUH... NOT HERE.
GRRR!!! THAT WAS A PERFECT OPPORTUNITY!
Wan!
AJI
KENTA'S MOM IS ENTERING A BUILDING TO INQUIRE ABOUT A JOB.

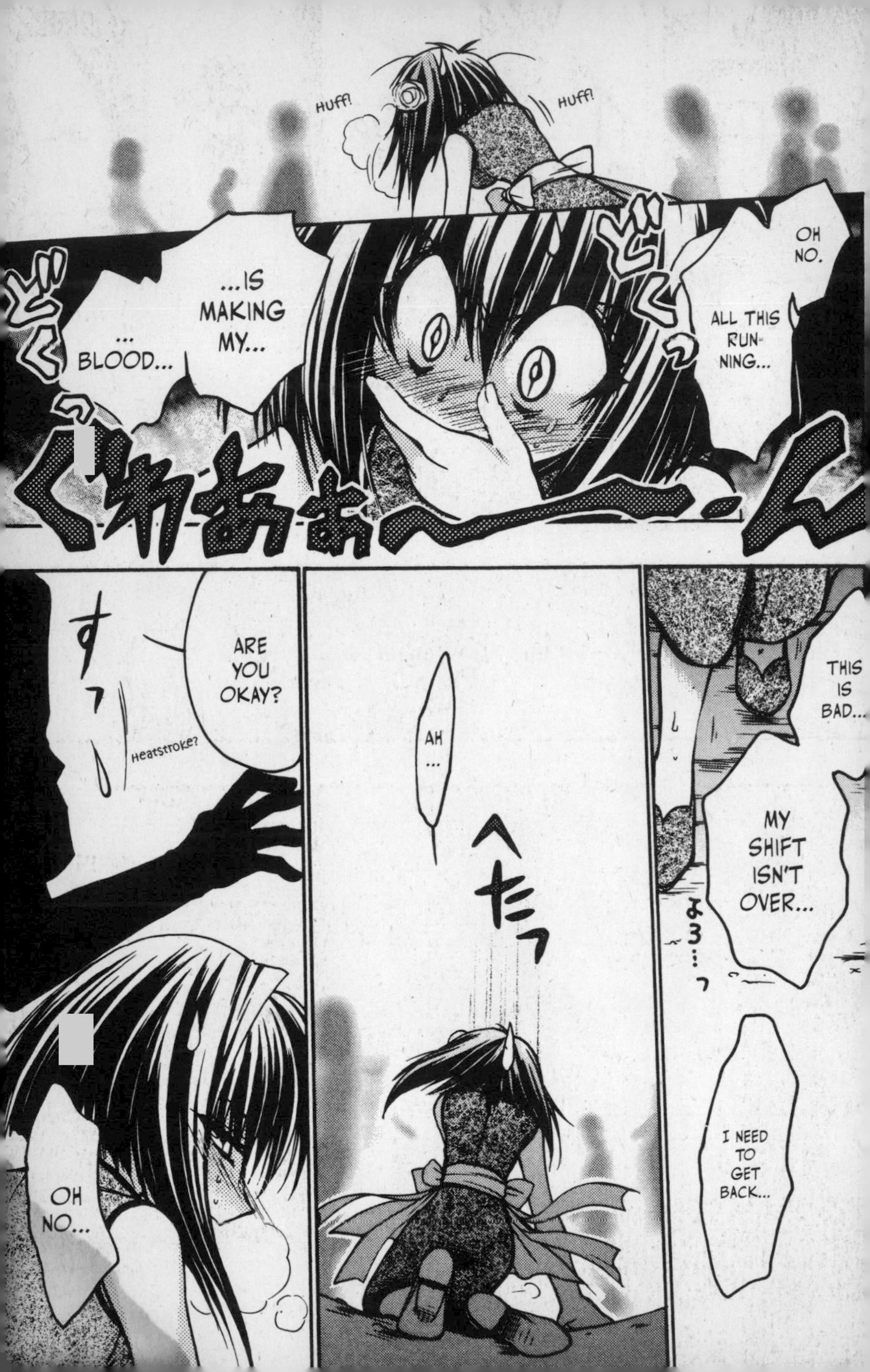
HUFF!
HUFF!
OH NO.
ALL THIS RUNNING...
...IS MAKING MY...
... BLOOD...
THIS IS BAD...
MY SHIFT ISN'T OVER...
I NEED TO GET BACK...
AH ...
ARE YOU OKAY?
Heatstroke?
OH NO...

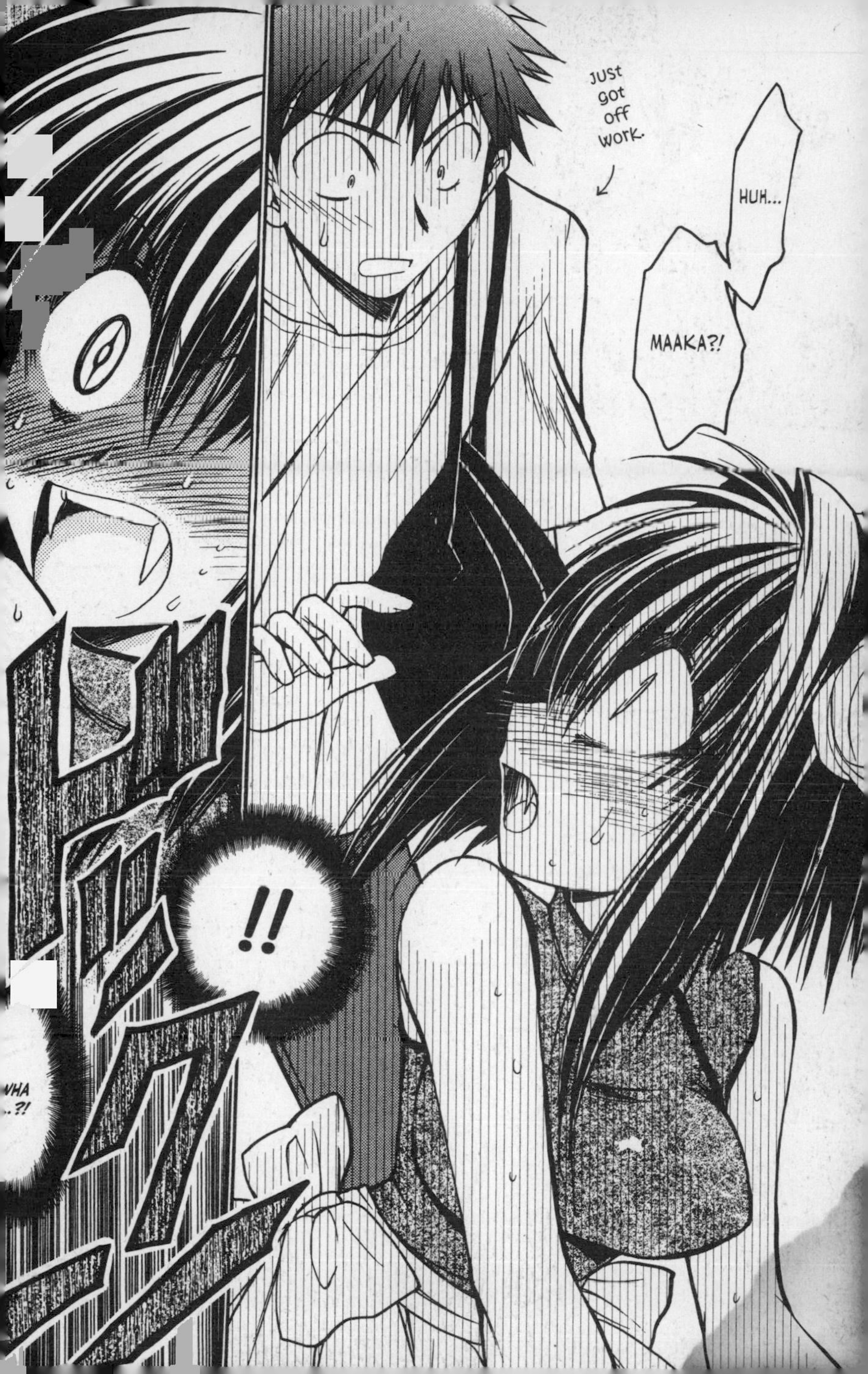
HUH...
MAAKA?!
JUST got off work.
!!
WHA ..?!

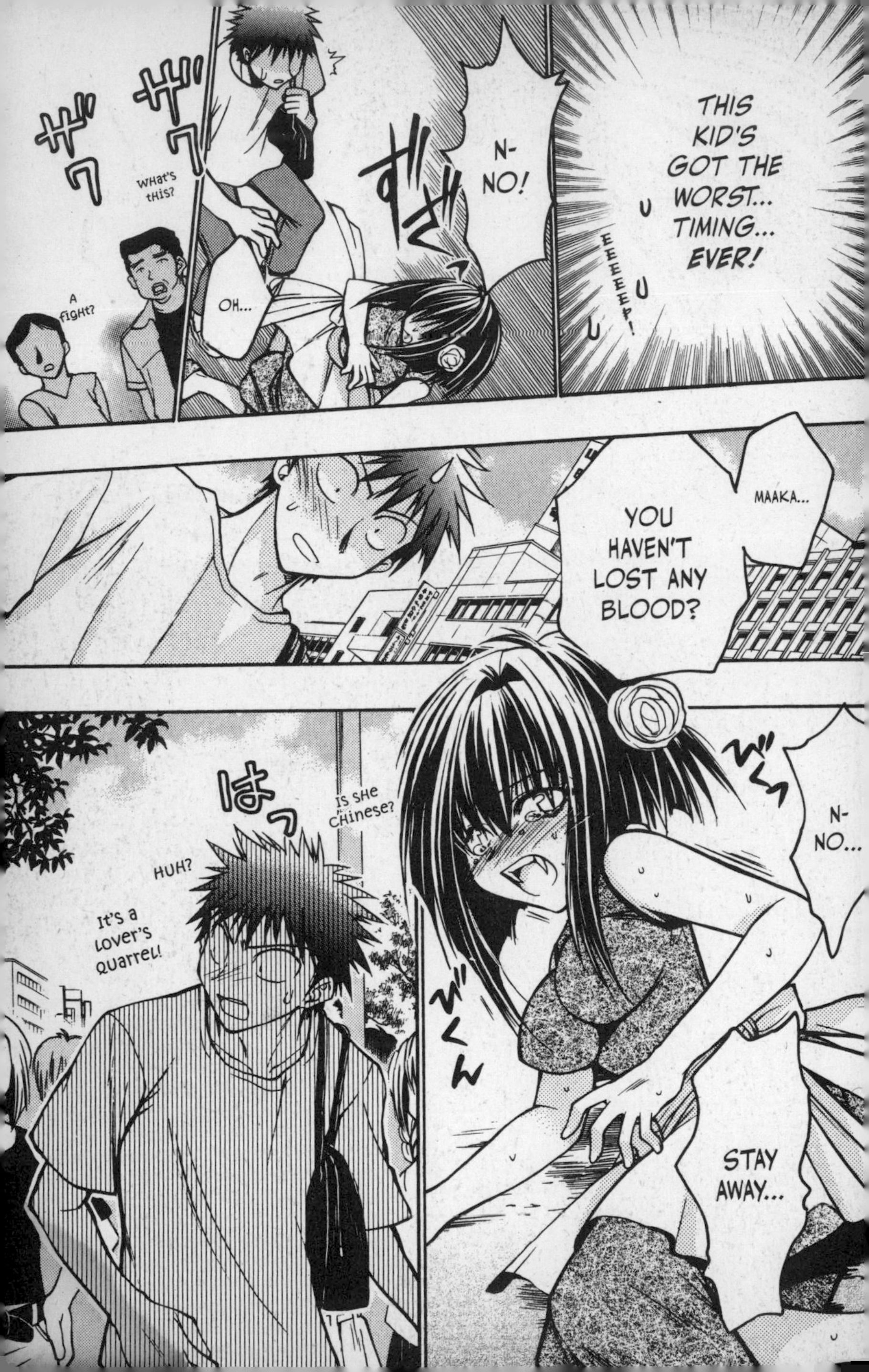
THIS KID'S GOT THE WORST... TIMING... EVER!
EEEEEEP!
N- NO!
OH...
What's this?
A fight?
MAAKA...
YOU HAVEN'T LOST ANY BLOOD?
N- NO...
STAY AWAY...
Is she Chinese?
はっ
HUH?
It's a lover's quarrel!

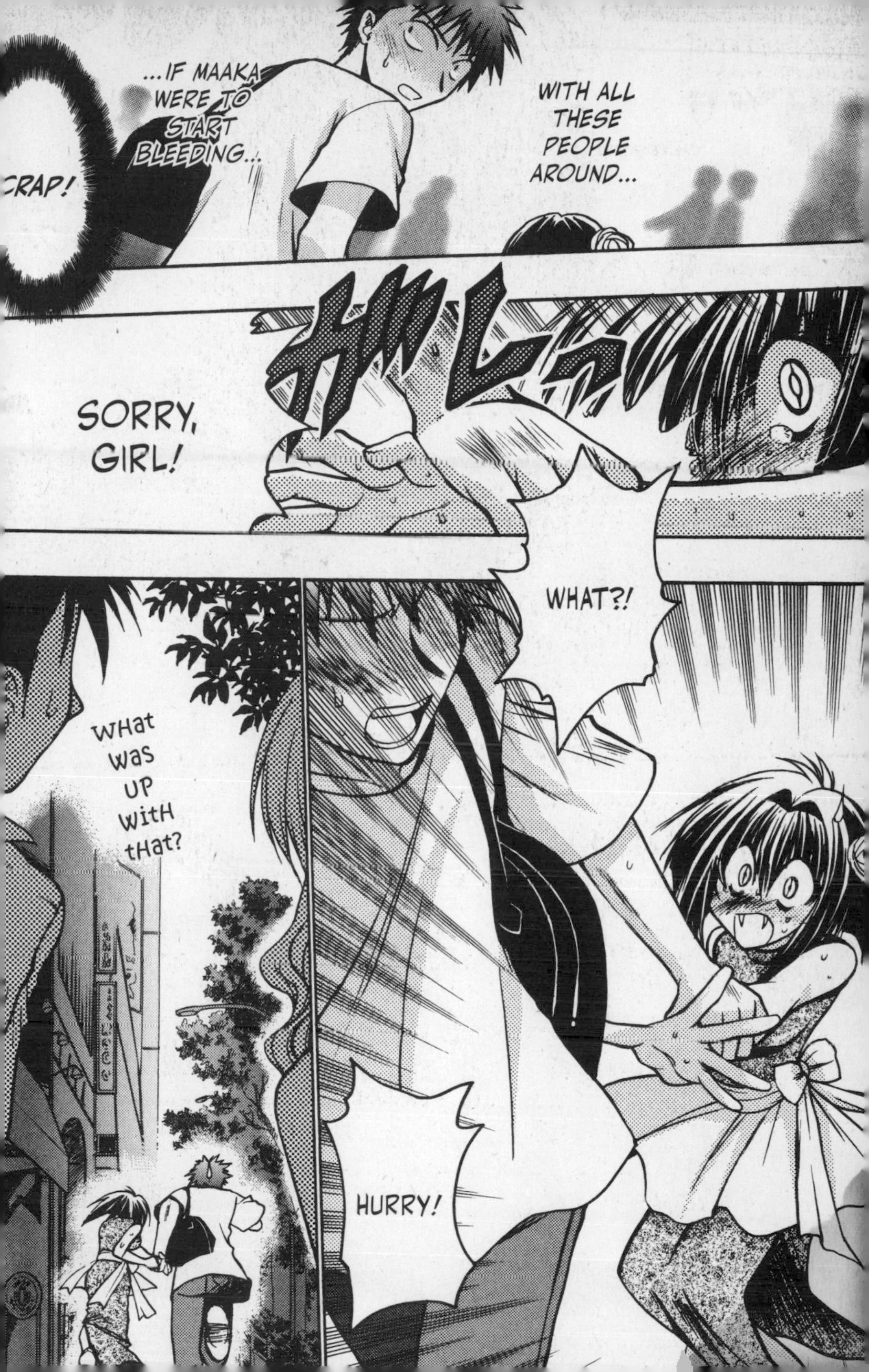
WITH ALL THESE PEOPLE AROUND...
...IF MAAKA WERE TO START BLEEDING...
CRAP!
SORRY, GIRL!
WHAT?!
HURRY!
WHAT WAS UP WITH THAT?

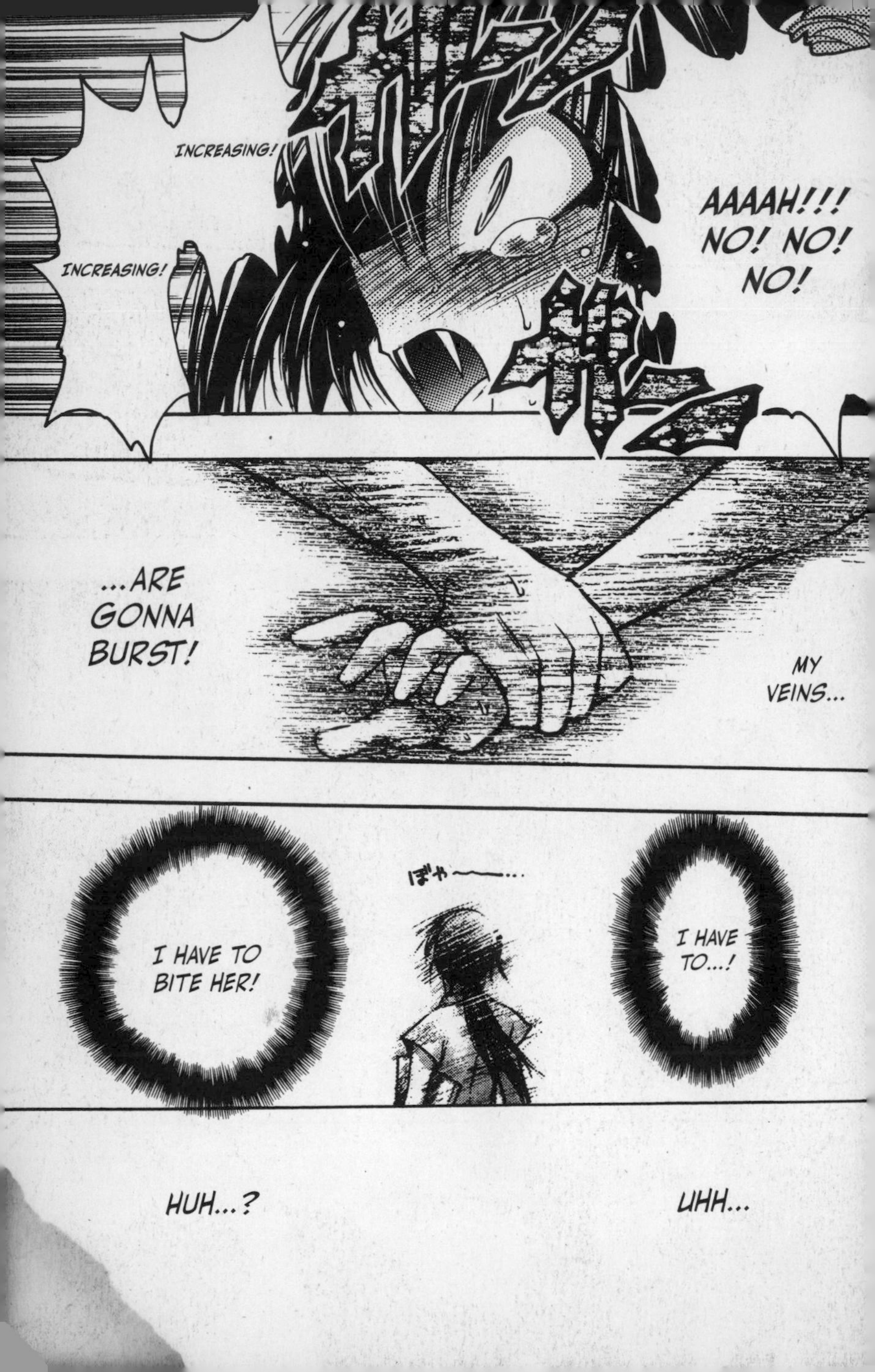
AAAAH!!! NO! NO! NO!
INCREASING!
INCREASING!
MY VEINS...
...ARE GONNA BURST!
ぼや～～…
I HAVE TO...!
I HAVE TO BITE HER!
UHH...
HUH...?

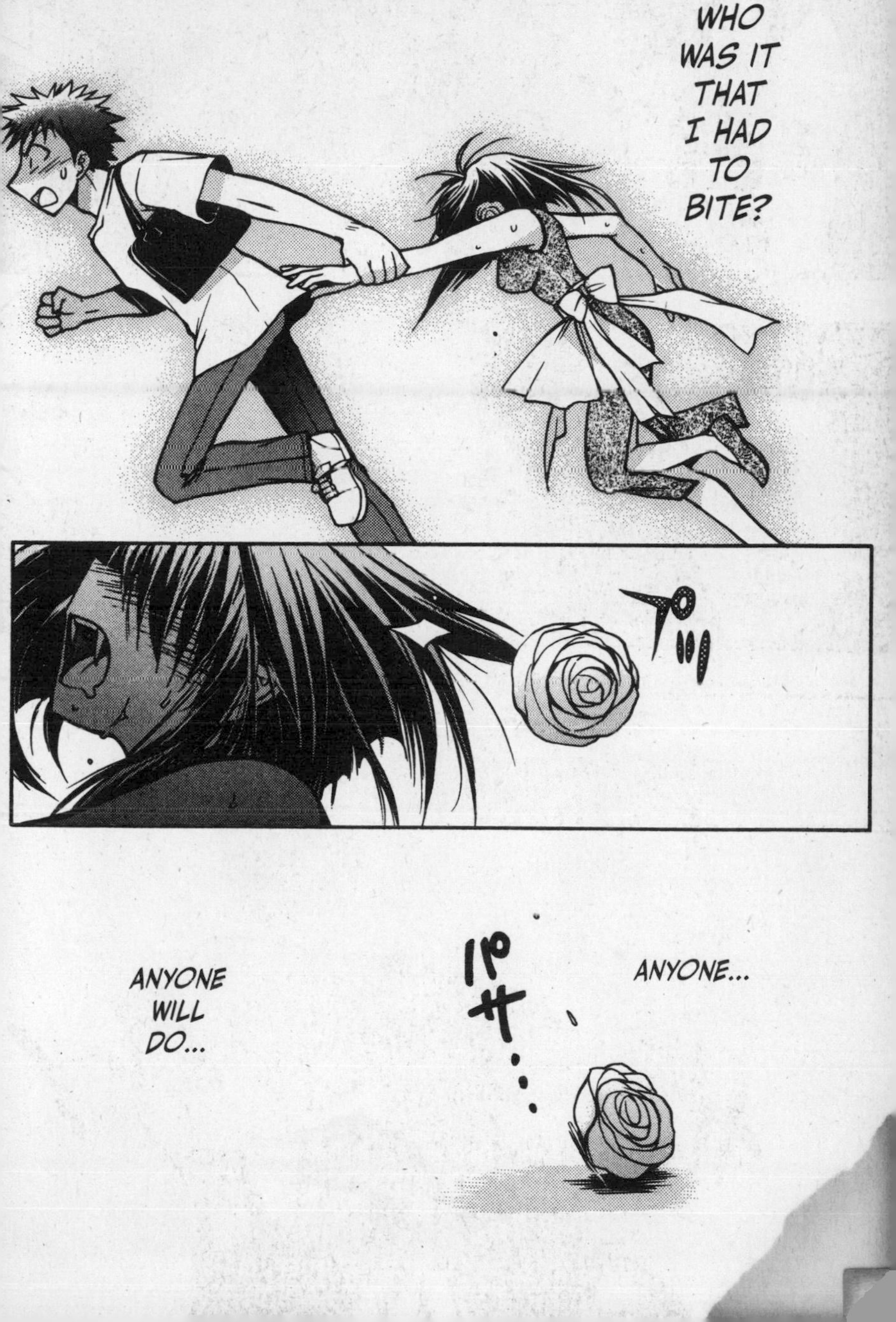
WHO WAS IT THAT I HAD TO BITE?
プッ
ANYONE...
パサ…
ANYONE WILL DO...

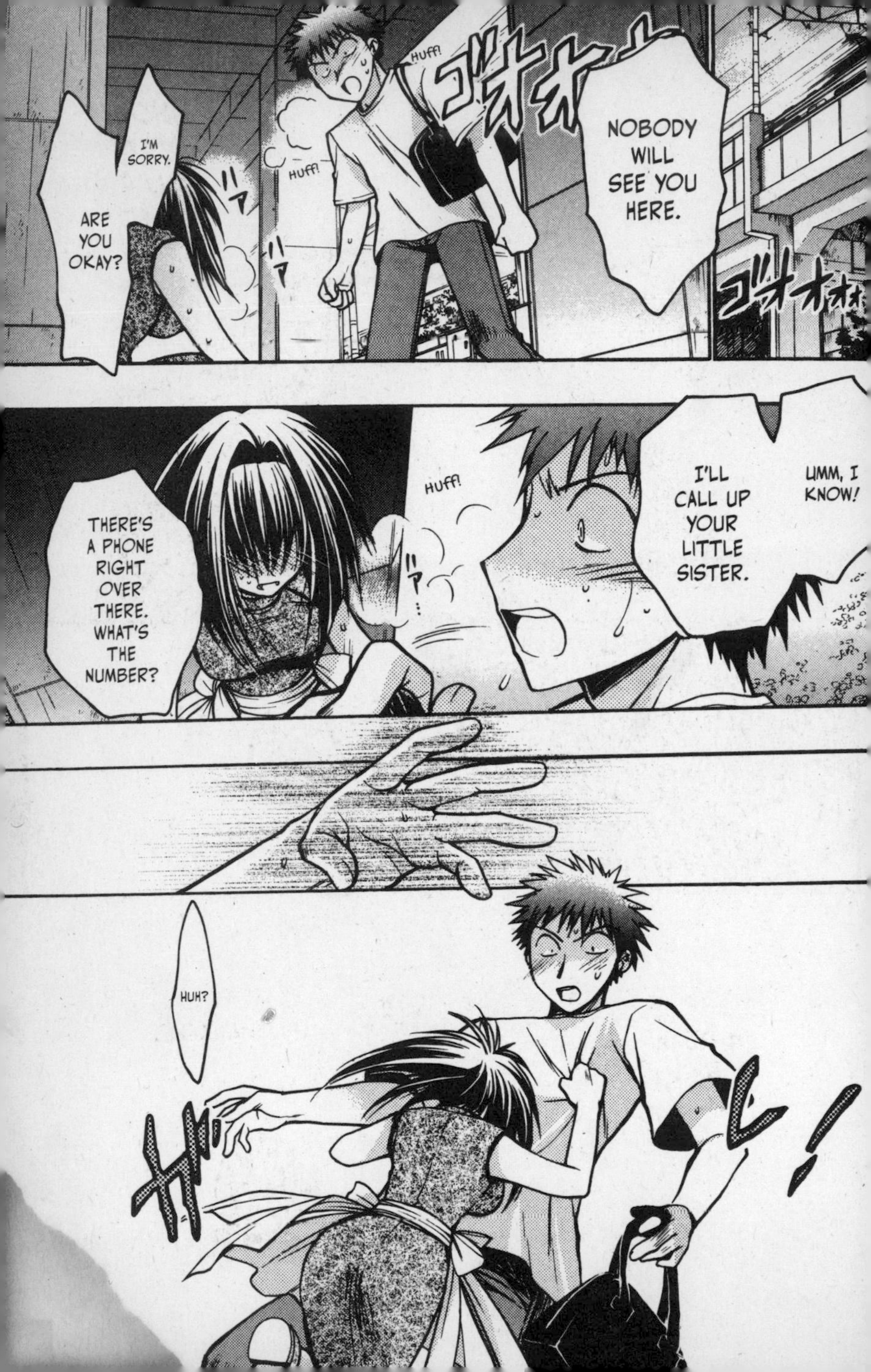
NOBODY WILL SEE YOU HERE.
HUFF!
HUFF!
I'M SORRY.
ARE YOU OKAY?
UMM, I KNOW!
I'LL CALL UP YOUR LITTLE SISTER.
HUFF!
THERE'S A PHONE RIGHT OVER THERE. WHAT'S THE NUMBER?
HUH?

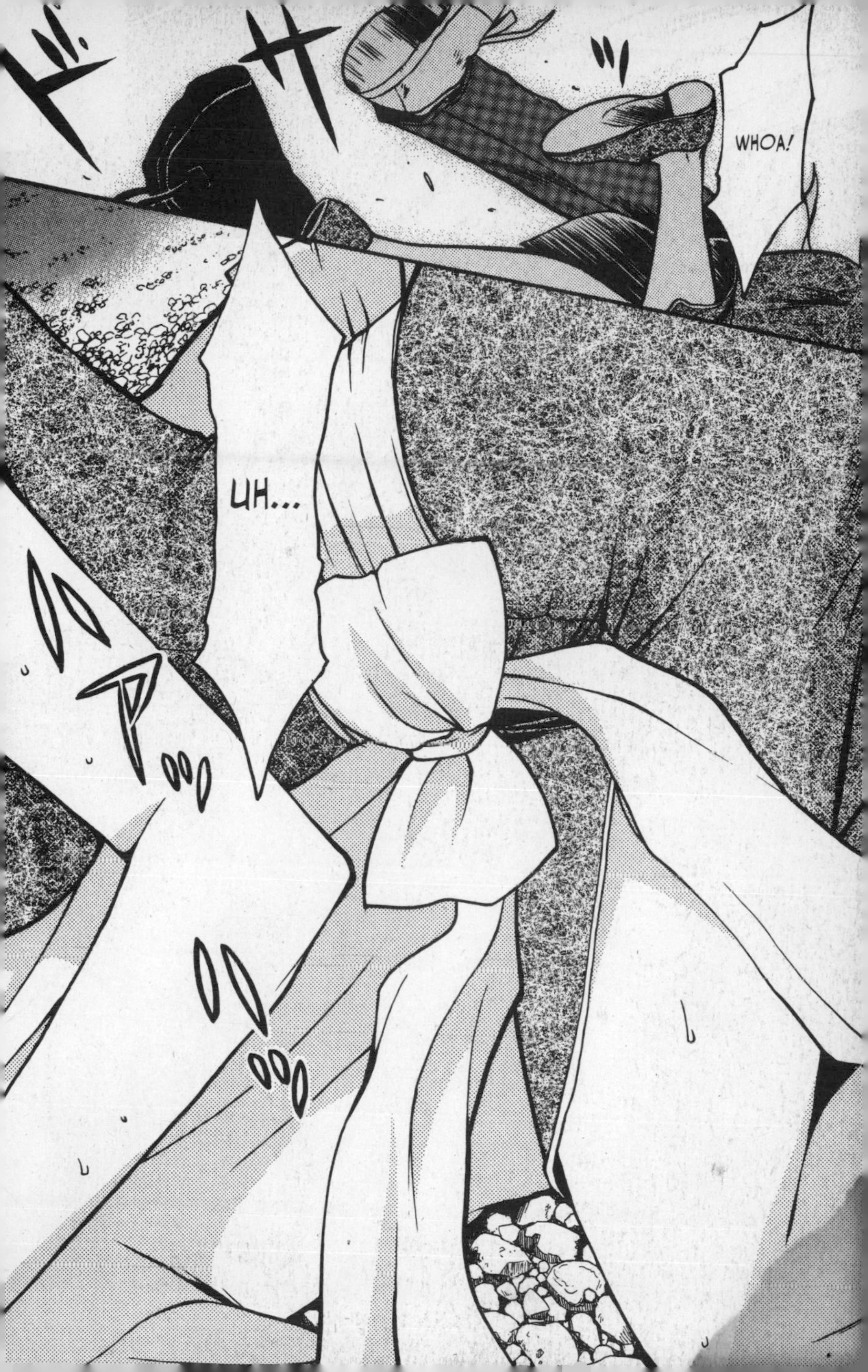
WHOA!
UH...

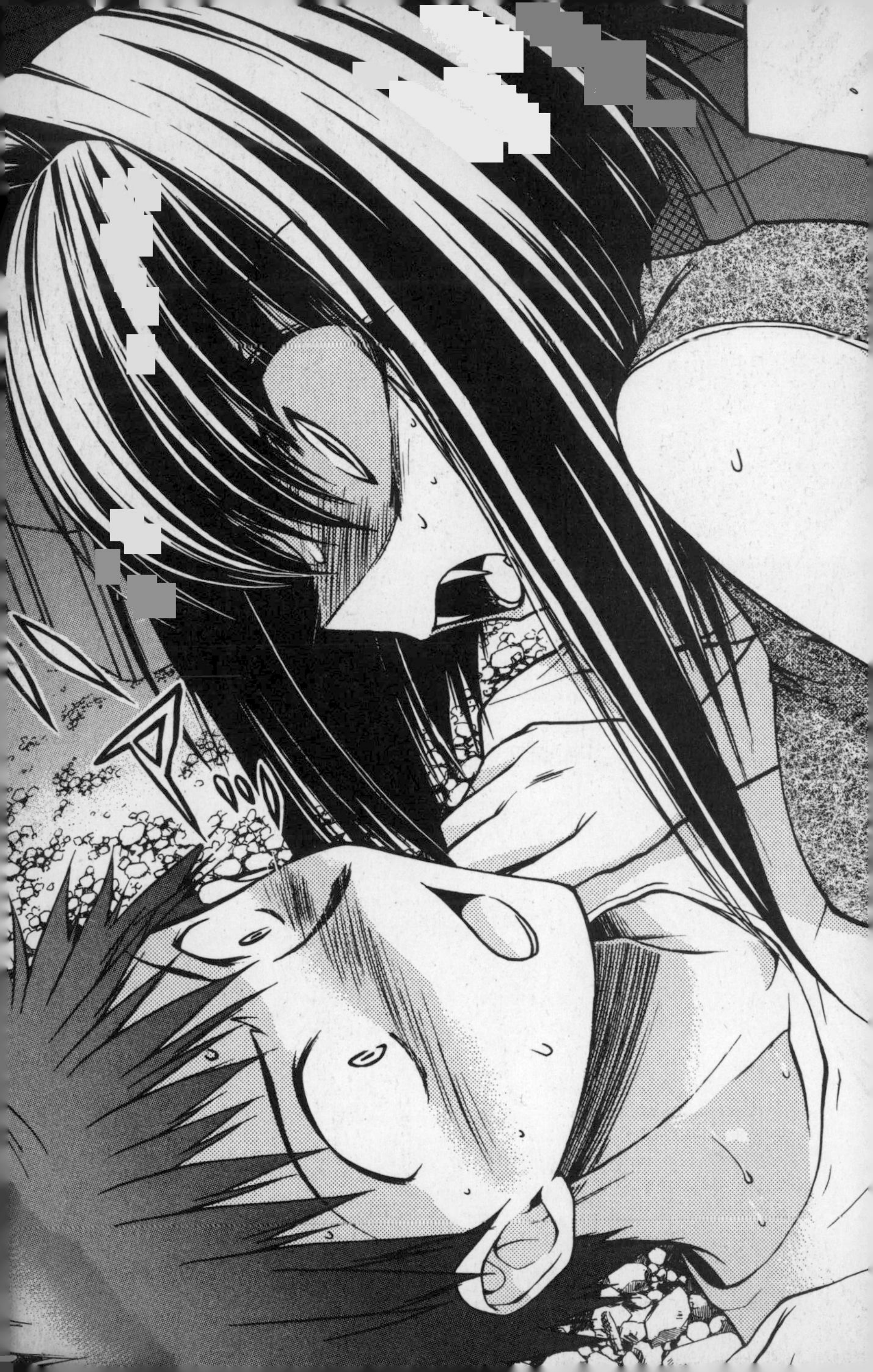

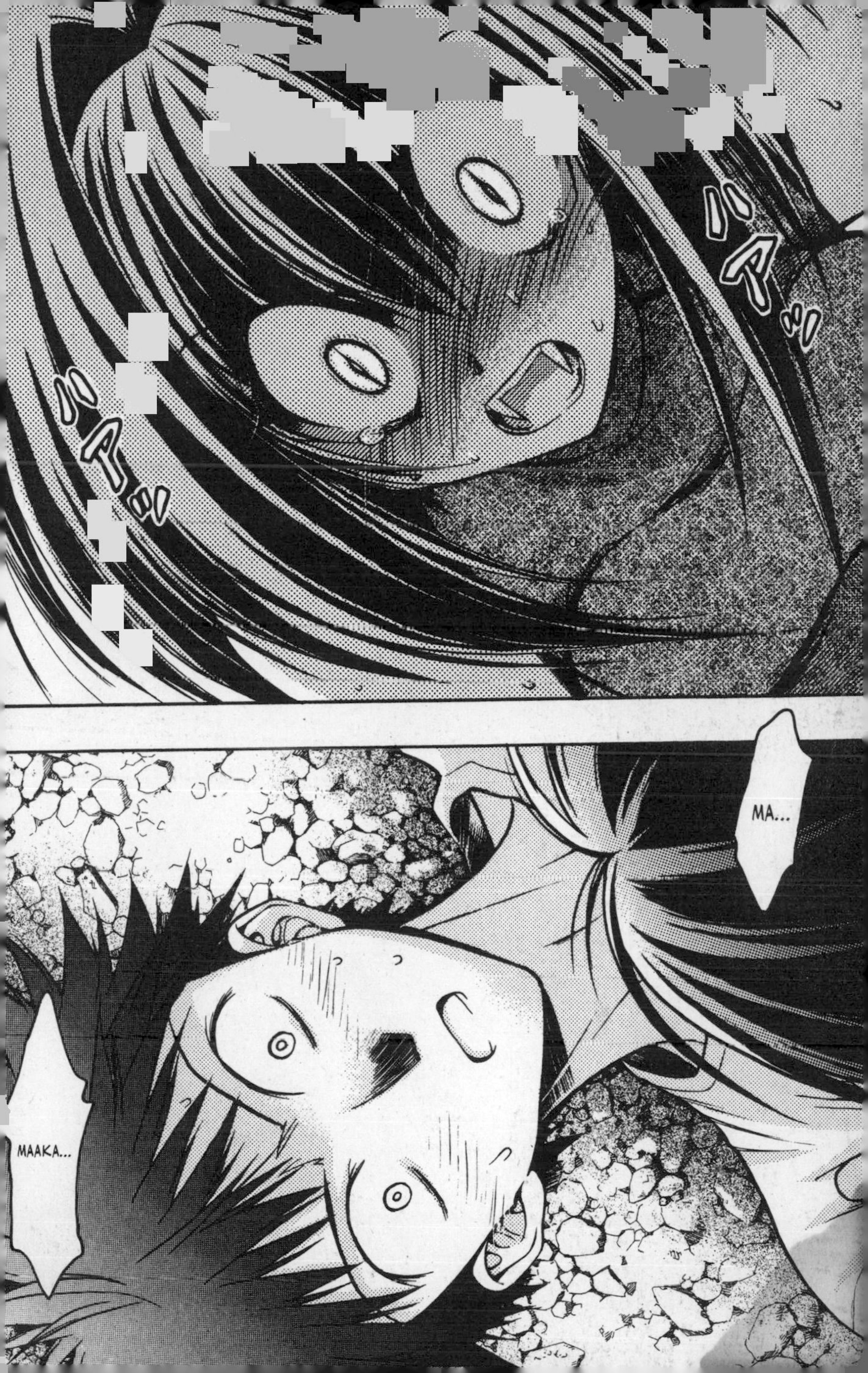
MA...
MAAKA...

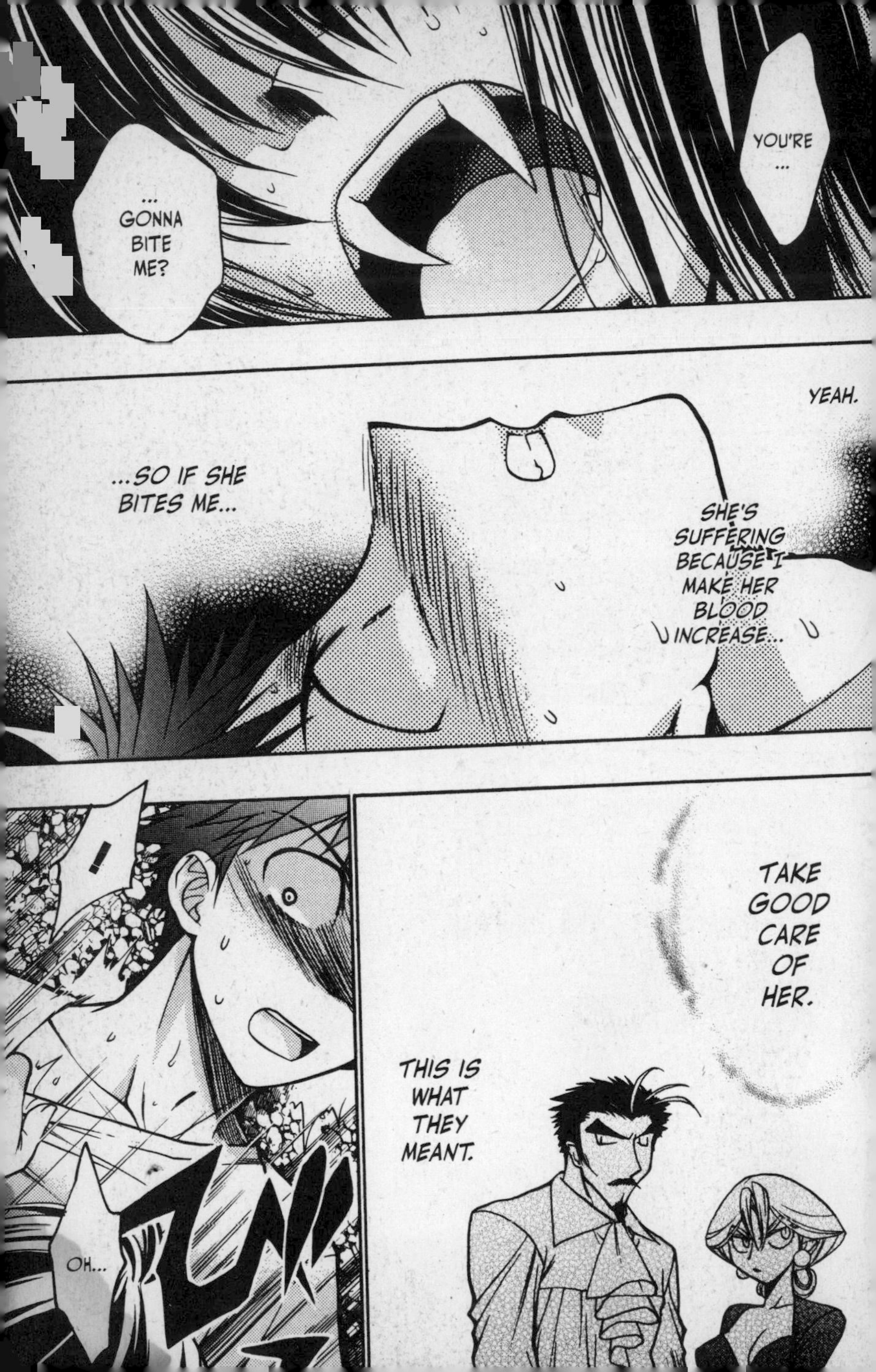

YOU'RE ...
... GONNA BITE ME?
YEAH.
SHE'S SUFFERING BECAUSE I MAKE HER BLOOD INCREASE...
...SO IF SHE BITES ME...
TAKE GOOD CARE OF HER.
THIS IS WHAT THEY MEANT.
!
OH...

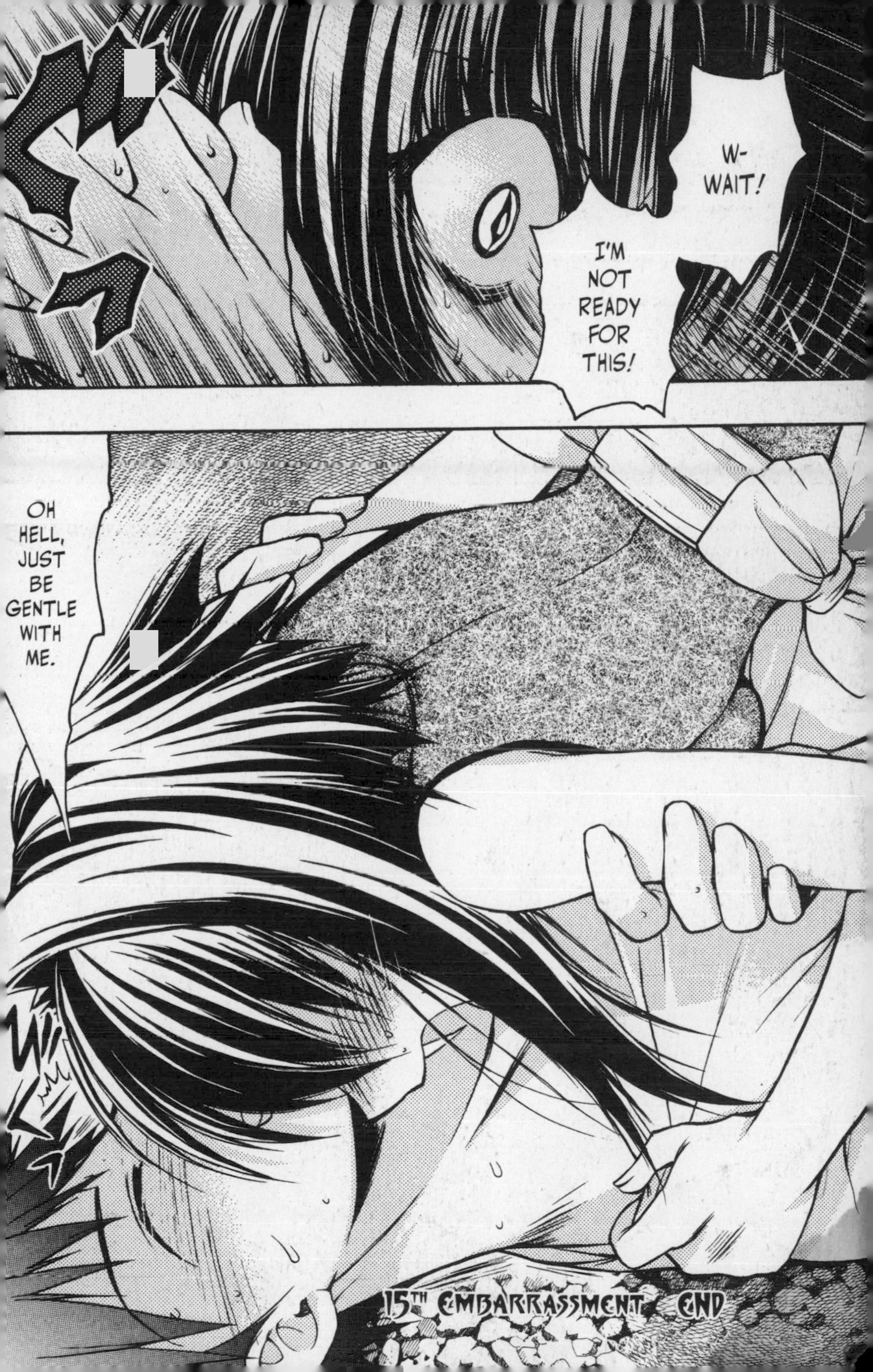
W-WAIT!
I'M NOT READY FOR THIS!
OH HELL, JUST BE GENTLE WITH ME.
15TH EMBARRASSMENT END

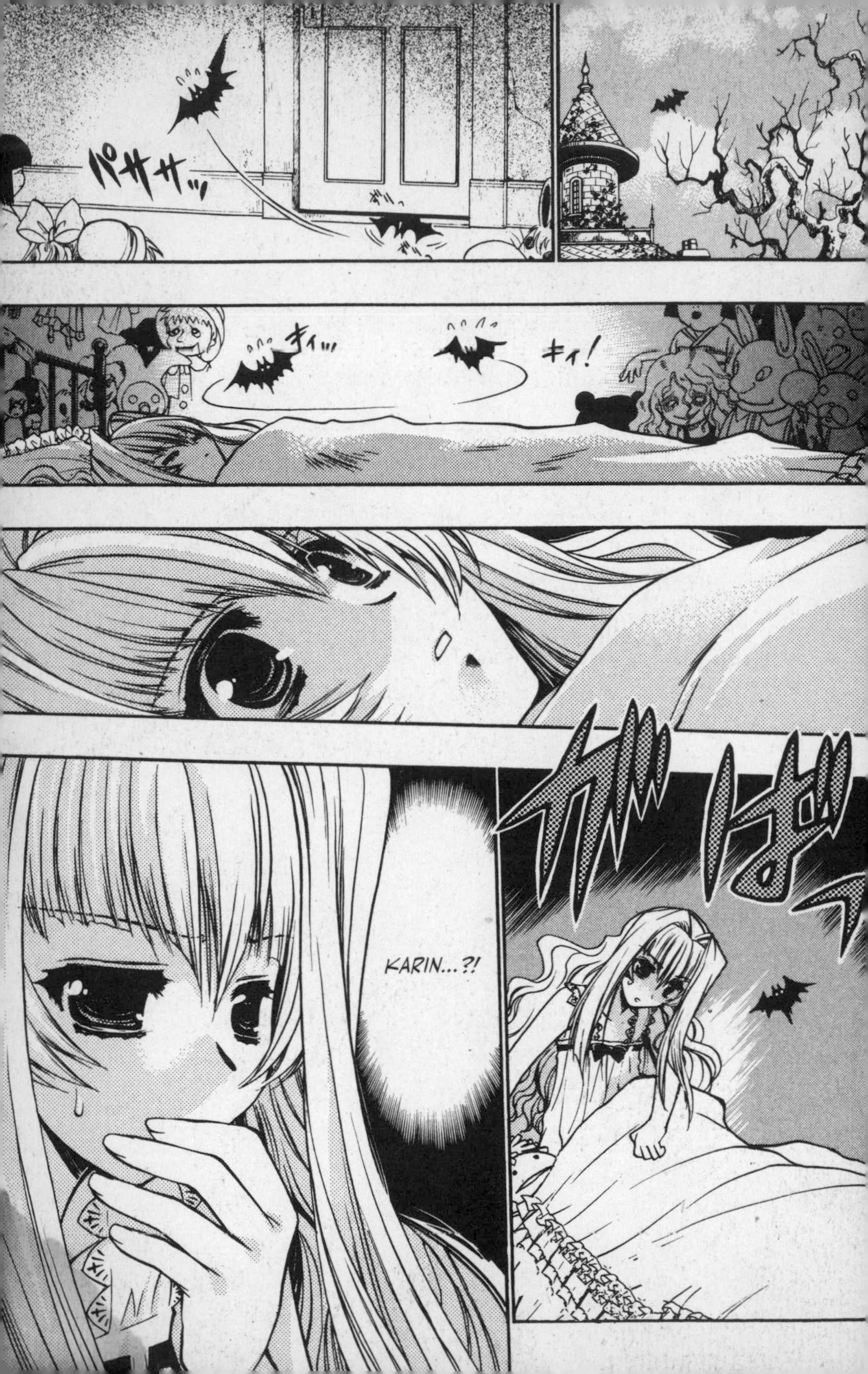
パササッ
キィ!
ギィッ
KARIN...?!

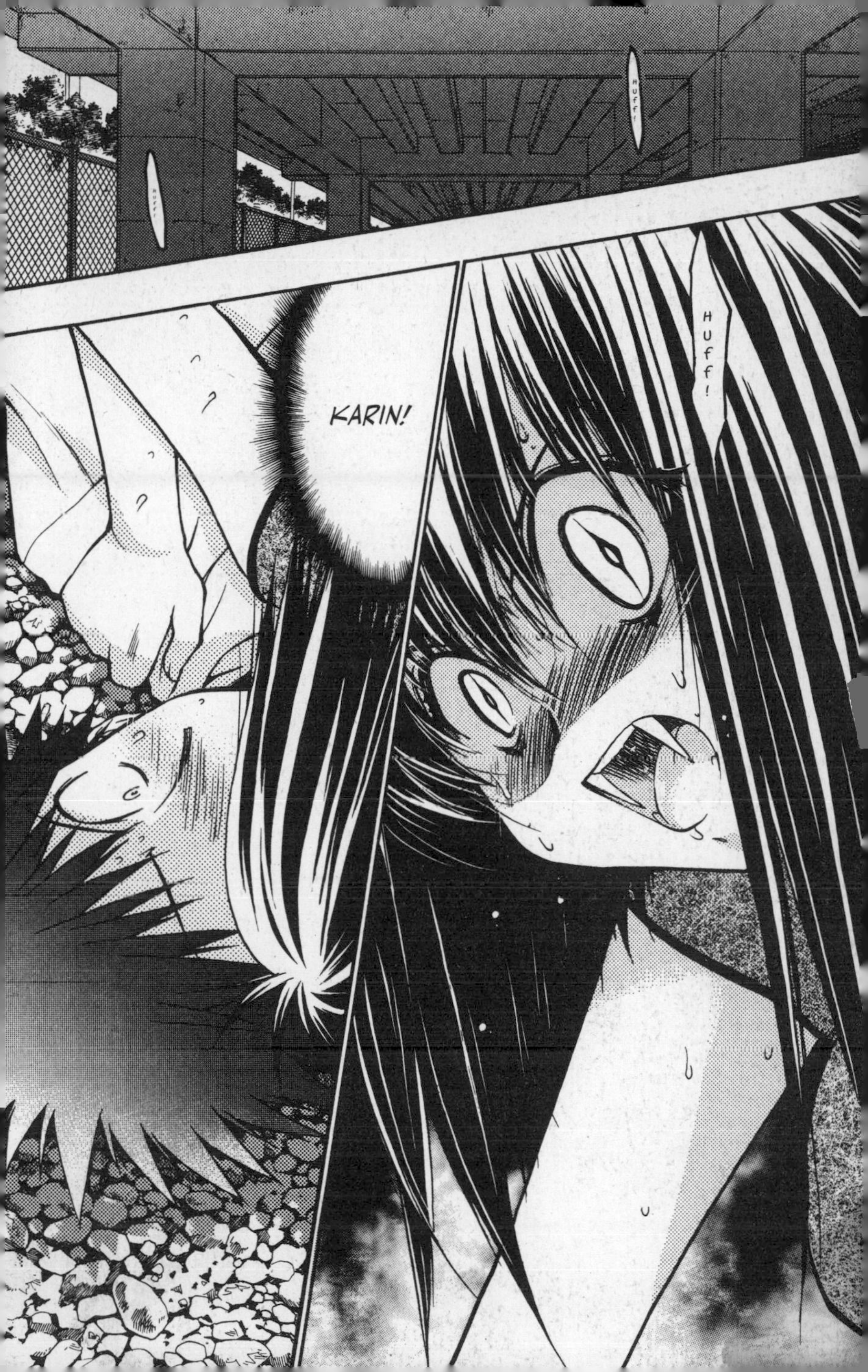
HUFF!
HUFF
Huff!
KARIN!

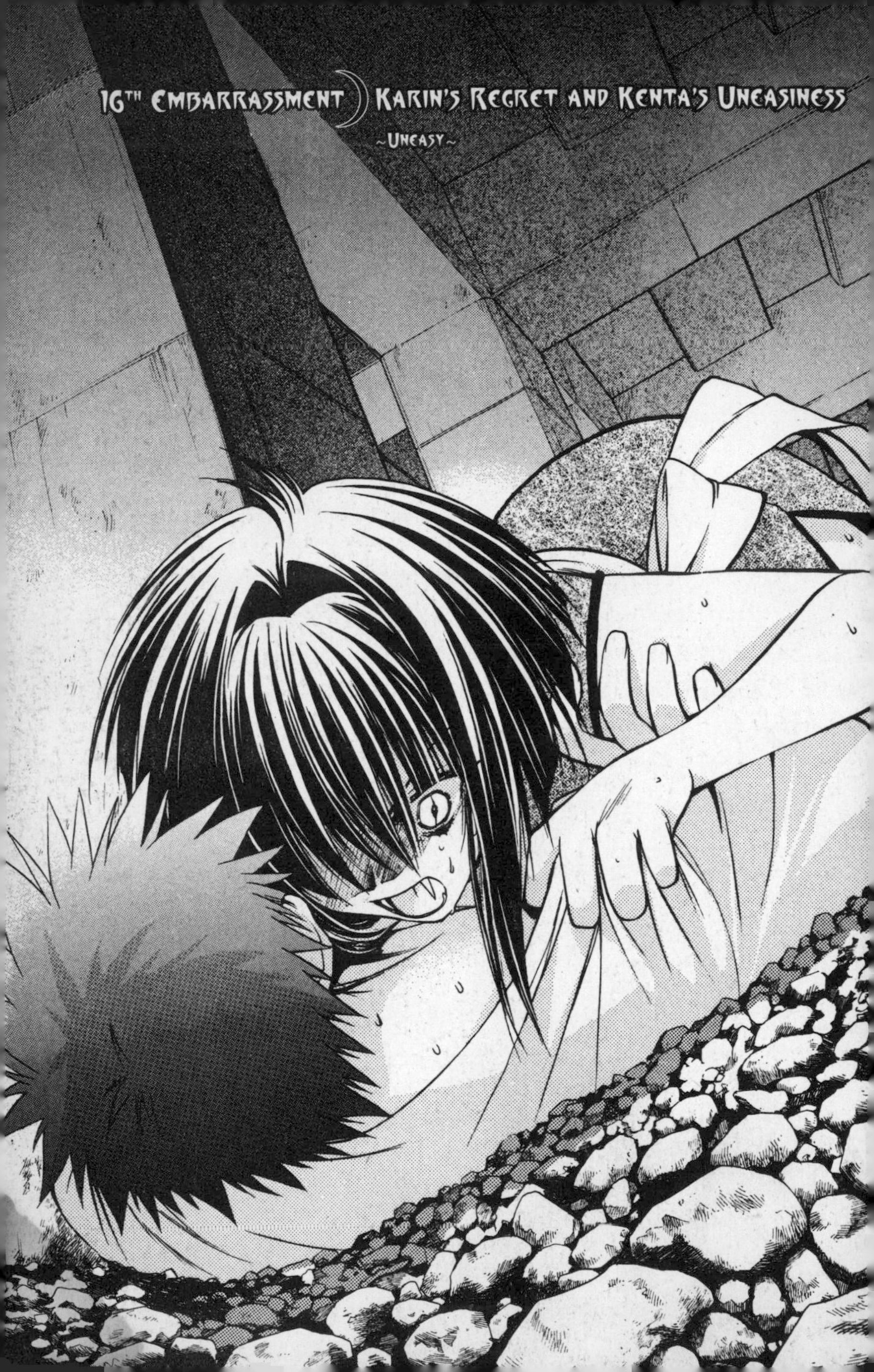
16TH EMBARRASSMENT Karin's Regret and Kenta's Uneasiness
~Uneasy~

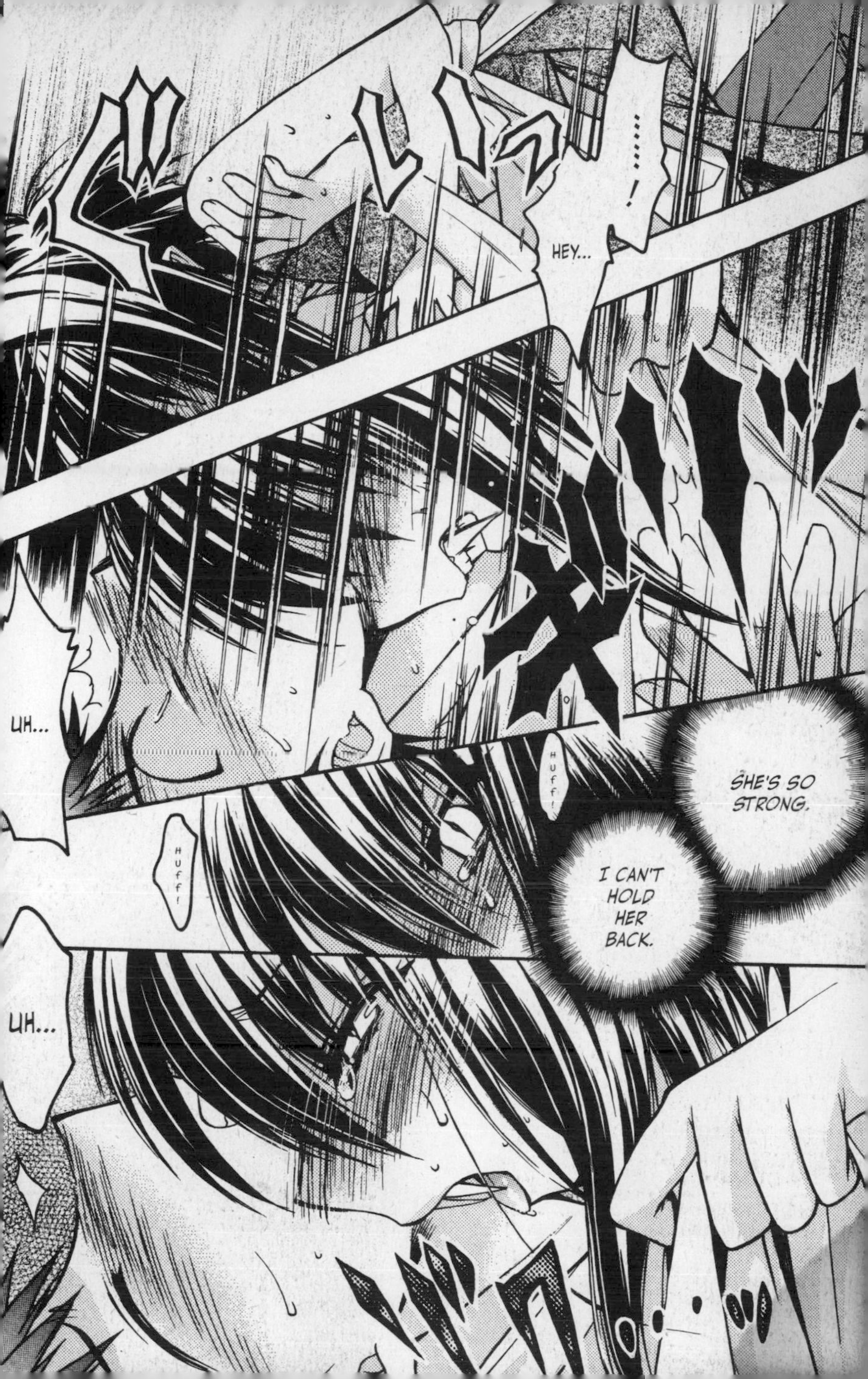
......!
HEY...
UH...
Huff!
SHE'S SO STRONG.
I CAN'T HOLD HER BACK.
Huff!
UH...

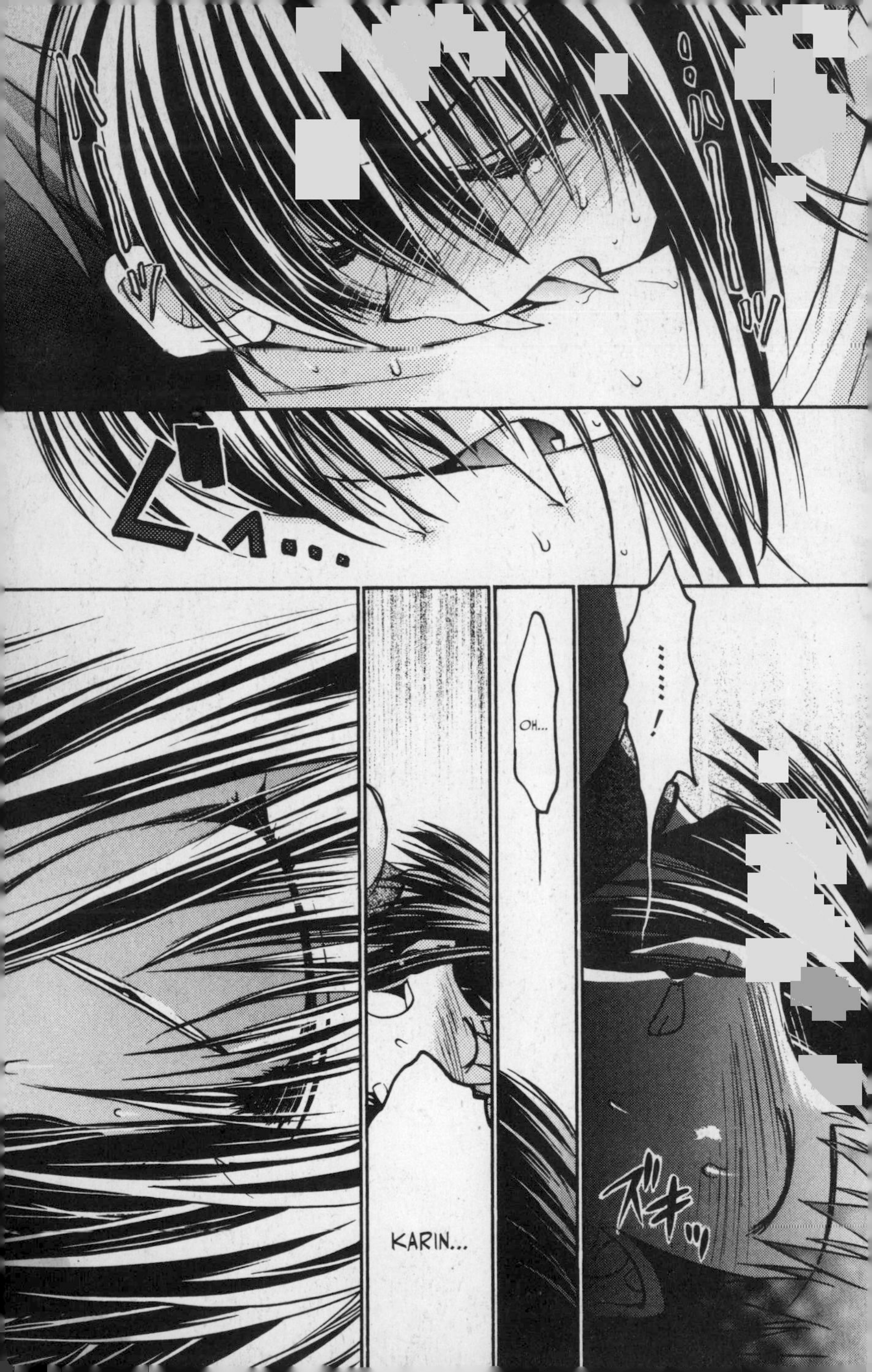
......!
OH...
KARIN...

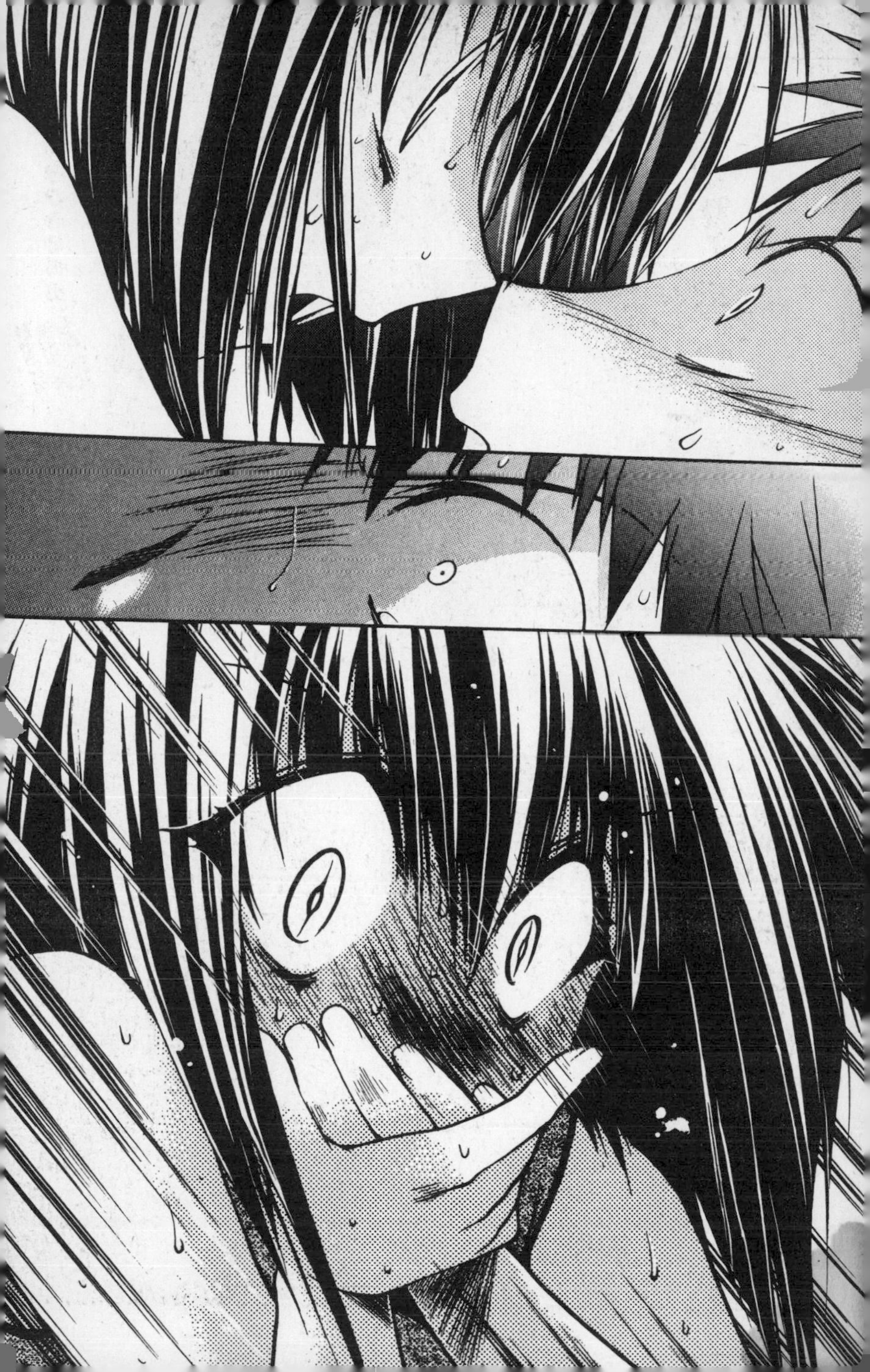

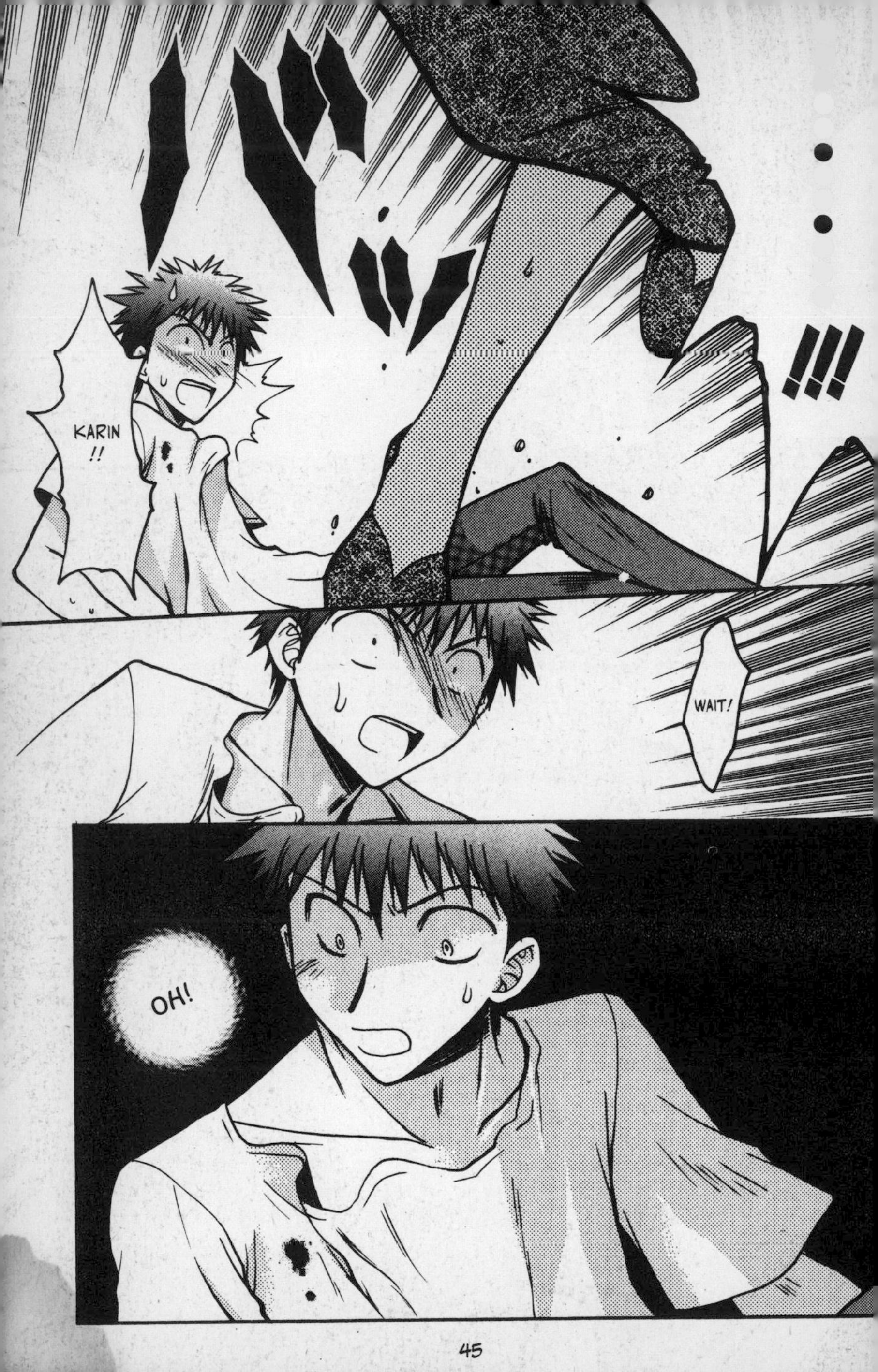
!!!!
KARIN !!
WAIT!
OH!

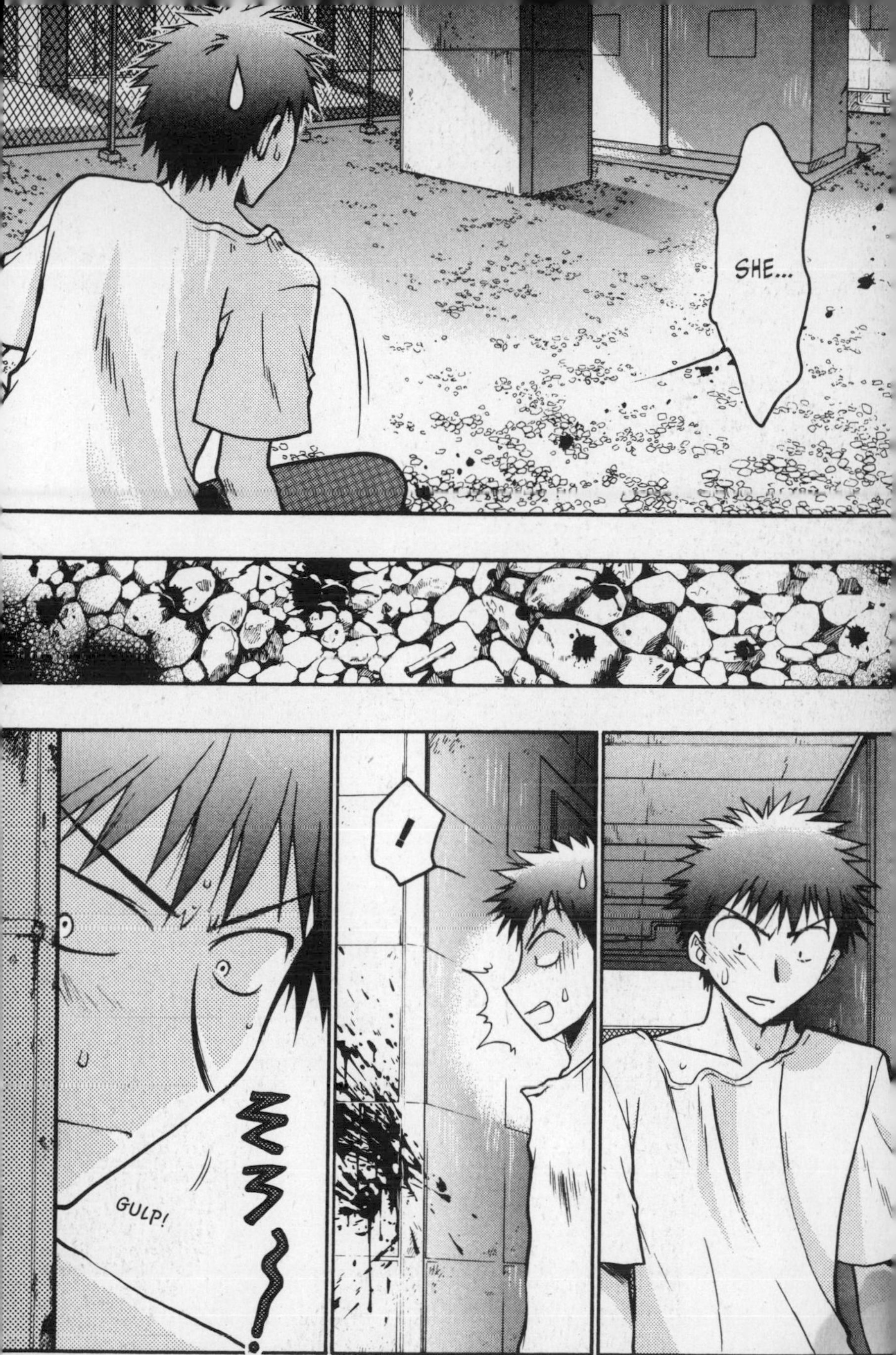
SHE...
!
GULP!

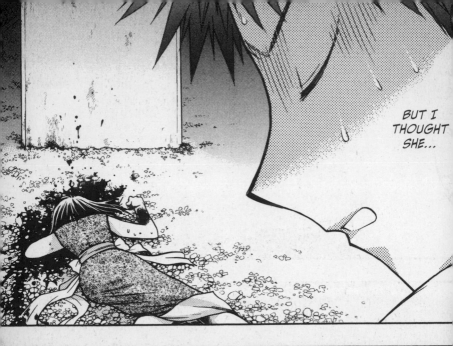

BUT I THOUGHT SHE...

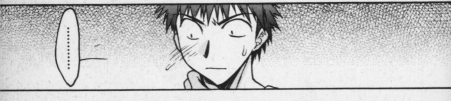

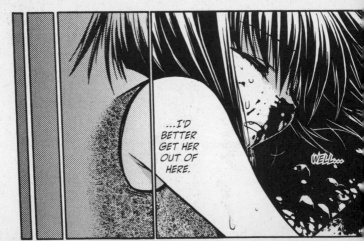

SO COLD...

...I'D BETTER GET HER OUT OF HERE.

WELL...

47

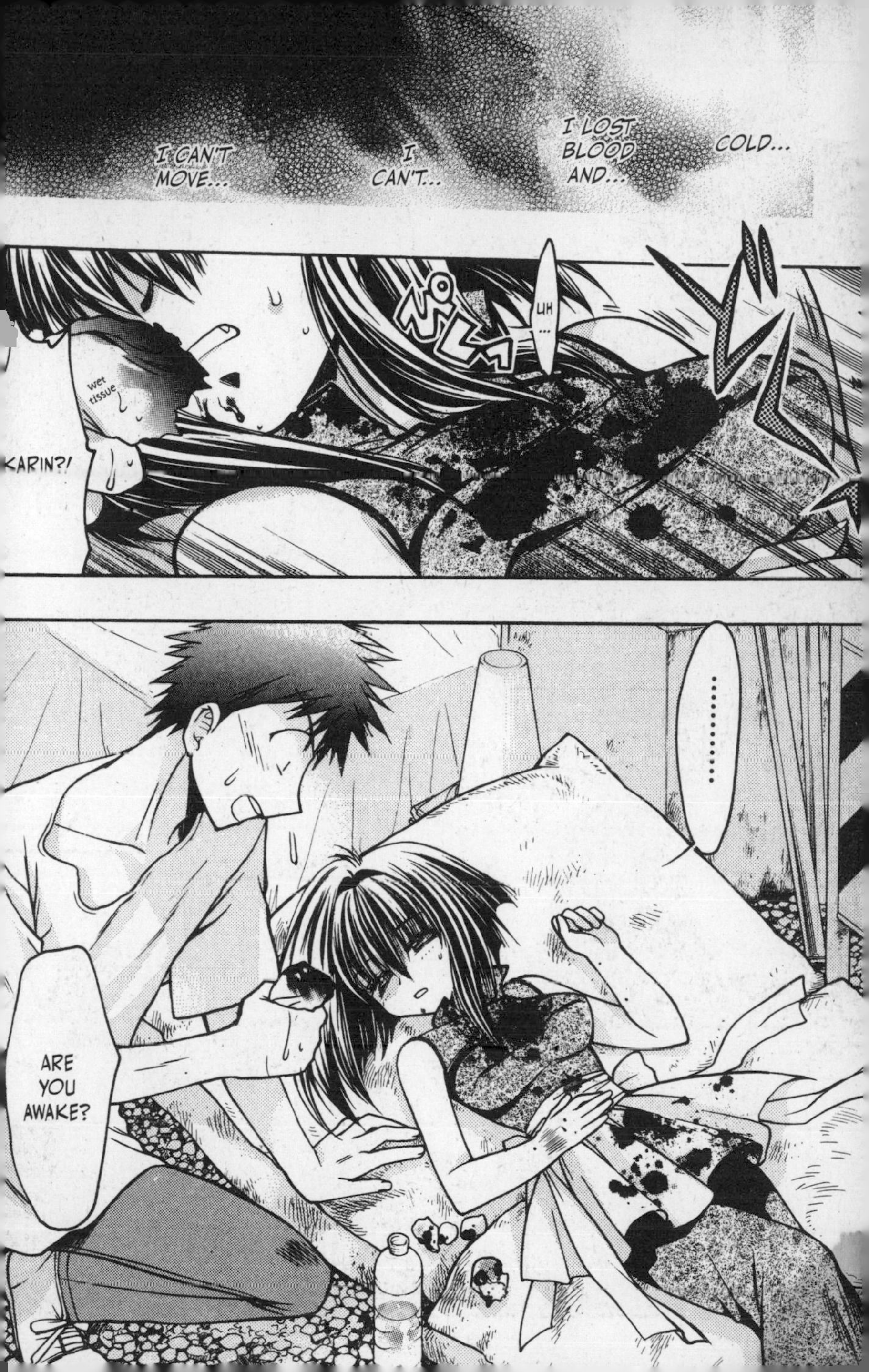
COLD...
I LOST BLOOD AND...
I CAN'T...
I CAN'T MOVE...
UH ...
wet tissue
KARIN?!
......
ARE YOU AWAKE?

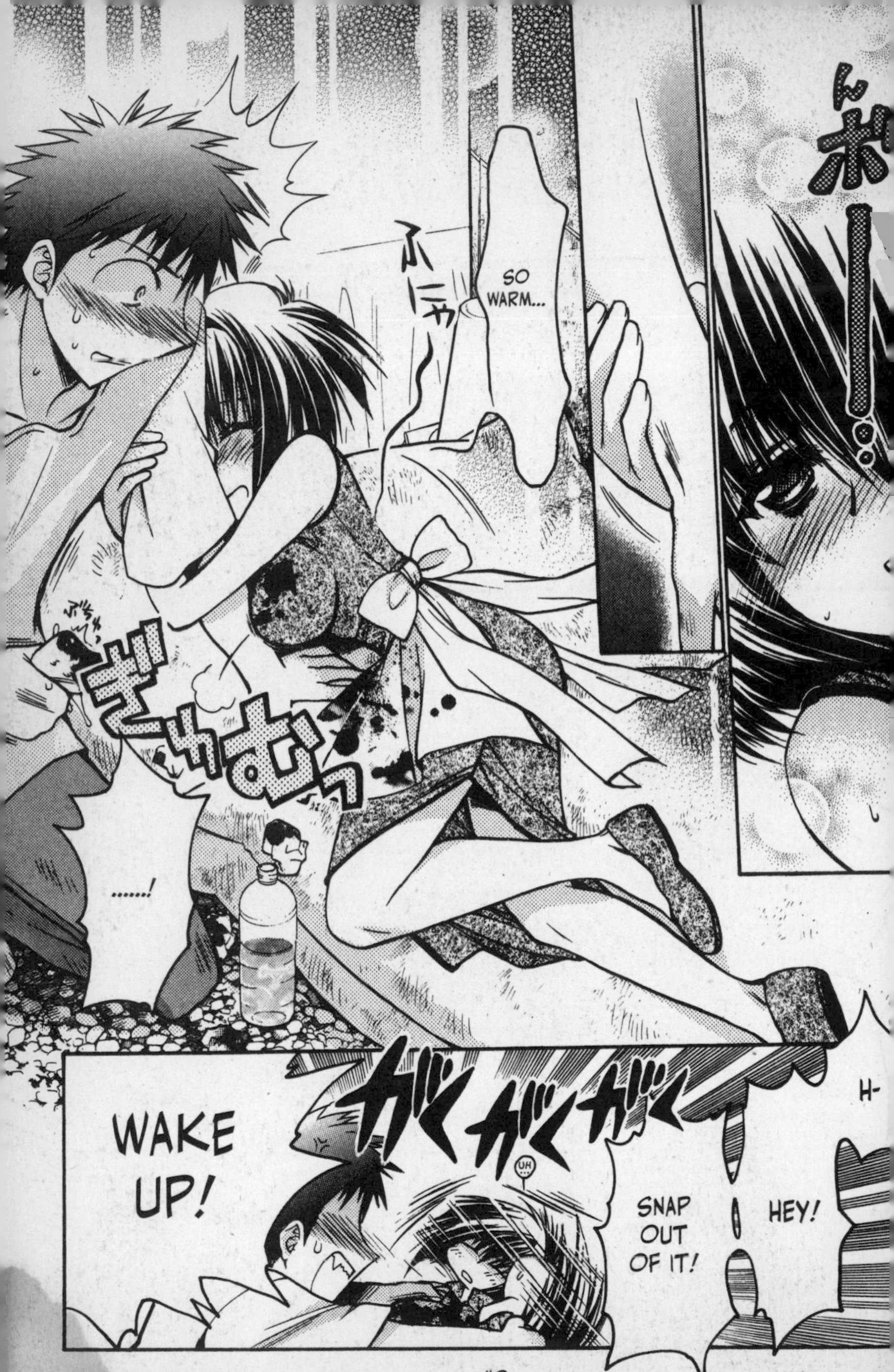
んボー！
ふにゃ
SO WARM...
ぎゅむっ
......!
H-
HEY!
SNAP OUT OF IT!
UH
がくがくがく
WAKE UP!

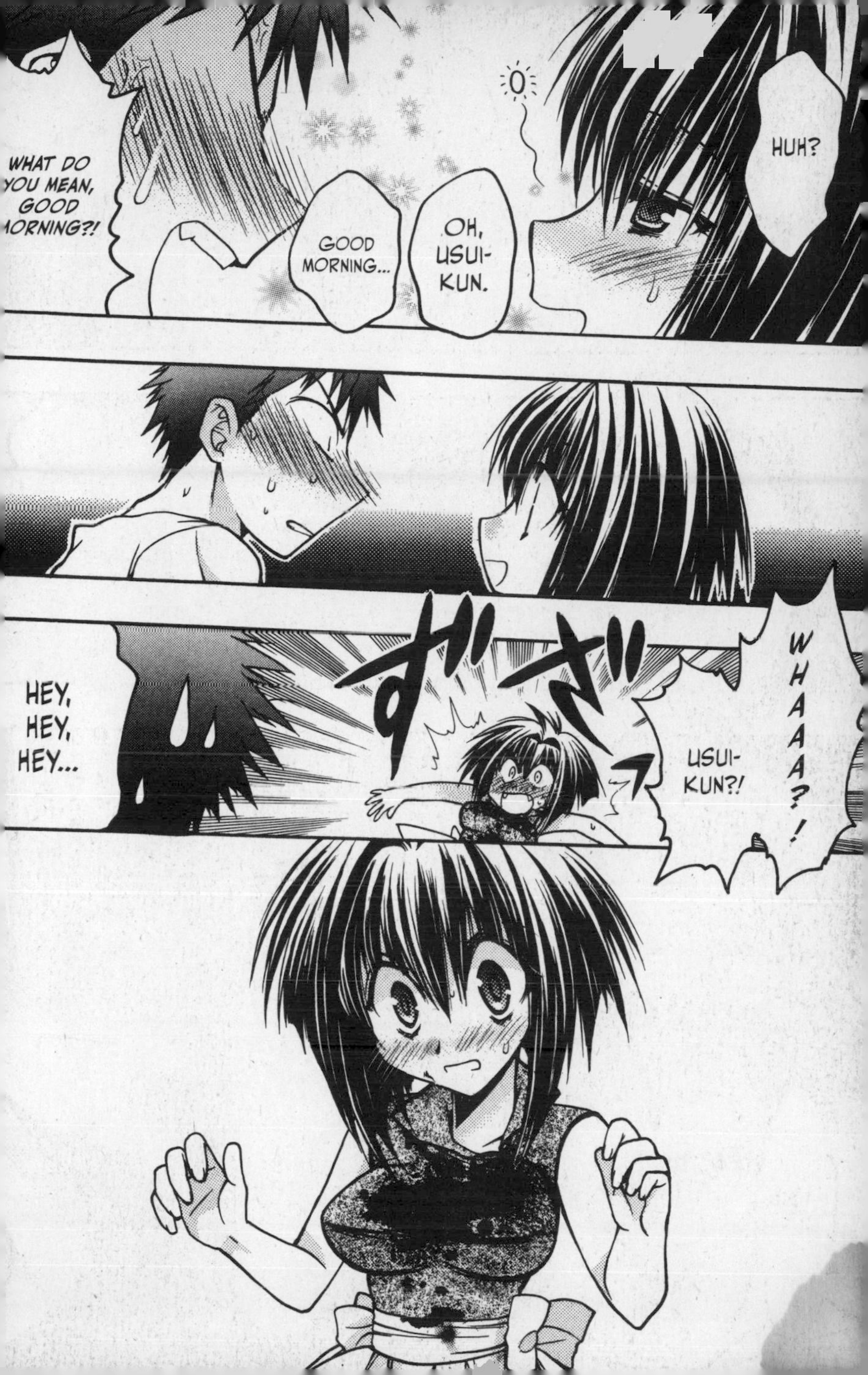
HUH?
OH, USUI-KUN.
GOOD MORNING...
WHAT DO YOU MEAN, GOOD MORNING?!
WHAAAA?!
USUI-KUN?!
ずざ
HEY, HEY, HEY...

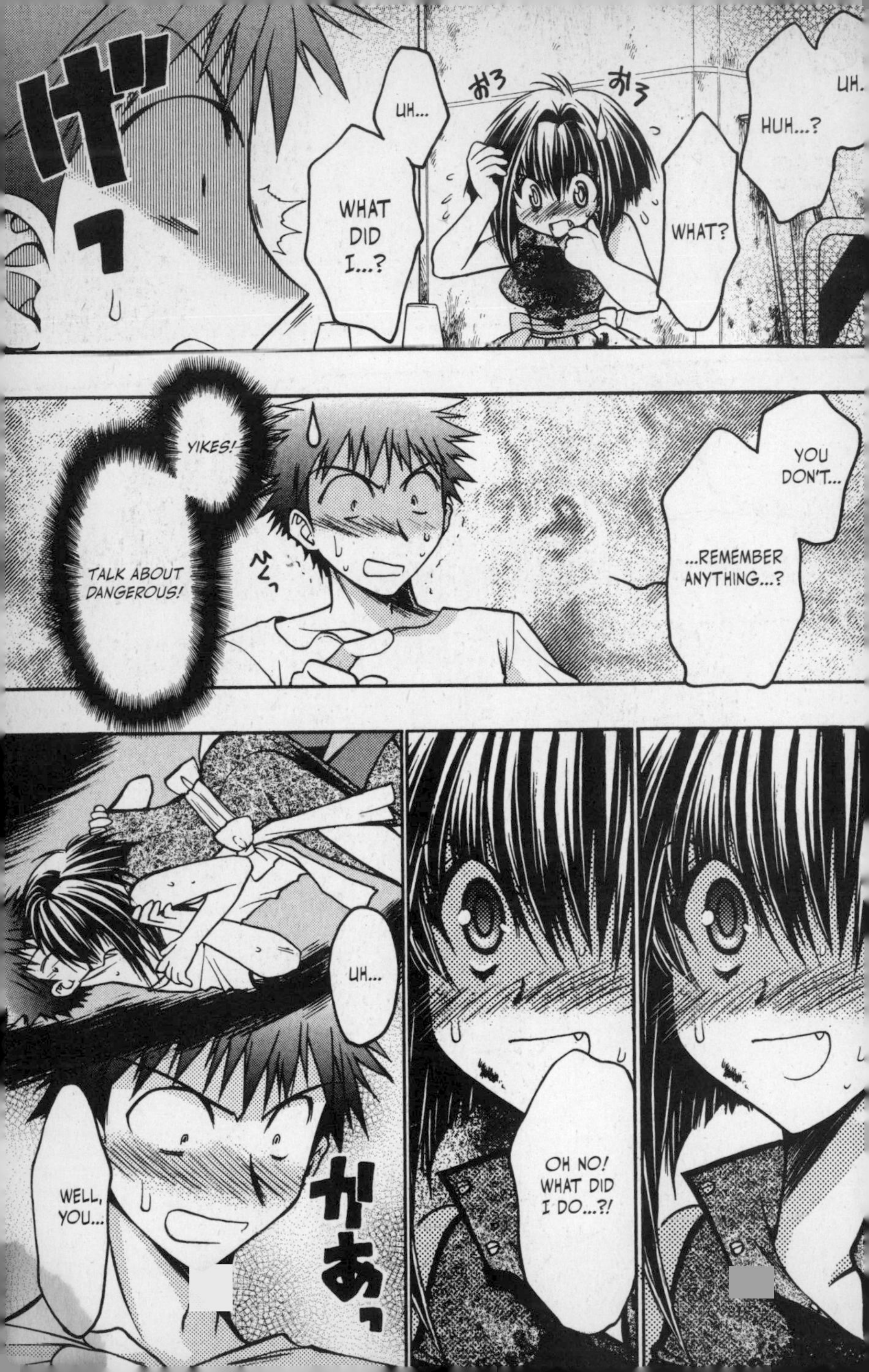
UH.
HUH...?
WHAT?
おろ
おろ
UH...
WHAT DID I...?
ゲッ
YOU DON'T...
...REMEMBER ANYTHING...?
YIKES!
TALK ABOUT DANGEROUS!
OH NO! WHAT DID I DO...?!
UH...
WELL, YOU...
かあっ

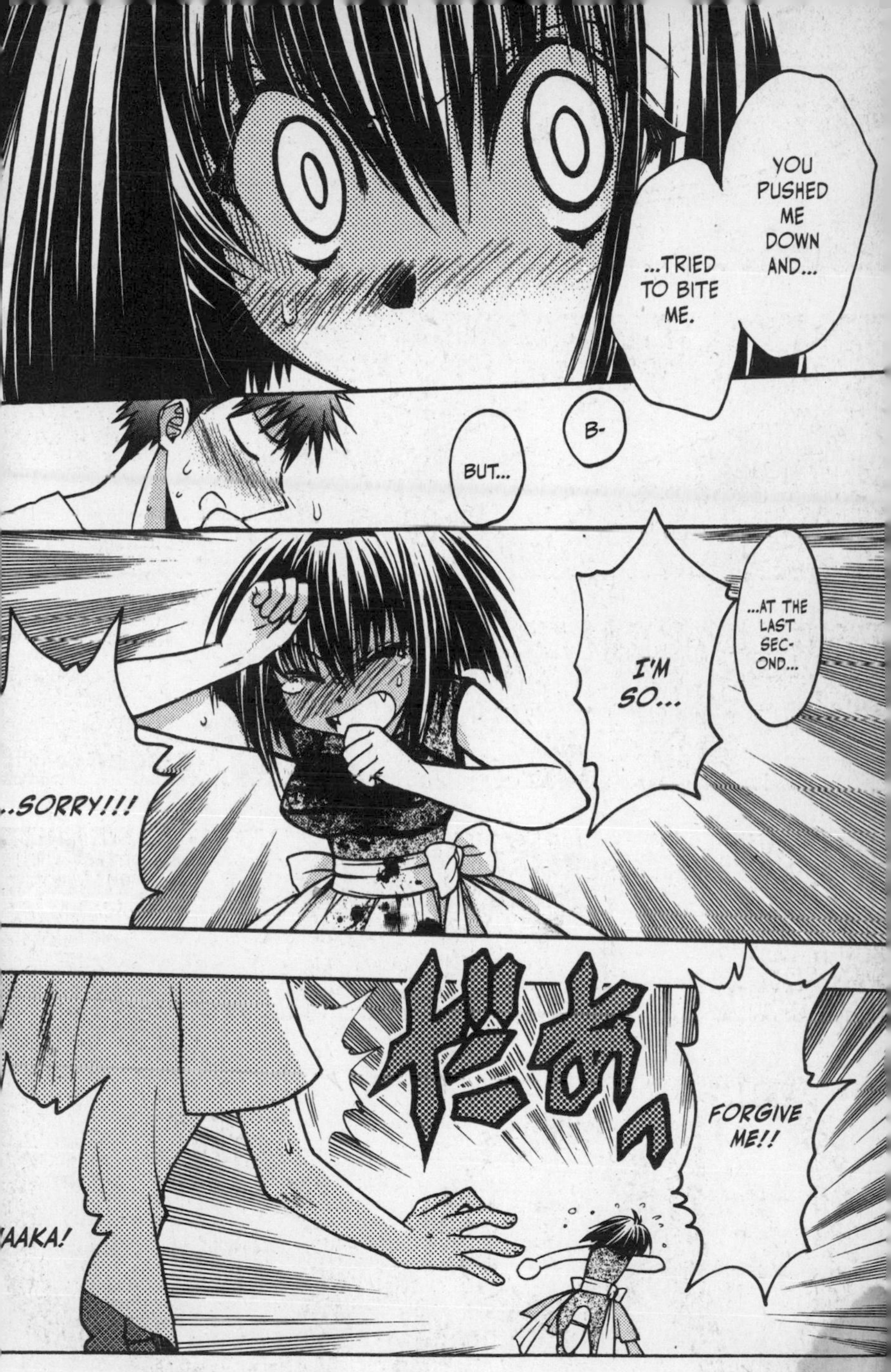
YOU PUSHED ME DOWN AND...
...TRIED TO BITE ME.
B-
BUT...
...AT THE LAST SEC- OND...
I'M SO...
..SORRY!!!
FORGIVE ME!!
AAKA!

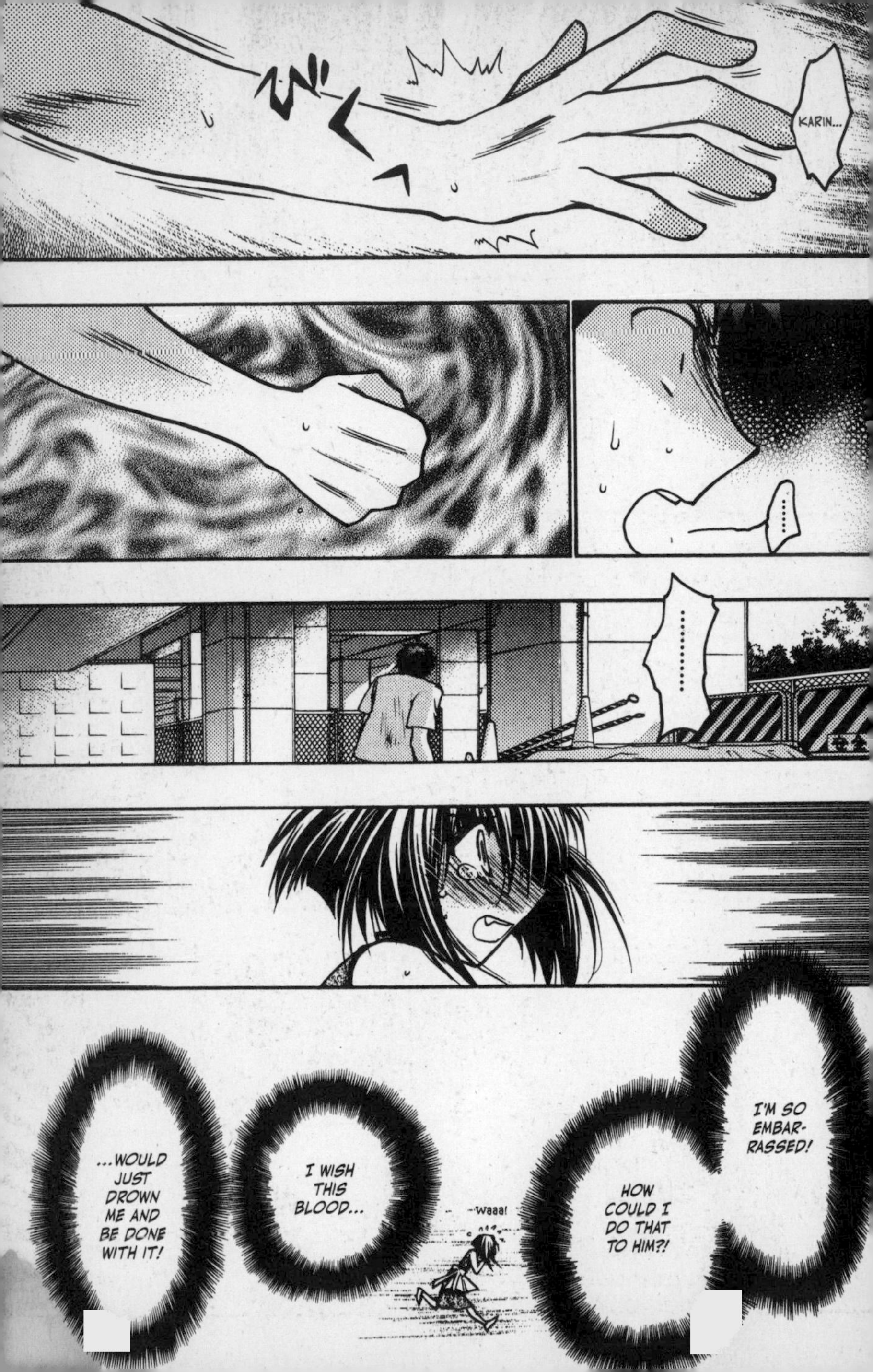
KARIN...
......
......
I'M SO EMBARRASSED!
HOW COULD I DO THAT TO HIM?!
--Waaa!
I WISH THIS BLOOD...
...WOULD JUST DROWN ME AND BE DONE WITH IT!

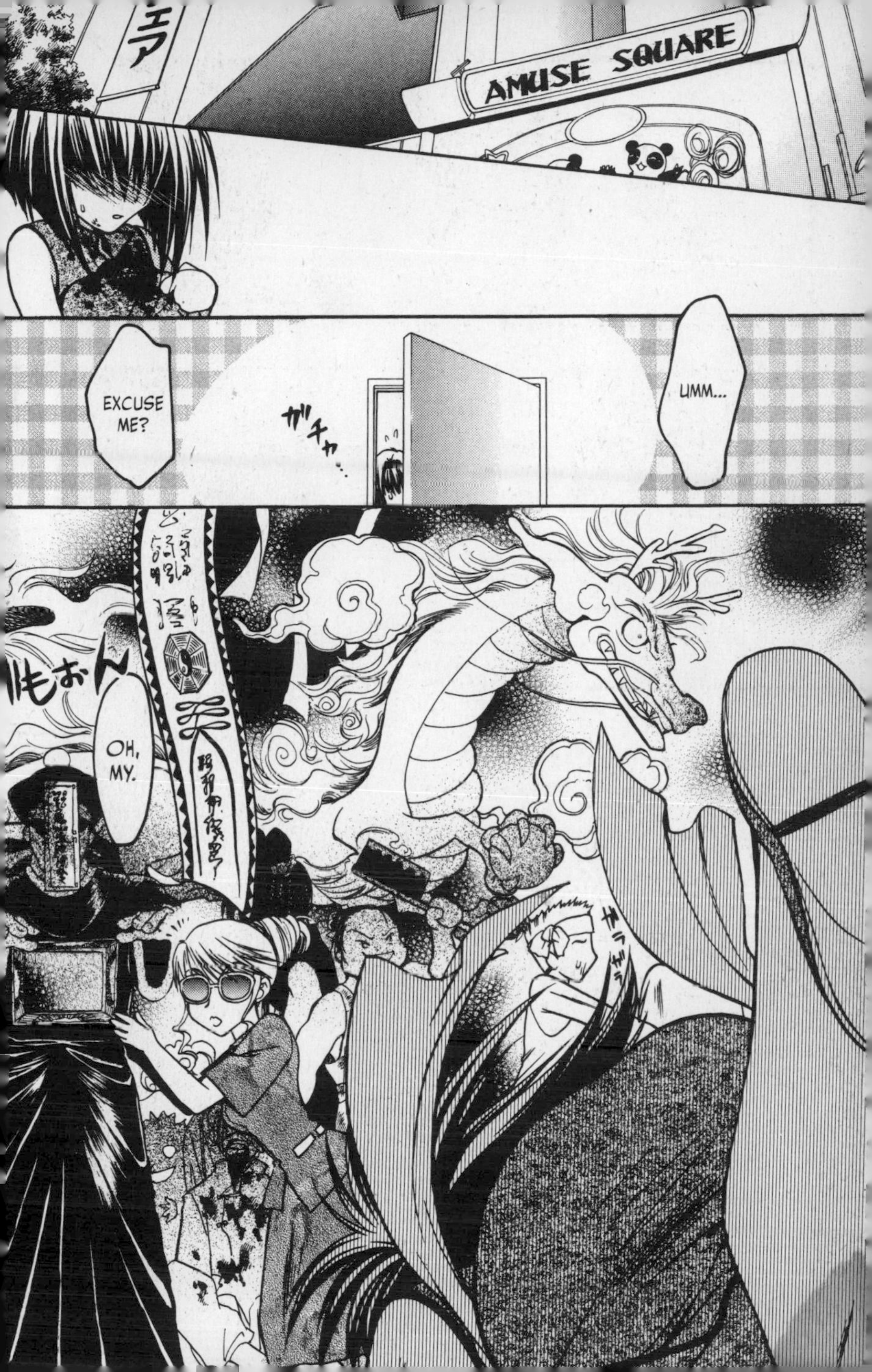
エア
AMUSE SQUARE
UMM...
ガチャ...
EXCUSE ME?
ガラガラ
もおん
OH, MY.

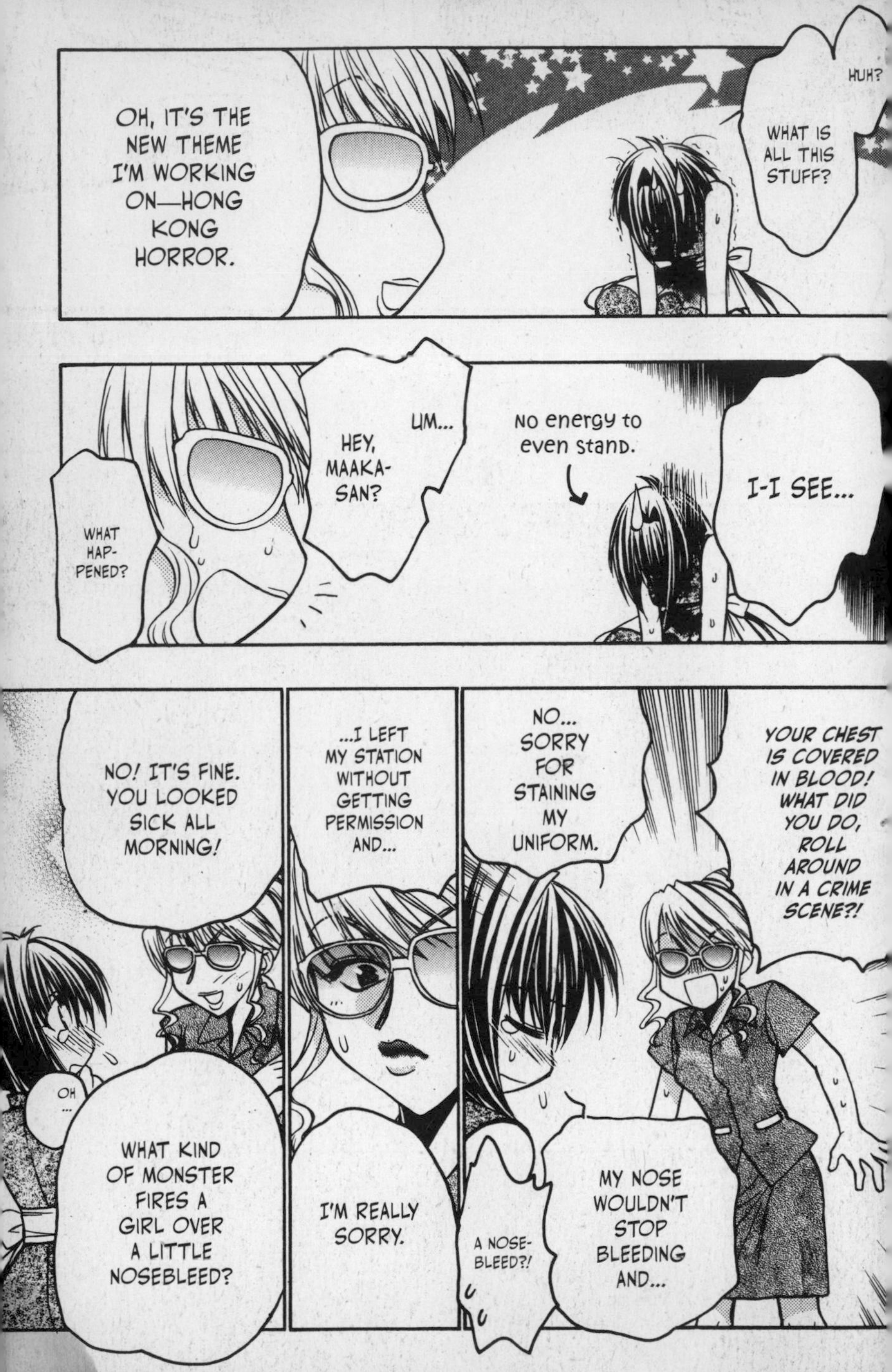
HUH?
WHAT IS ALL THIS STUFF?
OH, IT'S THE NEW THEME I'M WORKING ON—HONG KONG HORROR.
I-I SEE...
No energy to even stand.
UM...
HEY, MAAKA-SAN?
WHAT HAP-PENED?
YOUR CHEST IS COVERED IN BLOOD! WHAT DID YOU DO, ROLL AROUND IN A CRIME SCENE?!
NO... SORRY FOR STAINING MY UNIFORM.
MY NOSE WOULDN'T STOP BLEEDING AND...
A NOSE-BLEED?!
...I LEFT MY STATION WITHOUT GETTING PERMISSION AND...
I'M REALLY SORRY.
NO! IT'S FINE. YOU LOOKED SICK ALL MORNING!
OH ...
WHAT KIND OF MONSTER FIRES A GIRL OVER A LITTLE NOSEBLEED?

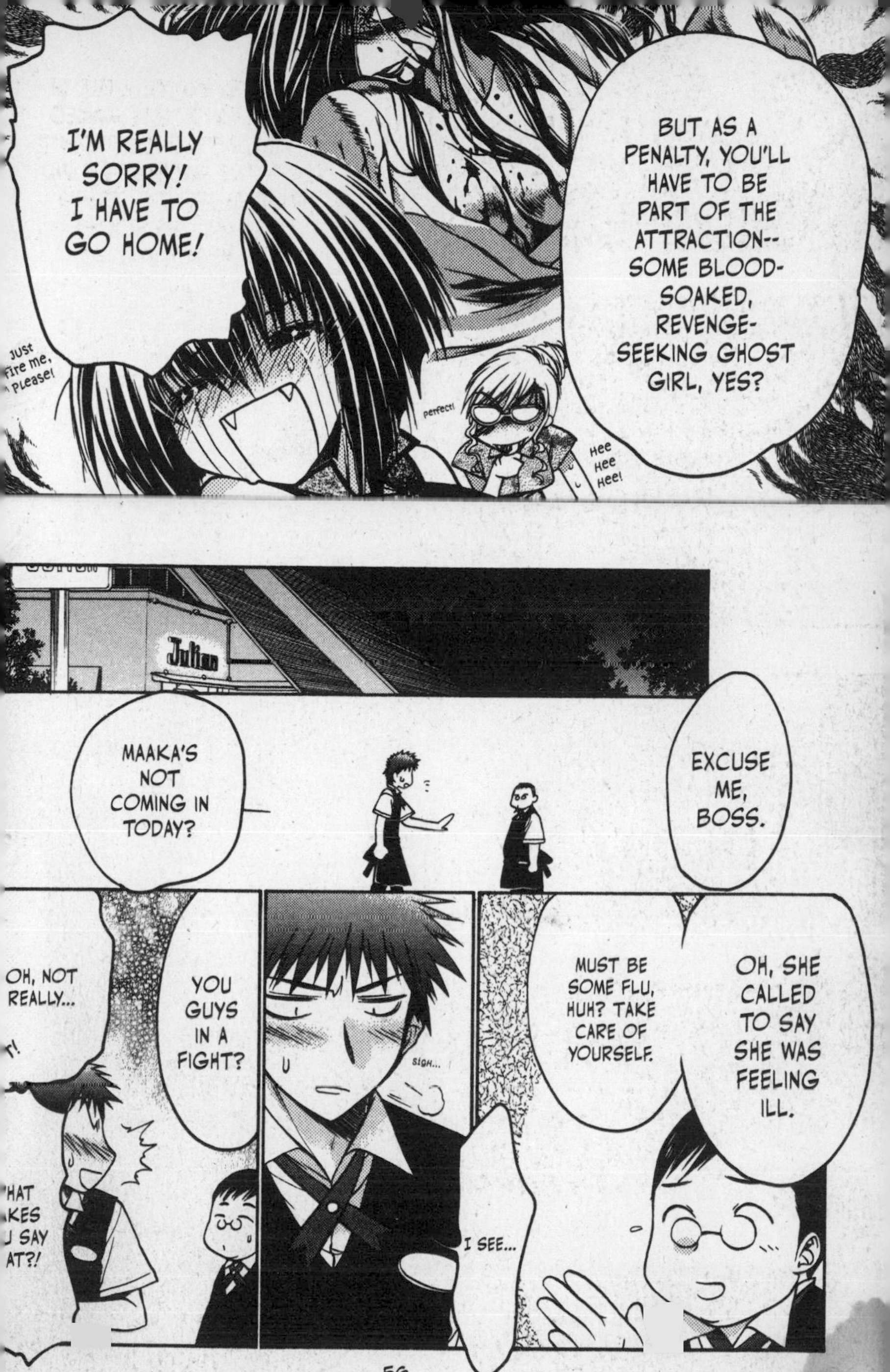
BUT AS A PENALTY, YOU'LL HAVE TO BE PART OF THE ATTRACTION--SOME BLOOD-SOAKED, REVENGE-SEEKING GHOST GIRL, YES?
Hee Hee Hee!
perfect!
I'M REALLY SORRY! I HAVE TO GO HOME!
Just fire me, please!
Julian
EXCUSE ME, BOSS.
MAAKA'S NOT COMING IN TODAY?
OH, SHE CALLED TO SAY SHE WAS FEELING ILL.
MUST BE SOME FLU, HUH? TAKE CARE OF YOURSELF.
SIGH...
I SEE...
YOU GUYS IN A FIGHT?
OH, NOT REALLY...
T!
HAT AKES U SAY AT?!

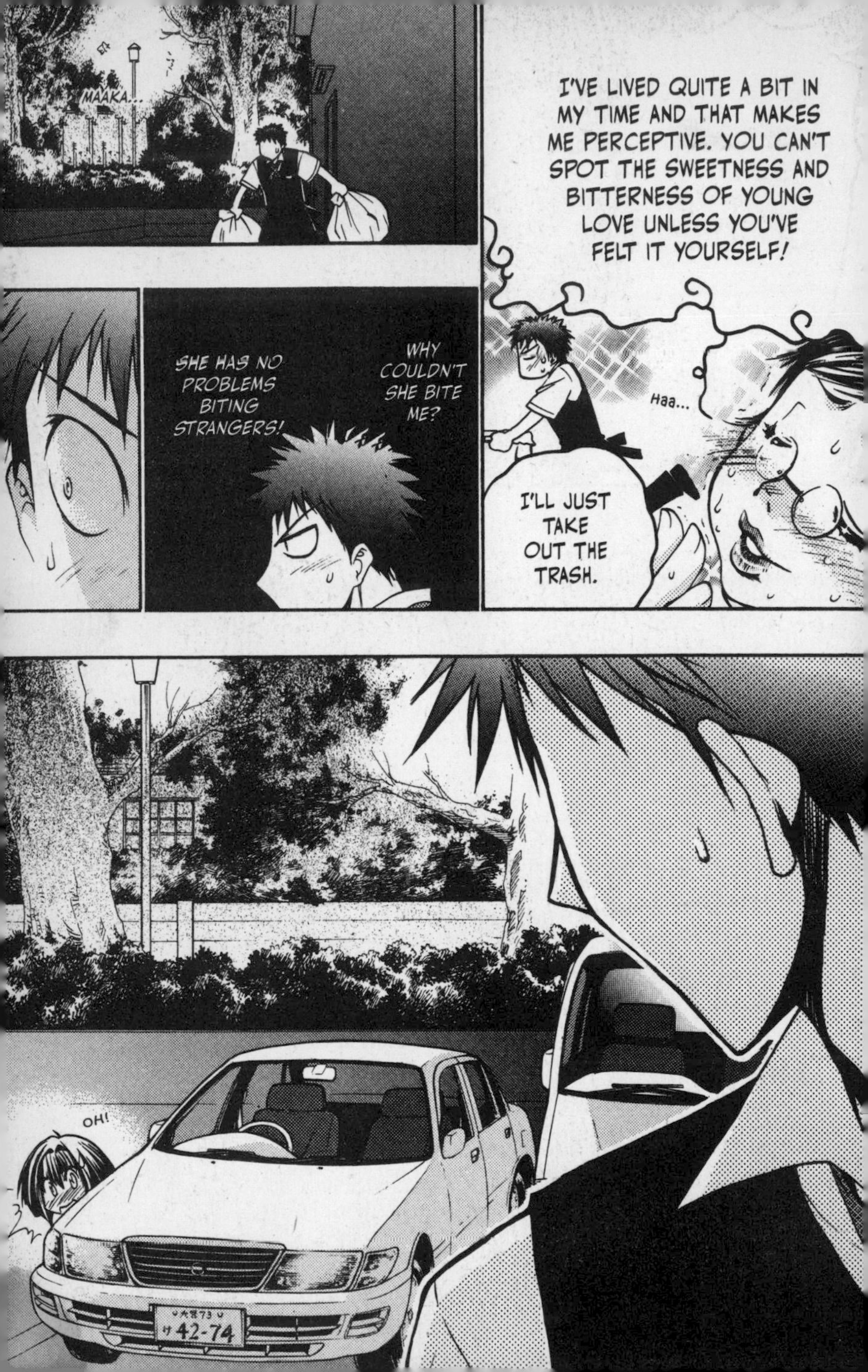
I'VE LIVED QUITE A BIT IN MY TIME AND THAT MAKES ME PERCEPTIVE. YOU CAN'T SPOT THE SWEETNESS AND BITTERNESS OF YOUNG LOVE UNLESS YOU'VE FELT IT YOURSELF!
Haa...
I'LL JUST TAKE OUT THE TRASH.
MAAKA...
WHY COULDN'T SHE BITE ME?
SHE HAS NO PROBLEMS BITING STRANGERS!
OH!

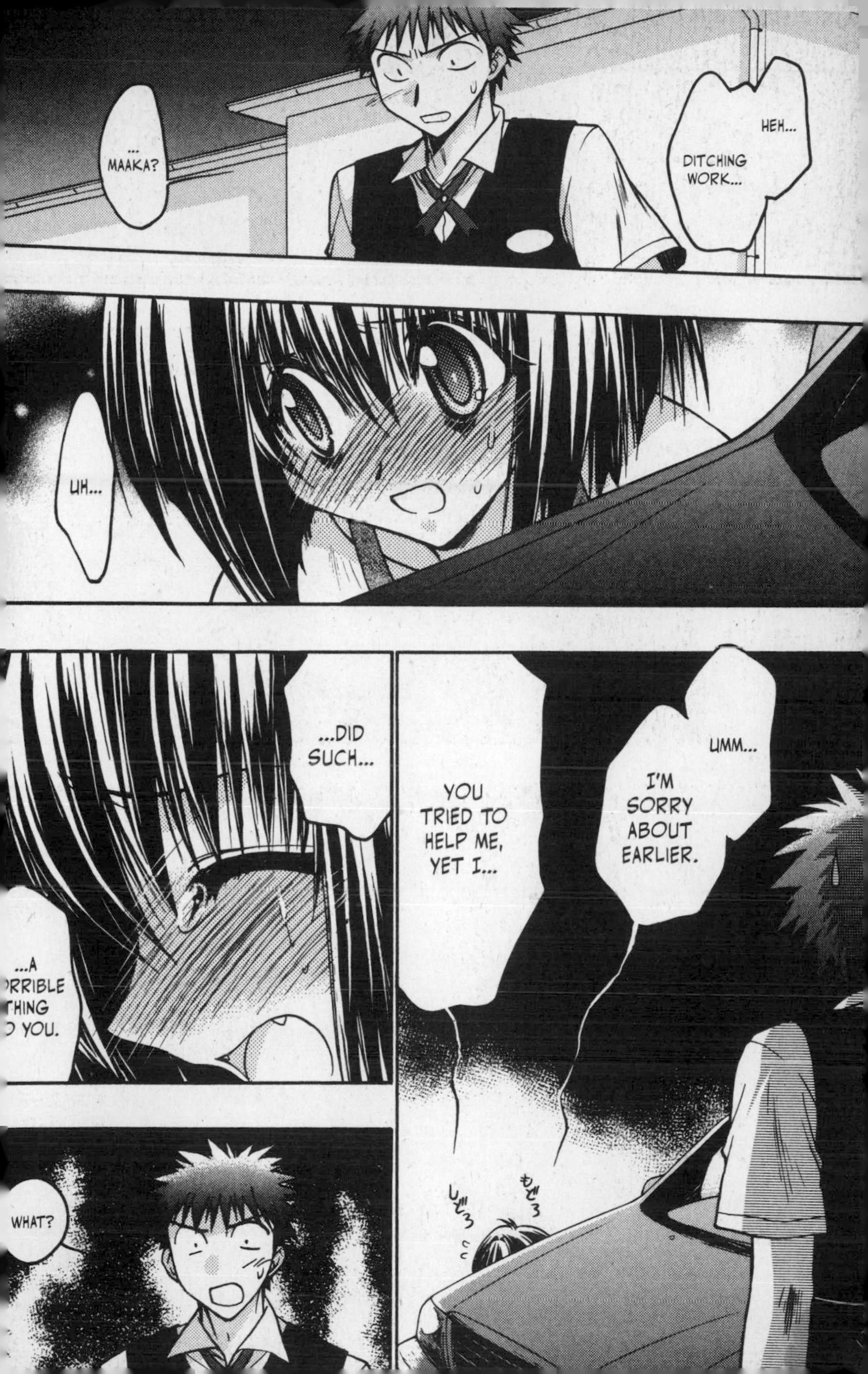
HEH... DITCHING WORK...
...MAAKA?
UH...
UMM... I'M SORRY ABOUT EARLIER.
YOU TRIED TO HELP ME, YET I...
...DID SUCH...
...A RRIBLE THING O YOU.
WHAT?

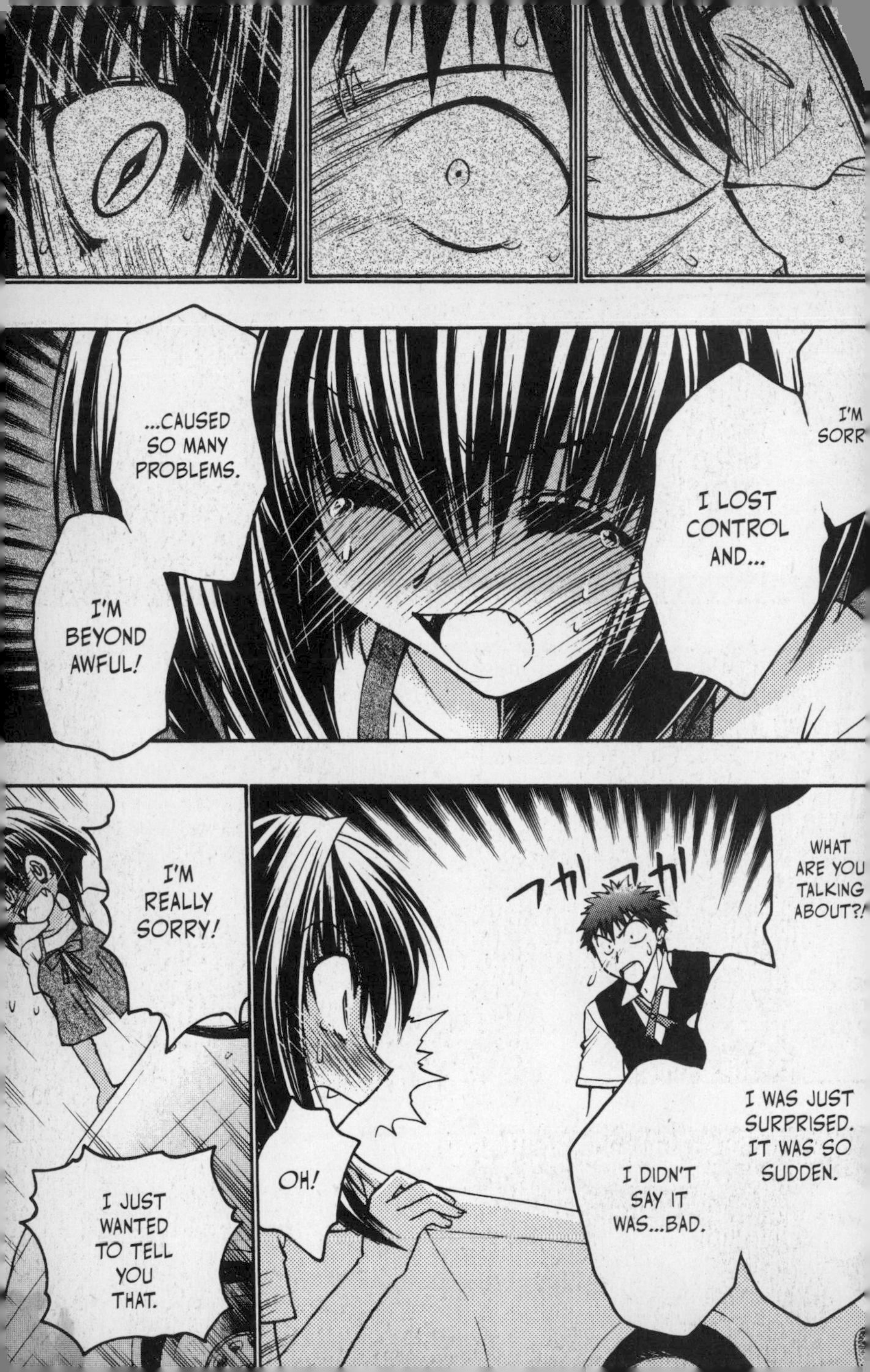
I'M SORR
I LOST CONTROL AND...
...CAUSED SO MANY PROBLEMS.
I'M BEYOND AWFUL!
WHAT ARE YOU TALKING ABOUT?!
I WAS JUST SURPRISED. IT WAS SO SUDDEN.
I DIDN'T SAY IT WAS...BAD.
OH!
I'M REALLY SORRY!
I JUST WANTED TO TELL YOU THAT.

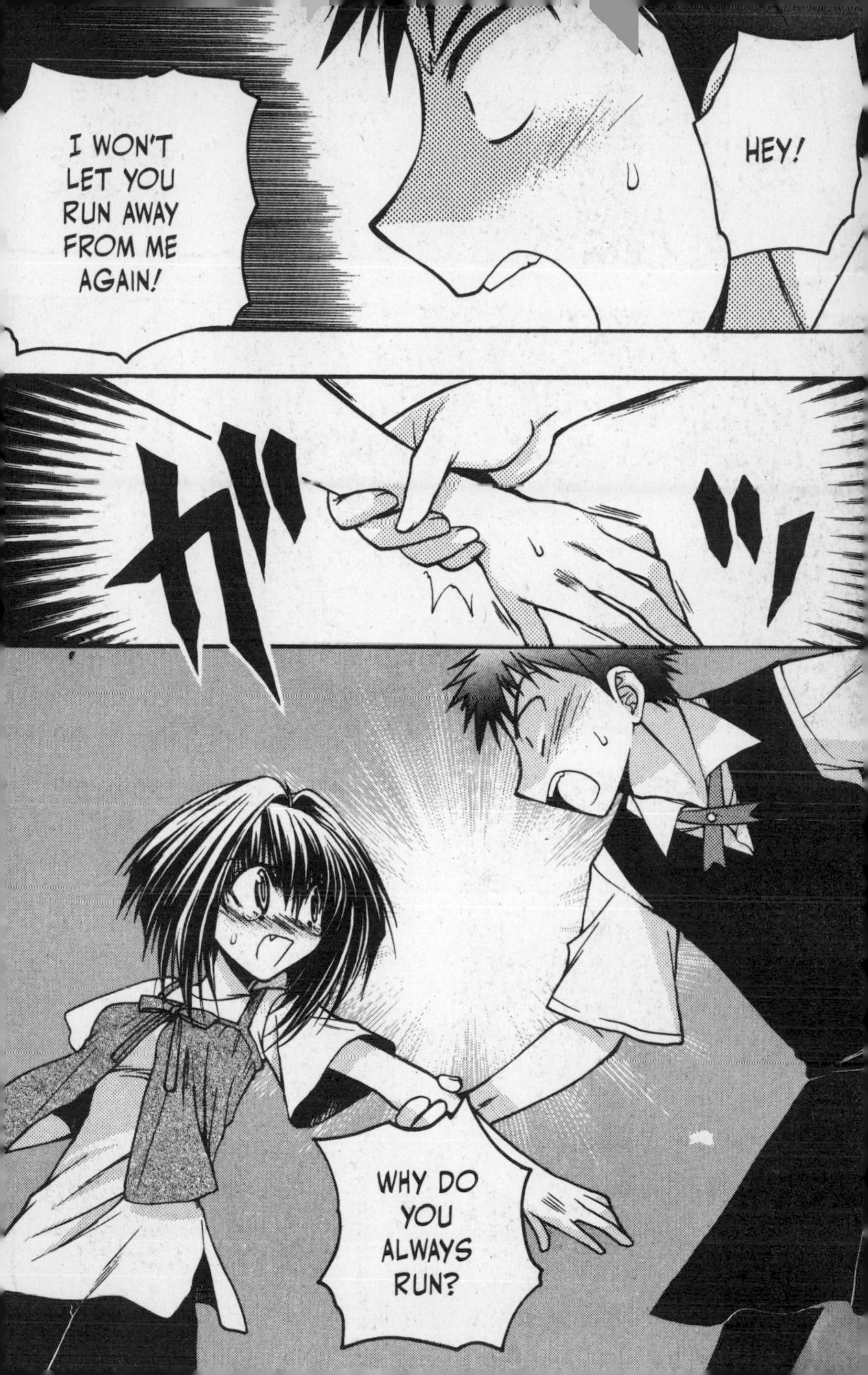
HEY!
I WON'T LET YOU RUN AWAY FROM ME AGAIN!
ガッ
WHY DO YOU ALWAYS RUN?

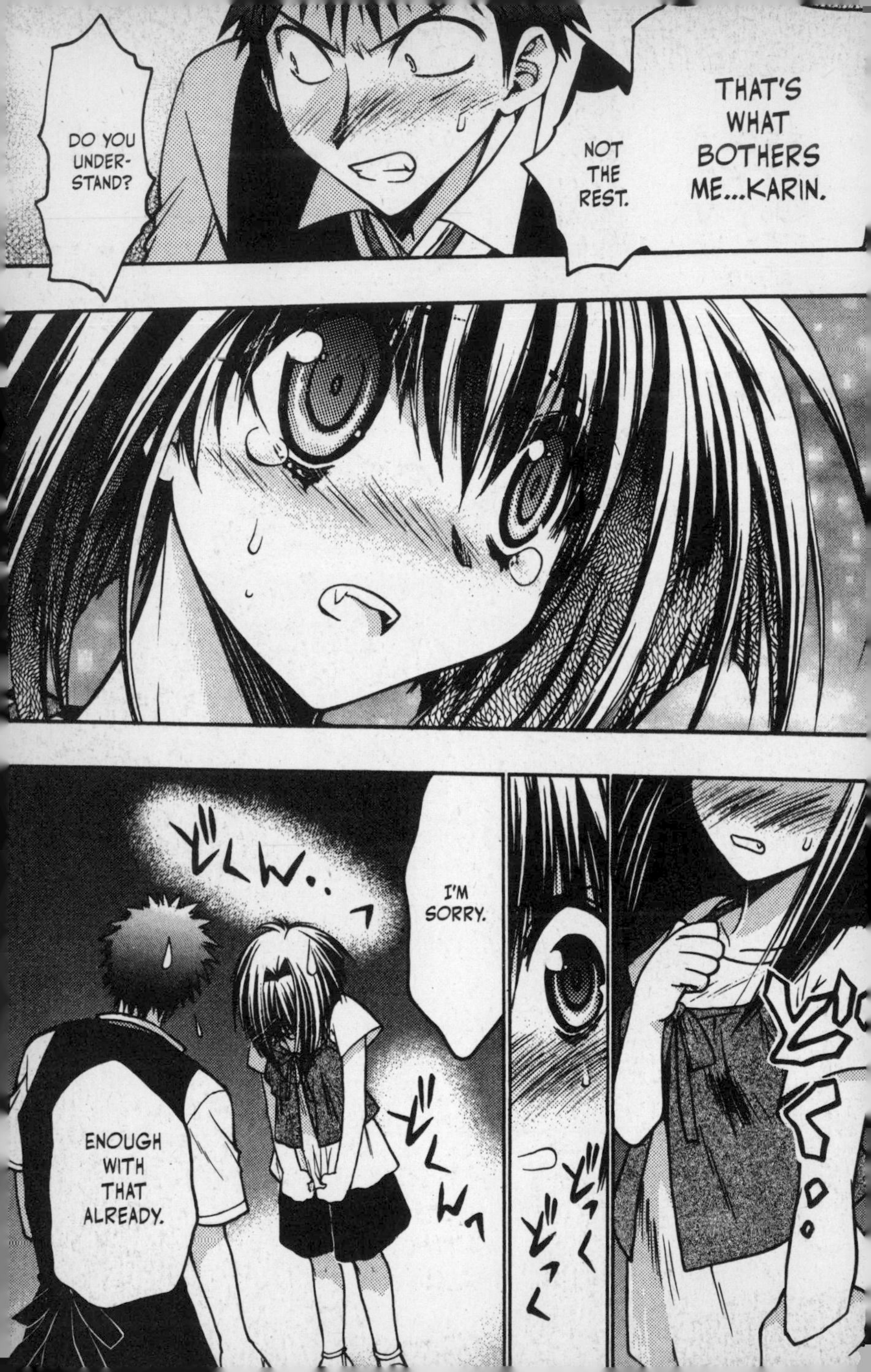
THAT'S WHAT BOTHERS ME...KARIN.
NOT THE REST.
DO YOU UNDER-STAND?
I'M SORRY.
ENOUGH WITH THAT ALREADY.

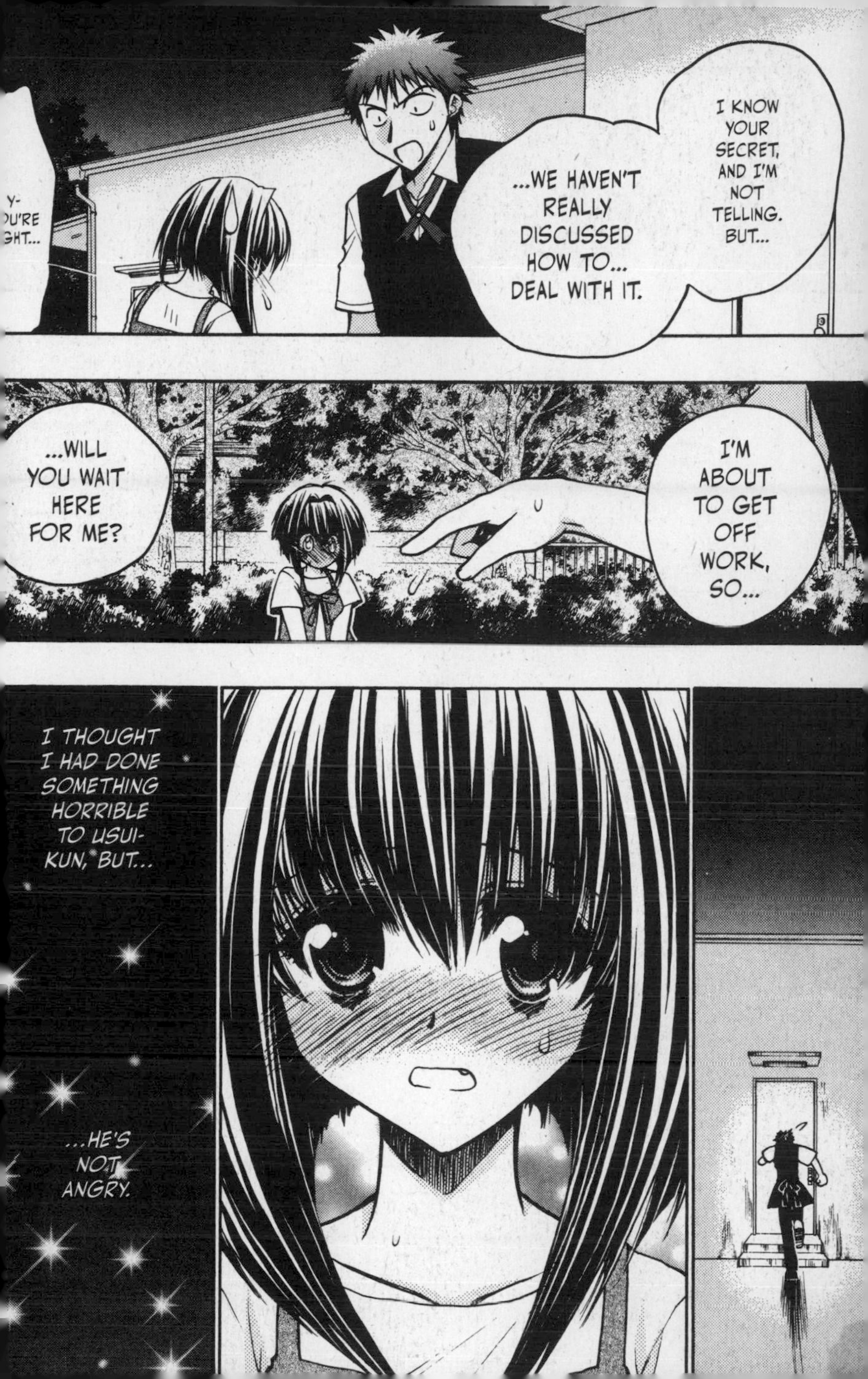
I KNOW YOUR SECRET, AND I'M NOT TELLING. BUT...
...WE HAVEN'T REALLY DISCUSSED HOW TO... DEAL WITH IT.
Y- OU'RE GHT...
I'M ABOUT TO GET OFF WORK, SO...
...WILL YOU WAIT HERE FOR ME?
I THOUGHT I HAD DONE SOMETHING HORRIBLE TO USUI-KUN, BUT...
...HE'S NOT ANGRY.

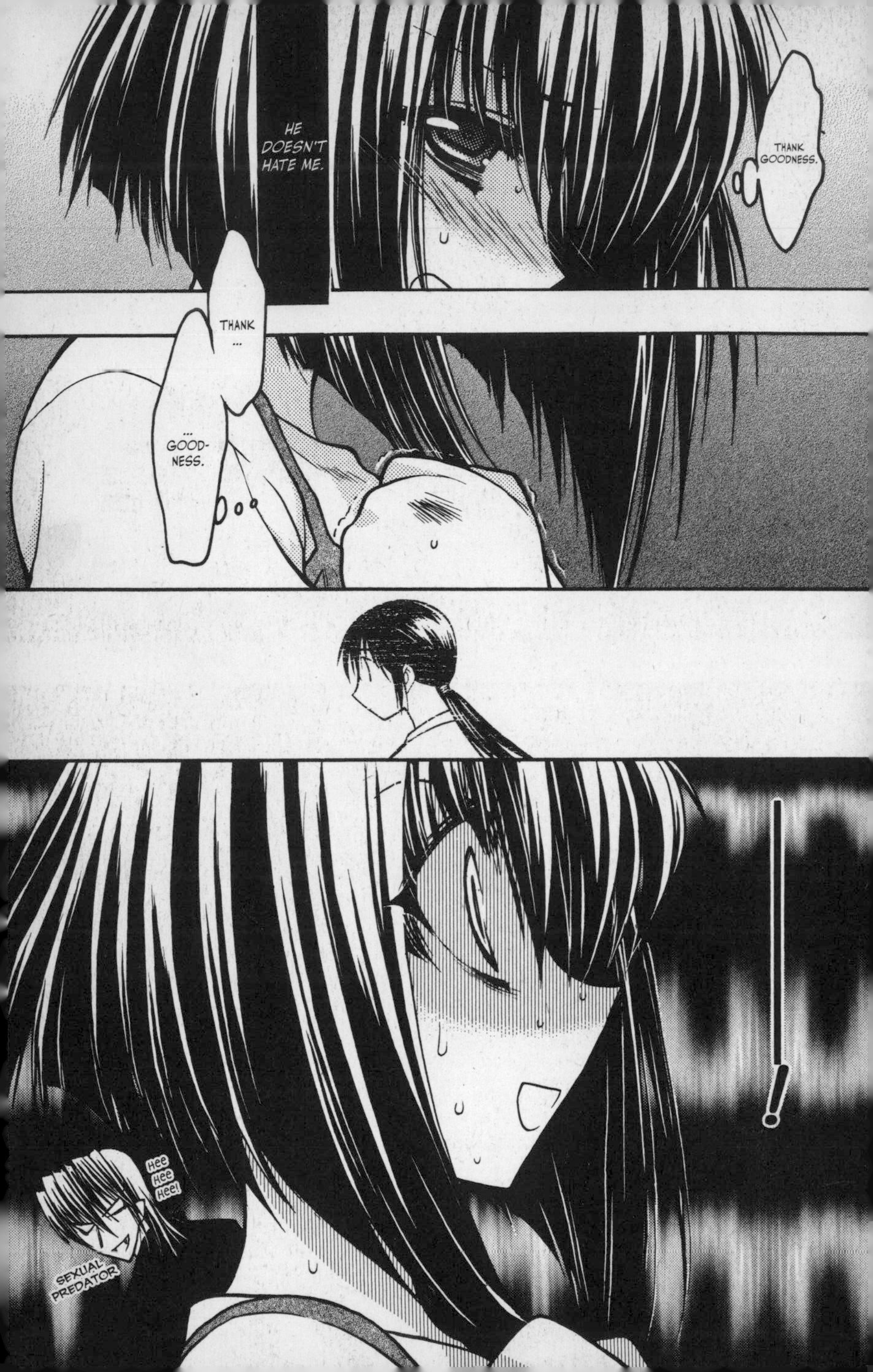
THANK GOODNESS.
HE DOESN'T HATE ME.
THANK ...
... GOOD-NESS.
Hee Hee Hee!
SEXUAL PREDATOR

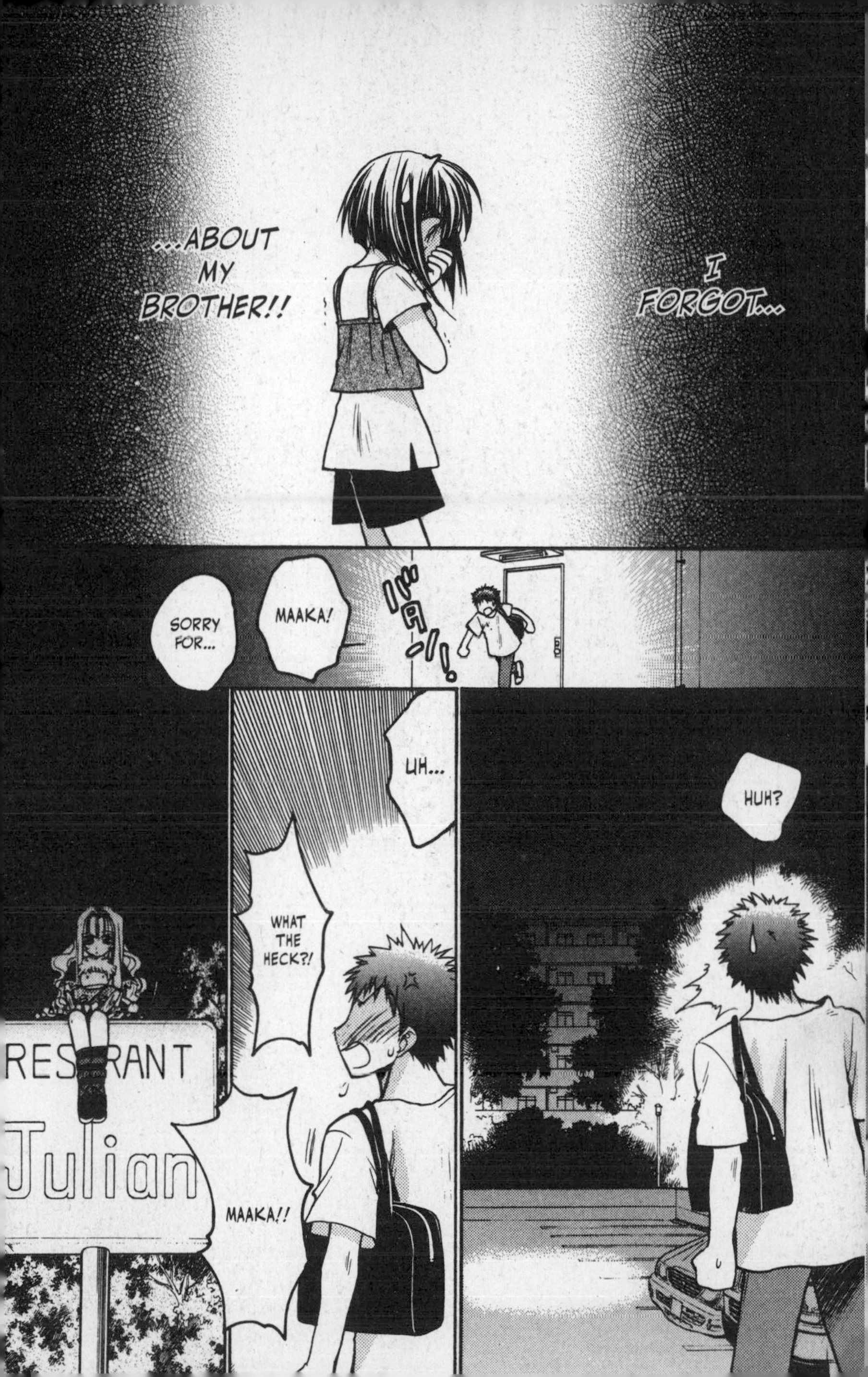
I FORGOT...
...ABOUT MY BROTHER!!
MAAKA!
SORRY FOR...
HUH?
UH...
WHAT THE HECK?!
RES RANT
Julian
MAAKA!!

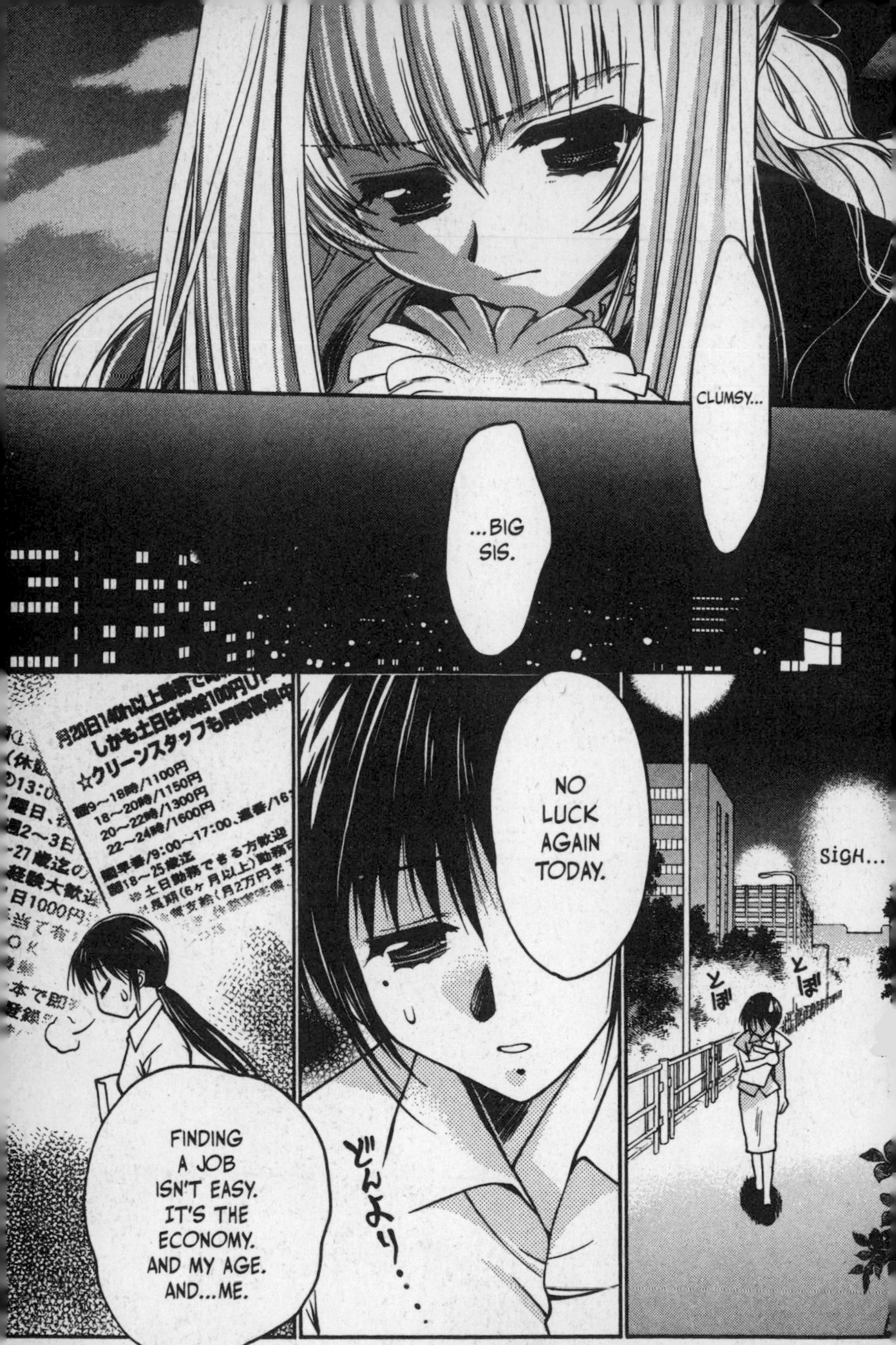
CLUMSY...
...BIG SIS.
SIGH...
とぼ
とぼ
NO LUCK AGAIN TODAY.
どんより・・・
FINDING A JOB ISN'T EASY. IT'S THE ECONOMY. AND MY AGE. AND...ME.

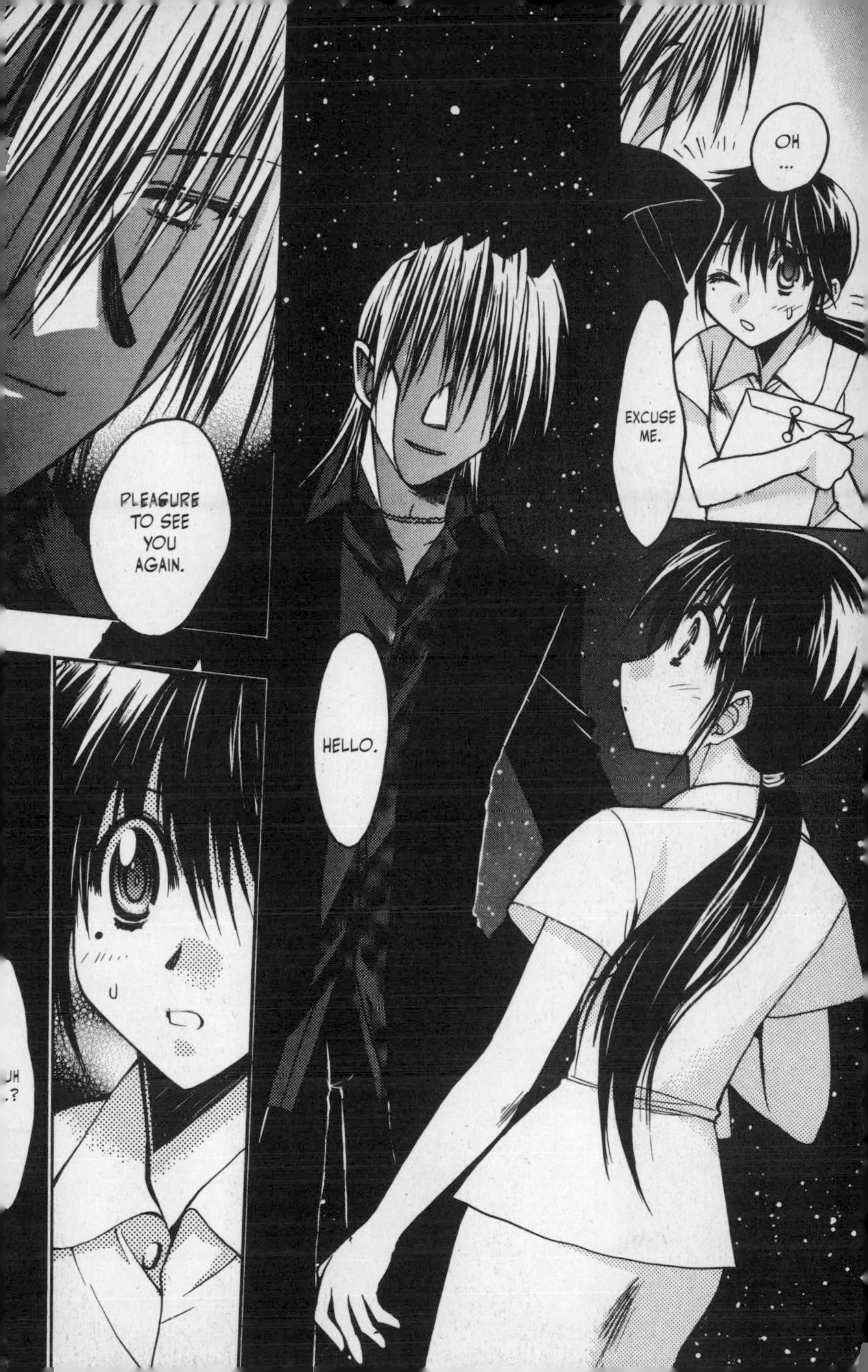
OH ...
EXCUSE ME.
HELLO.
PLEASURE TO SEE YOU AGAIN.
UH ...?

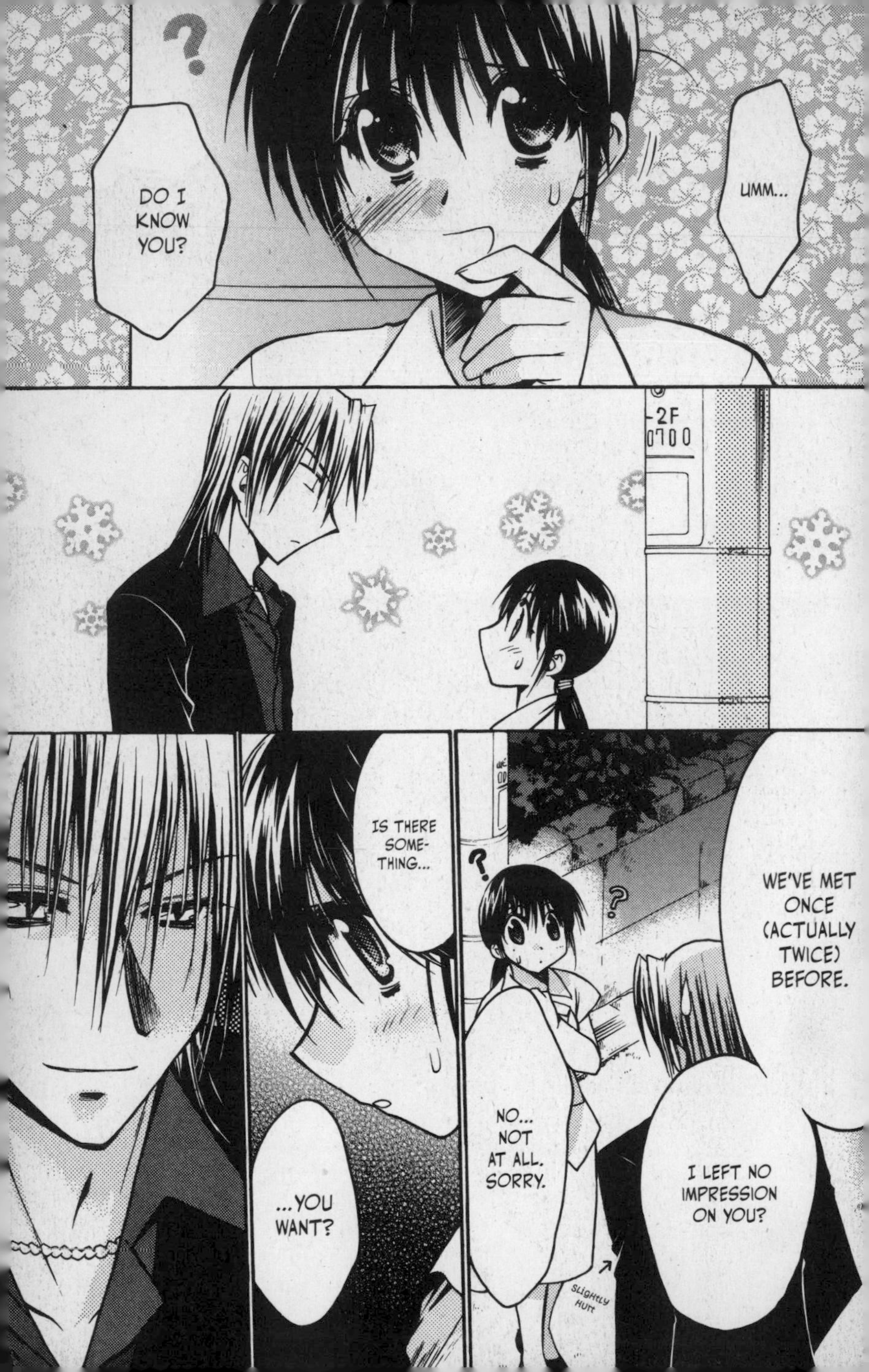
UMM...
DO I KNOW YOU?
2F
0700
WE'VE MET ONCE (ACTUALLY TWICE) BEFORE.
NO... NOT AT ALL. SORRY.
I LEFT NO IMPRESSION ON YOU?
SLIGHTLY HURT
IS THERE SOMETHING...
...YOU WANT?

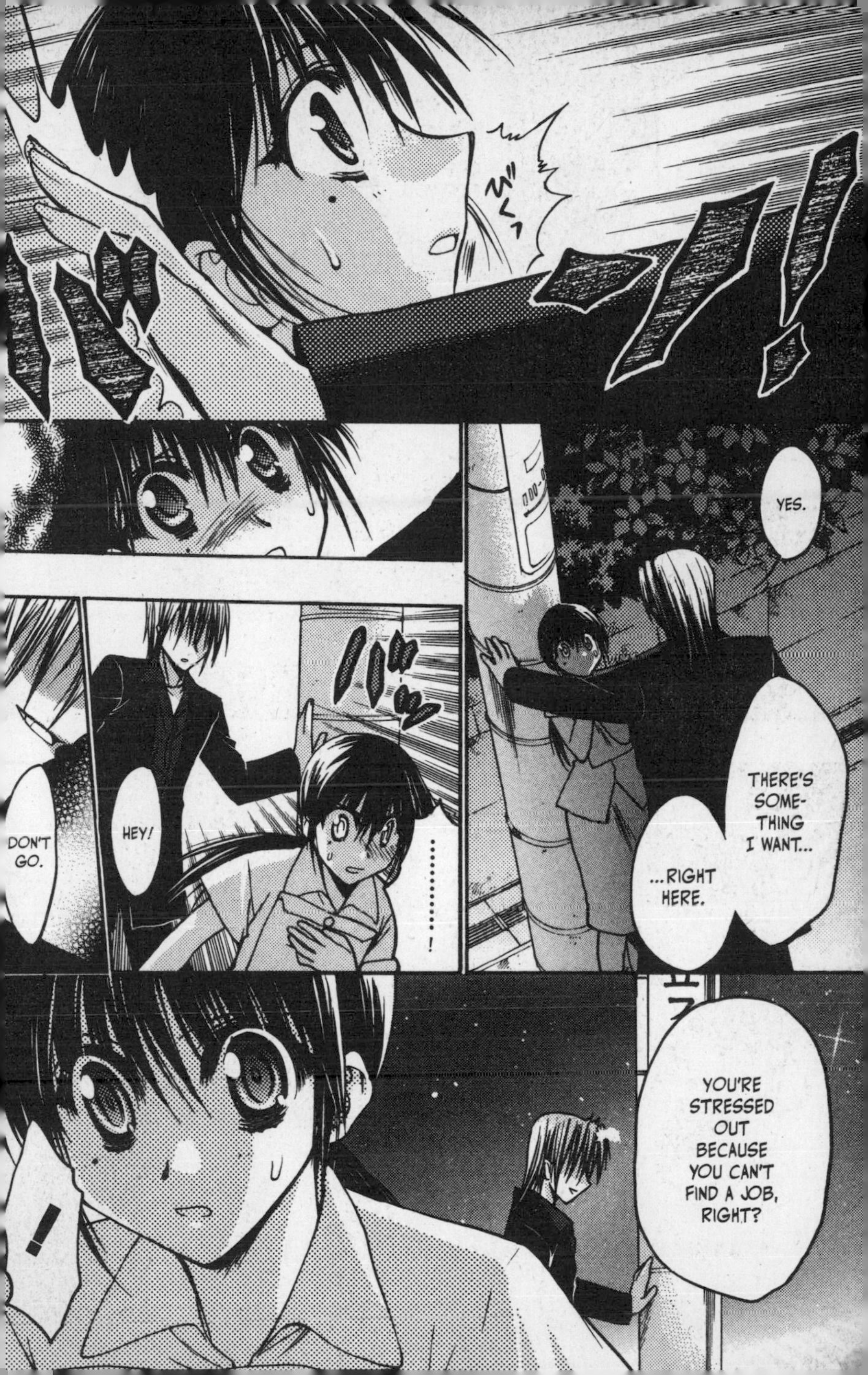
YES.
THERE'S SOME-THING I WANT...
...RIGHT HERE.
......!
HEY!
DON'T GO.
YOU'RE STRESSED OUT BECAUSE YOU CAN'T FIND A JOB, RIGHT?
!

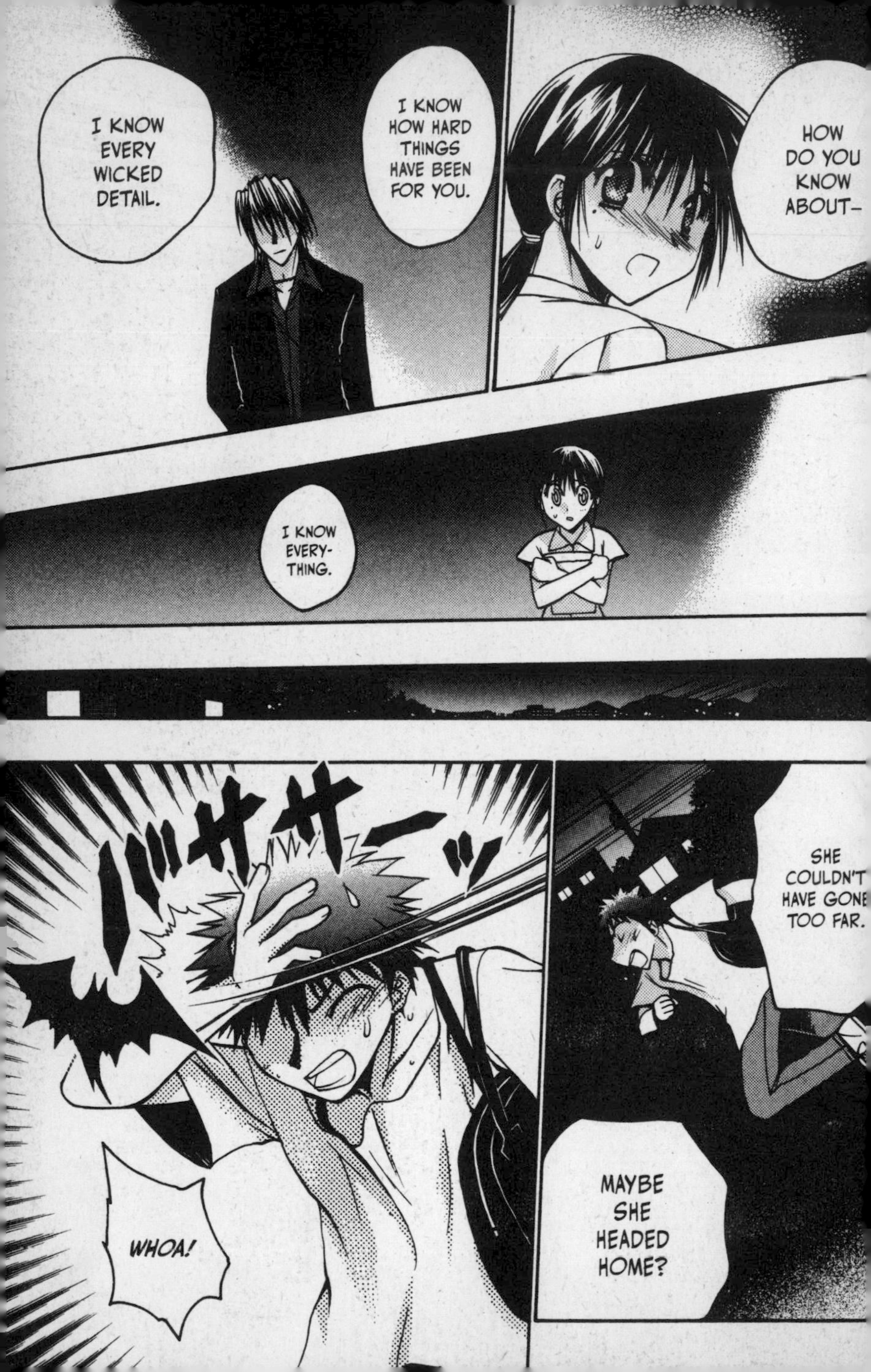
HOW DO YOU KNOW ABOUT–
I KNOW HOW HARD THINGS HAVE BEEN FOR YOU.
I KNOW EVERY WICKED DETAIL.
I KNOW EVERY-THING.
SHE COULDN'T HAVE GONE TOO FAR.
MAYBE SHE HEADED HOME?
WHOA!

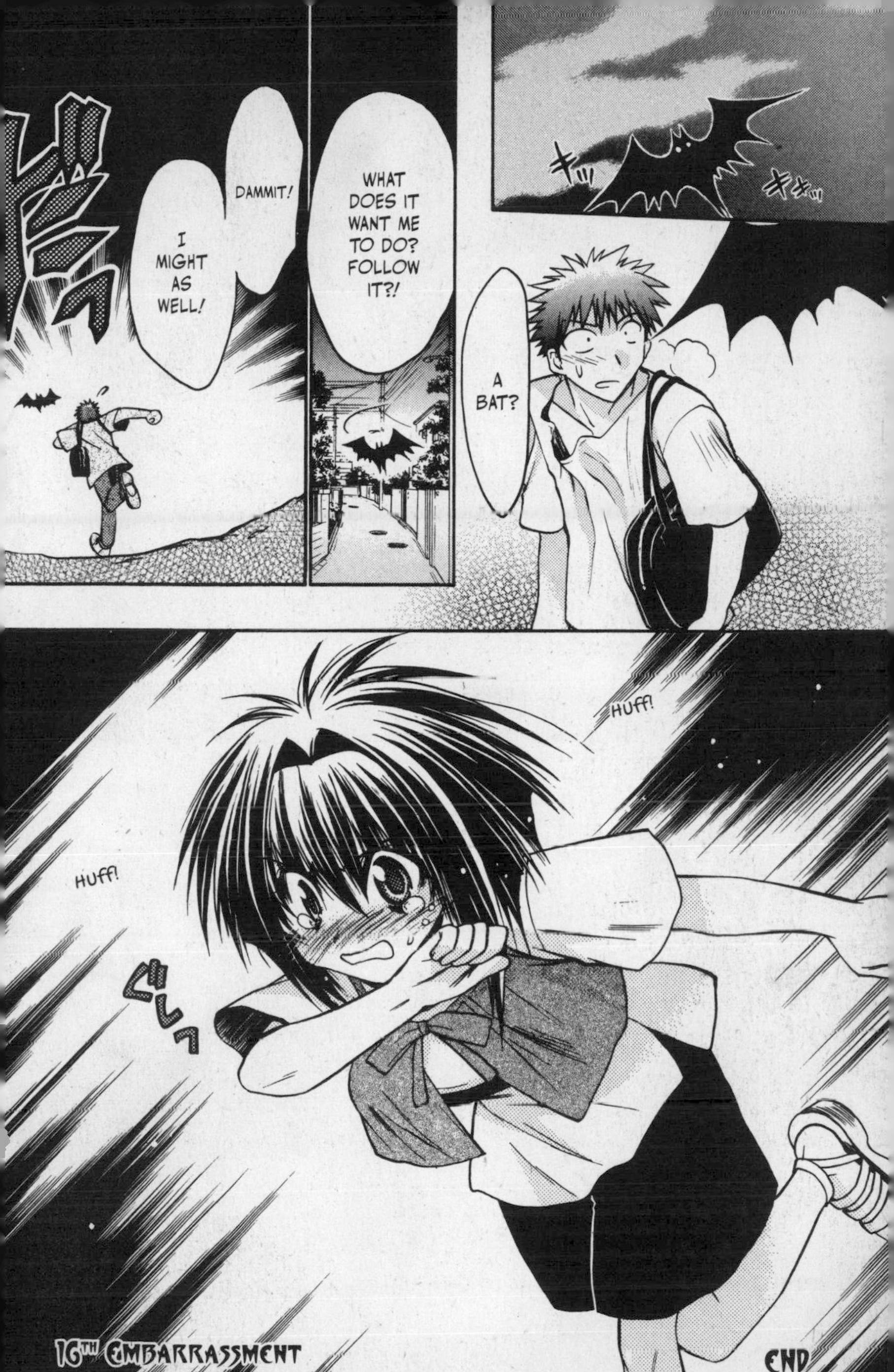
A BAT?
WHAT DOES IT WANT ME TO DO? FOLLOW IT?!
DAMMIT!
I MIGHT AS WELL!
HUFF!
HUFF!
16TH EMBARRASSMENT
END

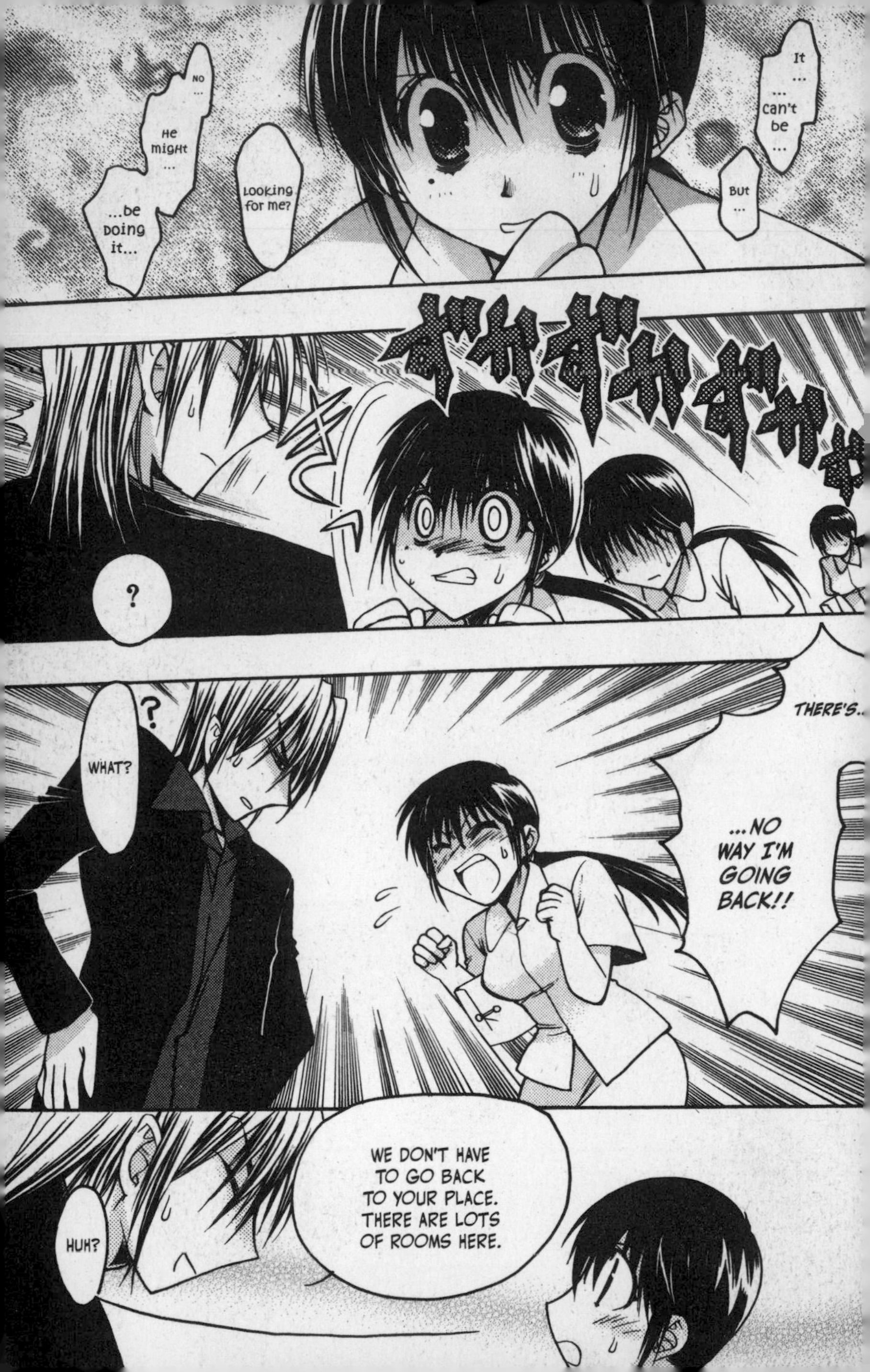
It ... ... can't be ...
But ...
Looking for me?
No ... He might ... ...be Doing it...
?
THERE'S...
...NO WAY I'M GOING BACK!!
WHAT?
WE DON'T HAVE TO GO BACK TO YOUR PLACE. THERE ARE LOTS OF ROOMS HERE.
HUH?

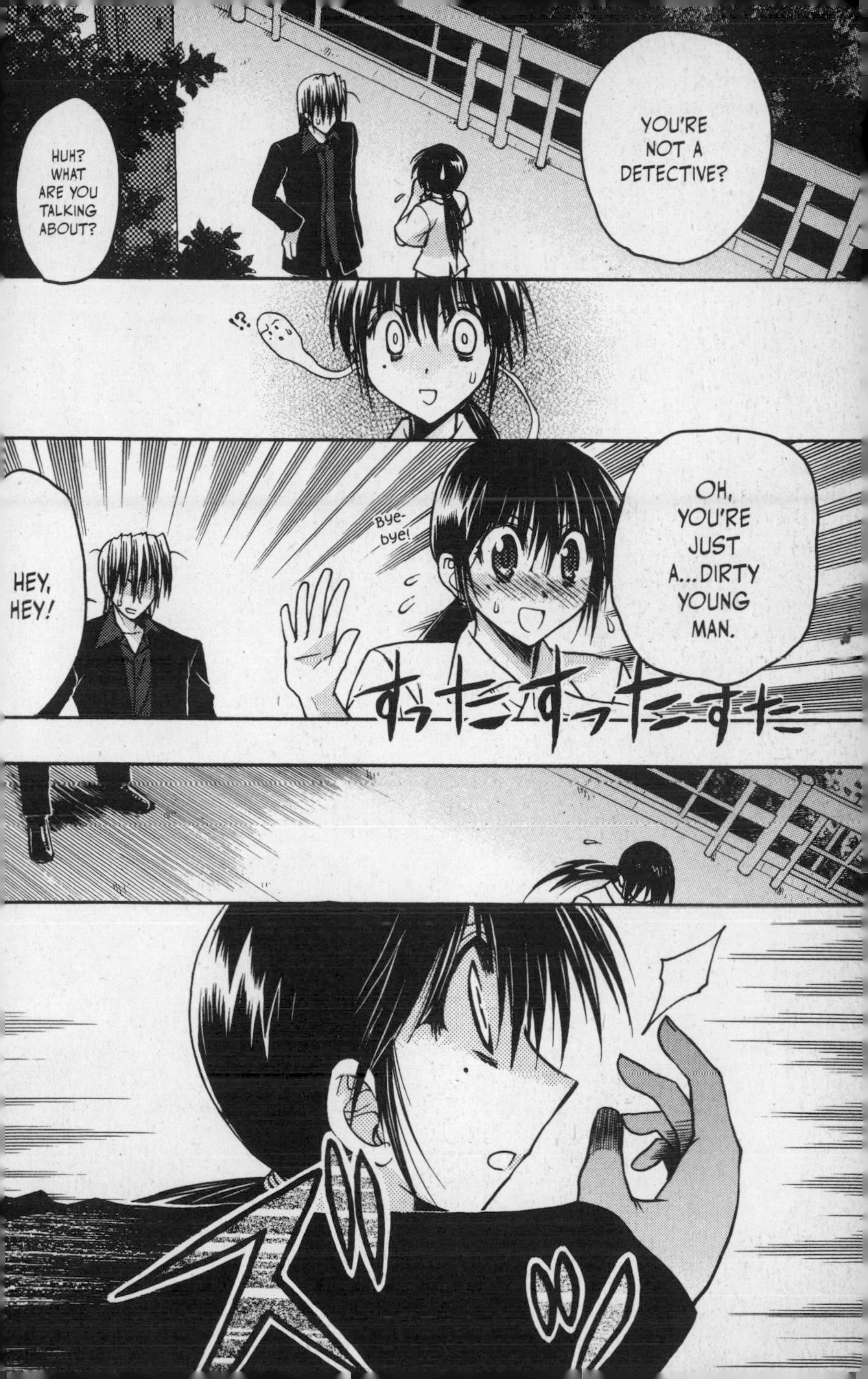
YOU'RE NOT A DETECTIVE?
HUH? WHAT ARE YOU TALKING ABOUT?
!?
OH, YOU'RE JUST A...DIRTY YOUNG MAN.
Bye-bye!
HEY, HEY!
すったすったすた

# 17th Embarrassment ) Karin's Feelings and Ren's Indignation

~Indignation~

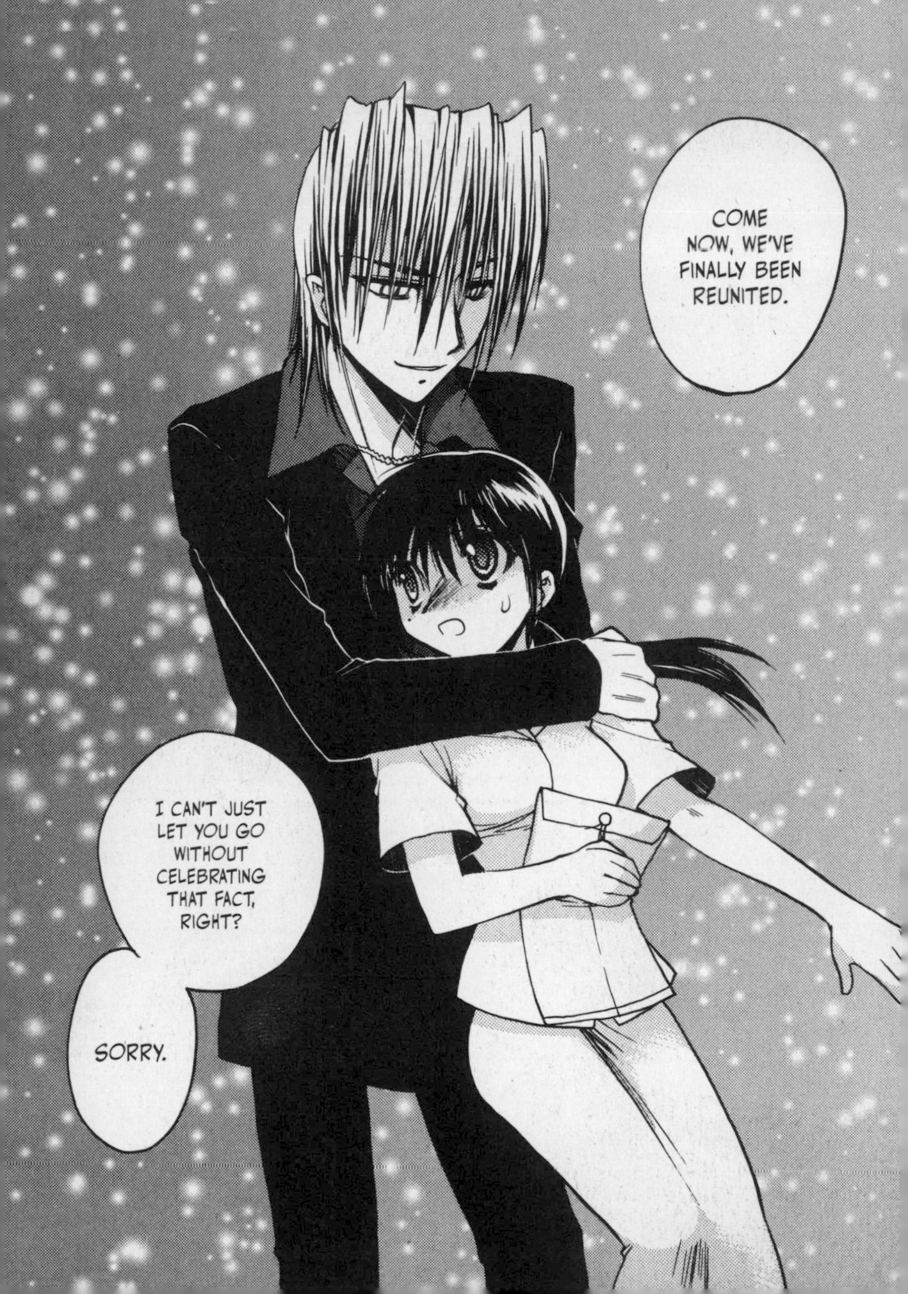
COME NOW, WE'VE FINALLY BEEN REUNITED.
I CAN'T JUST LET YOU GO WITHOUT CELEBRATING THAT FACT, RIGHT?
SORRY.

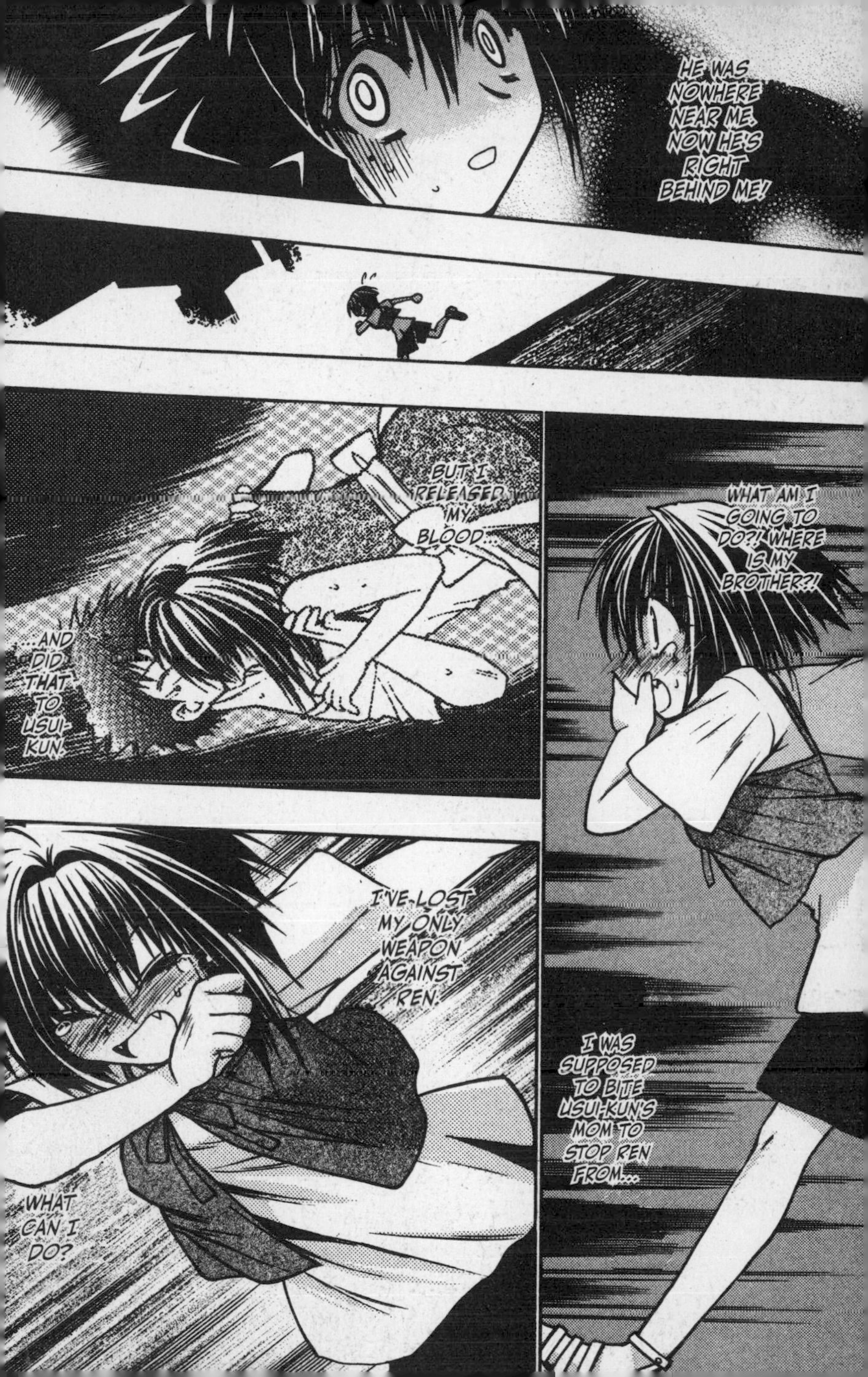
HE WAS NOWHERE NEAR ME. NOW HE'S RIGHT BEHIND ME!
WHAT AM I GOING TO DO?! WHERE IS MY BROTHER?!
I WAS SUPPOSED TO BITE USUI-KUN'S MOM TO STOP REN FROM...
BUT I RELEASED MY BLOOD...
...AND DID THAT TO USUI-KUN.
I'VE LOST MY ONLY WEAPON AGAINST REN.
WHAT CAN I DO?

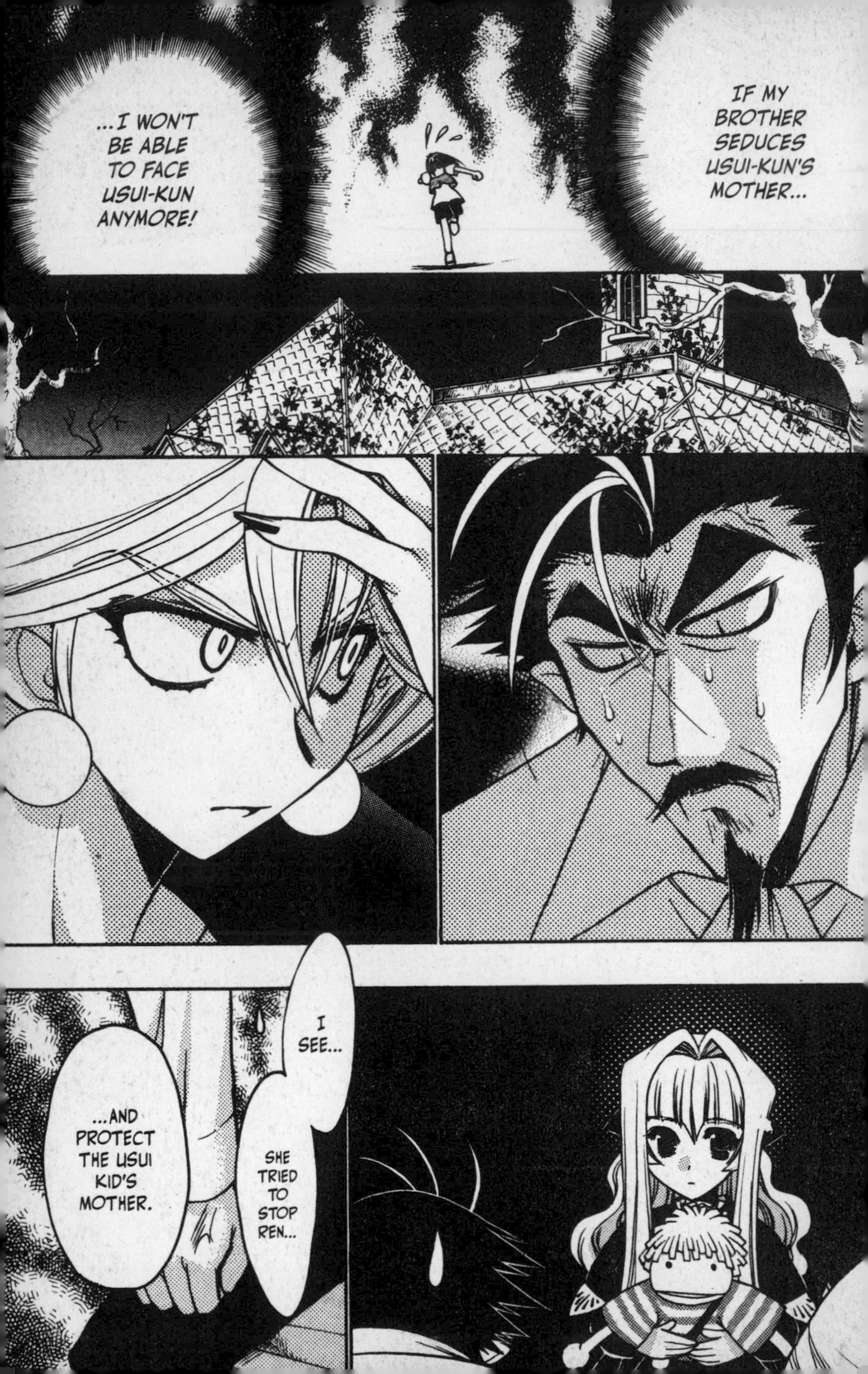
IF MY BROTHER SEDUCES USUI-KUN'S MOTHER...
...I WON'T BE ABLE TO FACE USUI-KUN ANYMORE!
I SEE...
SHE TRIED TO STOP REN...
...AND PROTECT THE USUI KID'S MOTHER.

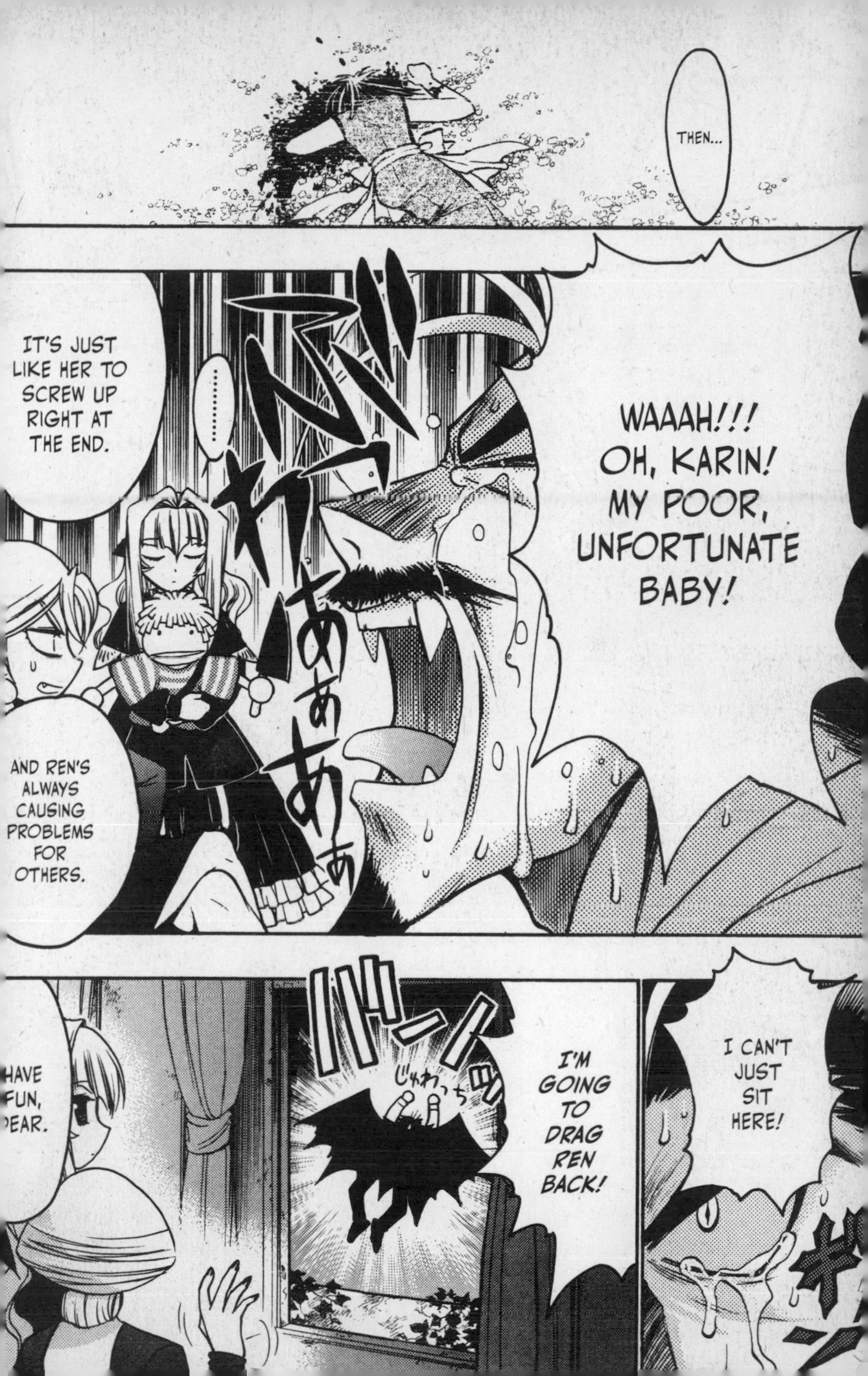

THEN...
WAAAH!!! OH, KARIN! MY POOR, UNFORTUNATE BABY!
......
IT'S JUST LIKE HER TO SCREW UP RIGHT AT THE END.
AND REN'S ALWAYS CAUSING PROBLEMS FOR OTHERS.
I CAN'T JUST SIT HERE!
I'M GOING TO DRAG REN BACK!
HAVE FUN, EAR.

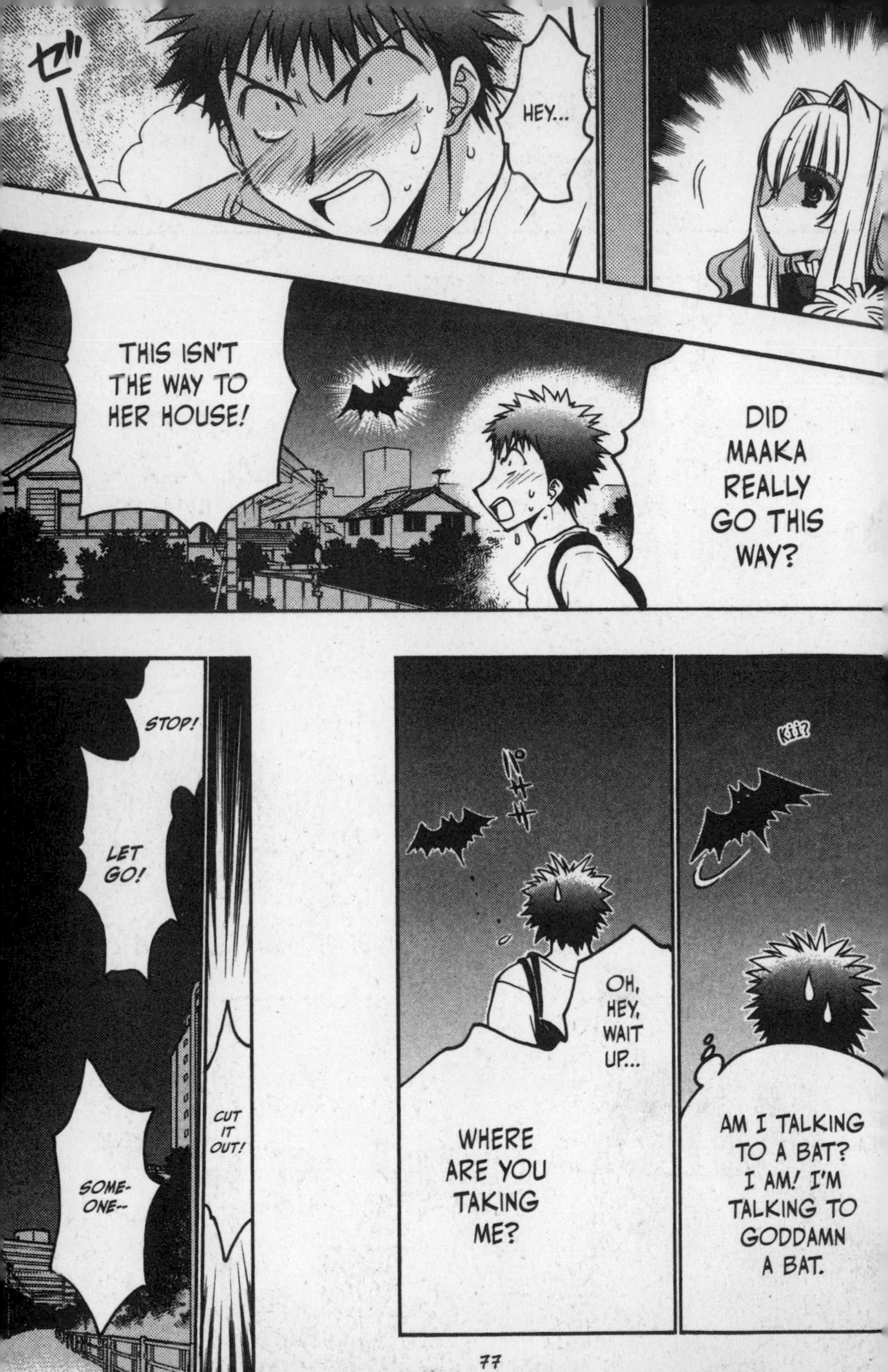
ゼ
HEY...
DID MAAKA REALLY GO THIS WAY?
THIS ISN'T THE WAY TO HER HOUSE!
Kiii?
AM I TALKING TO A BAT? I AM! I'M TALKING TO GODDAMN A BAT.
OH, HEY, WAIT UP...
WHERE ARE YOU TAKING ME?
STOP!
LET GO!
CUT IT OUT!
SOME-ONE--

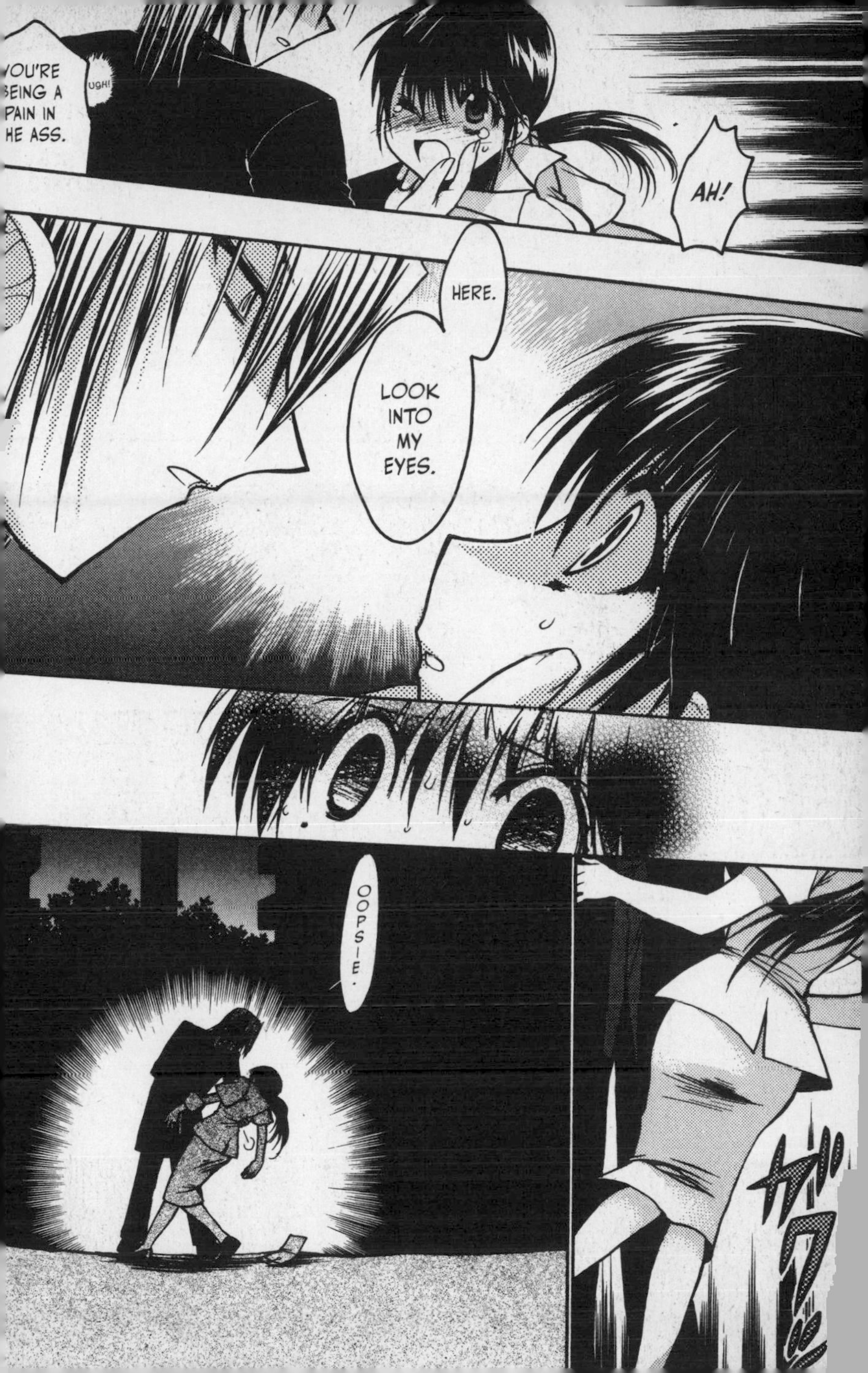
AH!
YOU'RE BEING A PAIN IN HE ASS.
UGH!
HERE.
LOOK INTO MY EYES.
OOPSIE.

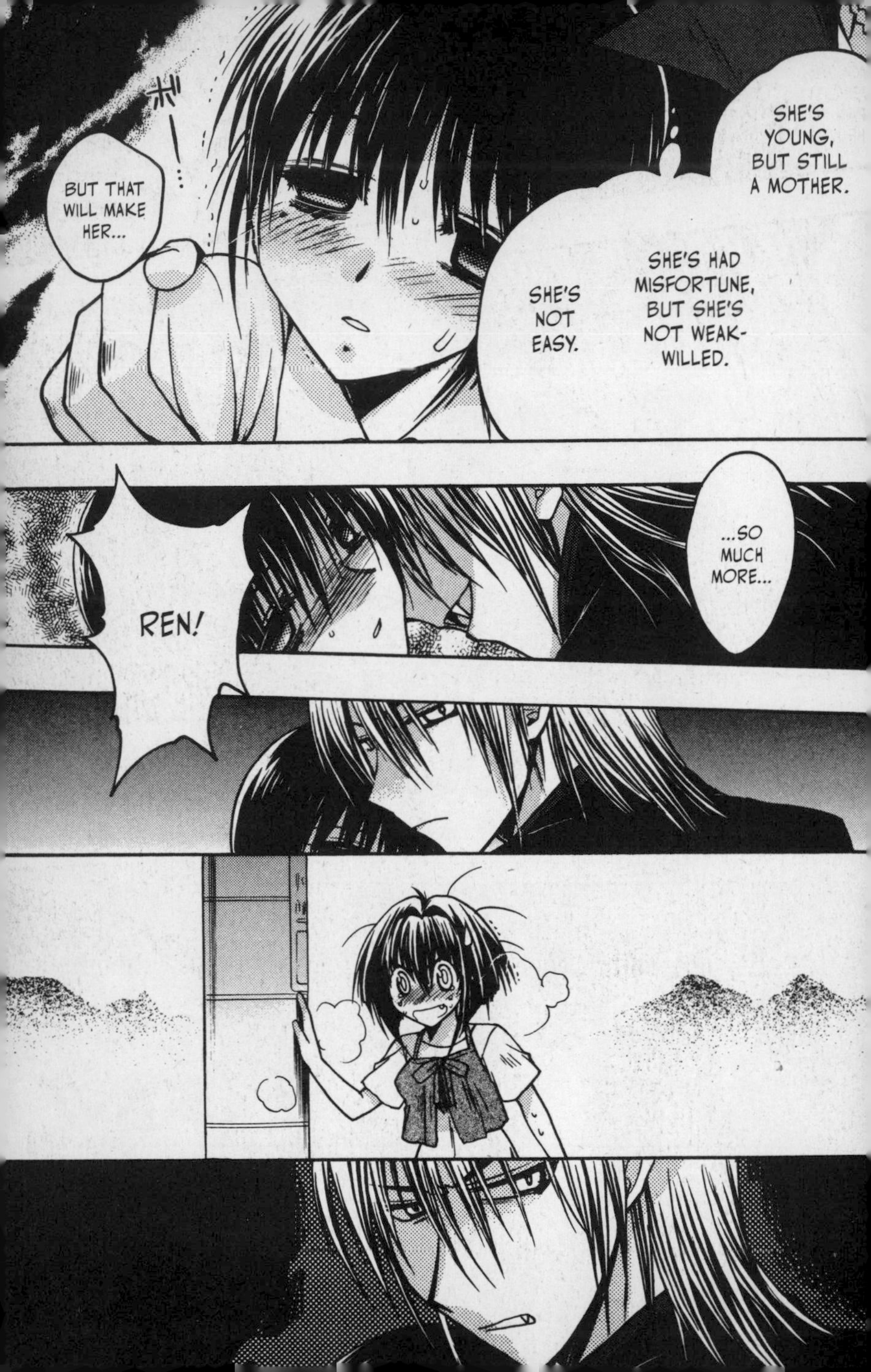
SHE'S YOUNG, BUT STILL A MOTHER.
SHE'S HAD MISFORTUNE, BUT SHE'S NOT WEAK-WILLED.
SHE'S NOT EASY.
BUT THAT WILL MAKE HER...
ボー
...SO MUCH MORE...
REN!

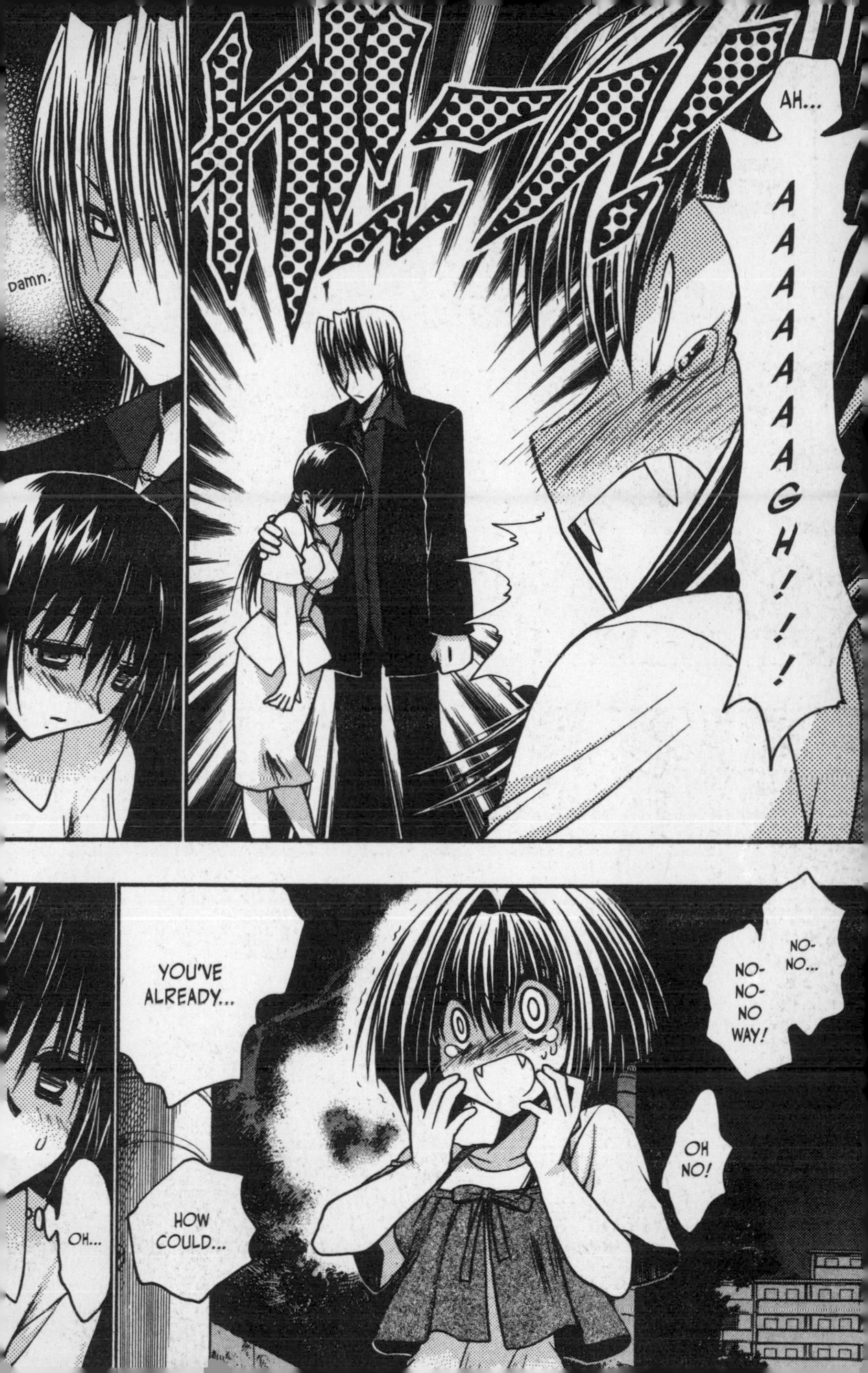
AH...
AAAAAAAAGH!!!
Damn.
NO-
NO...
NO-
NO-
NO
WAY!
OH
NO!
YOU'VE
ALREADY...
HOW
COULD...
OH...

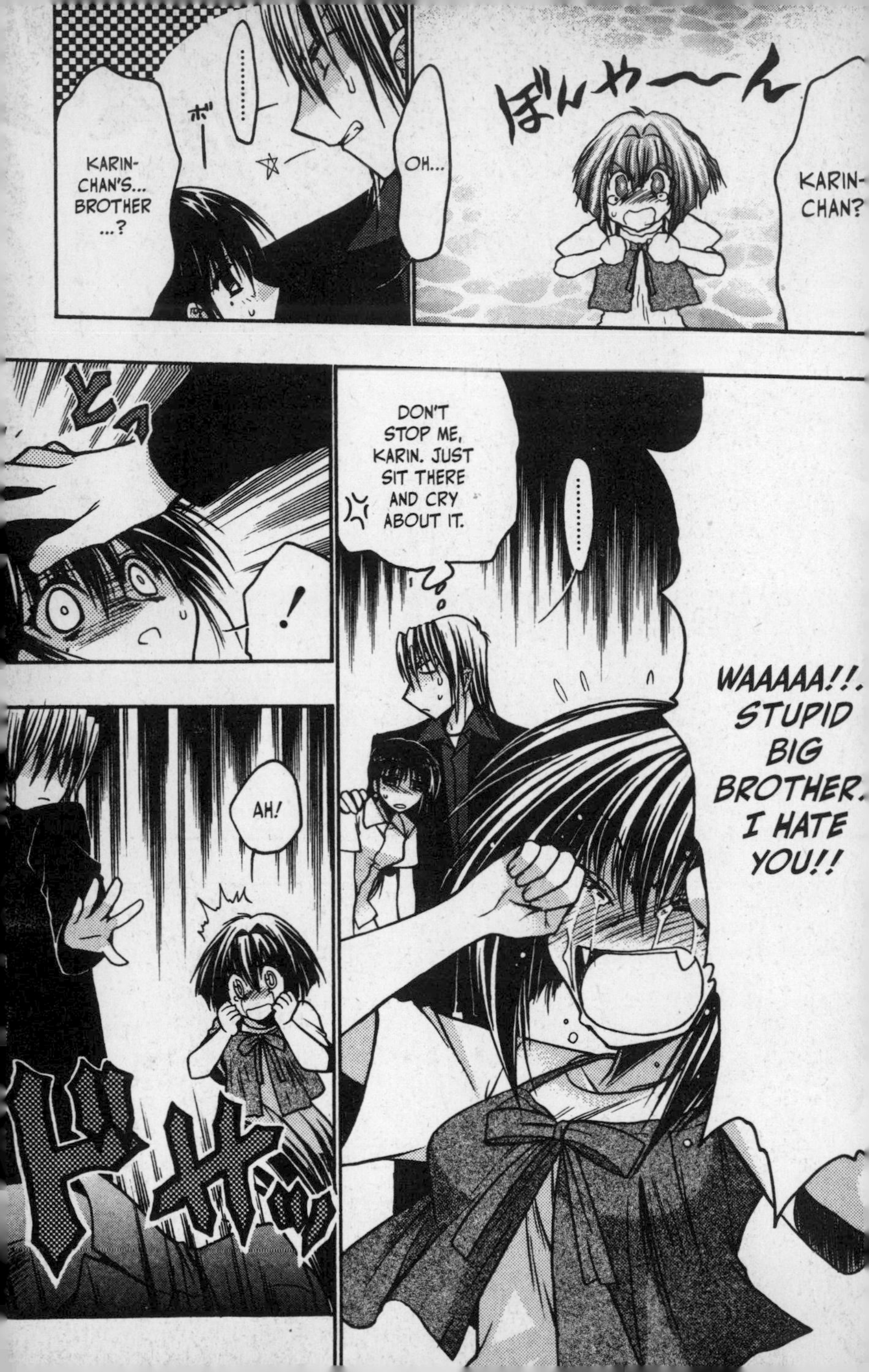
ぼんやーーん
KARIN-CHAN?
......
OH...
ボー
KARIN-CHAN'S... BROTHER ...?
WAAAAA!!. STUPID BIG BROTHER. I HATE YOU!!
......
DON'T STOP ME, KARIN. JUST SIT THERE AND CRY ABOUT IT.
!
AH!
ドサッ

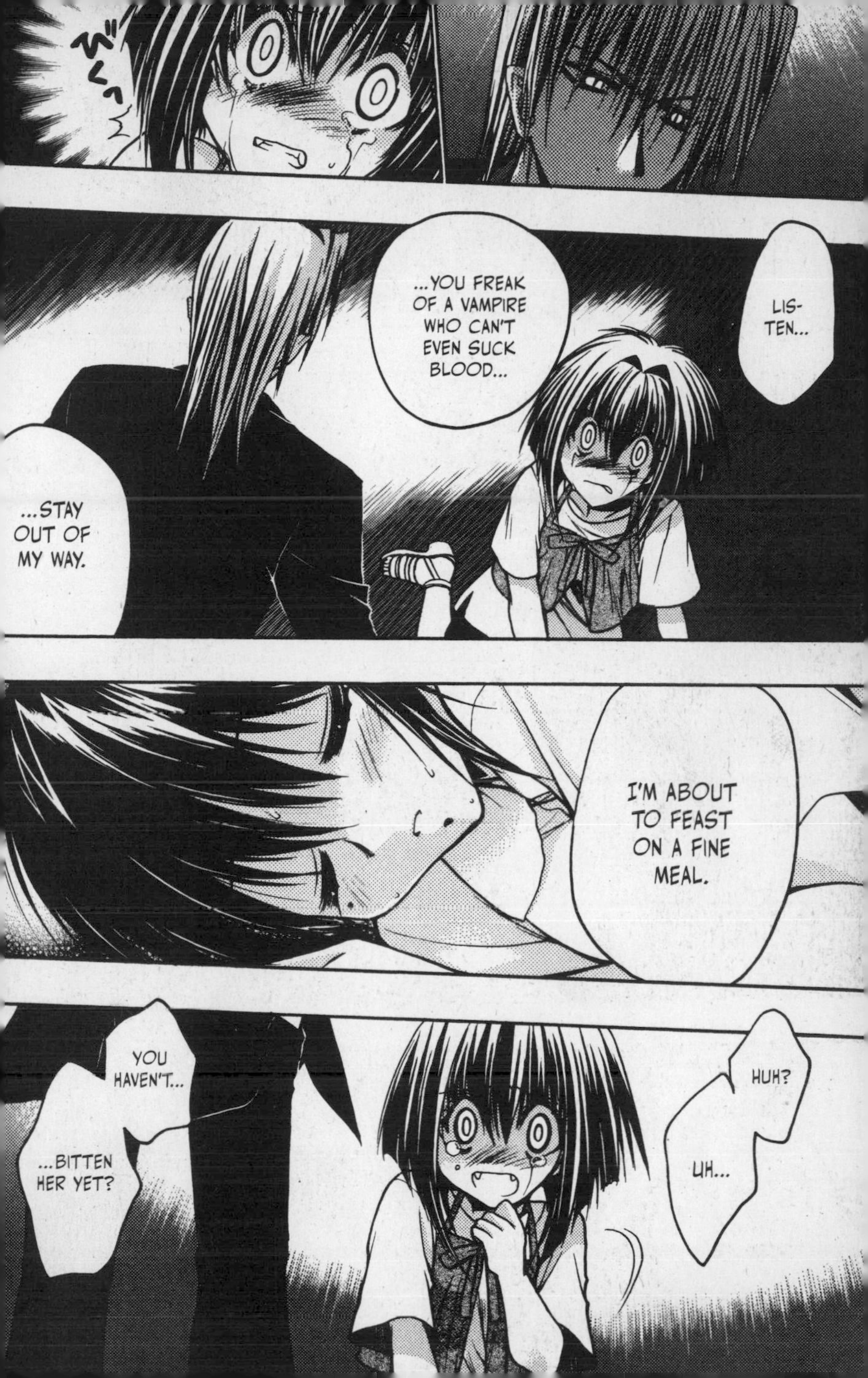
びくっ
LIS-TEN...
...YOU FREAK OF A VAMPIRE WHO CAN'T EVEN SUCK BLOOD...
...STAY OUT OF MY WAY.
I'M ABOUT TO FEAST ON A FINE MEAL.
HUH?
UH...
YOU HAVEN'T...
...BITTEN HER YET?

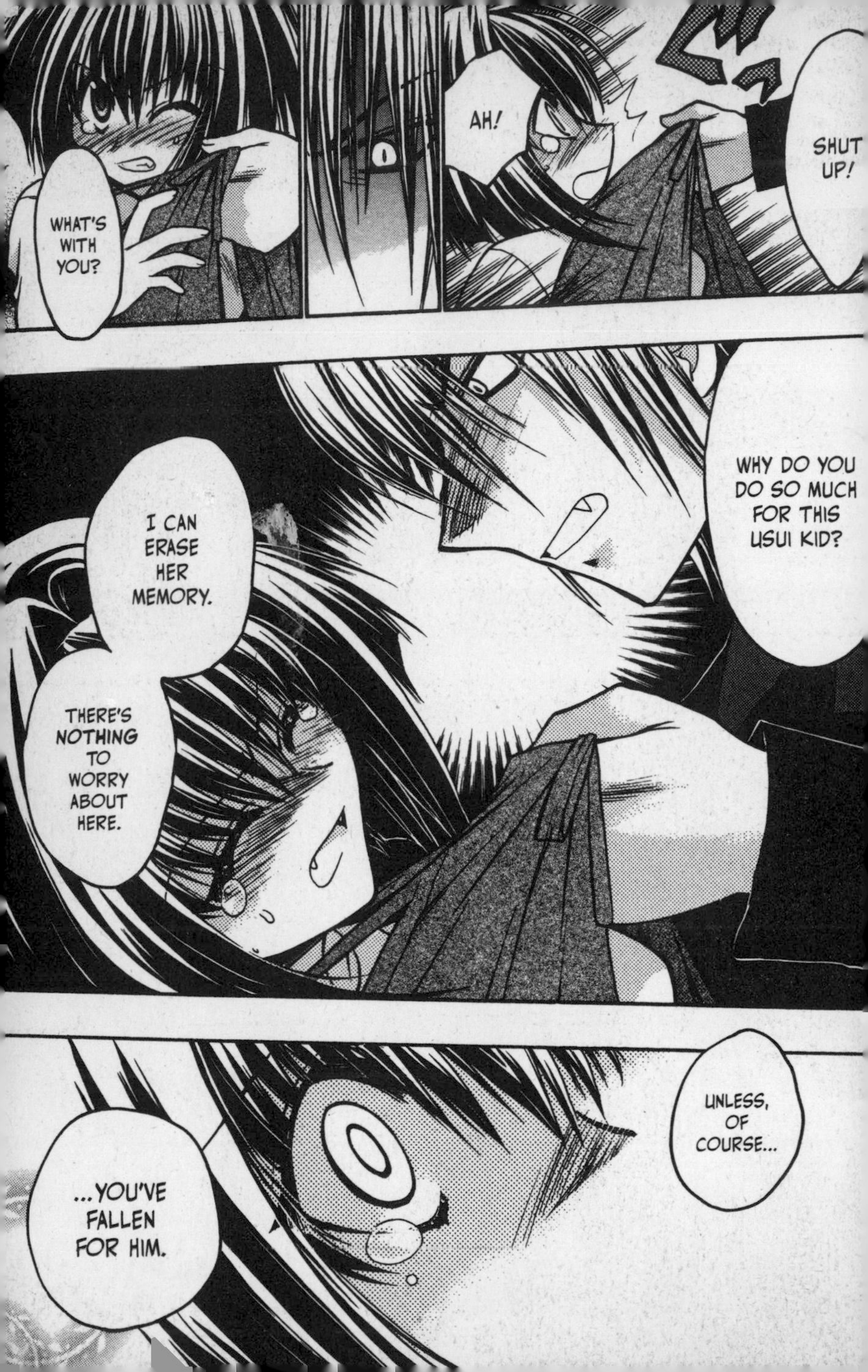
SHUT UP!
AH!
WHAT'S WITH YOU?
WHY DO YOU DO SO MUCH FOR THIS USUI KID?
I CAN ERASE HER MEMORY.
THERE'S NOTHING TO WORRY ABOUT HERE.
UNLESS, OF COURSE...
...YOU'VE FALLEN FOR HIM.

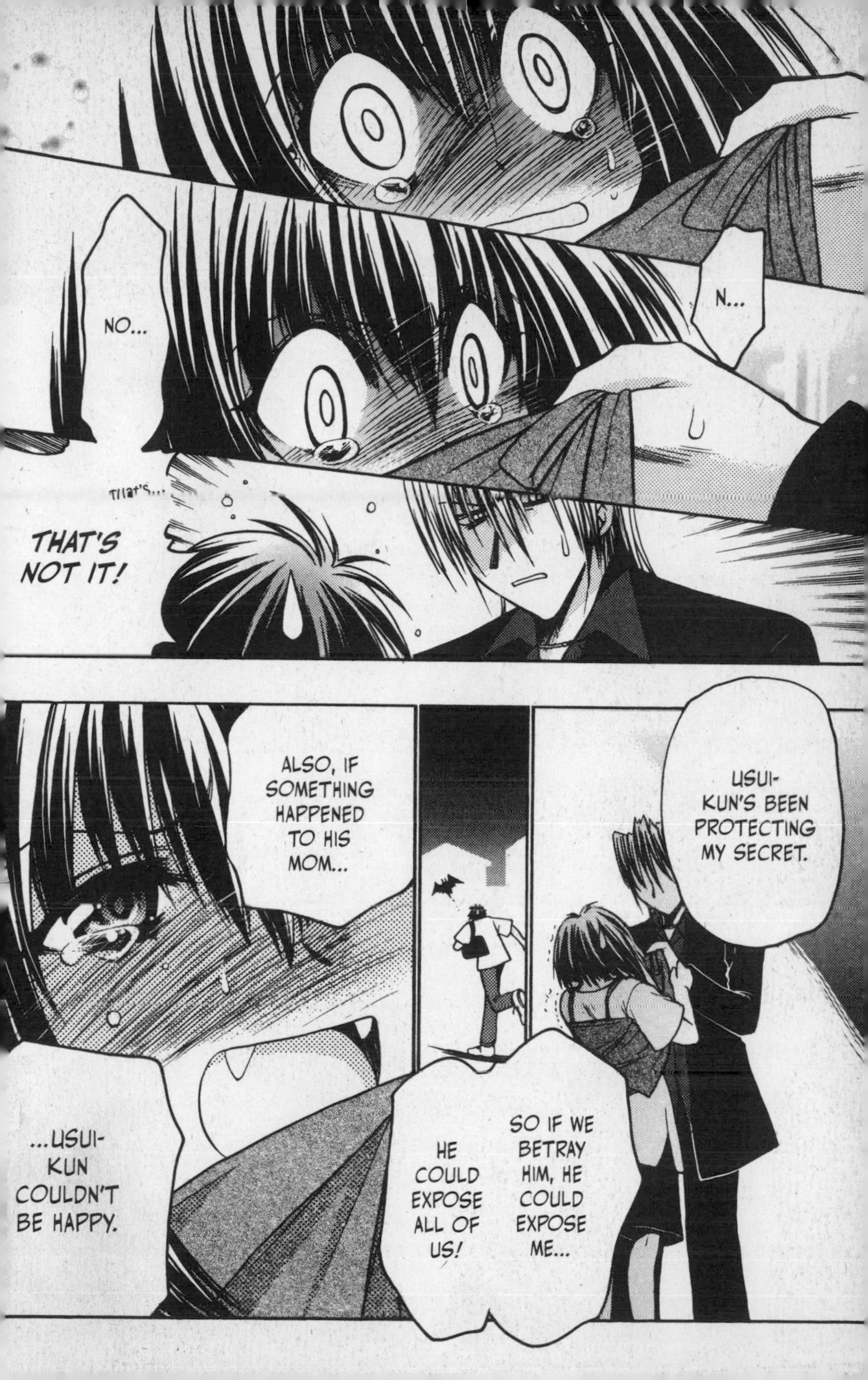
N...
NO...
That's...
THAT'S NOT IT!
USUI-KUN'S BEEN PROTECTING MY SECRET.
SO IF WE BETRAY HIM, HE COULD EXPOSE ME...
HE COULD EXPOSE ALL OF US!
ALSO, IF SOMETHING HAPPENED TO HIS MOM...
...USUI-KUN COULDN'T BE HAPPY.

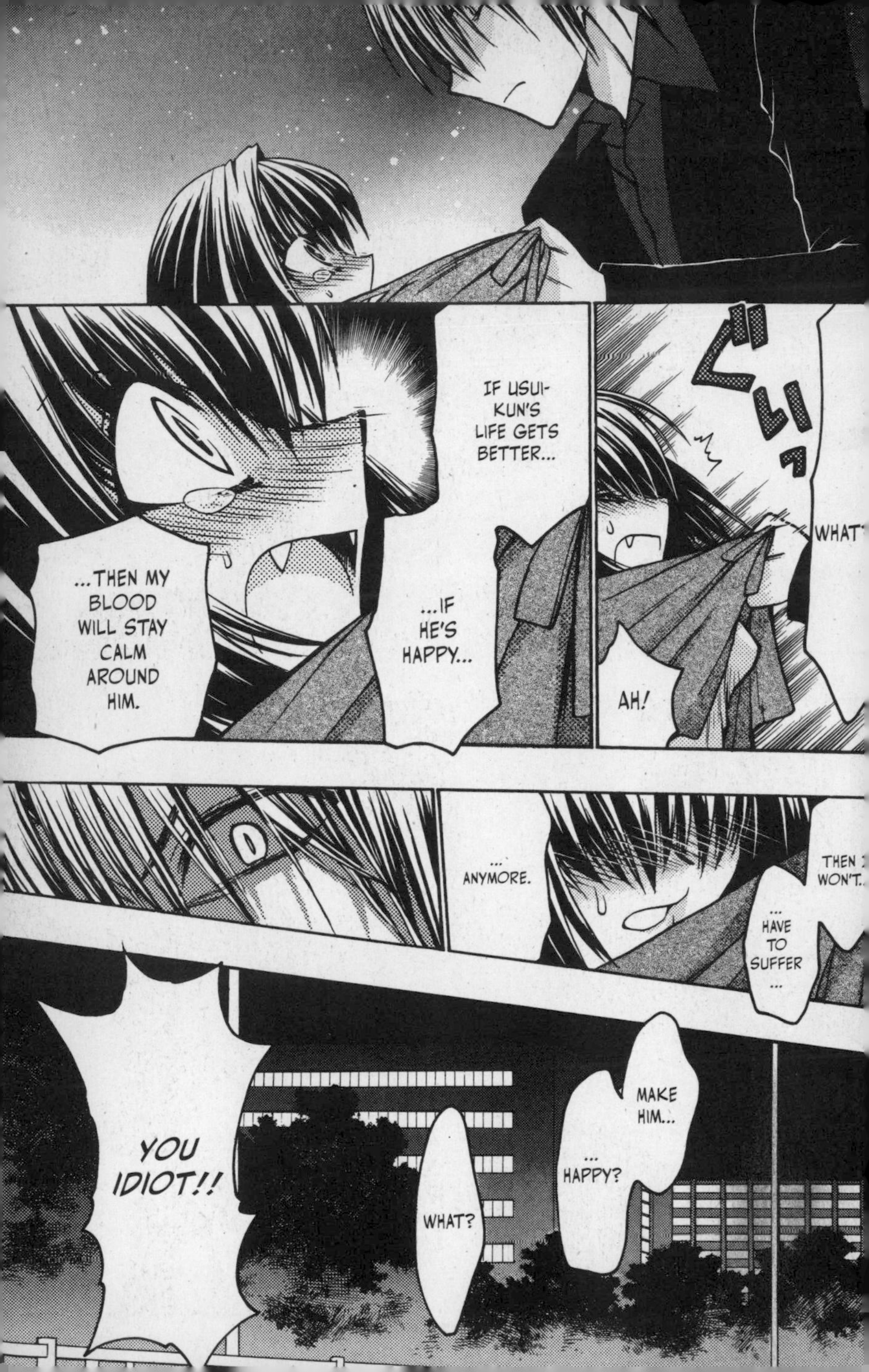
ぐいっ
WHAT?
AH!
IF USUI-KUN'S LIFE GETS BETTER...
...IF HE'S HAPPY...
...THEN MY BLOOD WILL STAY CALM AROUND HIM.
THEN I WON'T...
...HAVE TO SUFFER...
...ANYMORE.
MAKE HIM...
...HAPPY?
WHAT?
YOU IDIOT!!

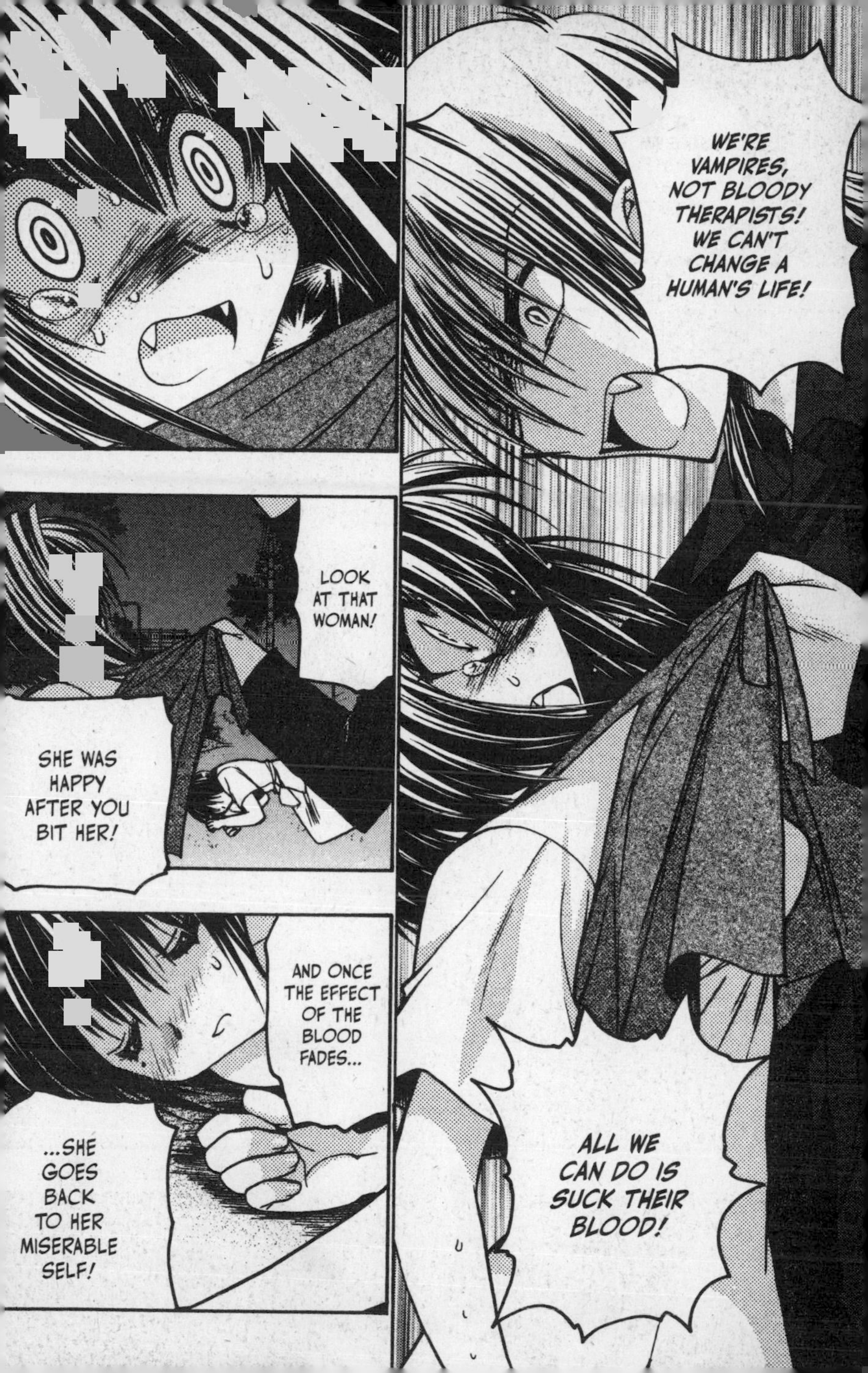
WE'RE VAMPIRES, NOT BLOODY THERAPISTS! WE CAN'T CHANGE A HUMAN'S LIFE!
ALL WE CAN DO IS SUCK THEIR BLOOD!
LOOK AT THAT WOMAN!
SHE WAS HAPPY AFTER YOU BIT HER!
AND ONCE THE EFFECT OF THE BLOOD FADES...
...SHE GOES BACK TO HER MISERABLE SELF!

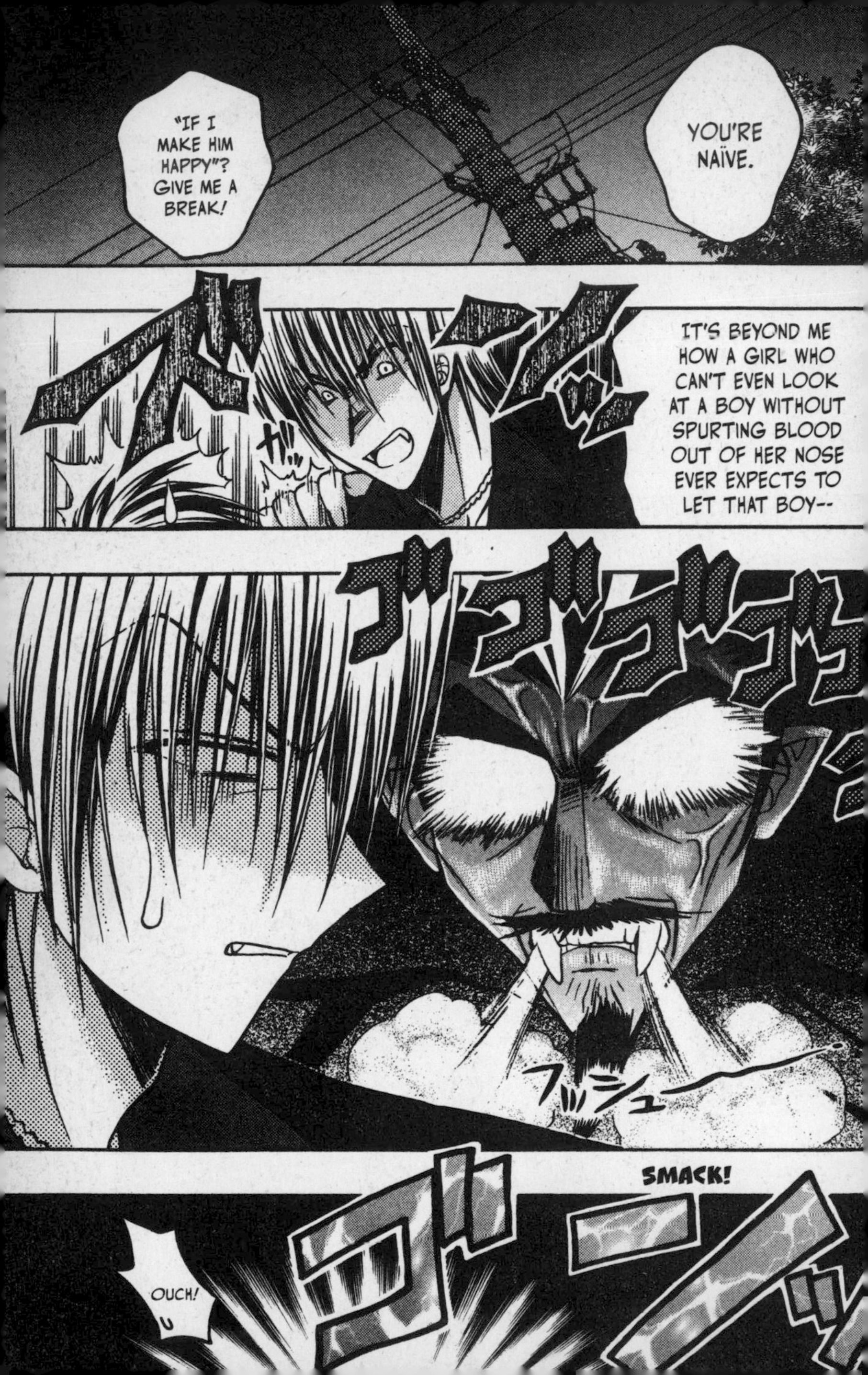
YOU'RE NAÏVE.
"IF I MAKE HIM HAPPY"? GIVE ME A BREAK!
IT'S BEYOND ME HOW A GIRL WHO CAN'T EVEN LOOK AT A BOY WITHOUT SPURTING BLOOD OUT OF HER NOSE EVER EXPECTS TO LET THAT BOY--
SMACK!
OUCH!

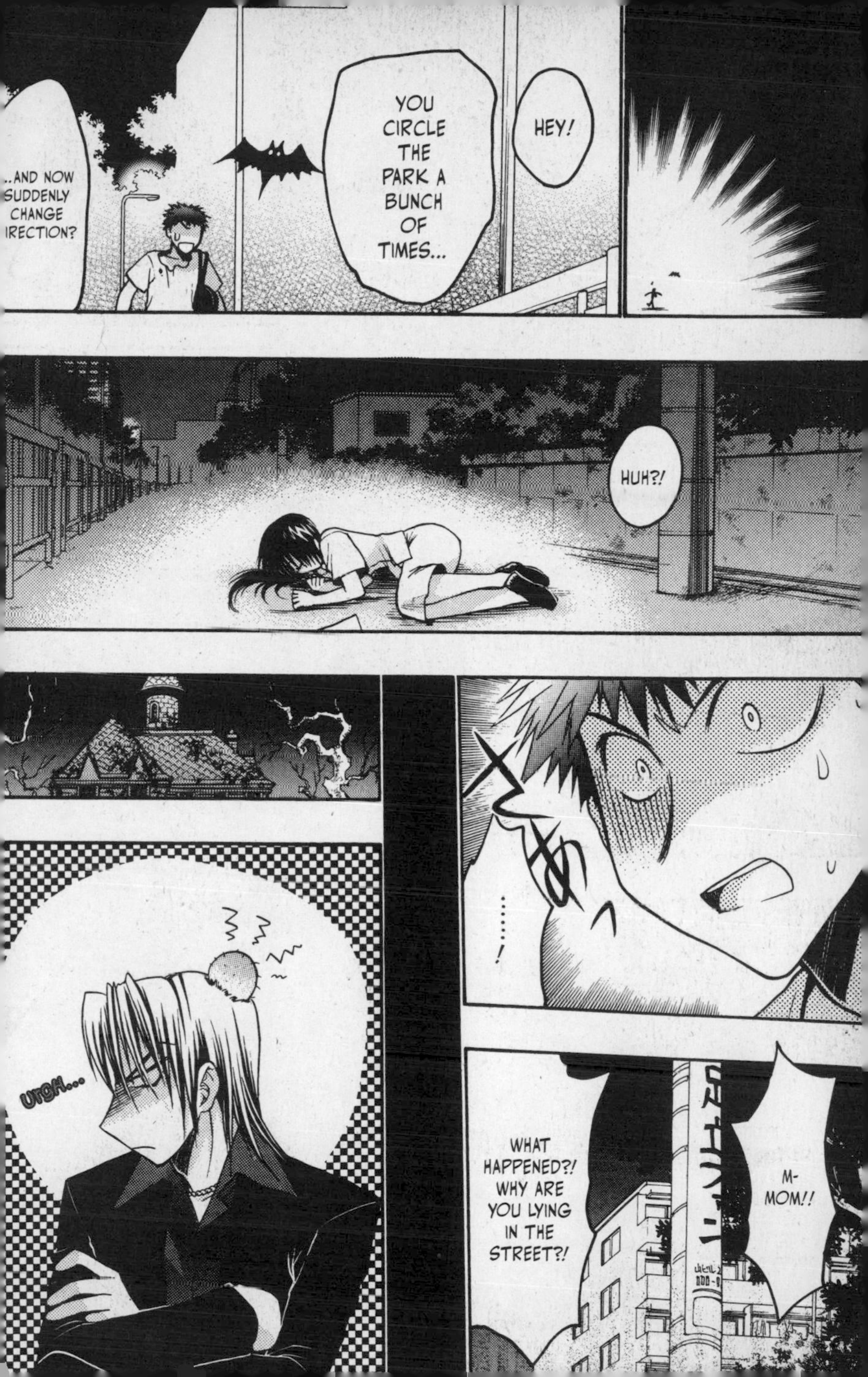
HEY!
YOU CIRCLE THE PARK A BUNCH OF TIMES...
..AND NOW SUDDENLY CHANGE IRECTION?
HUH?!
......!
M-MOM!!
WHAT HAPPENED?! WHY ARE YOU LYING IN THE STREET?!
UrGH...

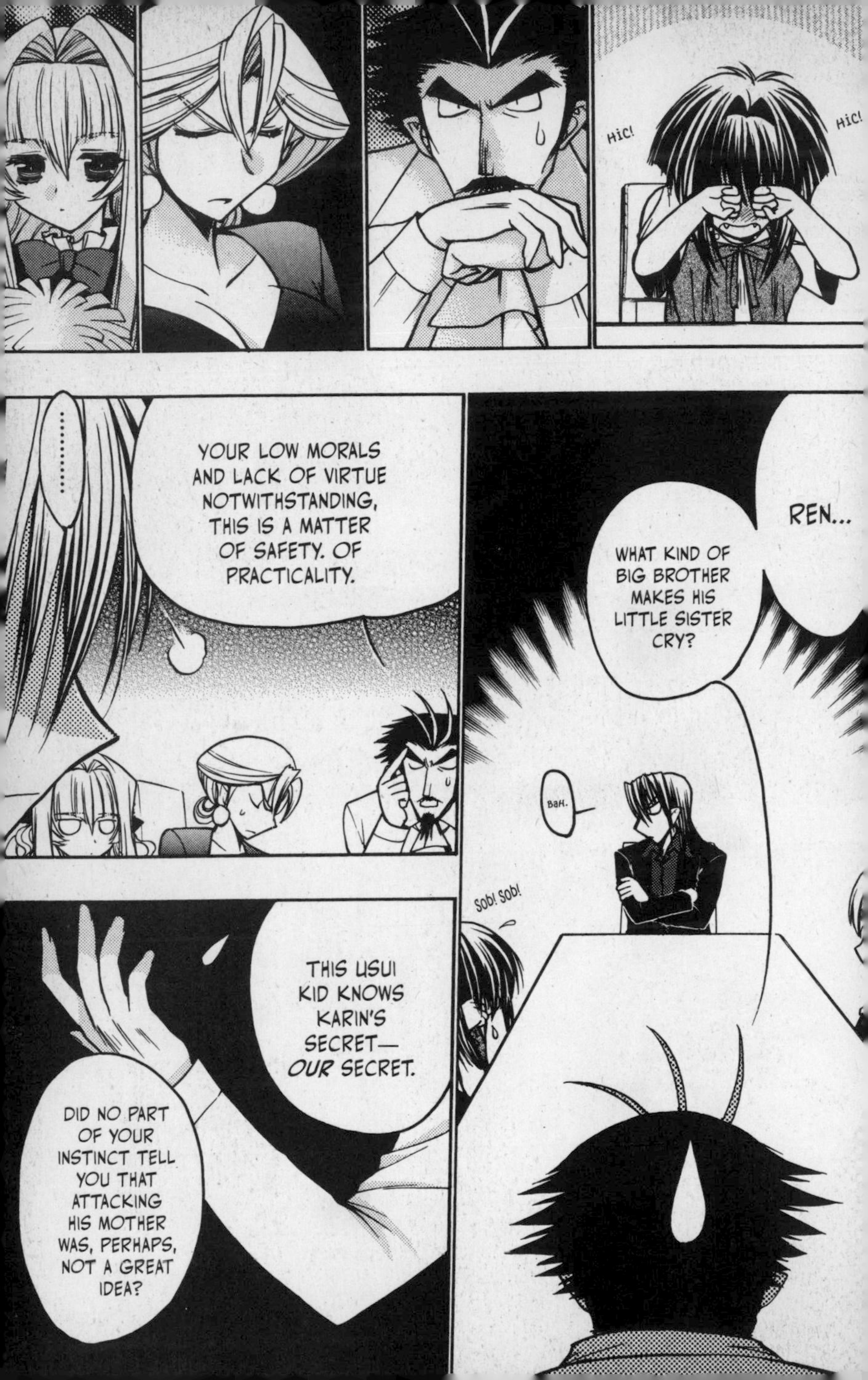
HIC!
HIC!
REN...
WHAT KIND OF BIG BROTHER MAKES HIS LITTLE SISTER CRY?
BAH.
SOB! SOB!
......
YOUR LOW MORALS AND LACK OF VIRTUE NOTWITHSTANDING, THIS IS A MATTER OF SAFETY. OF PRACTICALITY.
THIS USUI KID KNOWS KARIN'S SECRET— *OUR* SECRET.
DID NO PART OF YOUR INSTINCT TELL YOU THAT ATTACKING HIS MOTHER WAS, PERHAPS, NOT A GREAT IDEA?

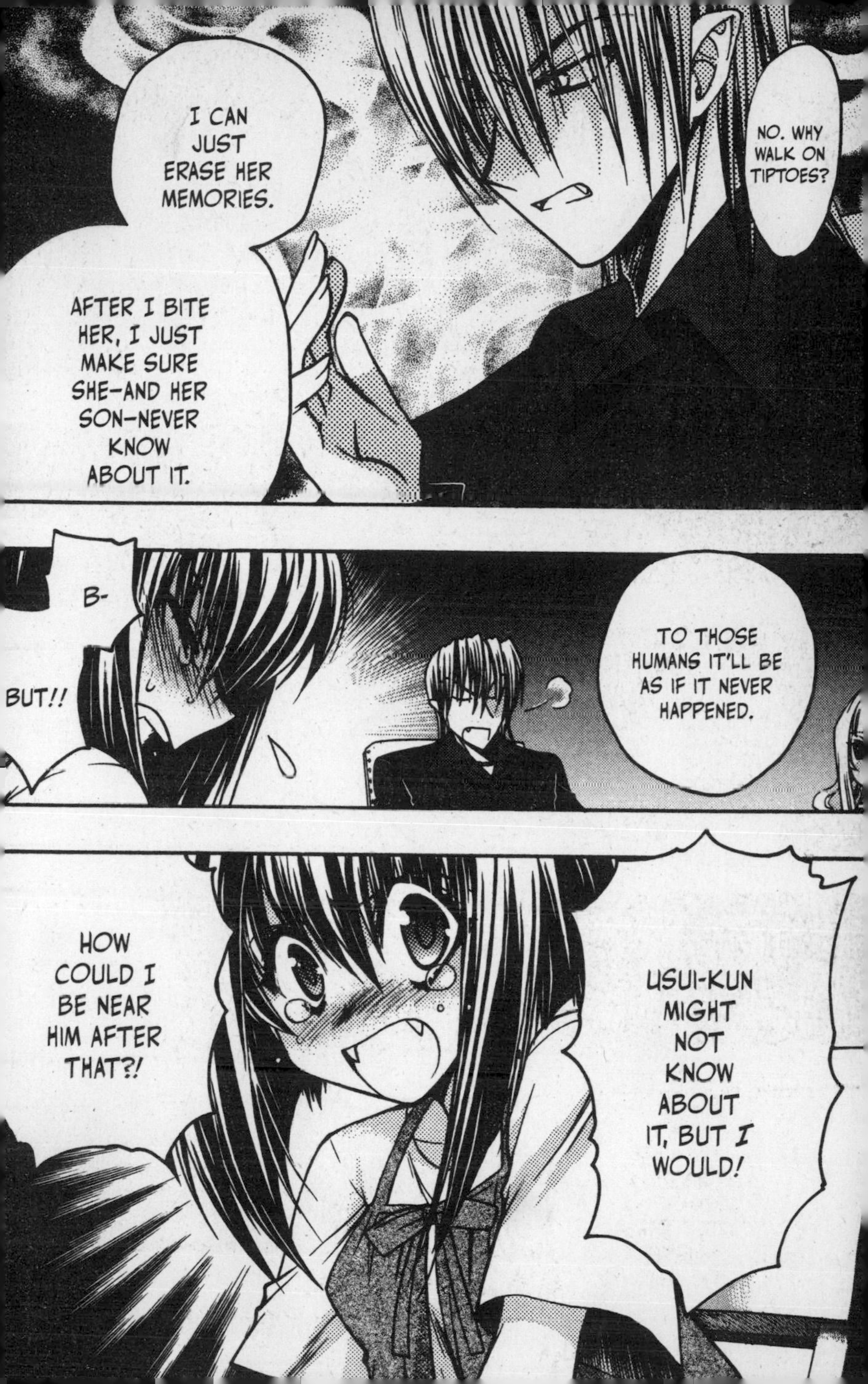
NO. WHY WALK ON TIPTOES?
I CAN JUST ERASE HER MEMORIES.
AFTER I BITE HER, I JUST MAKE SURE SHE—AND HER SON—NEVER KNOW ABOUT IT.
TO THOSE HUMANS IT'LL BE AS IF IT NEVER HAPPENED.
B-
BUT!!
USUI-KUN MIGHT NOT KNOW ABOUT IT, BUT I WOULD!
HOW COULD I BE NEAR HIM AFTER THAT?!

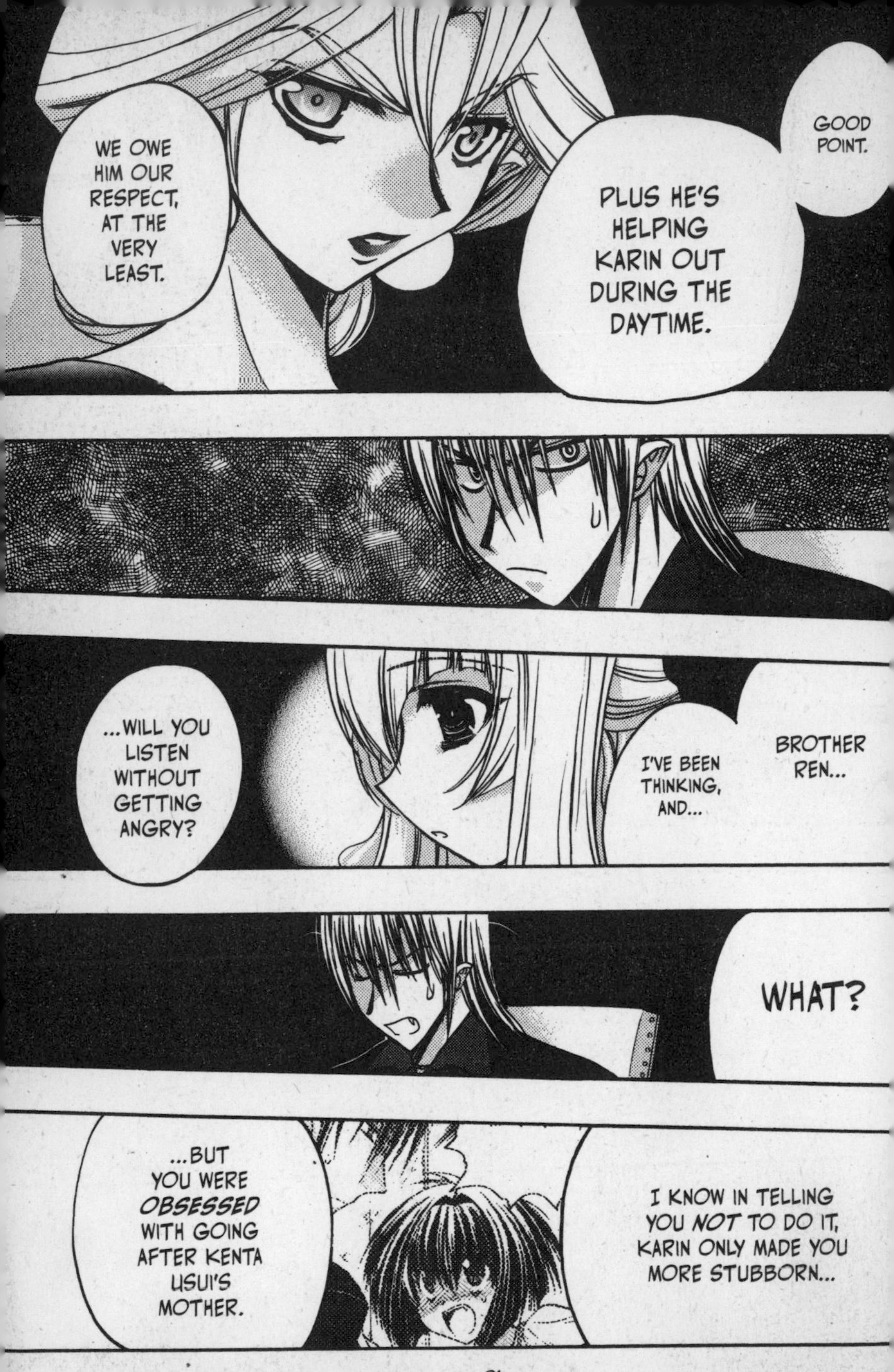
GOOD POINT.
PLUS HE'S HELPING KARIN OUT DURING THE DAYTIME.
WE OWE HIM OUR RESPECT, AT THE VERY LEAST.
BROTHER REN...
I'VE BEEN THINKING, AND...
...WILL YOU LISTEN WITHOUT GETTING ANGRY?
WHAT?
I KNOW IN TELLING YOU *NOT* TO DO IT, KARIN ONLY MADE YOU MORE STUBBORN...
...BUT YOU WERE *OBSESSED* WITH GOING AFTER KENTA USUI'S MOTHER.

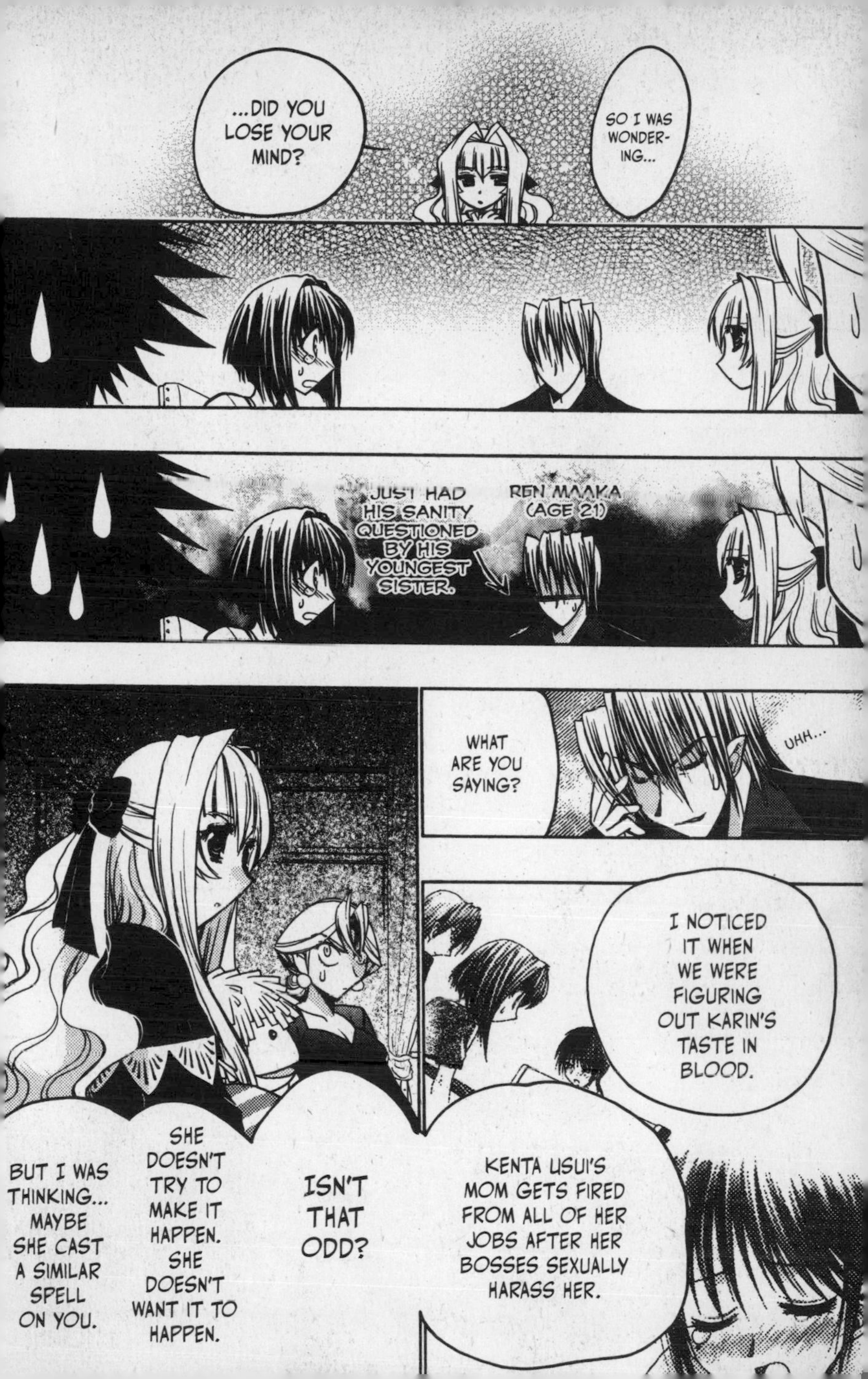
SO I WAS WONDERING...
...DID YOU LOSE YOUR MIND?
REN MAAKA (AGE 21)
JUST HAD HIS SANITY QUESTIONED BY HIS YOUNGEST SISTER.
UHH...
WHAT ARE YOU SAYING?
I NOTICED IT WHEN WE WERE FIGURING OUT KARIN'S TASTE IN BLOOD.
KENTA USUI'S MOM GETS FIRED FROM ALL OF HER JOBS AFTER HER BOSSES SEXUALLY HARASS HER.
ISN'T THAT ODD?
SHE DOESN'T TRY TO MAKE IT HAPPEN. SHE DOESN'T WANT IT TO HAPPEN.
BUT I WAS THINKING... MAYBE SHE CAST A SIMILAR SPELL ON YOU.

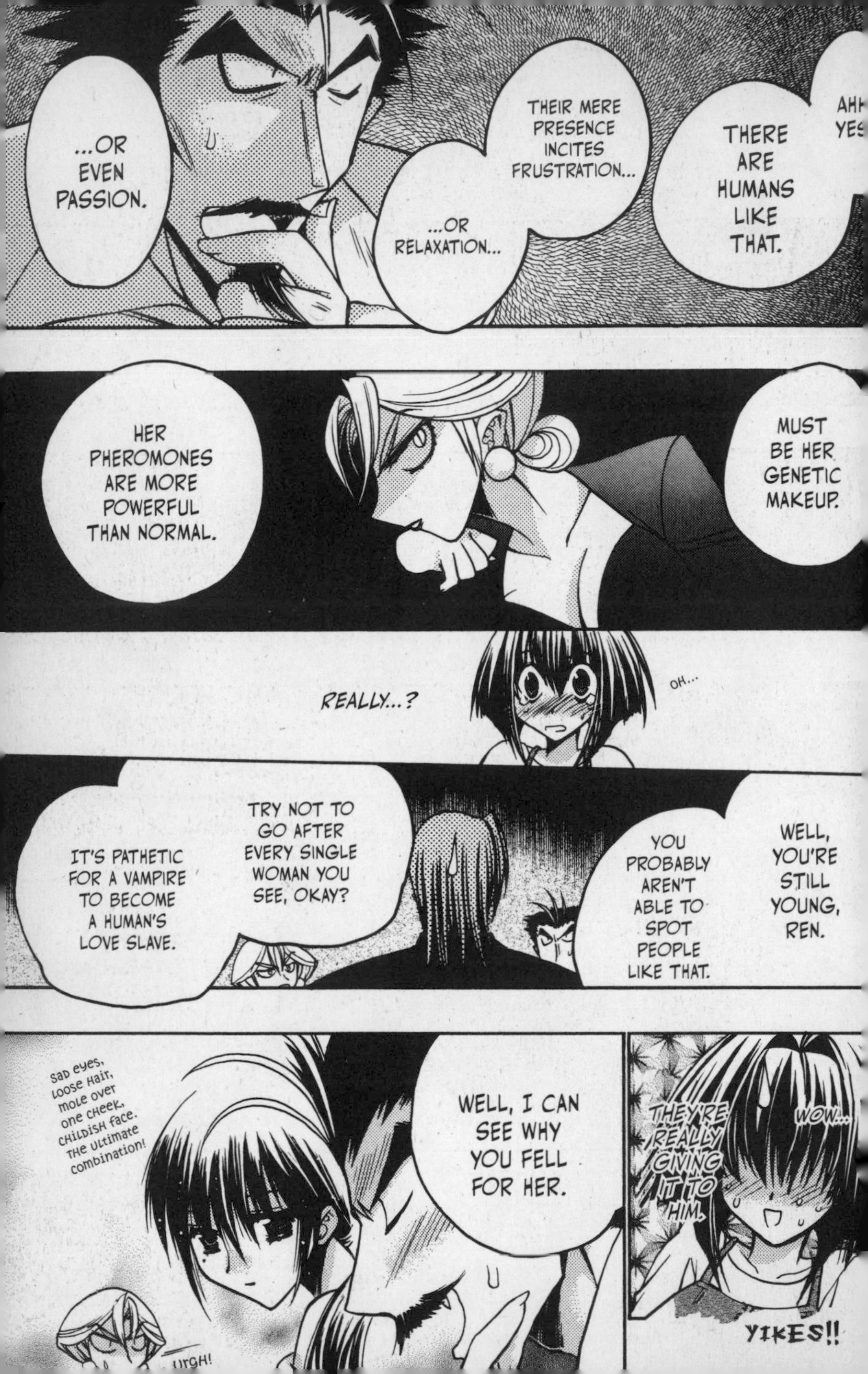
THERE ARE HUMANS LIKE THAT.
THEIR MERE PRESENCE INCITES FRUSTRATION...
...OR RELAXATION...
...OR EVEN PASSION.
MUST BE HER GENETIC MAKEUP.
HER PHEROMONES ARE MORE POWERFUL THAN NORMAL.
OH...
REALLY...?
WELL, YOU'RE STILL YOUNG, REN.
YOU PROBABLY AREN'T ABLE TO SPOT PEOPLE LIKE THAT.
TRY NOT TO GO AFTER EVERY SINGLE WOMAN YOU SEE, OKAY?
IT'S PATHETIC FOR A VAMPIRE TO BECOME A HUMAN'S LOVE SLAVE.
WOW...
THEY'RE REALLY GIVING IT TO HIM.
YIKES!!
WELL, I CAN SEE WHY YOU FELL FOR HER.
Sad eyes, loose hair, mole over one cheek, childish face. The ultimate combination!
URGH!

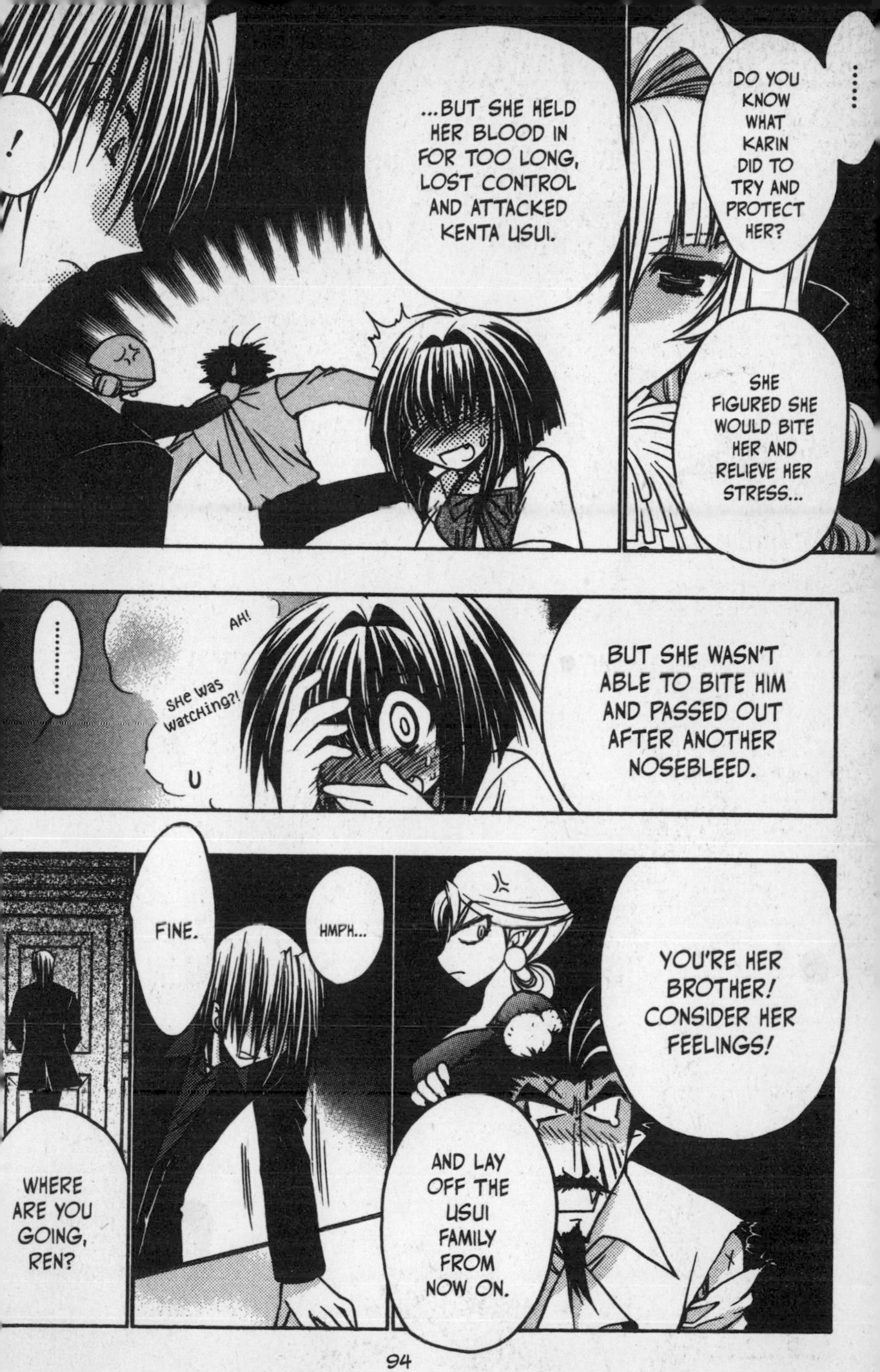

......
DO YOU KNOW WHAT KARIN DID TO TRY AND PROTECT HER?
SHE FIGURED SHE WOULD BITE HER AND RELIEVE HER STRESS...
...BUT SHE HELD HER BLOOD IN FOR TOO LONG, LOST CONTROL AND ATTACKED KENTA USUI.
!
BUT SHE WASN'T ABLE TO BITE HIM AND PASSED OUT AFTER ANOTHER NOSEBLEED.
AH!
SHE WAS WATCHING?!
U
.......
YOU'RE HER BROTHER! CONSIDER HER FEELINGS!
AND LAY OFF THE USUI FAMILY FROM NOW ON.
HMPH...
FINE.
WHERE ARE YOU GOING, REN?

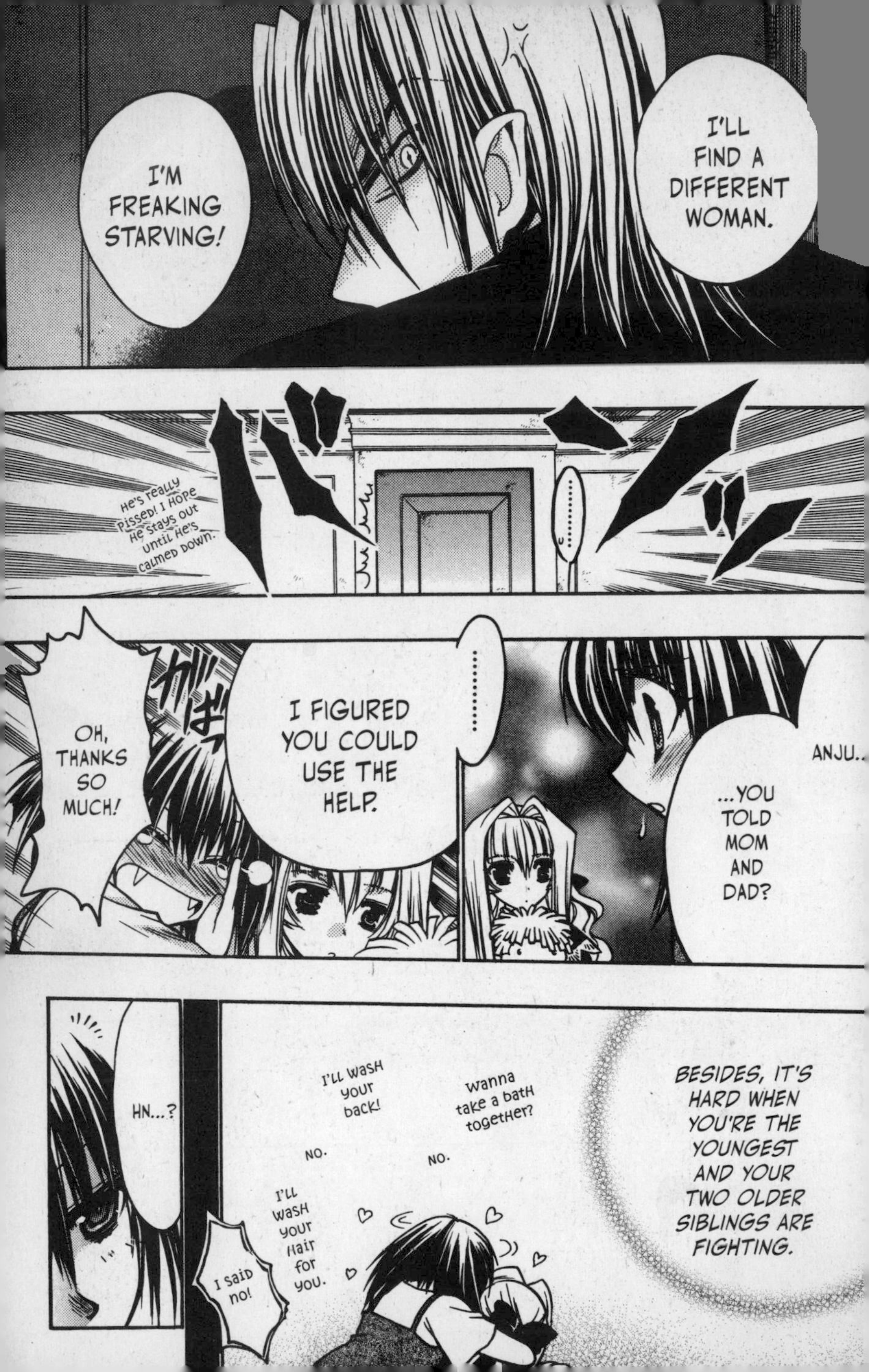
I'LL FIND A DIFFERENT WOMAN.
I'M FREAKING STARVING!
......
He's really pissed! I hope he stays out until he's calmed down.
ANJU...
...YOU TOLD MOM AND DAD?
......
I FIGURED YOU COULD USE THE HELP.
OH, THANKS SO MUCH!
BESIDES, IT'S HARD WHEN YOU'RE THE YOUNGEST AND YOUR TWO OLDER SIBLINGS ARE FIGHTING.
Wanna take a bath together?
NO.
I'll wash your back!
NO.
I'll wash your hair for you.
I said no!
HN...?

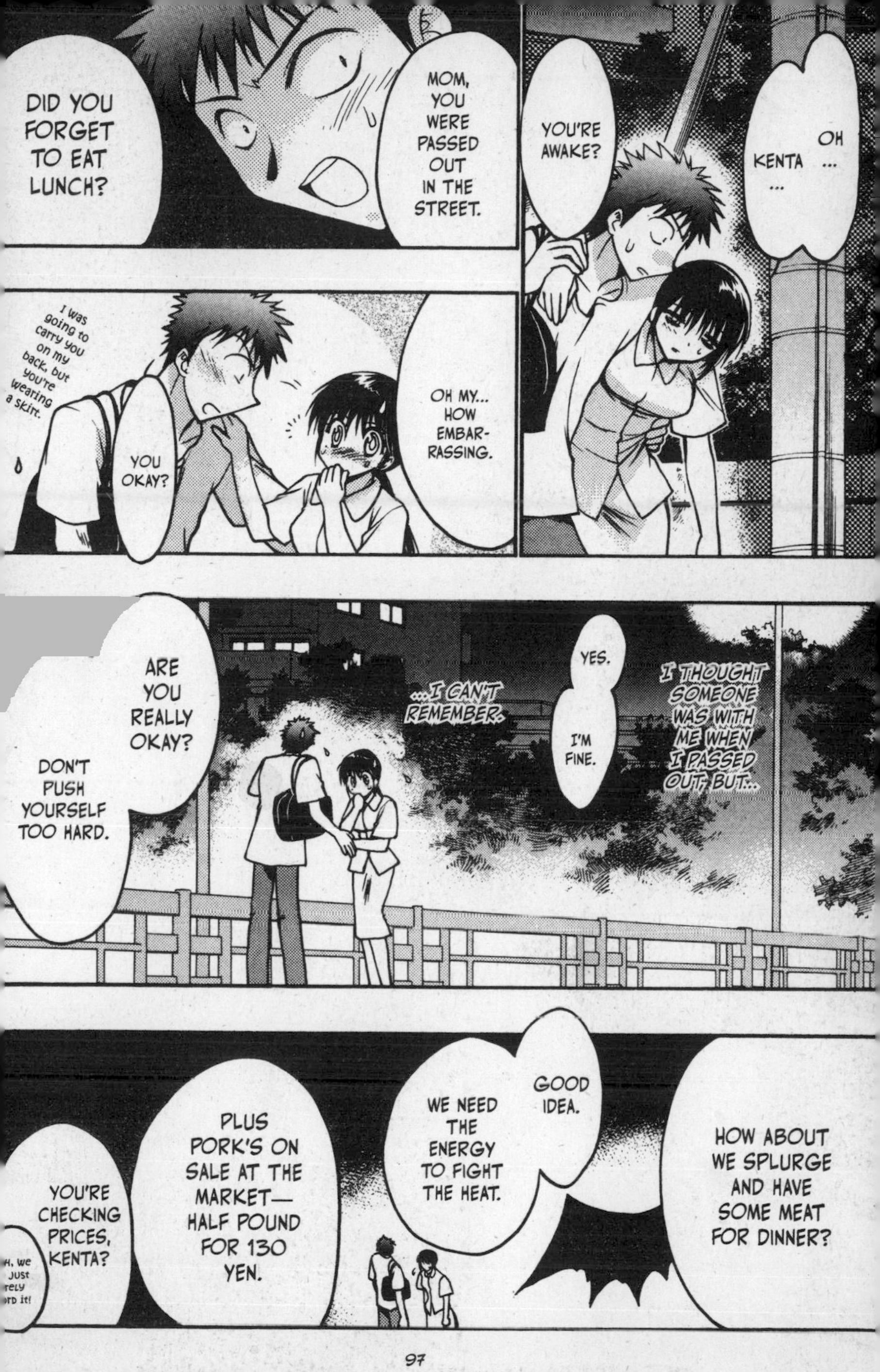
OH KENTA ... ...
YOU'RE AWAKE?
MOM, YOU WERE PASSED OUT IN THE STREET.
DID YOU FORGET TO EAT LUNCH?
OH MY... HOW EMBARRASSING.
YOU OKAY?
I was going to carry you on my back, but you're wearing a skirt.
I THOUGHT SOMEONE WAS WITH ME WHEN I PASSED OUT, BUT...
YES. I'M FINE.
...I CAN'T REMEMBER.
ARE YOU REALLY OKAY? DON'T PUSH YOURSELF TOO HARD.
HOW ABOUT WE SPLURGE AND HAVE SOME MEAT FOR DINNER?
GOOD IDEA.
WE NEED THE ENERGY TO FIGHT THE HEAT.
PLUS PORK'S ON SALE AT THE MARKET— HALF POUND FOR 130 YEN.
YOU'RE CHECKING PRICES, KENTA?

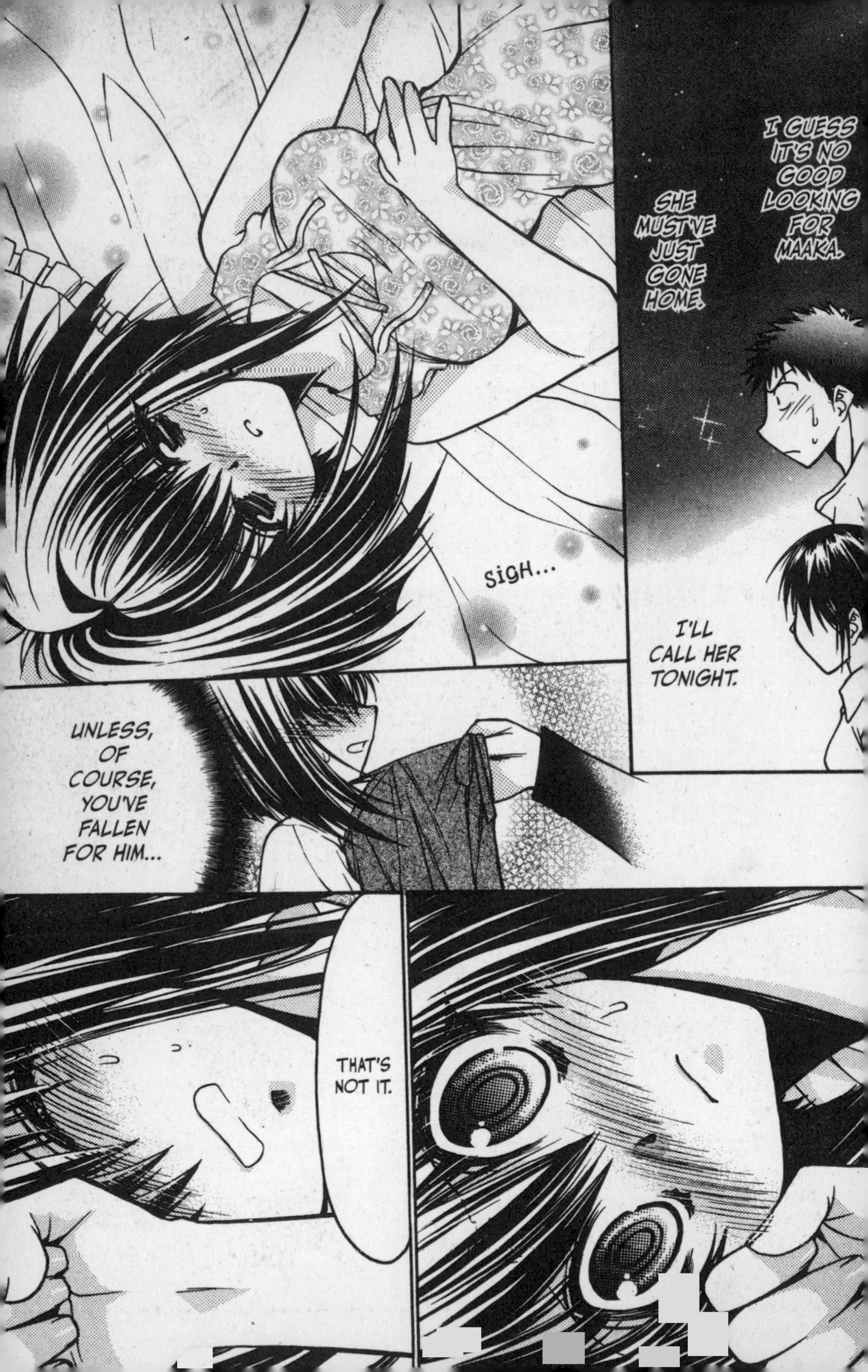
I GUESS IT'S NO GOOD LOOKING FOR MAAKA.
SHE MUST'VE JUST GONE HOME.
I'LL CALL HER TONIGHT.
SIGH...
UNLESS, OF COURSE, YOU'VE FALLEN FOR HIM...
THAT'S NOT IT.

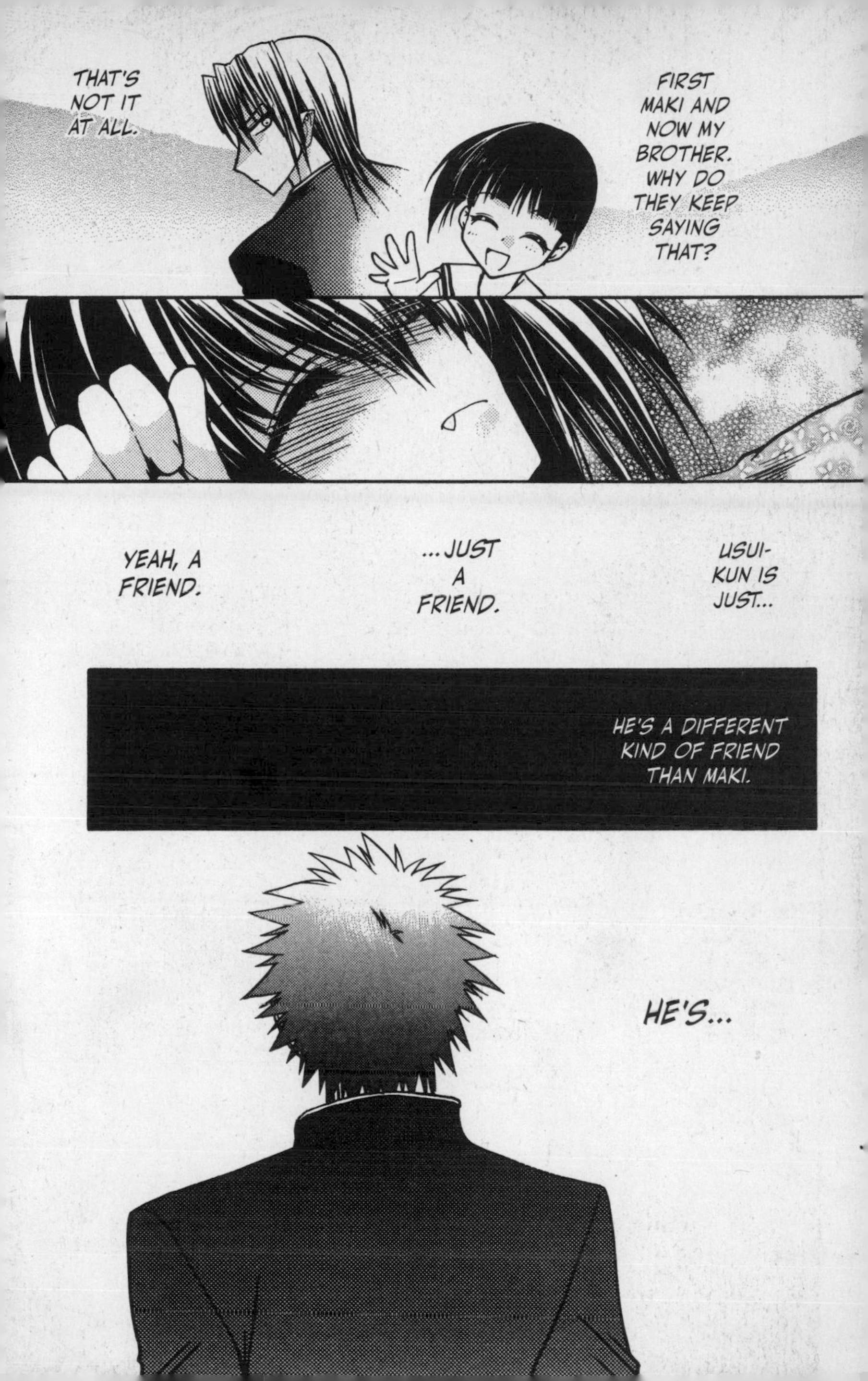
FIRST MAKI AND NOW MY BROTHER. WHY DO THEY KEEP SAYING THAT?
THAT'S NOT IT AT ALL.
USUI-KUN IS JUST...
...JUST A FRIEND.
YEAH, A FRIEND.
HE'S A DIFFERENT KIND OF FRIEND THAN MAKI.
HE'S...

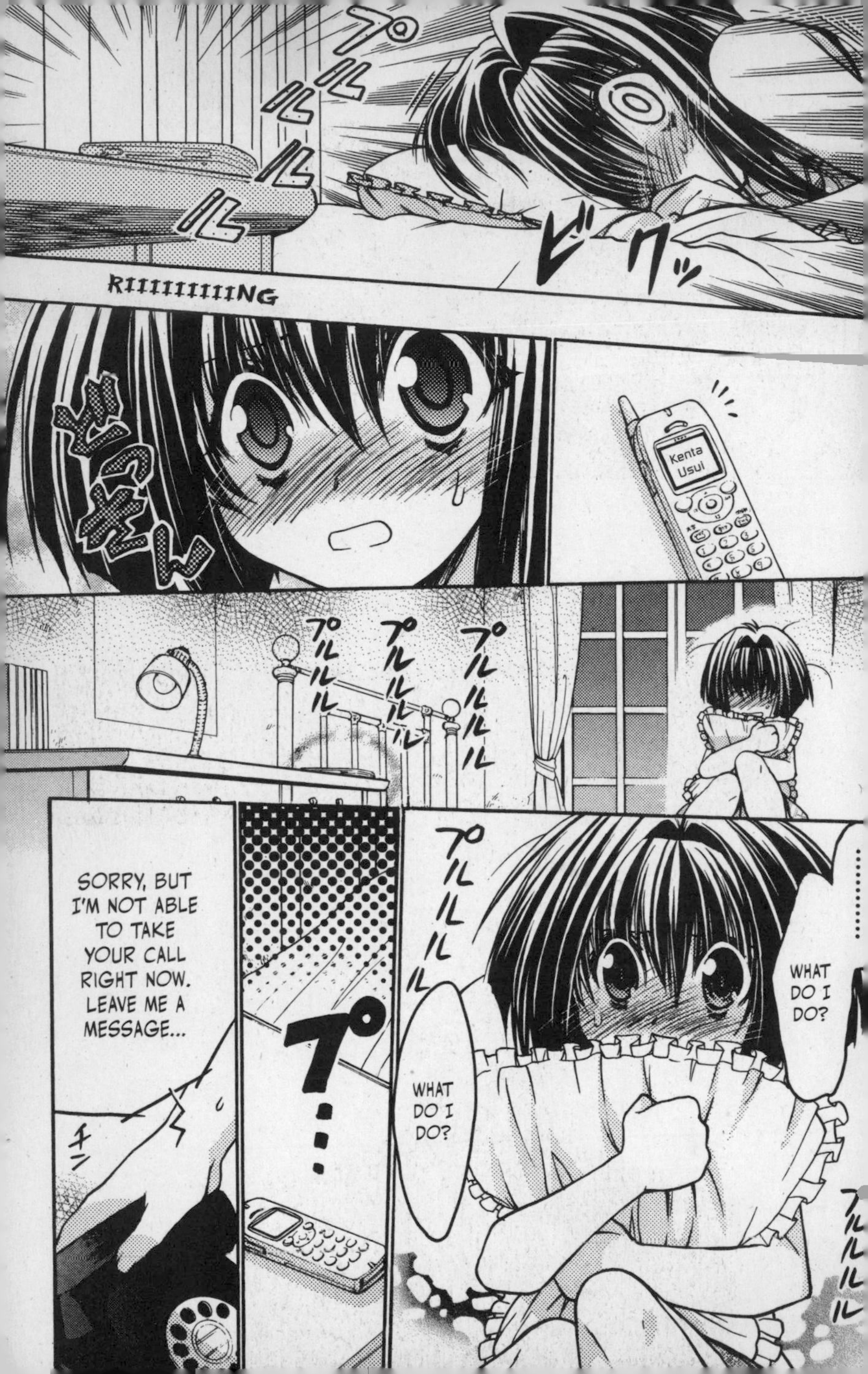
プルルルル
ビクッ
RIIIIIIIIIING
Kenta Usui
プルルル
プルルルル
プルルルル
......
WHAT DO I DO?
プルルルル
WHAT DO I DO?
プルルルル
プ...
SORRY, BUT I'M NOT ABLE TO TAKE YOUR CALL RIGHT NOW. LEAVE ME A MESSAGE...
チン

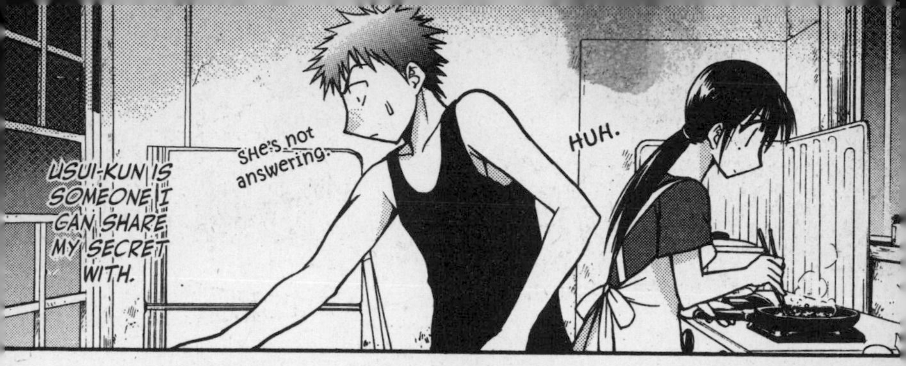
HUH.
SHE'S not answering.
USUI-KUN IS SOMEONE I CAN SHARE MY SECRET WITH.

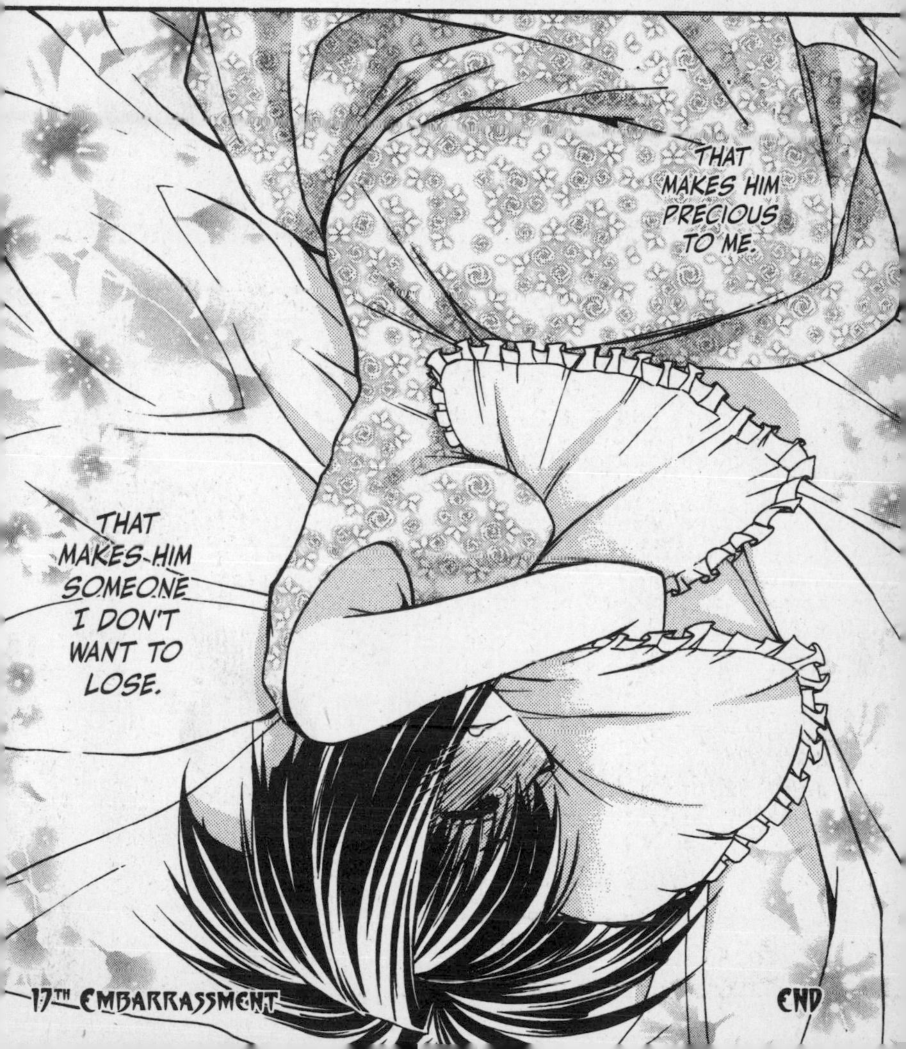
THAT MAKES HIM PRECIOUS TO ME.
THAT MAKES HIM SOMEONE I DON'T WANT TO LOSE.

17TH EMBARRASSMENT END

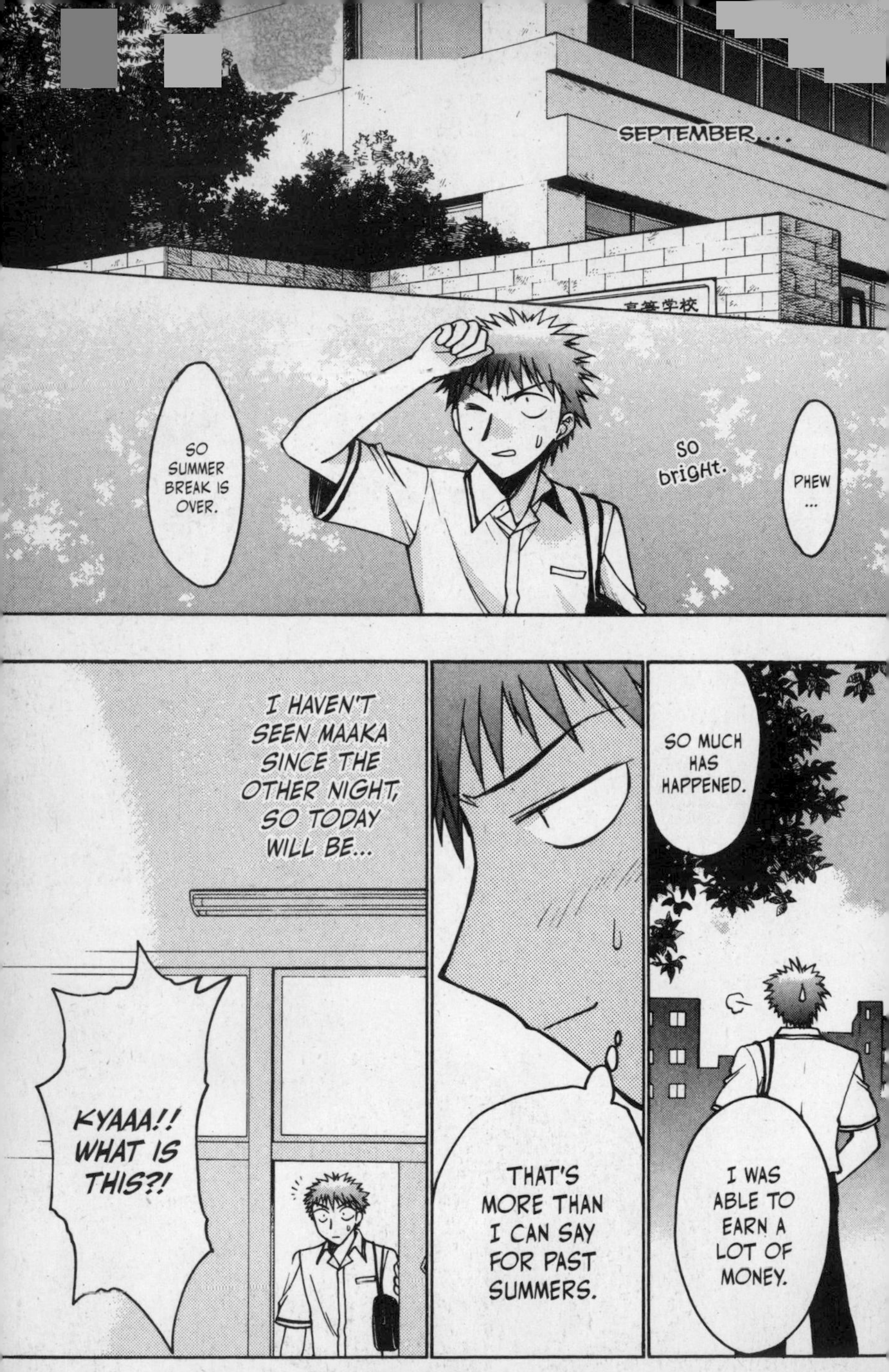
SEPTEMBER...
PHEW...
SO bright.
SO SUMMER BREAK IS OVER.
SO MUCH HAS HAPPENED.
I WAS ABLE TO EARN A LOT OF MONEY.
THAT'S MORE THAN I CAN SAY FOR PAST SUMMERS.
I HAVEN'T SEEN MAAKA SINCE THE OTHER NIGHT, SO TODAY WILL BE...
KYAAA!! WHAT IS THIS?!

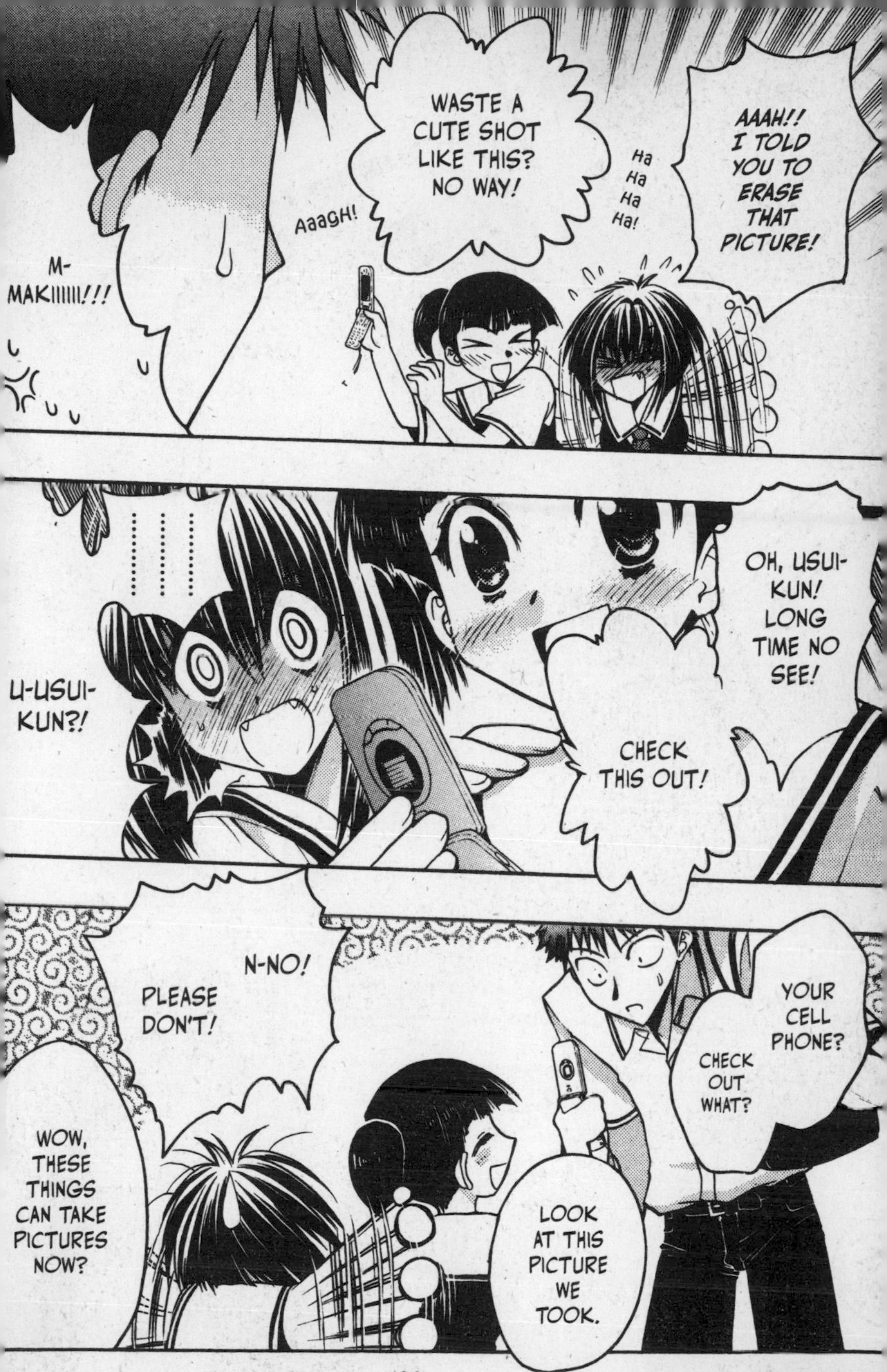
AAAH!! I TOLD YOU TO ERASE THAT PICTURE!
Ha Ha Ha Ha!
WASTE A CUTE SHOT LIKE THIS? NO WAY!
Aaagh!
M-MAKIIIIII!!!
OH, USUI-KUN! LONG TIME NO SEE!
CHECK THIS OUT!
U-USUI-KUN?!
YOUR CELL PHONE?
CHECK OUT WHAT?
N-NO! PLEASE DON'T!
LOOK AT THIS PICTURE WE TOOK.
WOW, THESE THINGS CAN TAKE PICTURES NOW?

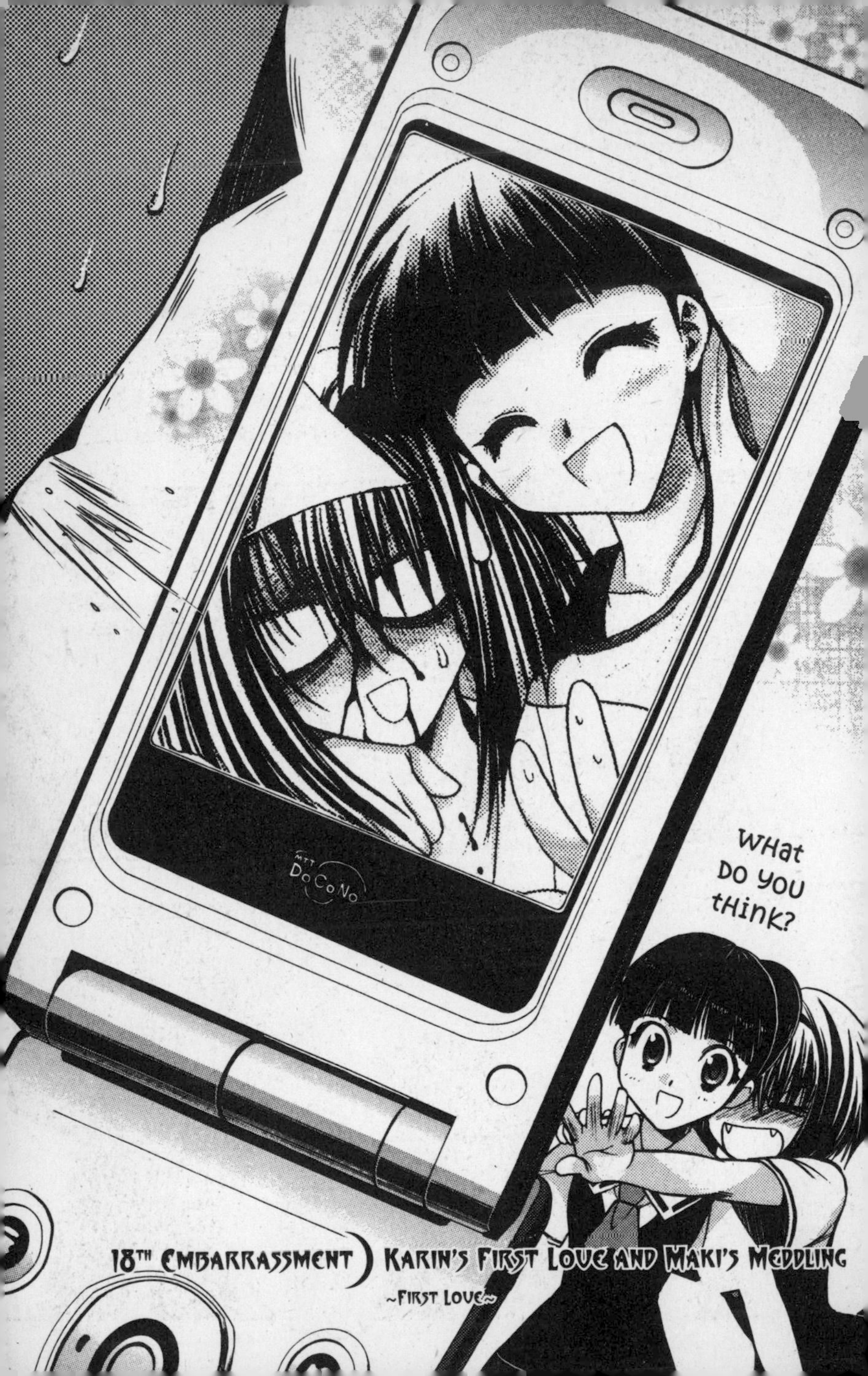
DoCoNo
WHAT DO YOU THINK?
18TH EMBARRASSMENT KARIN'S FIRST LOVE AND MAKI'S MEDDLING
~FIRST LOVE~

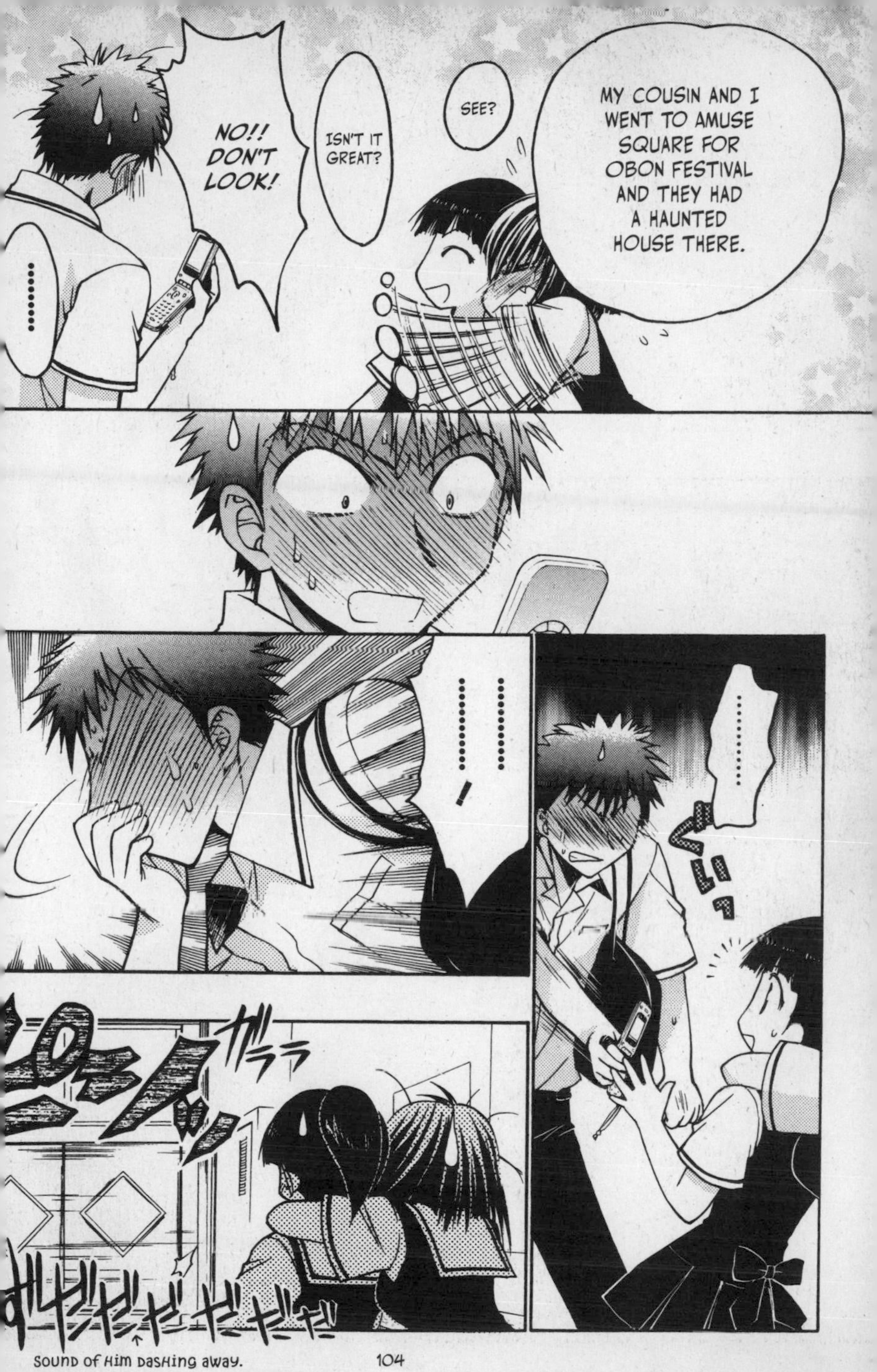
MY COUSIN AND I WENT TO AMUSE SQUARE FOR OBON FESTIVAL AND THEY HAD A HAUNTED HOUSE THERE.
SEE?
ISN'T IT GREAT?
NO!! DON'T LOOK!
........
........
........!
ガララ

Sound of him dashing away.

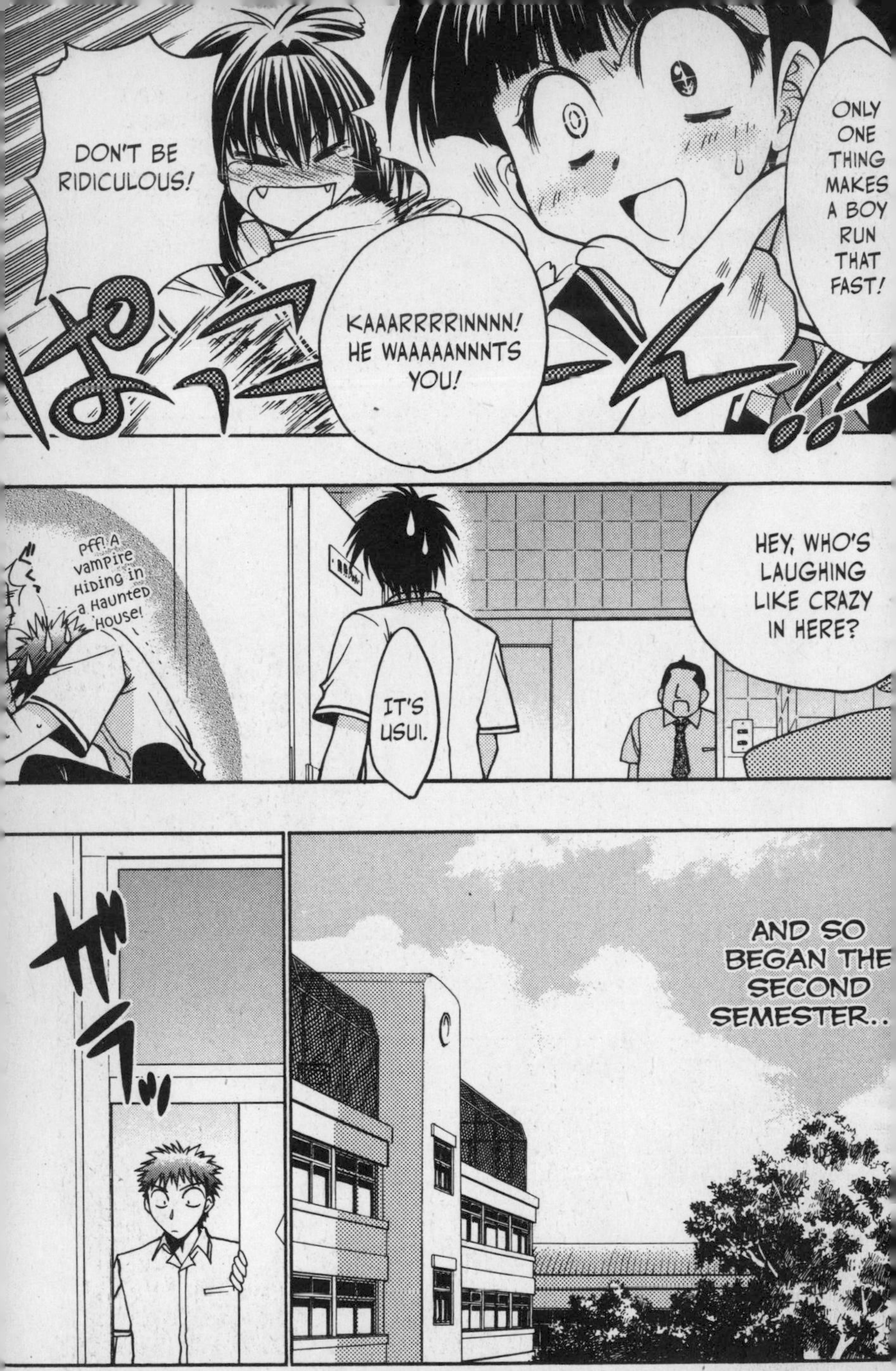
ONLY ONE THING MAKES A BOY RUN THAT FAST!
KAAARRRRINNNN! HE WAAAAANNNTS YOU!
DON'T BE RIDICULOUS!
HEY, WHO'S LAUGHING LIKE CRAZY IN HERE?
IT'S USUI.
Pff! A vampire Hiding in a Haunted House!
AND SO BEGAN THE SECOND SEMESTER...

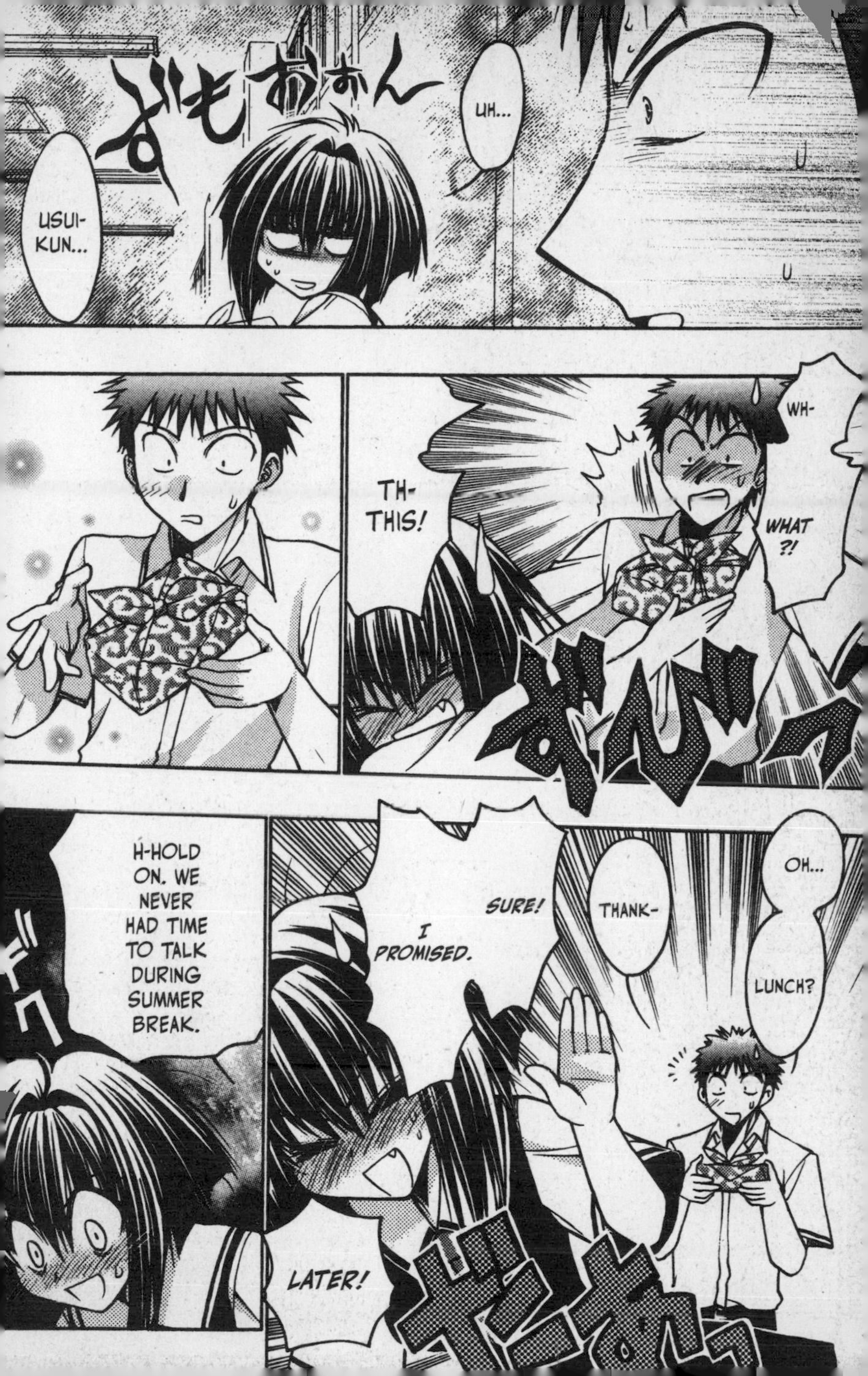
UH...
USUI-KUN...
WH-
WHAT?!
TH- THIS!
OH...
LUNCH?
THANK-
SURE!
I PROMISED.
LATER!
H-HOLD ON. WE NEVER HAD TIME TO TALK DURING SUMMER BREAK.

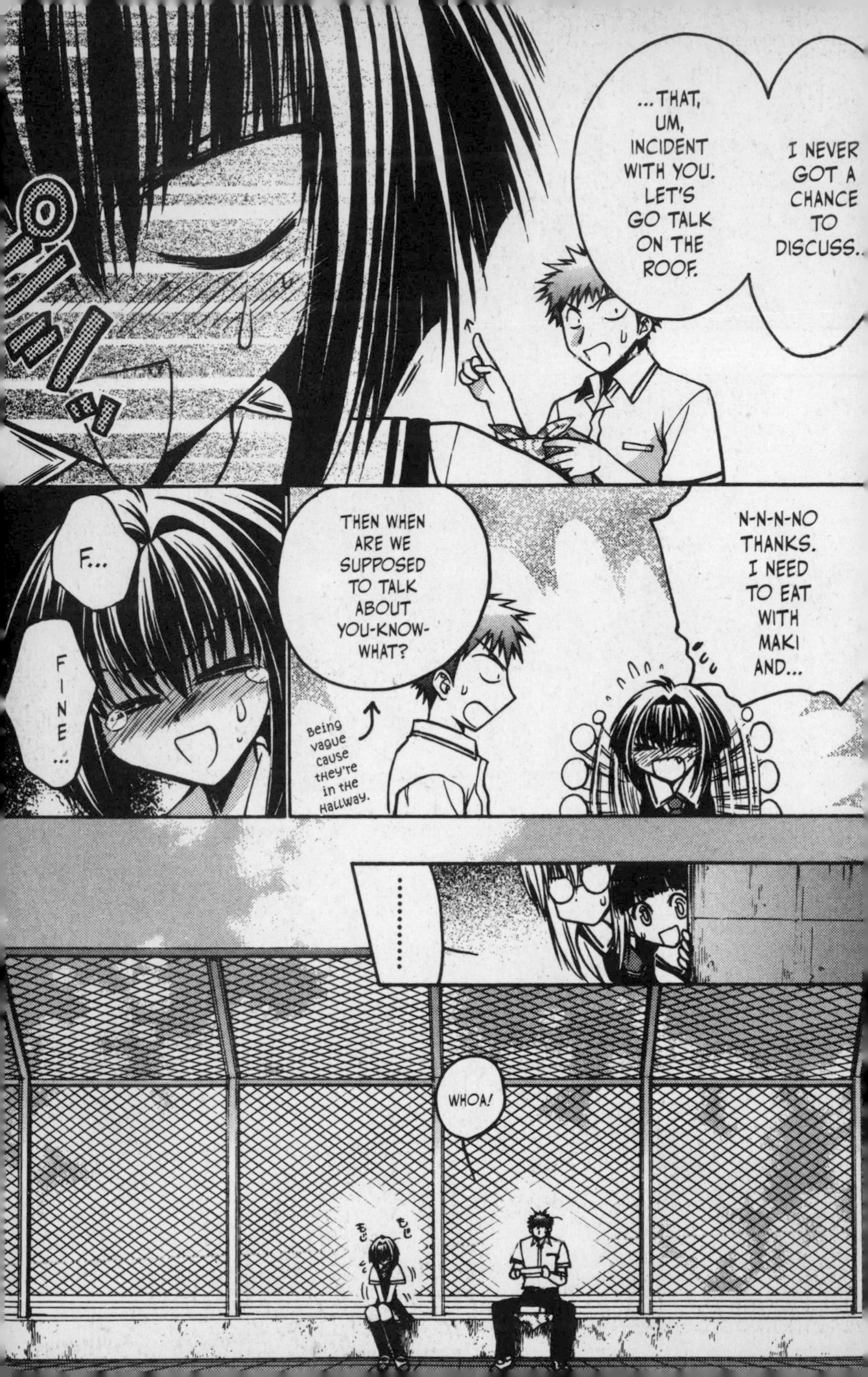

I NEVER GOT A CHANCE TO DISCUSS..
...THAT, UM, INCIDENT WITH YOU. LET'S GO TALK ON THE ROOF.
N-N-N-NO THANKS. I NEED TO EAT WITH MAKI AND...
THEN WHEN ARE WE SUPPOSED TO TALK ABOUT YOU-KNOW-WHAT?
Being vague cause they're in the Hallway.
F...
FINE...
........
WHOA!

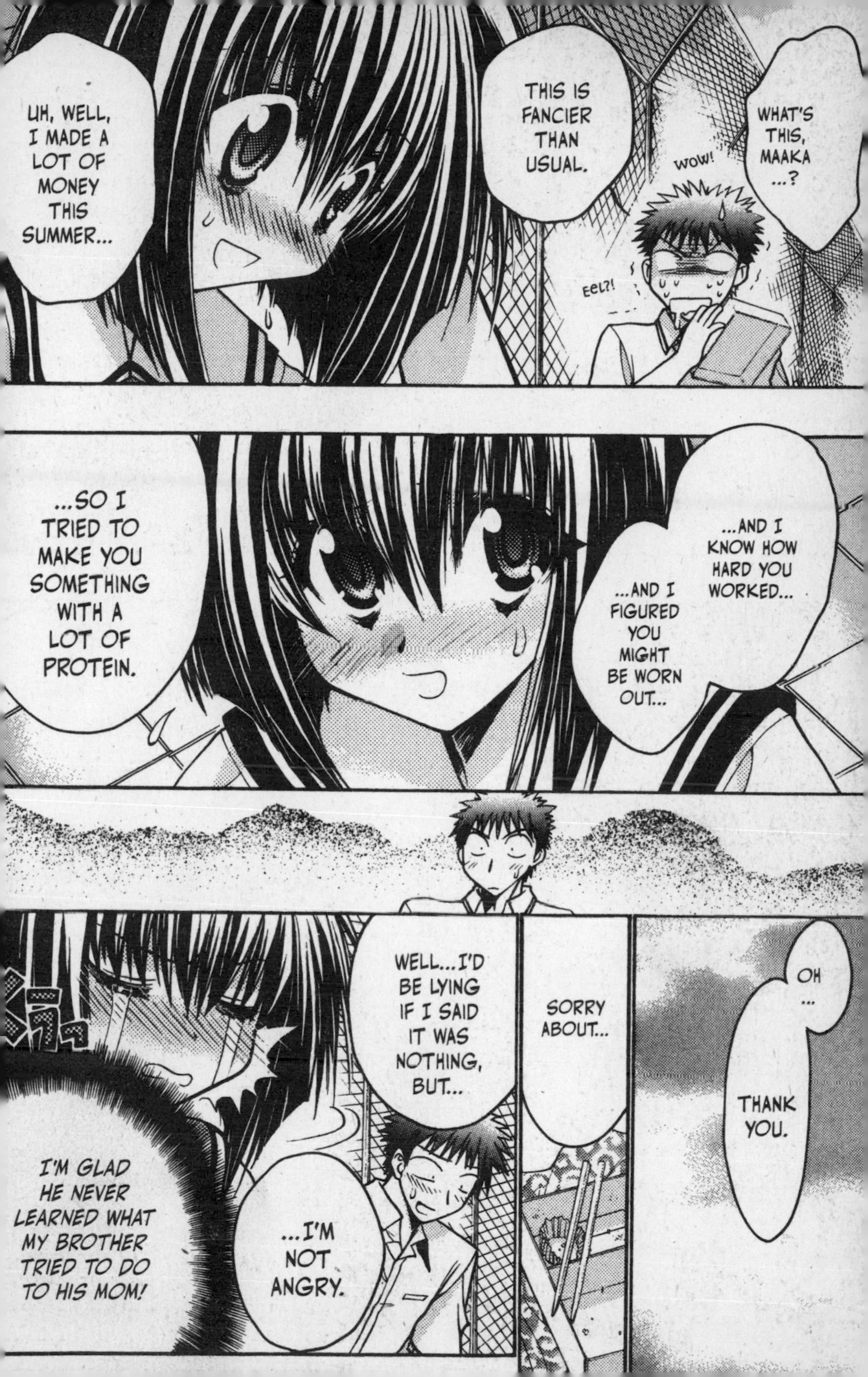
WHAT'S THIS, MAAKA ...?
WOW!
EEL?!
THIS IS FANCIER THAN USUAL.
UH, WELL, I MADE A LOT OF MONEY THIS SUMMER...
...AND I KNOW HOW HARD YOU WORKED...
...AND I FIGURED YOU MIGHT BE WORN OUT...
...SO I TRIED TO MAKE YOU SOMETHING WITH A LOT OF PROTEIN.
OH ...
THANK YOU.
SORRY ABOUT...
WELL...I'D BE LYING IF I SAID IT WAS NOTHING, BUT...
...I'M NOT ANGRY.
I'M GLAD HE NEVER LEARNED WHAT MY BROTHER TRIED TO DO TO HIS MOM!

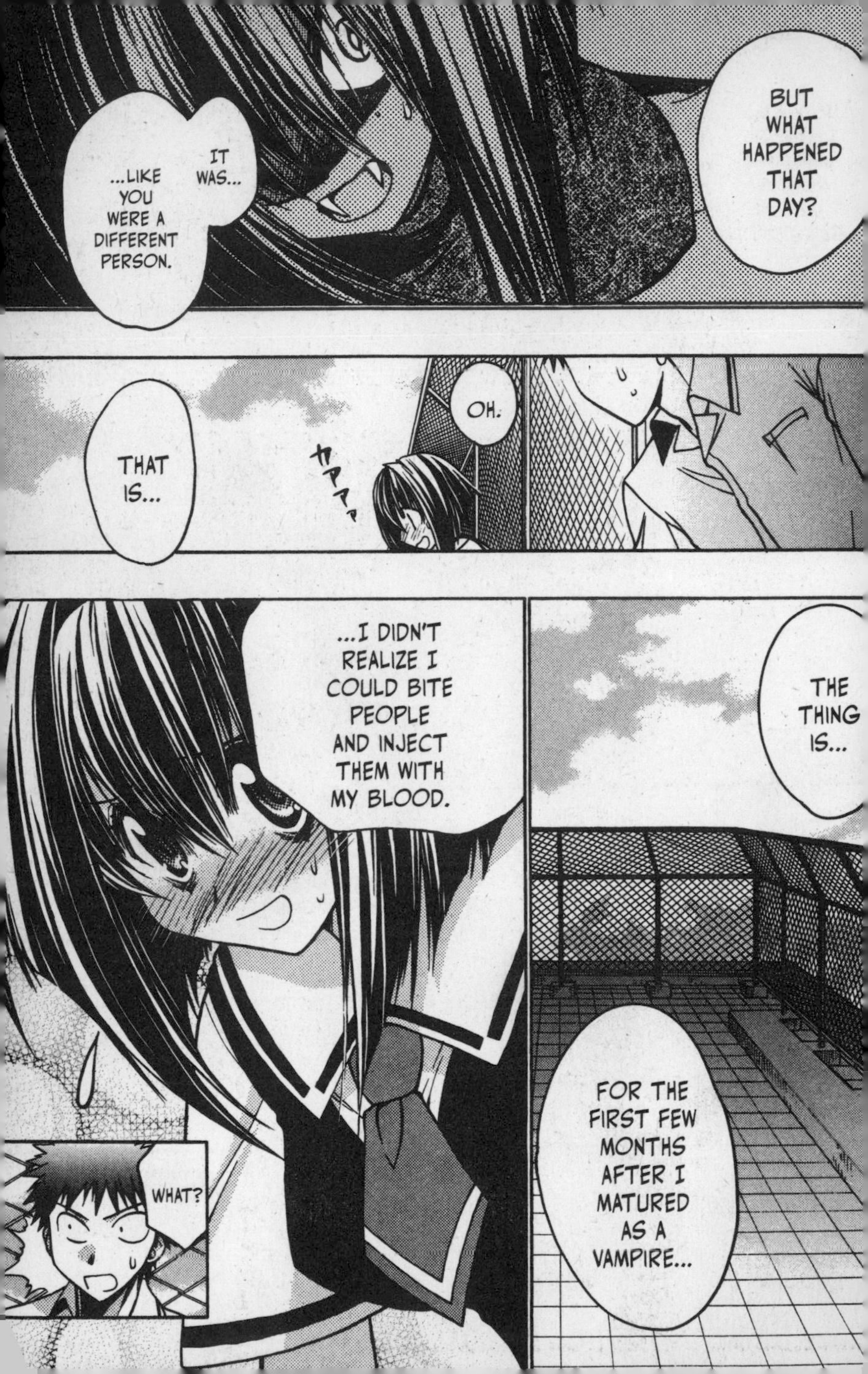
BUT WHAT HAPPENED THAT DAY?
IT WAS...
...LIKE YOU WERE A DIFFERENT PERSON.
OH.
カァァァ
THAT IS...
THE THING IS...
FOR THE FIRST FEW MONTHS AFTER I MATURED AS A VAMPIRE...
...I DIDN'T REALIZE I COULD BITE PEOPLE AND INJECT THEM WITH MY BLOOD.
WHAT?

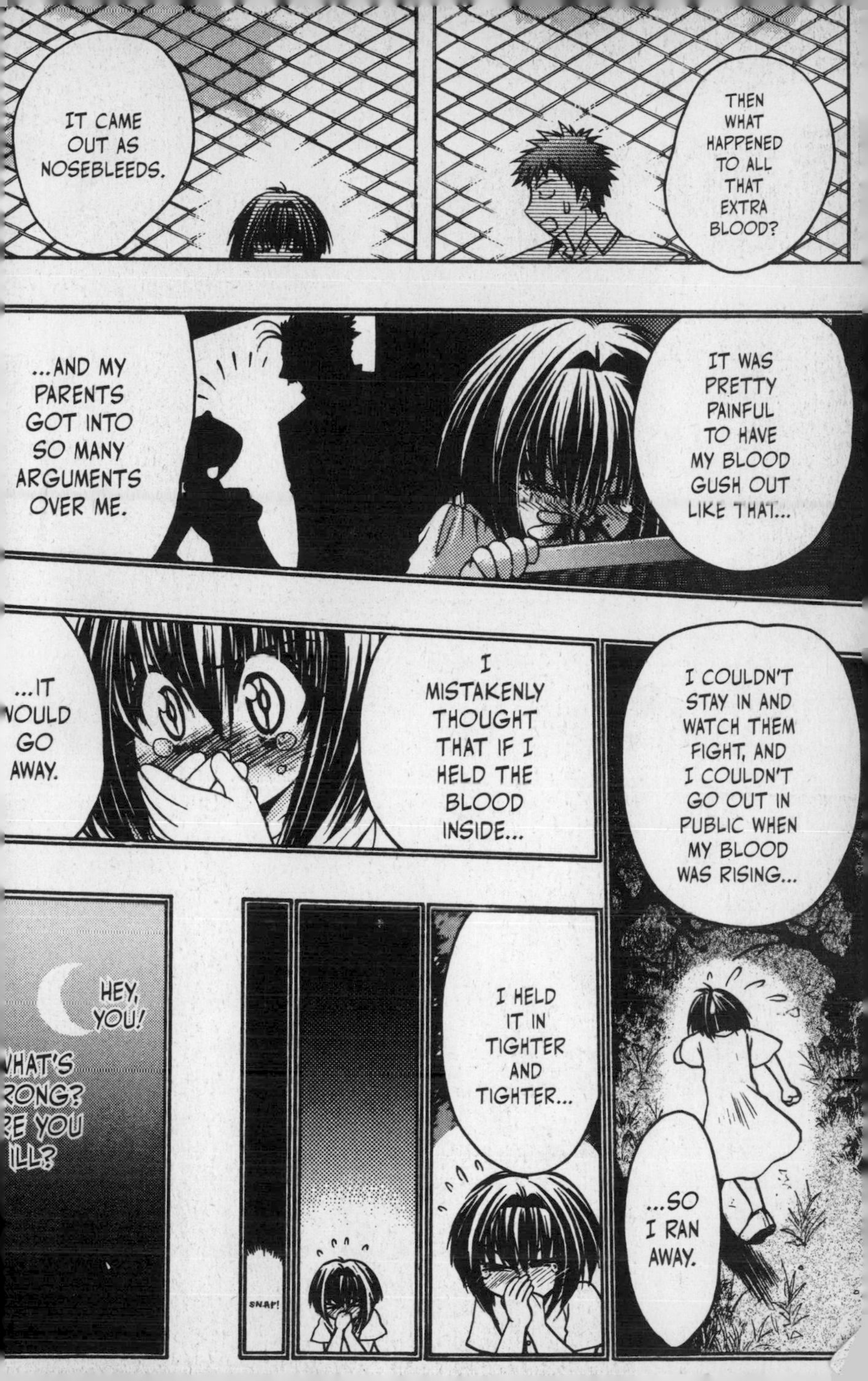
THEN WHAT HAPPENED TO ALL THAT EXTRA BLOOD?
IT CAME OUT AS NOSEBLEEDS.
IT WAS PRETTY PAINFUL TO HAVE MY BLOOD GUSH OUT LIKE THAT...
...AND MY PARENTS GOT INTO SO MANY ARGUMENTS OVER ME.
I COULDN'T STAY IN AND WATCH THEM FIGHT, AND I COULDN'T GO OUT IN PUBLIC WHEN MY BLOOD WAS RISING...
...SO I RAN AWAY.
I MISTAKENLY THOUGHT THAT IF I HELD THE BLOOD INSIDE...
...IT WOULD GO AWAY.
I HELD IT IN TIGHTER AND TIGHTER...
SNAP!
HEY, YOU!

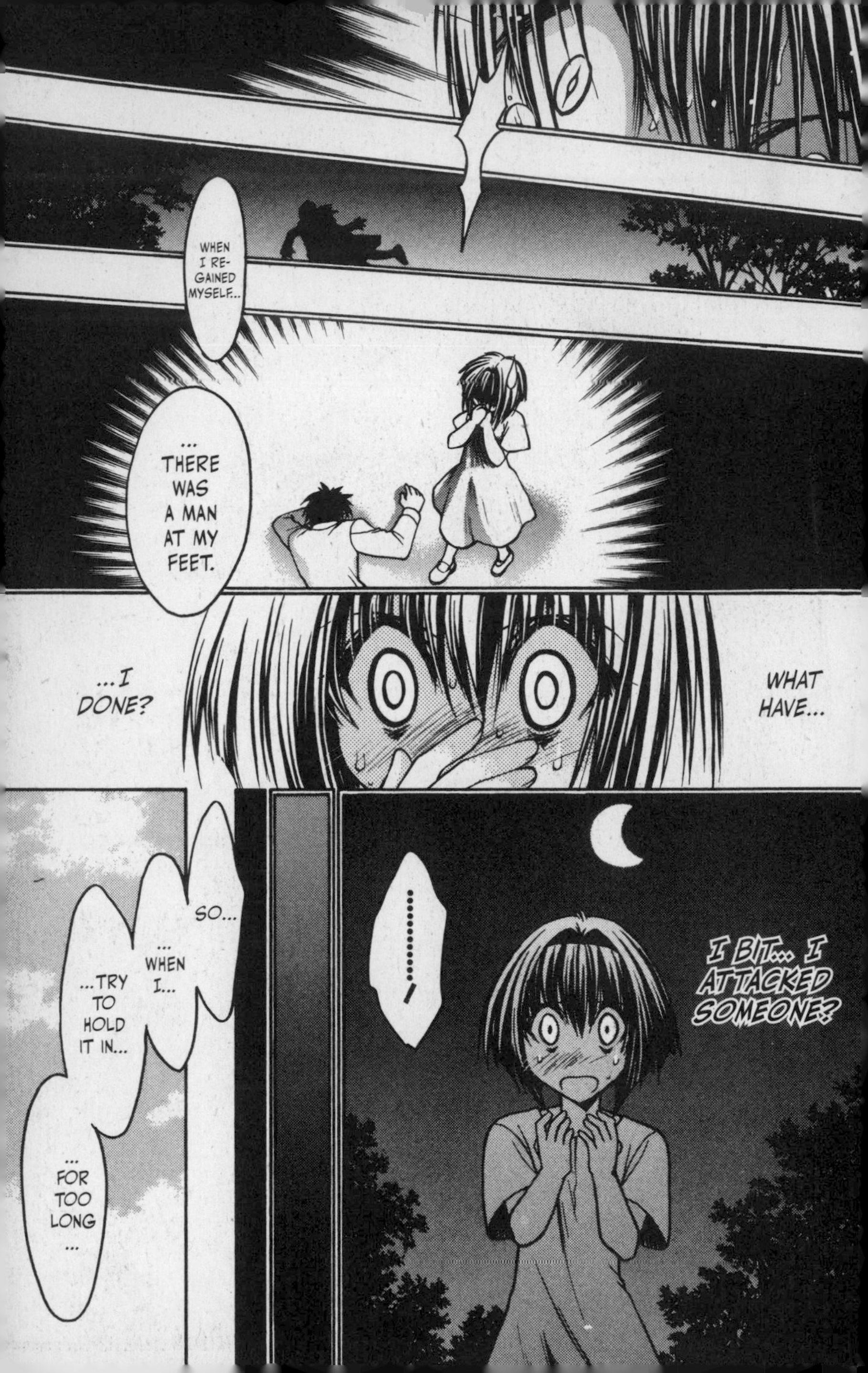
WHEN I RE-GAINED MYSELF...
...THERE WAS A MAN AT MY FEET.
WHAT HAVE...
...I DONE?
......!
I BIT... I ATTACKED SOMEONE?
SO...
...WHEN I...
...TRY TO HOLD IT IN...
...FOR TOO LONG...

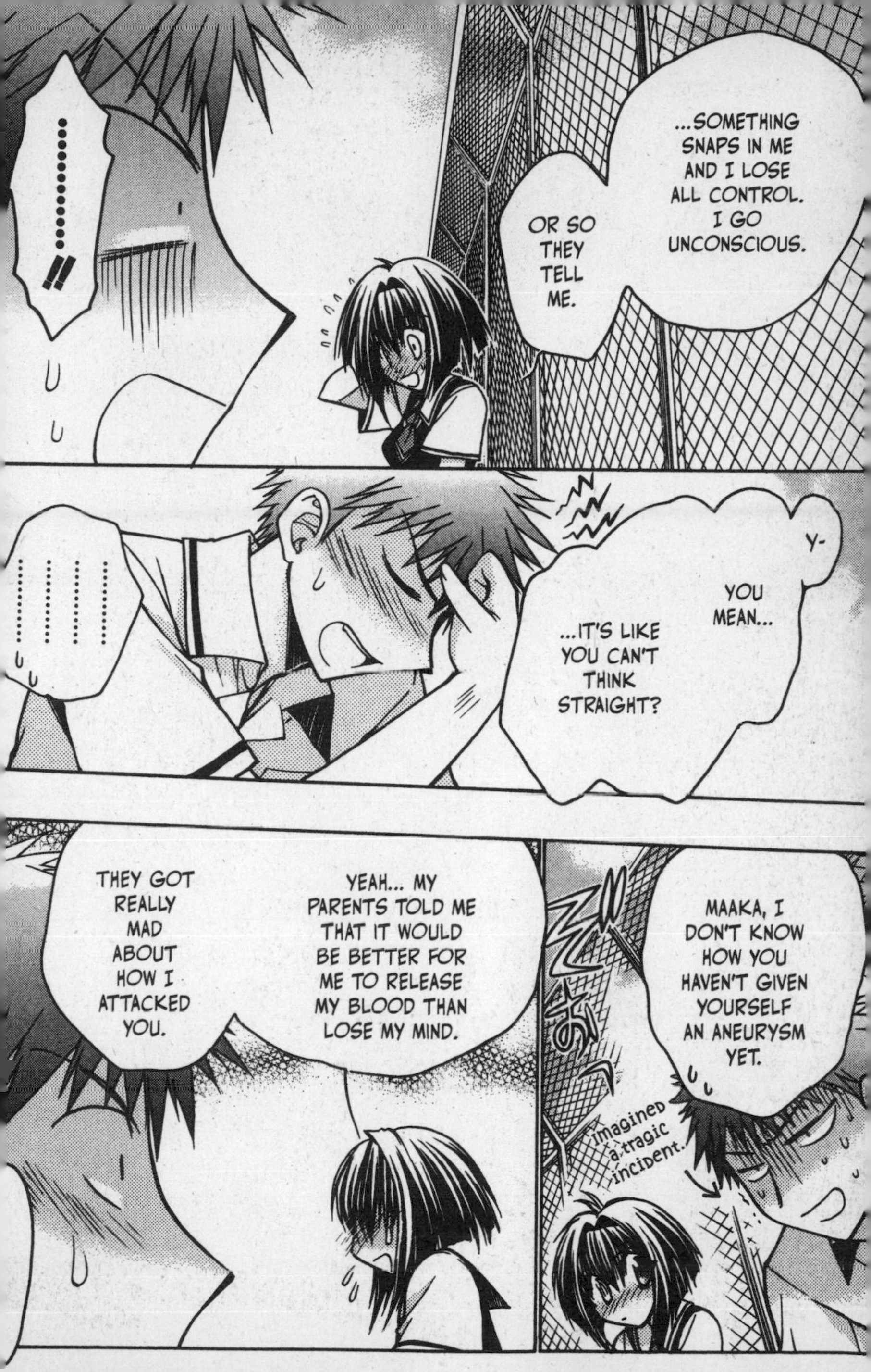
...SOMETHING SNAPS IN ME AND I LOSE ALL CONTROL. I GO UNCONSCIOUS.
OR SO THEY TELL ME.
......!!
Y-
YOU MEAN...
...IT'S LIKE YOU CAN'T THINK STRAIGHT?
......
MAAKA, I DON'T KNOW HOW YOU HAVEN'T GIVEN YOURSELF AN ANEURYSM YET.
imagined a tragic incident.
YEAH... MY PARENTS TOLD ME THAT IT WOULD BE BETTER FOR ME TO RELEASE MY BLOOD THAN LOSE MY MIND.
THEY GOT REALLY MAD ABOUT HOW I ATTACKED YOU.

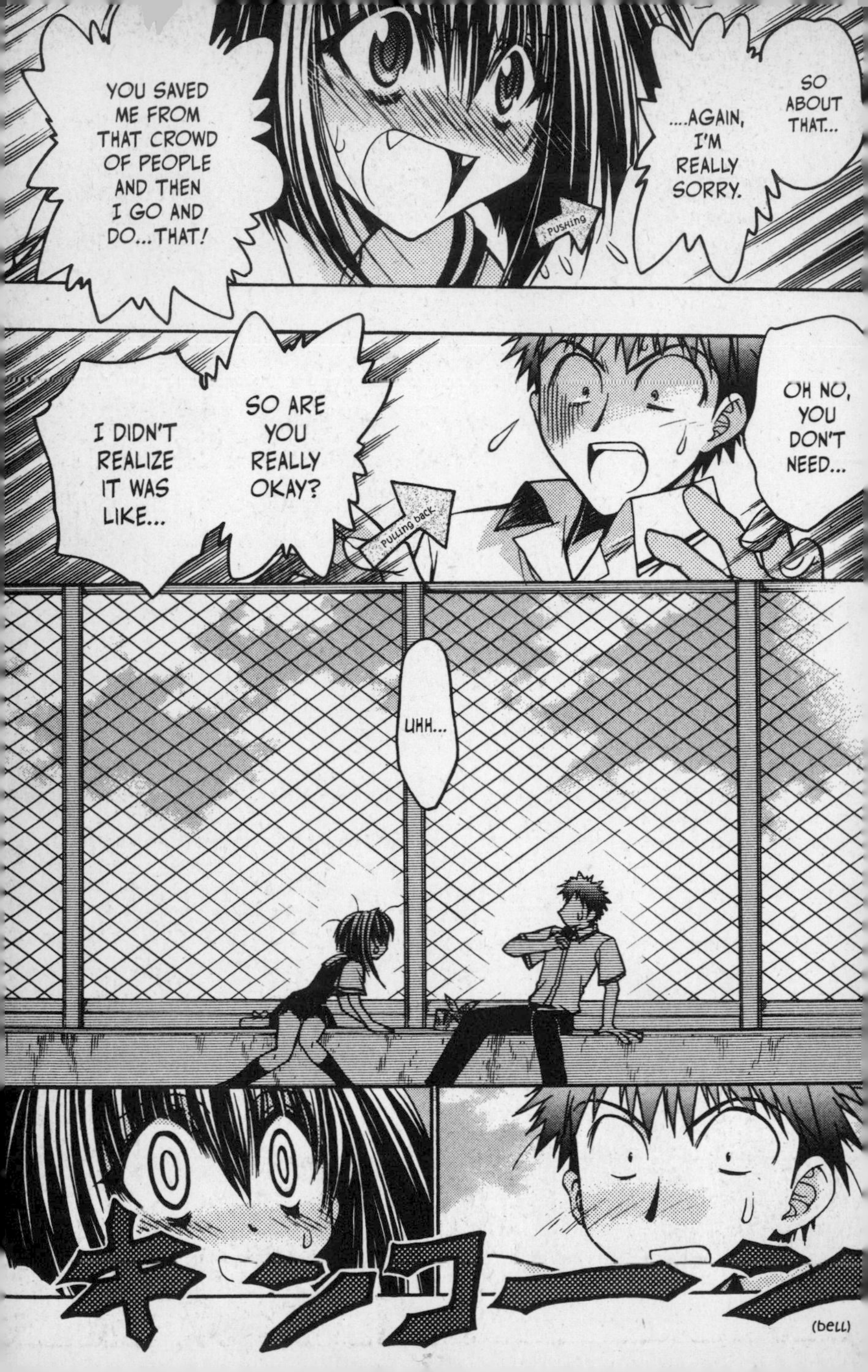
SO ABOUT THAT...
....AGAIN, I'M REALLY SORRY.
Pushing
YOU SAVED ME FROM THAT CROWD OF PEOPLE AND THEN I GO AND DO...THAT!
OH NO, YOU DON'T NEED...
Pulling back
SO ARE YOU REALLY OKAY?
I DIDN'T REALIZE IT WAS LIKE...
UHH...
(bell)

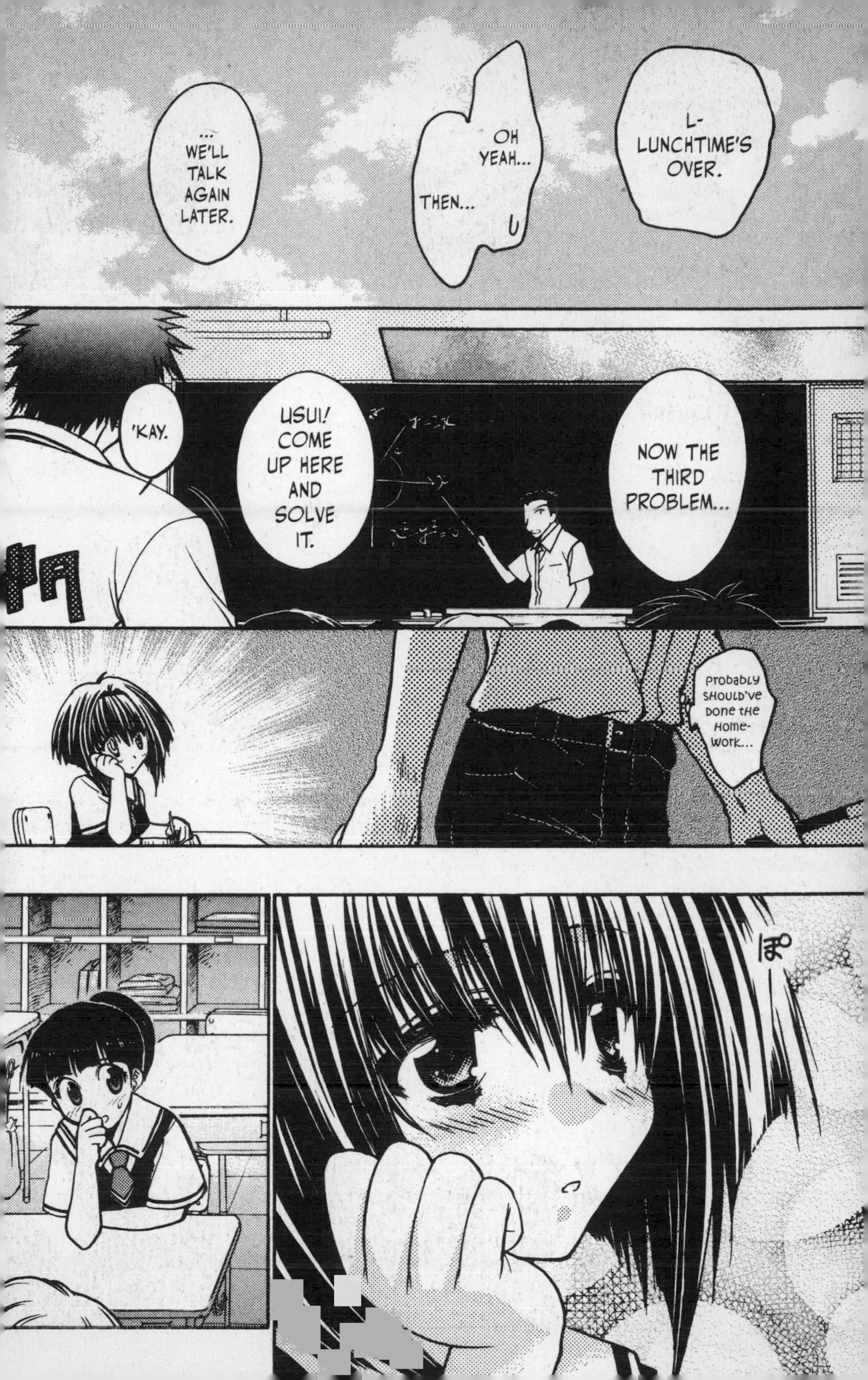
L-LUNCHTIME'S OVER.
OH YEAH... THEN...
... WE'LL TALK AGAIN LATER.
NOW THE THIRD PROBLEM...
USUI! COME UP HERE AND SOLVE IT.
'KAY.
Probably SHOULD've Done the Home-work...
ぽ

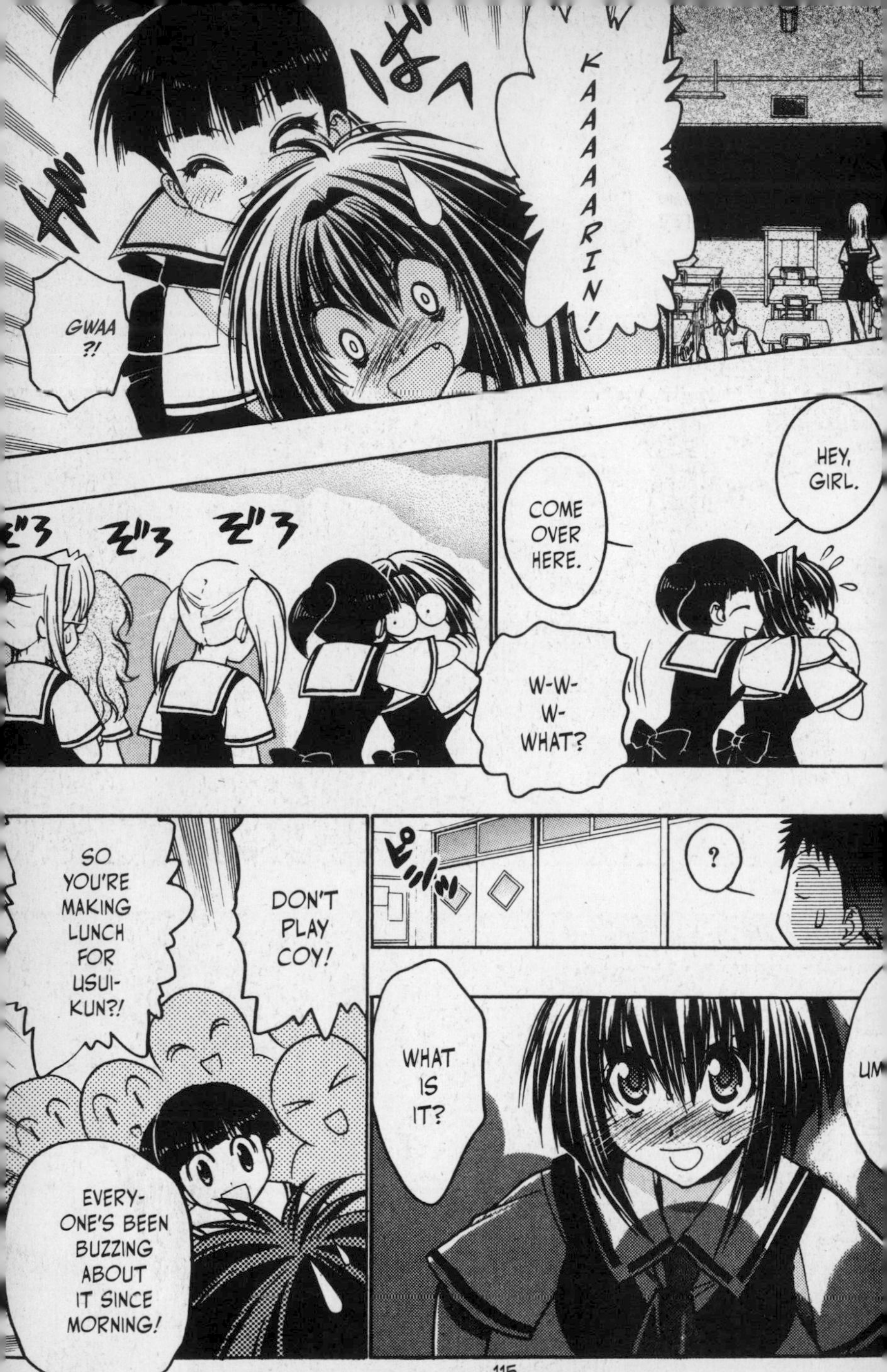
KAAAAARIN!
GWAA ?!
HEY, GIRL.
COME OVER HERE.
W-W-W-WHAT?
ぞろ ぞろ ぞろ
?
UM
WHAT IS IT?
DON'T PLAY COY!
SO YOU'RE MAKING LUNCH FOR USUI-KUN?!
EVERY-ONE'S BEEN BUZZING ABOUT IT SINCE MORNING!

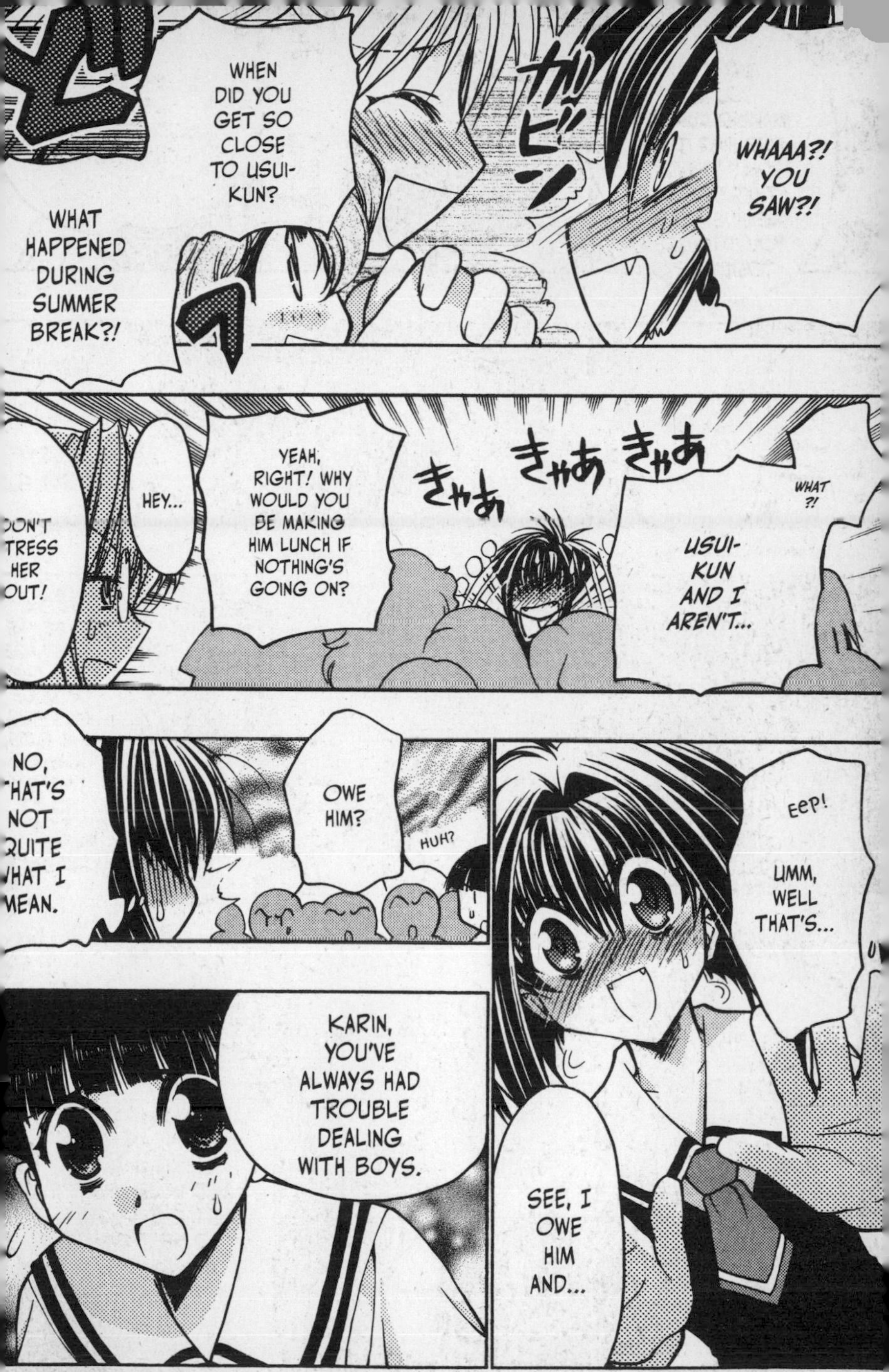
WHAAA?! YOU SAW?!
WHEN DID YOU GET SO CLOSE TO USUI-KUN?
WHAT HAPPENED DURING SUMMER BREAK?!
WHAT ?!
USUI-KUN AND I AREN'T...
きゃあ きゃあ きゃあ
YEAH, RIGHT! WHY WOULD YOU BE MAKING HIM LUNCH IF NOTHING'S GOING ON?
HEY...
ON'T TRESS HER OUT!
EEP!
UMM, WELL THAT'S...
SEE, I OWE HIM AND...
OWE HIM?
HUH?
NO, HAT'S NOT UITE HAT I MEAN.
KARIN, YOU'VE ALWAYS HAD TROUBLE DEALING WITH BOYS.

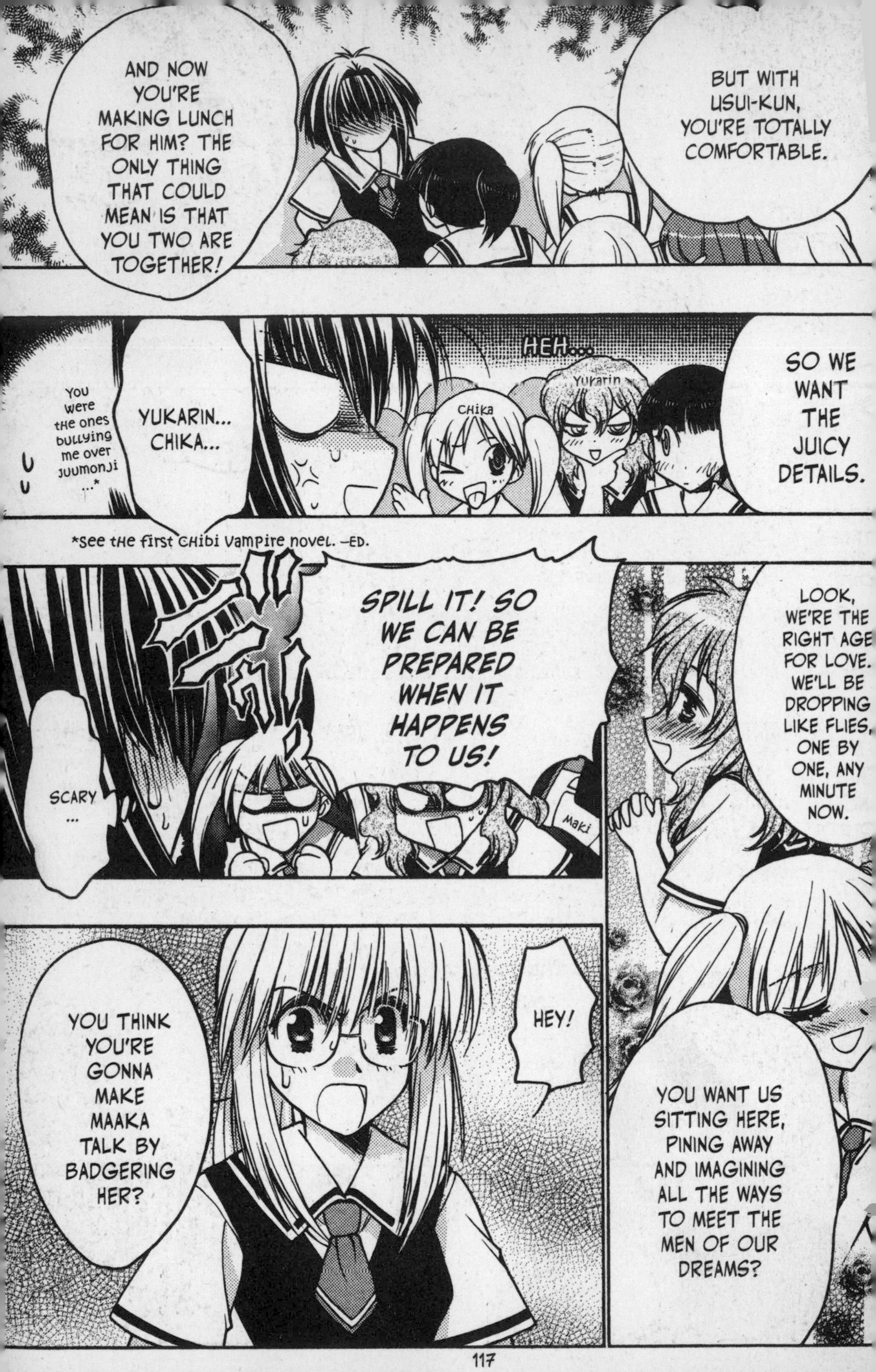
BUT WITH USUI-KUN, YOU'RE TOTALLY COMFORTABLE.
AND NOW YOU'RE MAKING LUNCH FOR HIM? THE ONLY THING THAT COULD MEAN IS THAT YOU TWO ARE TOGETHER!
SO WE WANT THE JUICY DETAILS.
HEH...
Yukarin
Chika
YUKARIN... CHIKA...
You were the ones bullying me over Juumonji ...*
*See the first Chibi Vampire novel. –ED.
LOOK, WE'RE THE RIGHT AGE FOR LOVE. WE'LL BE DROPPING LIKE FLIES, ONE BY ONE, ANY MINUTE NOW.
YOU WANT US SITTING HERE, PINING AWAY AND IMAGINING ALL THE WAYS TO MEET THE MEN OF OUR DREAMS?
SPILL IT! SO WE CAN BE PREPARED WHEN IT HAPPENS TO US!
Maki
SCARY ...
HEY!
YOU THINK YOU'RE GONNA MAKE MAAKA TALK BY BADGERING HER?

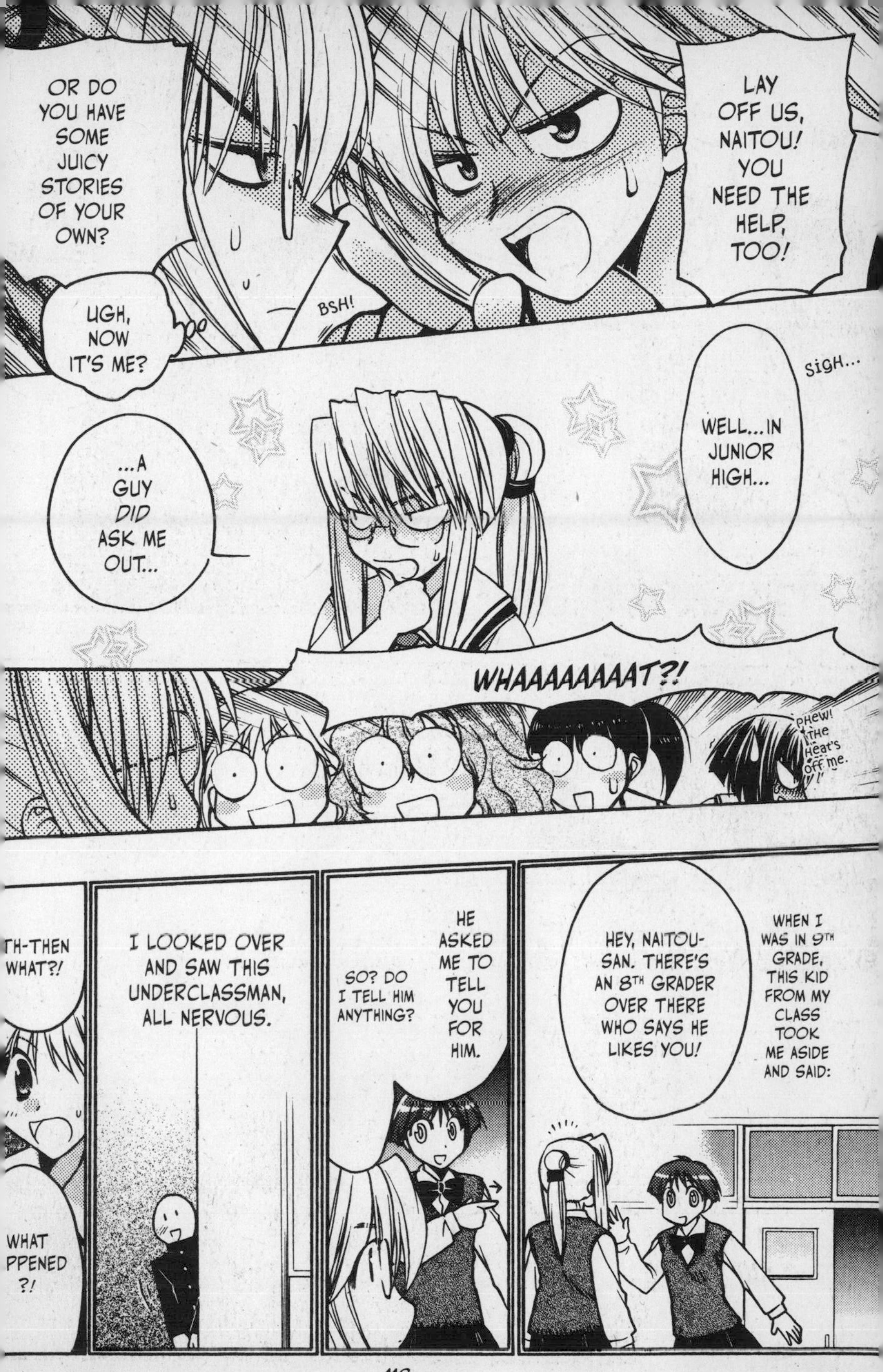

LAY OFF US, NAITOU! YOU NEED THE HELP, TOO!
OR DO YOU HAVE SOME JUICY STORIES OF YOUR OWN?
BSH!
UGH, NOW IT'S ME?
SIGH...
WELL...IN JUNIOR HIGH...
...A GUY *DID* ASK ME OUT...
WHAAAAAAAAT?!
PHEW! THE HEAT'S OFF ME.
WHEN I WAS IN 9TH GRADE, THIS KID FROM MY CLASS TOOK ME ASIDE AND SAID:
HEY, NAITOU-SAN. THERE'S AN 8TH GRADER OVER THERE WHO SAYS HE LIKES YOU!
HE ASKED ME TO TELL YOU FOR HIM.
SO? DO I TELL HIM ANYTHING?
I LOOKED OVER AND SAW THIS UNDERCLASSMAN, ALL NERVOUS.
TH-THEN WHAT?!
WHAT PPENED ?!

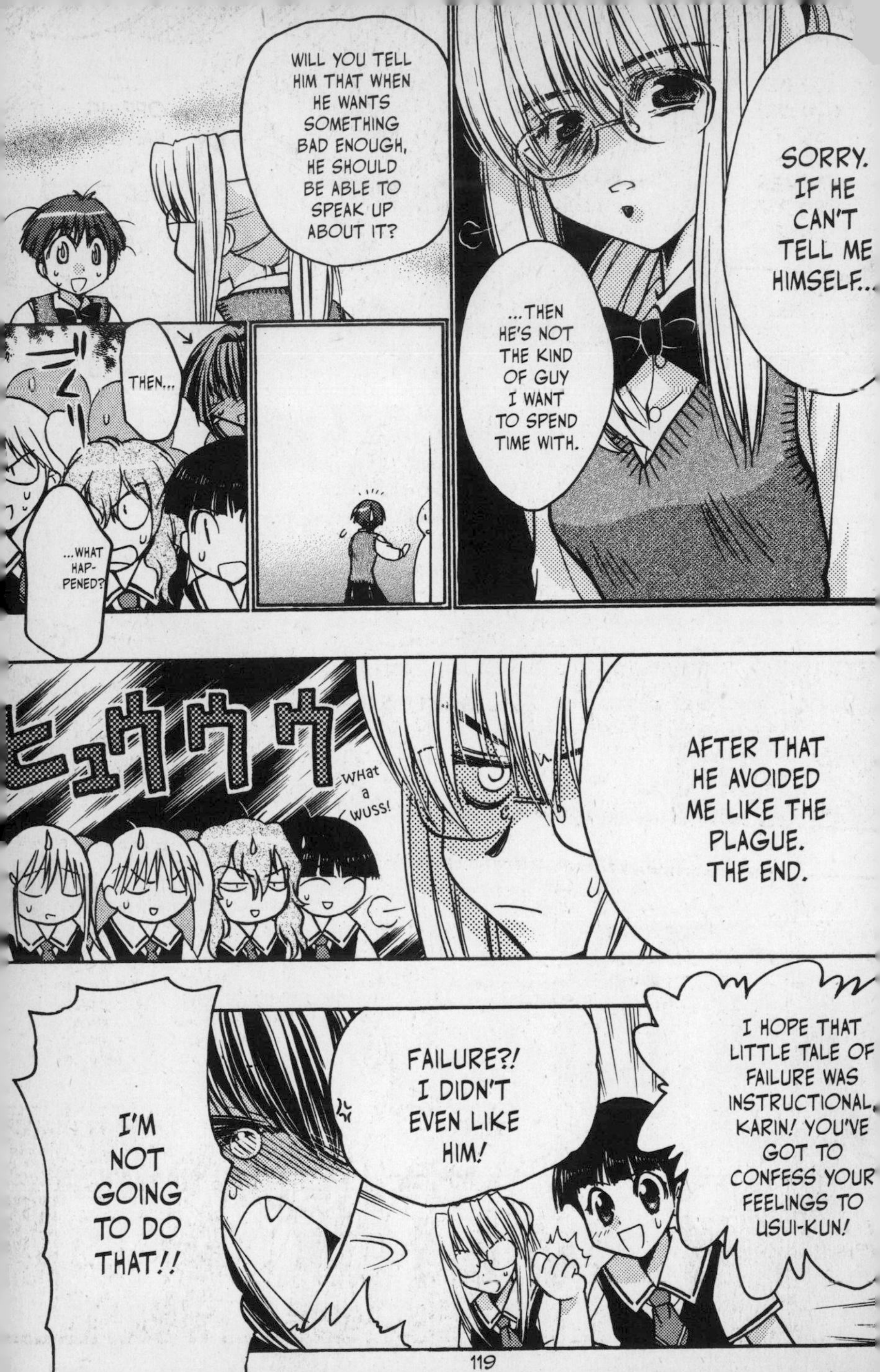

SORRY. IF HE CAN'T TELL ME HIMSELF...
...THEN HE'S NOT THE KIND OF GUY I WANT TO SPEND TIME WITH.
WILL YOU TELL HIM THAT WHEN HE WANTS SOMETHING BAD ENOUGH, HE SHOULD BE ABLE TO SPEAK UP ABOUT IT?
THEN...
...WHAT HAP-PENED?
AFTER THAT HE AVOIDED ME LIKE THE PLAGUE. THE END.
ヒュウウウ
WHAt a WUSS!
I HOPE THAT LITTLE TALE OF FAILURE WAS INSTRUCTIONAL, KARIN! YOU'VE GOT TO CONFESS YOUR FEELINGS TO USUI-KUN!
FAILURE?! I DIDN'T EVEN LIKE HIM!
I'M NOT GOING TO DO THAT!!

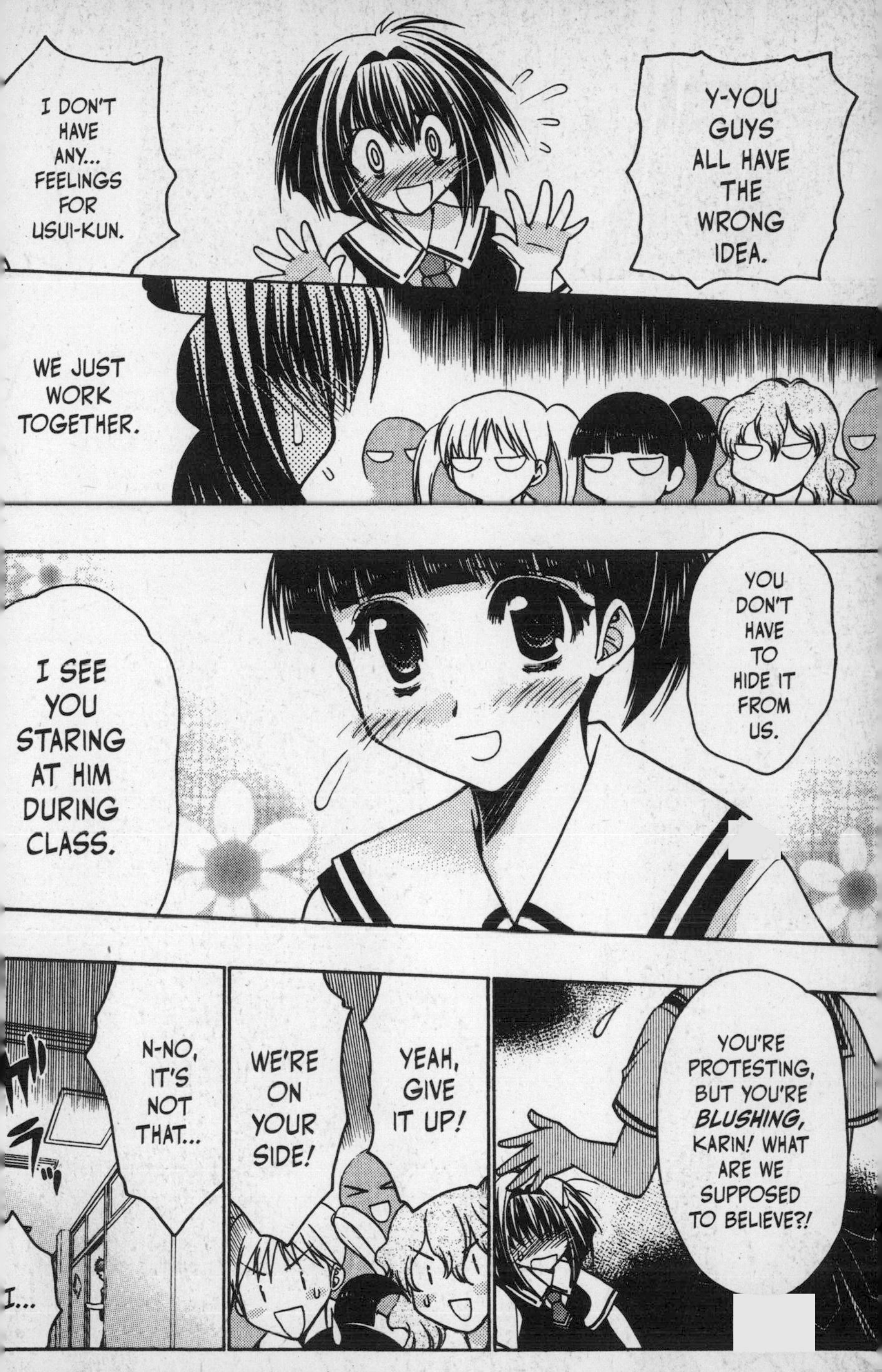
Y-YOU GUYS ALL HAVE THE WRONG IDEA.
I DON'T HAVE ANY... FEELINGS FOR USUI-KUN.
WE JUST WORK TOGETHER.
YOU DON'T HAVE TO HIDE IT FROM US.
I SEE YOU STARING AT HIM DURING CLASS.
YOU'RE PROTESTING, BUT YOU'RE *BLUSHING*, KARIN! WHAT ARE WE SUPPOSED TO BELIEVE?!
YEAH, GIVE IT UP!
WE'RE ON YOUR SIDE!
N-NO, IT'S NOT THAT...
I...

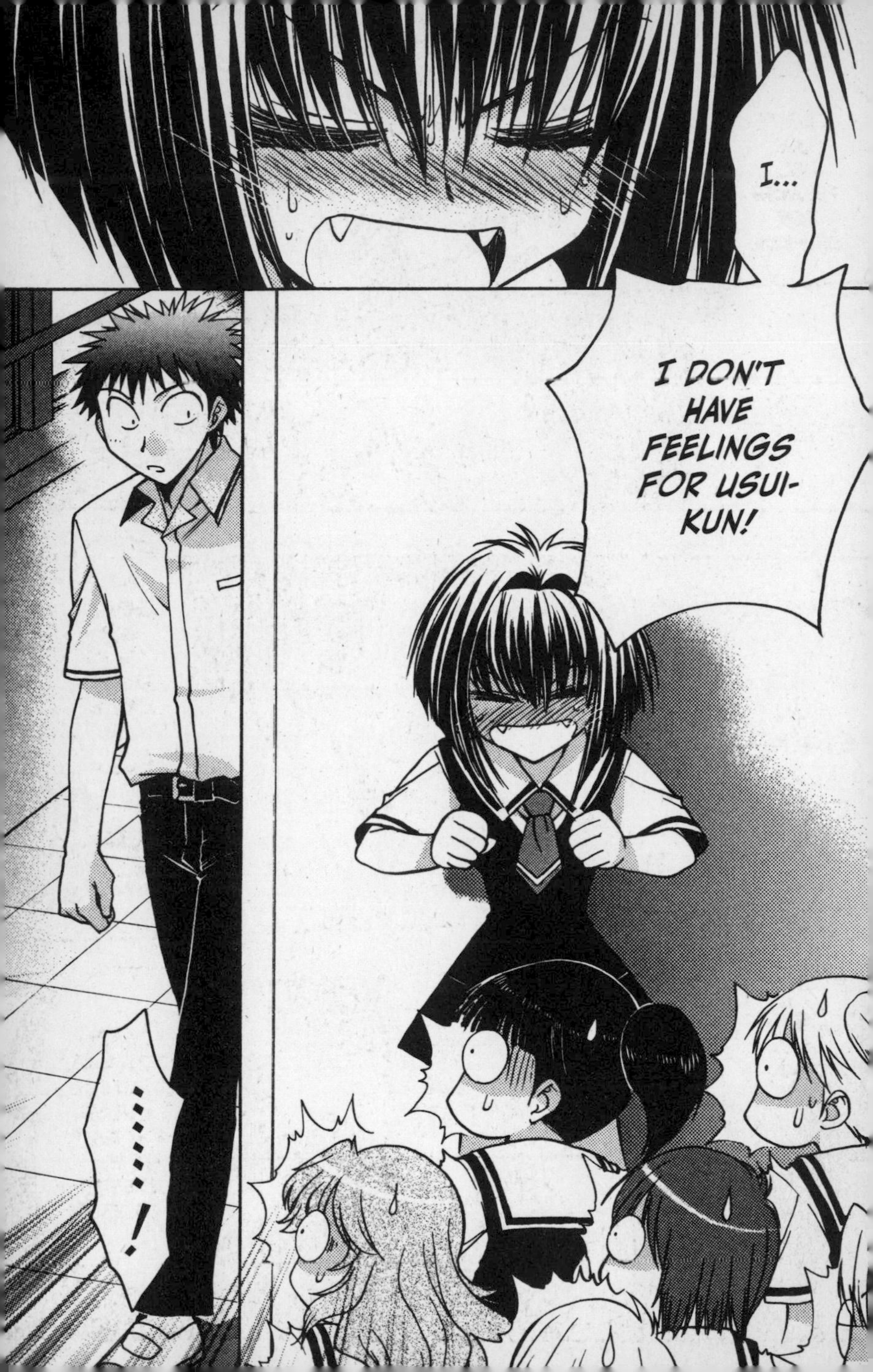
I...
I DON'T HAVE FEELINGS FOR USUI-KUN!
......!

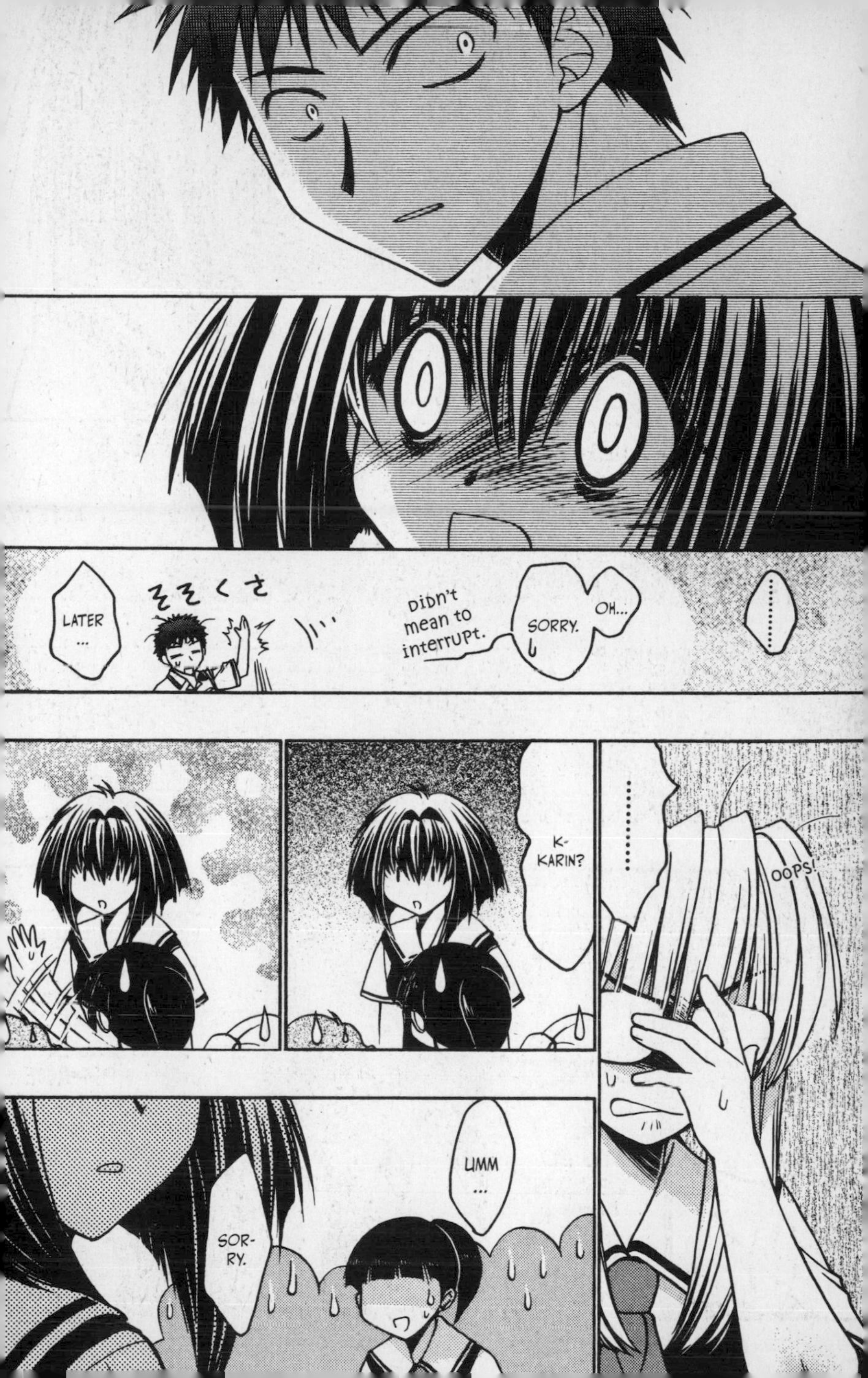
......
OH...
SORRY.
DIDN'T mean to interrupt.
そそくさ
LATER ...
OOPS!
......
K-KARIN?
UMM ...
SOR-RY.

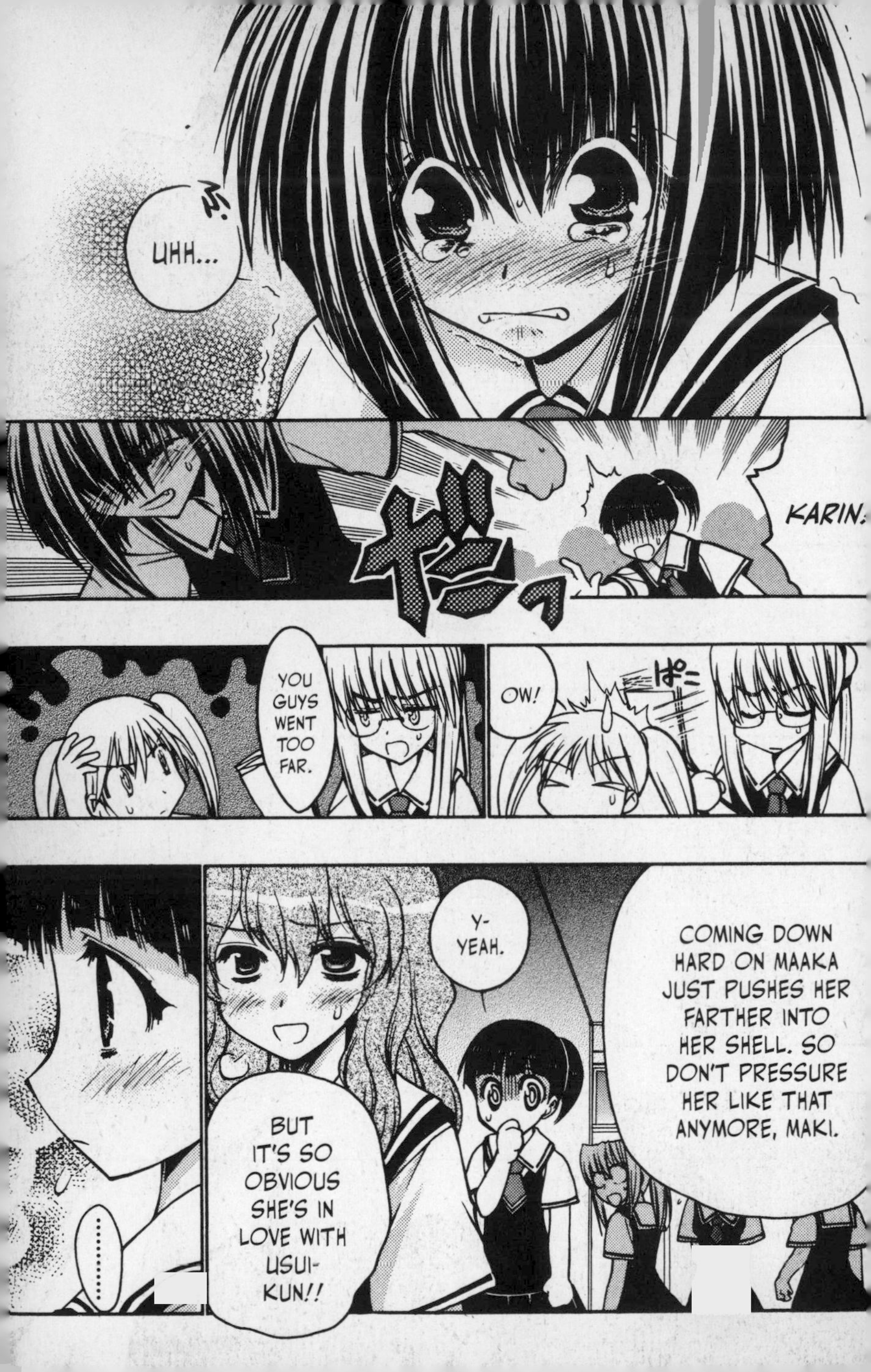
UHH...
KARIN!
OW!
YOU GUYS WENT TOO FAR.
COMING DOWN HARD ON MAAKA JUST PUSHES HER FARTHER INTO HER SHELL. SO DON'T PRESSURE HER LIKE THAT ANYMORE, MAKI.
Y-YEAH.
BUT IT'S SO OBVIOUS SHE'S IN LOVE WITH USUI-KUN!!
......

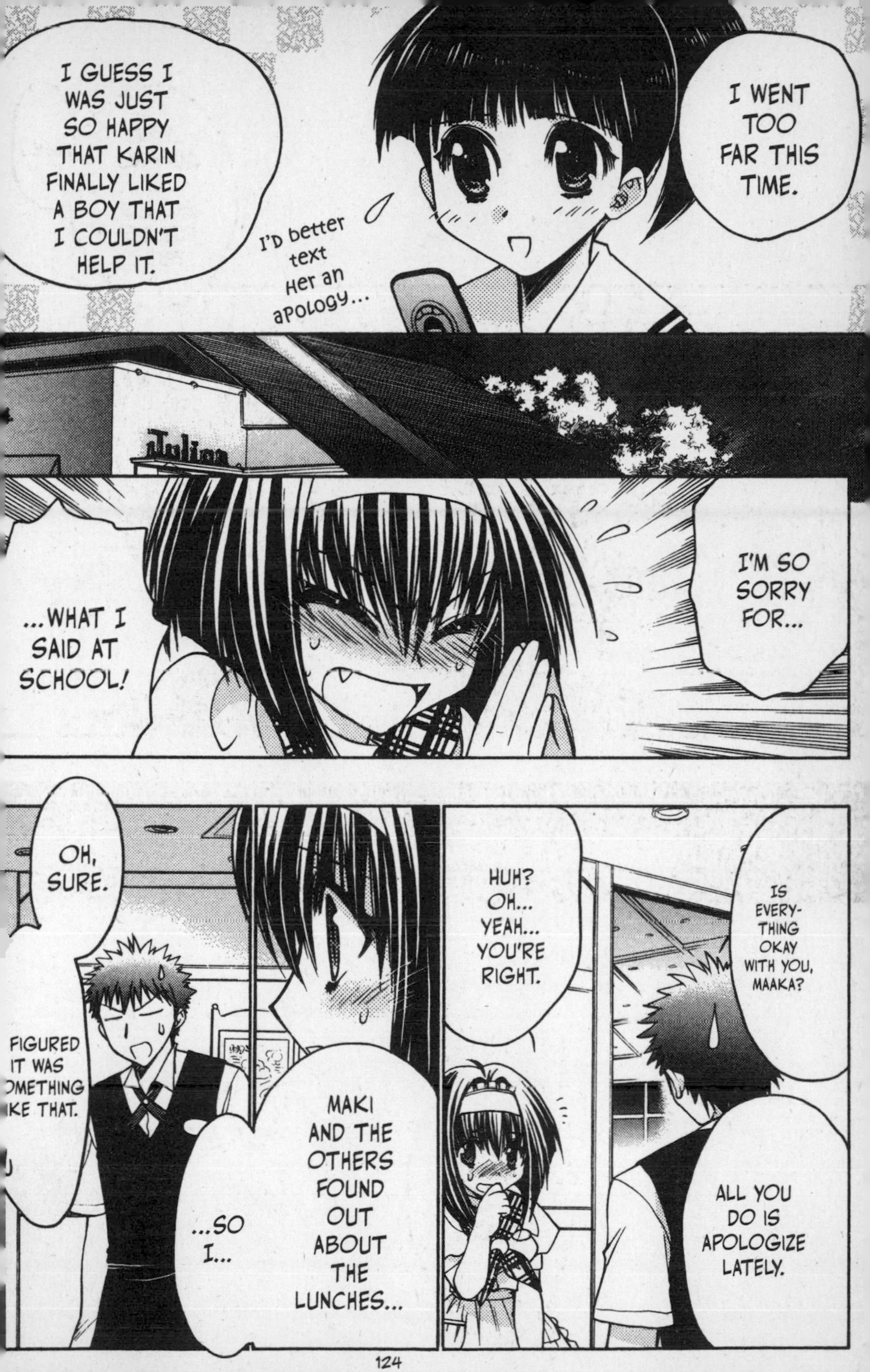
I WENT TOO FAR THIS TIME.
I GUESS I WAS JUST SO HAPPY THAT KARIN FINALLY LIKED A BOY THAT I COULDN'T HELP IT.
I'D better text Her an apology...
I'M SO SORRY FOR...
...WHAT I SAID AT SCHOOL!
IS EVERY-THING OKAY WITH YOU, MAAKA?
HUH? OH... YEAH... YOU'RE RIGHT.
ALL YOU DO IS APOLOGIZE LATELY.
MAKI AND THE OTHERS FOUND OUT ABOUT THE LUNCHES...
...SO I...
OH, SURE.
FIGURED IT WAS OMETHING KE THAT.

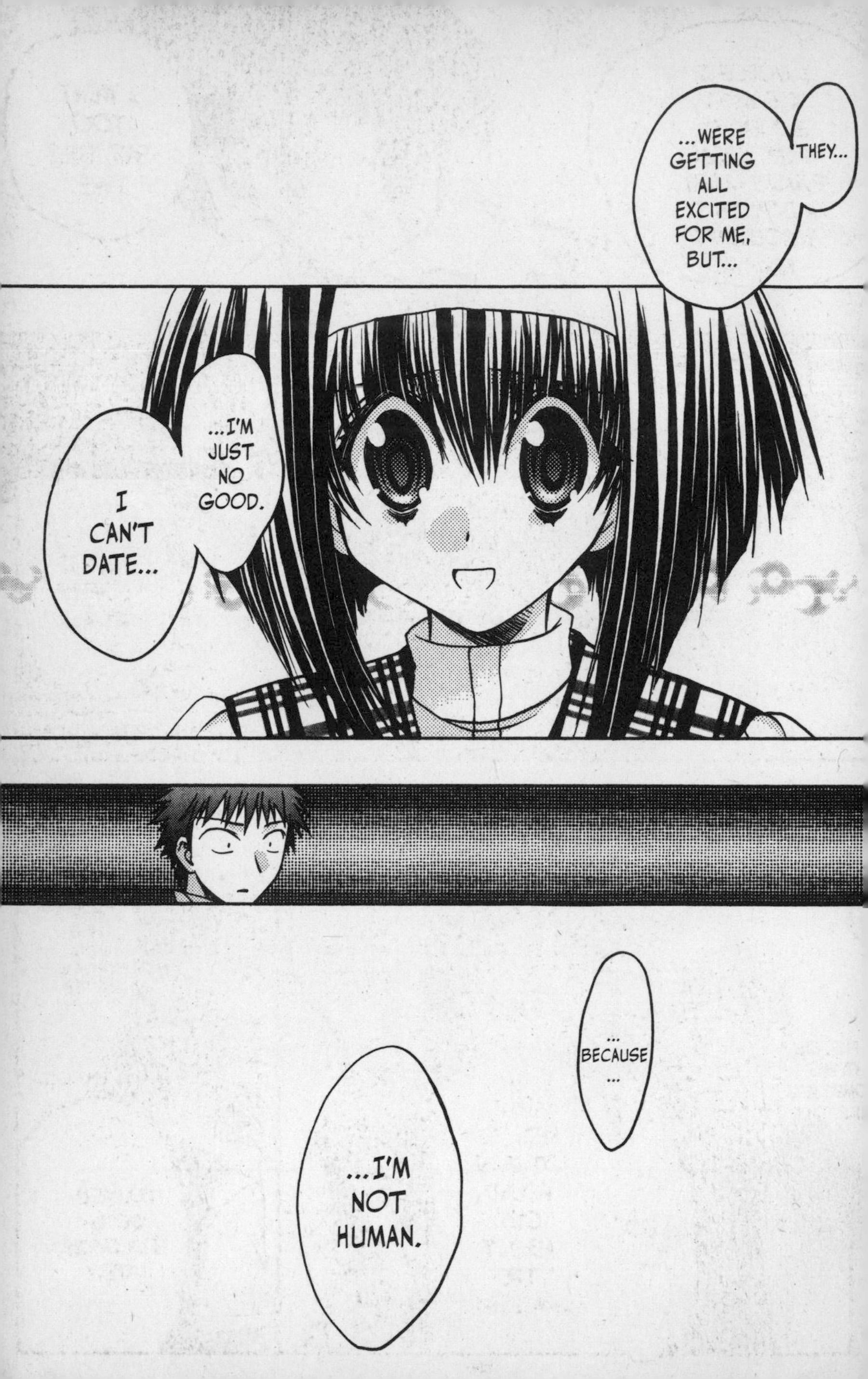
THEY...
...WERE GETTING ALL EXCITED FOR ME, BUT...
...I'M JUST NO GOOD.
I CAN'T DATE...
... BECAUSE ...
...I'M NOT HUMAN.

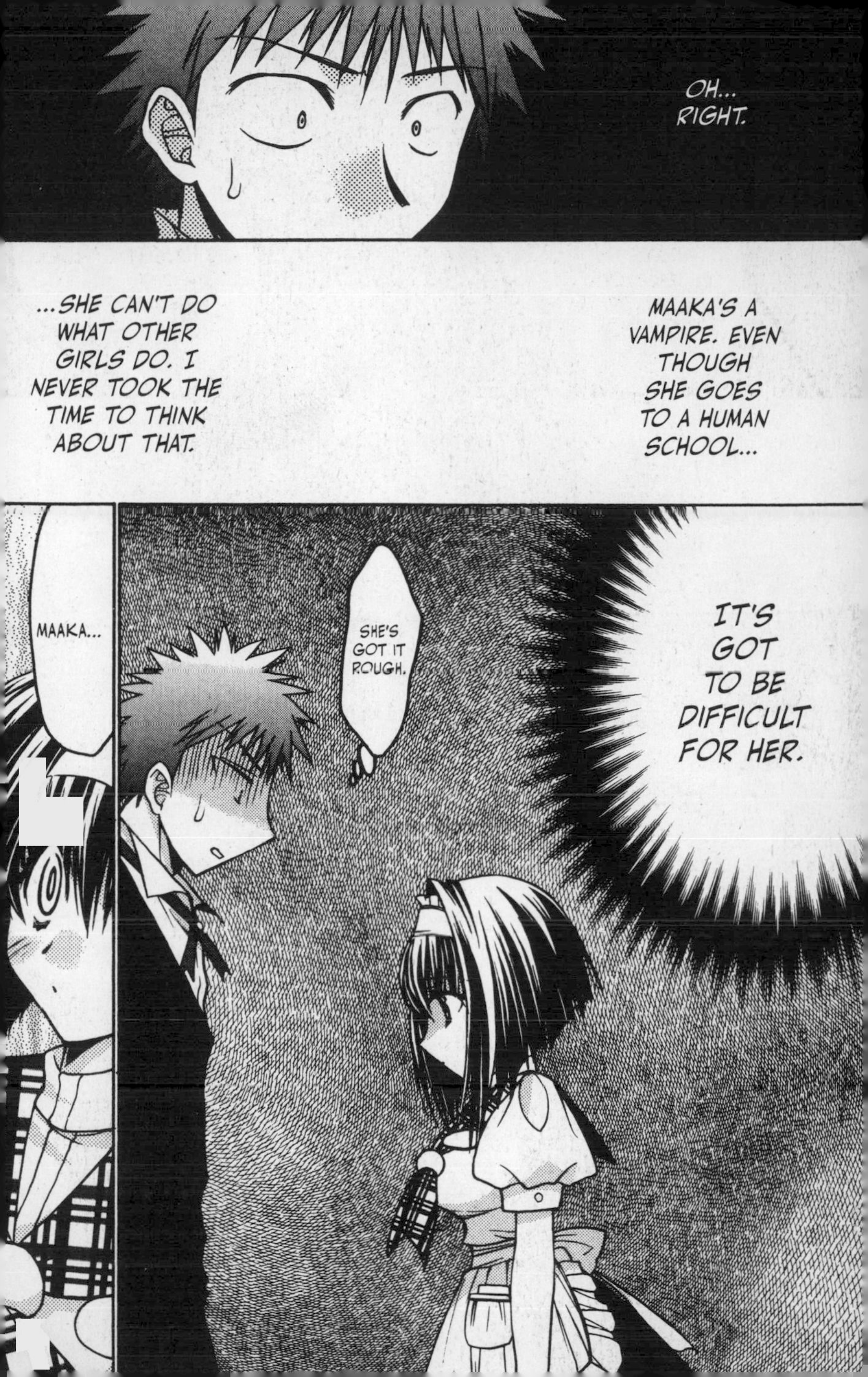
OH... RIGHT.
MAAKA'S A VAMPIRE. EVEN THOUGH SHE GOES TO A HUMAN SCHOOL...
...SHE CAN'T DO WHAT OTHER GIRLS DO. I NEVER TOOK THE TIME TO THINK ABOUT THAT.
IT'S GOT TO BE DIFFICULT FOR HER.
SHE'S GOT IT ROUGH.
MAAKA...

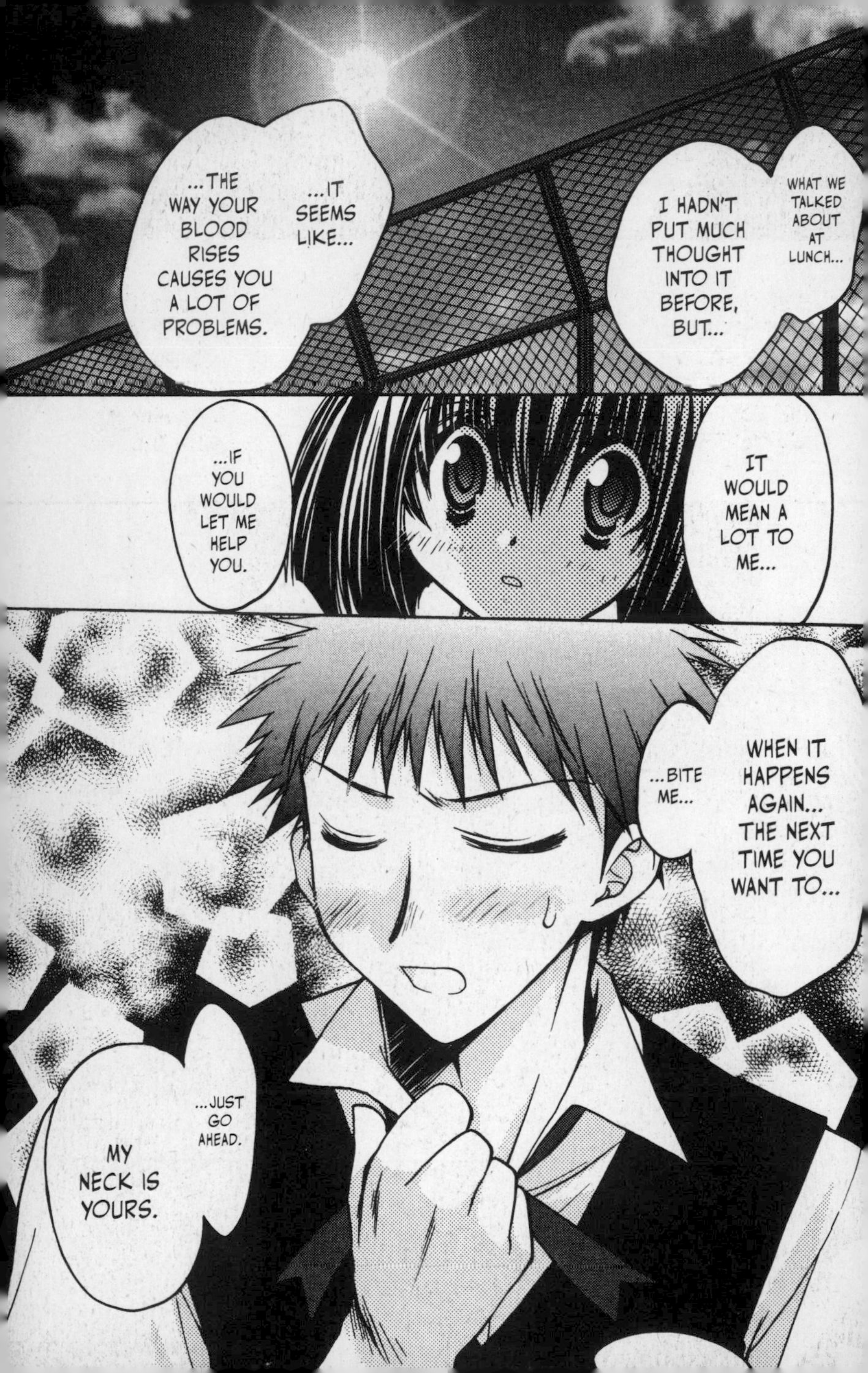
WHAT WE TALKED ABOUT AT LUNCH...
I HADN'T PUT MUCH THOUGHT INTO IT BEFORE, BUT...
...IT SEEMS LIKE...
...THE WAY YOUR BLOOD RISES CAUSES YOU A LOT OF PROBLEMS.
IT WOULD MEAN A LOT TO ME...
...IF YOU WOULD LET ME HELP YOU.
WHEN IT HAPPENS AGAIN... THE NEXT TIME YOU WANT TO...
...BITE ME...
...JUST GO AHEAD.
MY NECK IS YOURS.

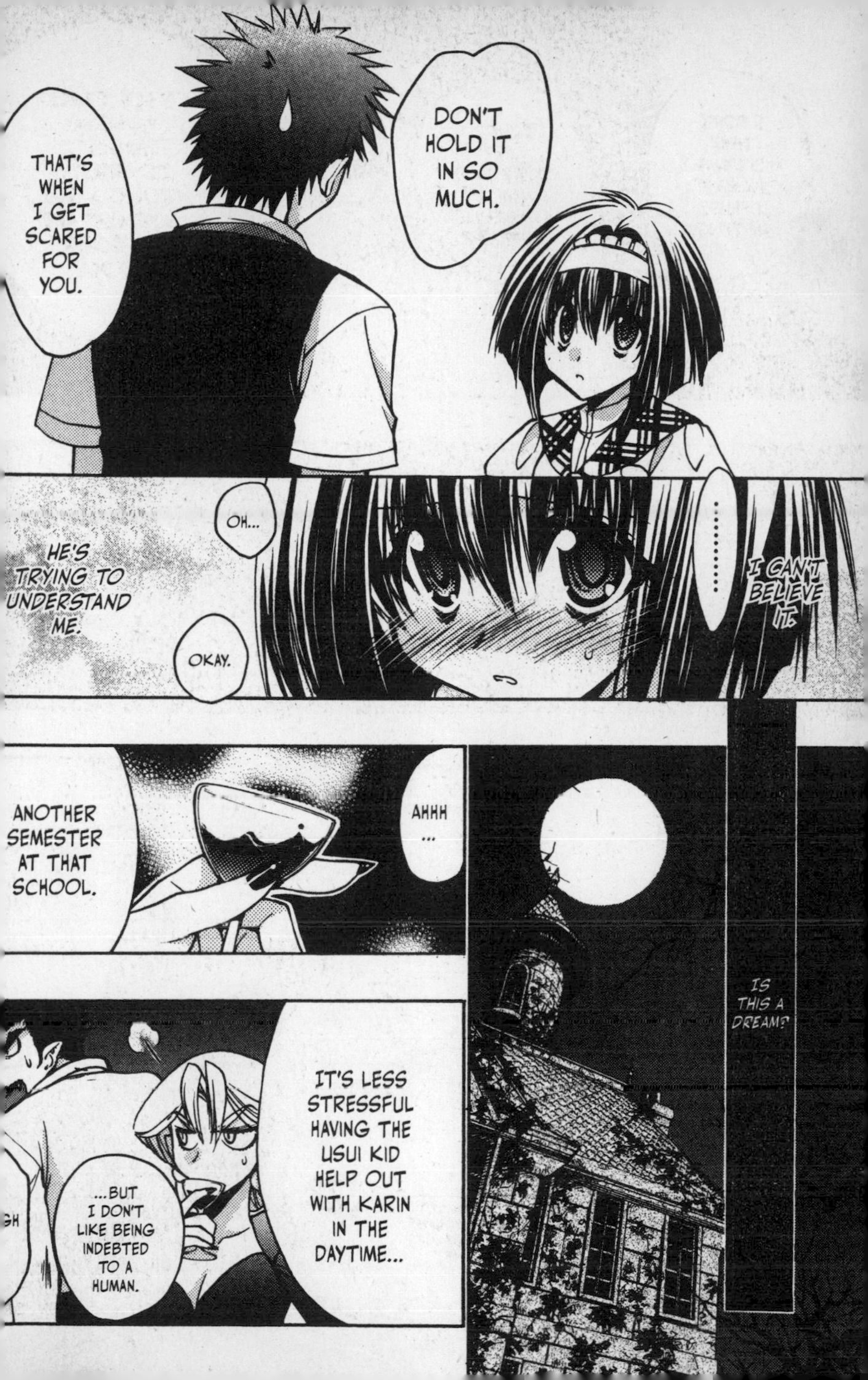
DON'T HOLD IT IN SO MUCH.
THAT'S WHEN I GET SCARED FOR YOU.
I CAN'T BELIEVE IT.
......
OH...
OKAY.
HE'S TRYING TO UNDERSTAND ME.
IS THIS A DREAM?
AHHH ...
ANOTHER SEMESTER AT THAT SCHOOL.
IT'S LESS STRESSFUL HAVING THE USUI KID HELP OUT WITH KARIN IN THE DAYTIME...
...BUT I DON'T LIKE BEING INDEBTED TO A HUMAN.

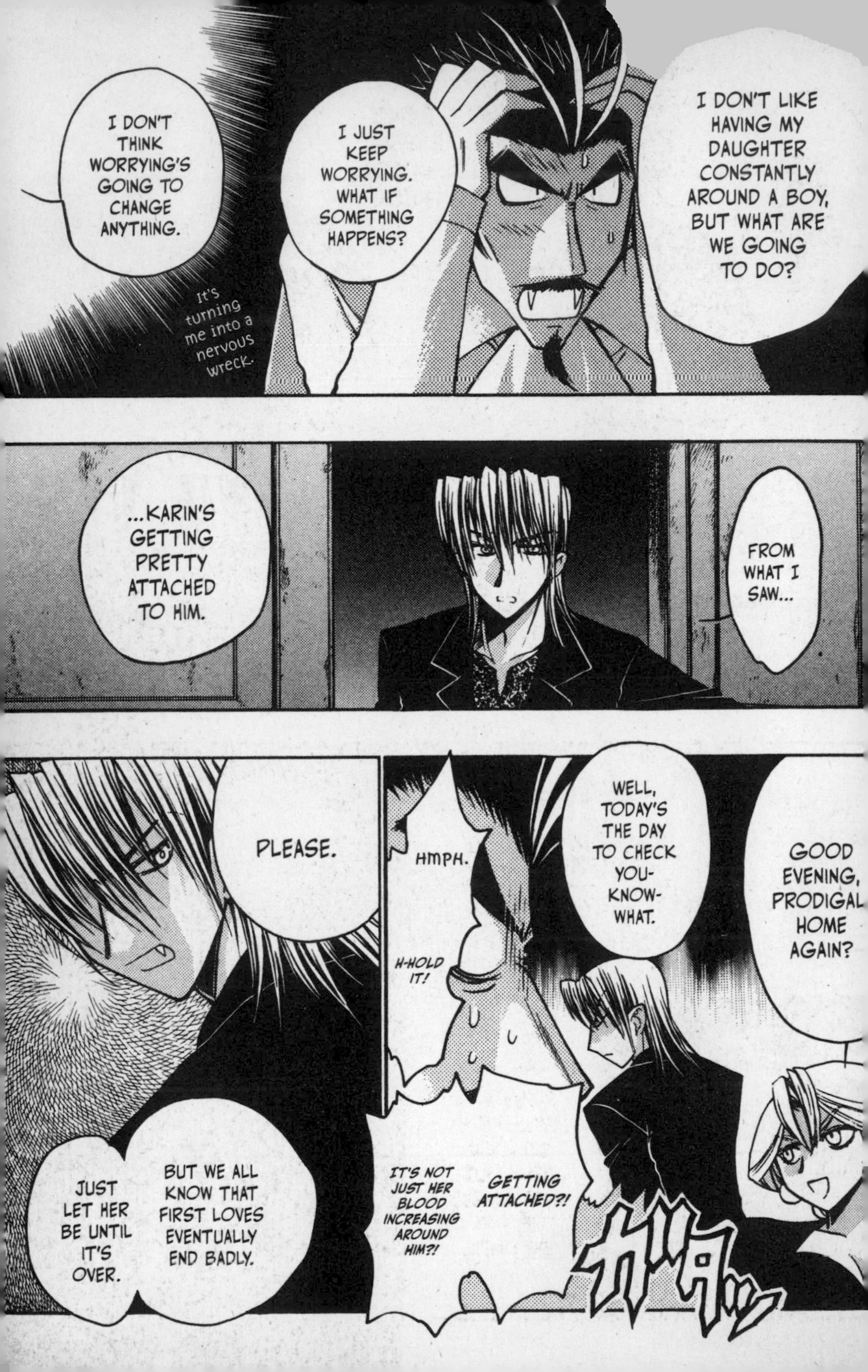
I DON'T LIKE HAVING MY DAUGHTER CONSTANTLY AROUND A BOY, BUT WHAT ARE WE GOING TO DO?
I JUST KEEP WORRYING. WHAT IF SOMETHING HAPPENS?
I DON'T THINK WORRYING'S GOING TO CHANGE ANYTHING.
It's turning me into a nervous wreck.
FROM WHAT I SAW...
...KARIN'S GETTING PRETTY ATTACHED TO HIM.
GOOD EVENING, PRODIGAL HOME AGAIN?
WELL, TODAY'S THE DAY TO CHECK YOU-KNOW-WHAT.
HMPH.
H-HOLD IT!
ガタ...
GETTING ATTACHED?!
IT'S NOT JUST HER BLOOD INCREASING AROUND HIM?!
PLEASE.
BUT WE ALL KNOW THAT FIRST LOVES EVENTUALLY END BADLY.
JUST LET HER BE UNTIL IT'S OVER.

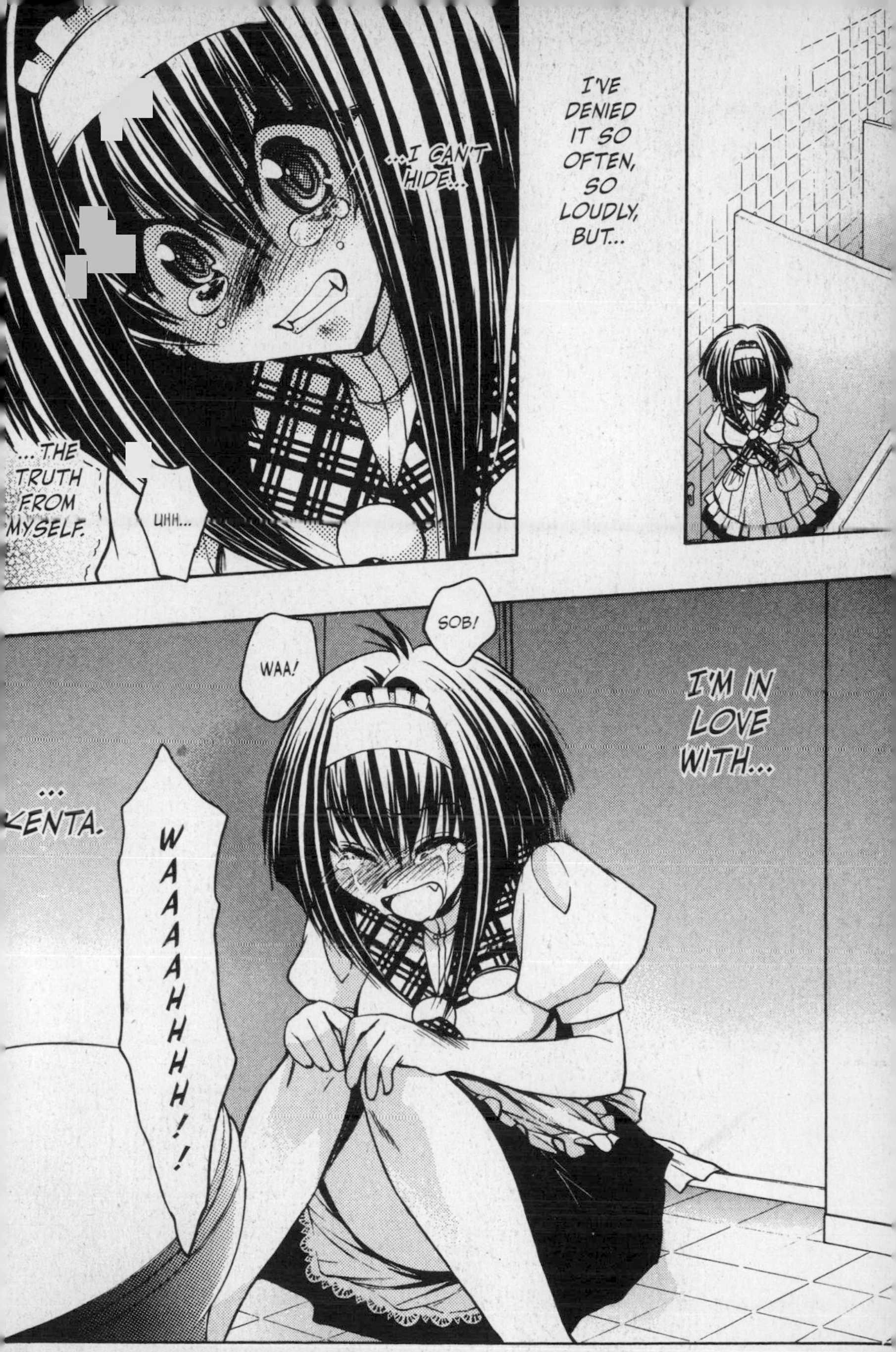
I'VE DENIED IT SO OFTEN, SO LOUDLY, BUT...
...I CAN'T HIDE...
...THE TRUTH FROM MYSELF.
UHH...
I'M IN LOVE WITH...
SOB!
WAA!
...KENTA.
WAAAAAHHHHH!!

TH EMBARRASSMENT END

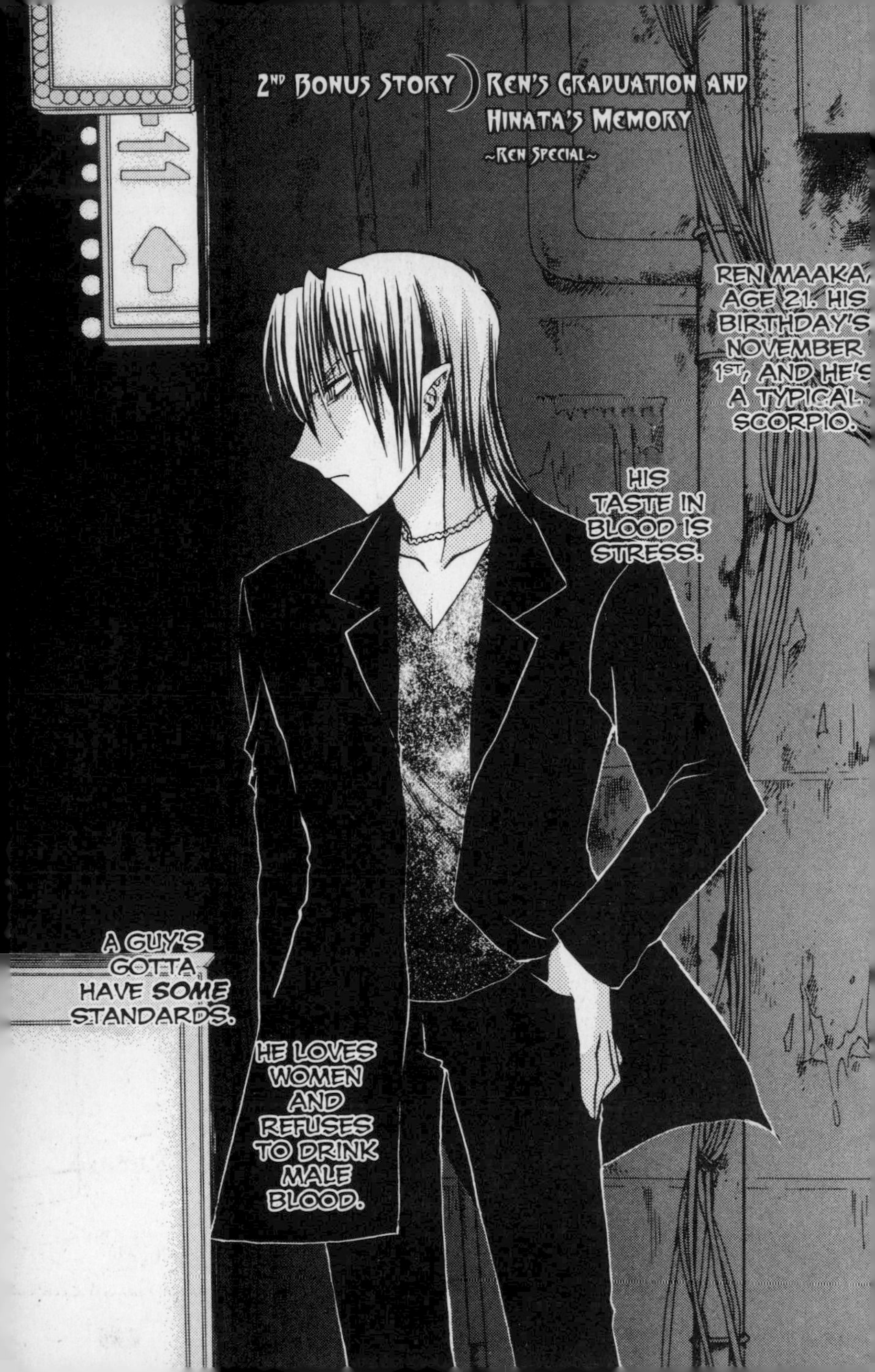
2ND BONUS STORY REN'S GRADUATION AND HINATA'S MEMORY
~REN SPECIAL~
REN MAAKA, AGE 21. HIS BIRTHDAY'S NOVEMBER 1ST, AND HE'S A TYPICAL SCORPIO.
HIS TASTE IN BLOOD IS STRESS.
HE LOVES WOMEN AND REFUSES TO DRINK MALE BLOOD.
A GUY'S GOTTA HAVE SOME STANDARDS.

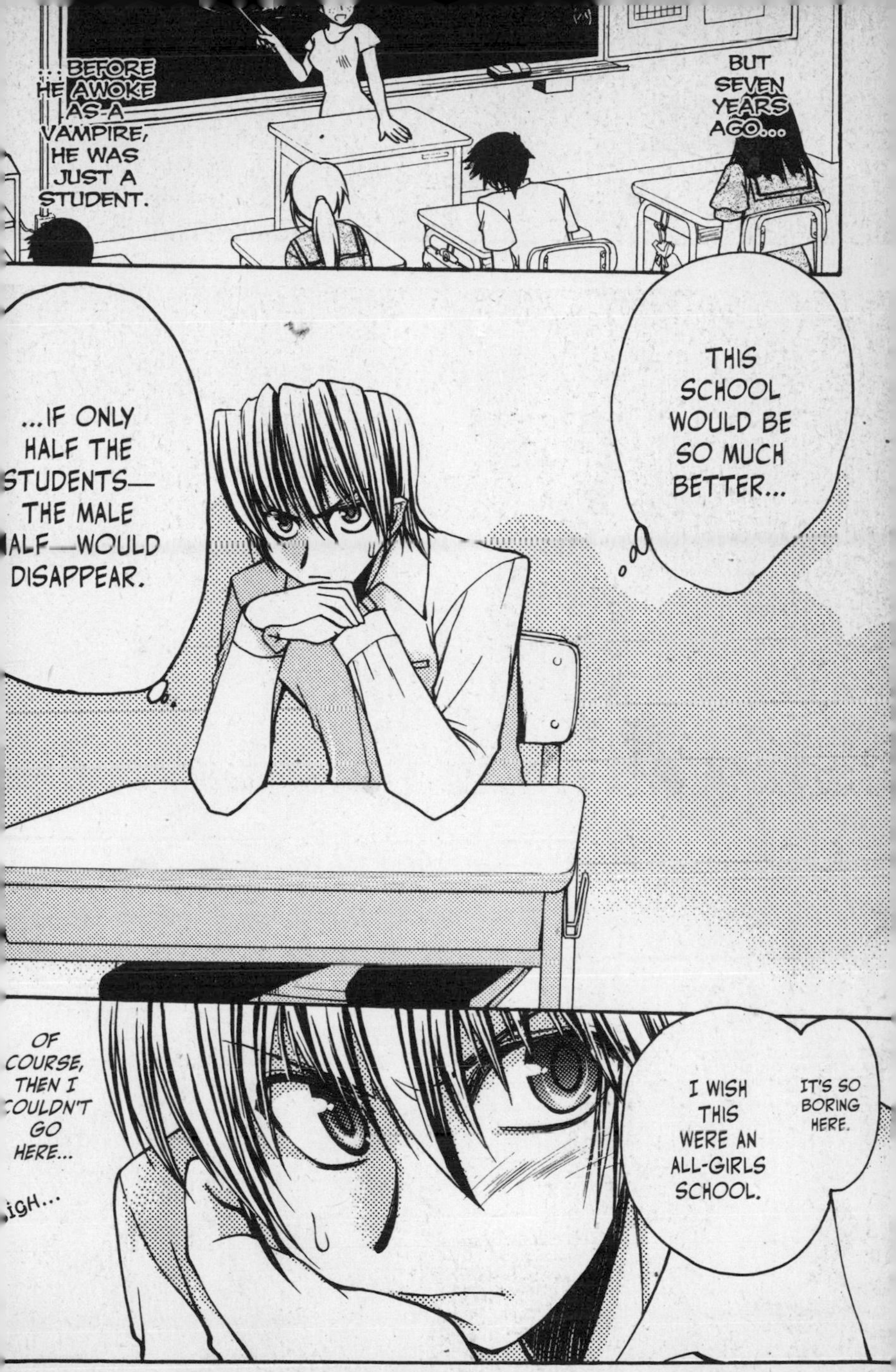
BUT SEVEN YEARS AGO...
...BEFORE HE AWOKE AS A VAMPIRE, HE WAS JUST A STUDENT.
THIS SCHOOL WOULD BE SO MUCH BETTER...
...IF ONLY HALF THE STUDENTS— THE MALE ALF—WOULD DISAPPEAR.
IT'S SO BORING HERE.
I WISH THIS WERE AN ALL-GIRLS SCHOOL.
OF COURSE, THEN I COULDN'T GO HERE...
IGH...

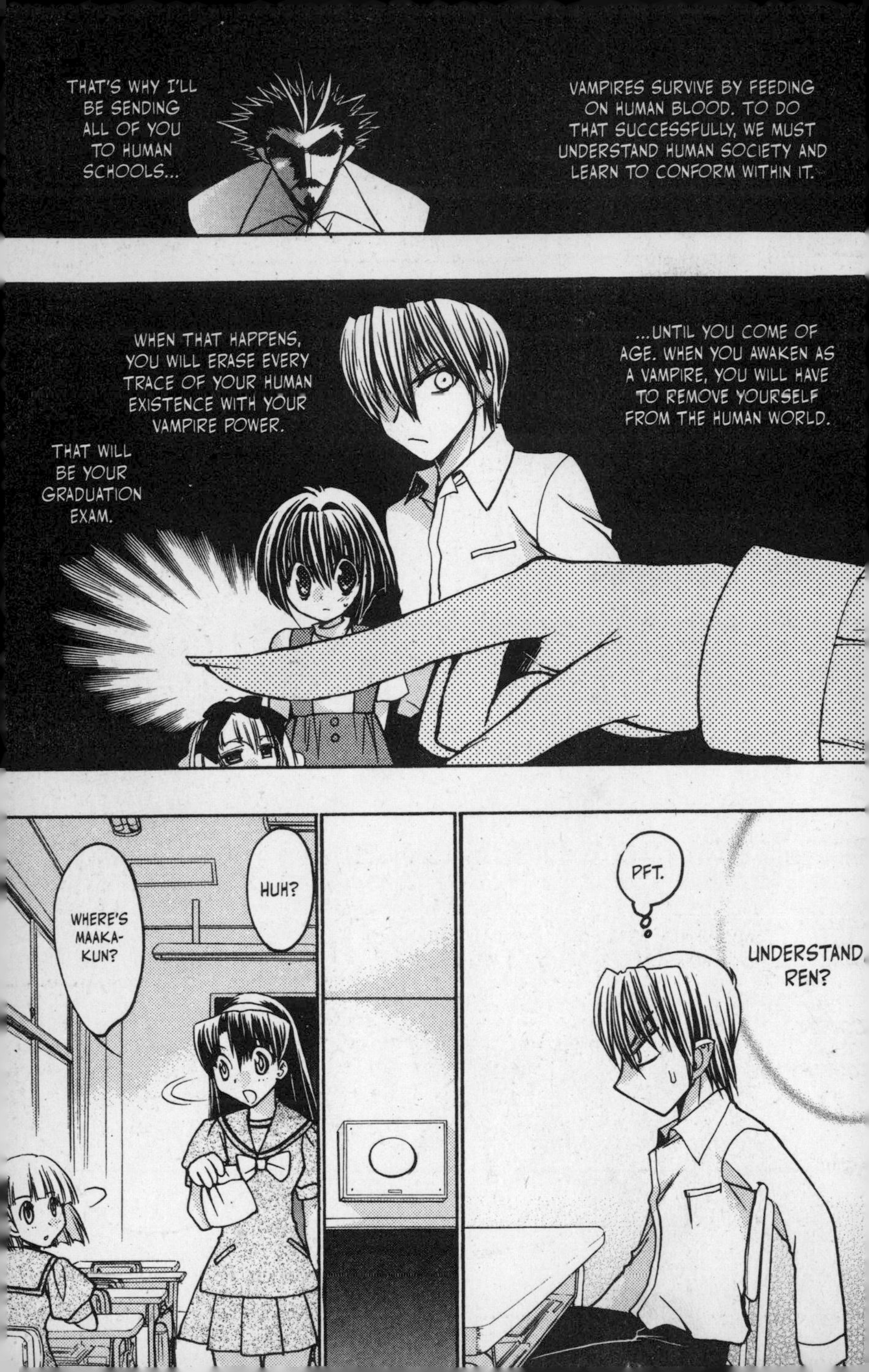
VAMPIRES SURVIVE BY FEEDING ON HUMAN BLOOD. TO DO THAT SUCCESSFULLY, WE MUST UNDERSTAND HUMAN SOCIETY AND LEARN TO CONFORM WITHIN IT.
THAT'S WHY I'LL BE SENDING ALL OF YOU TO HUMAN SCHOOLS...
...UNTIL YOU COME OF AGE. WHEN YOU AWAKEN AS A VAMPIRE, YOU WILL HAVE TO REMOVE YOURSELF FROM THE HUMAN WORLD.
WHEN THAT HAPPENS, YOU WILL ERASE EVERY TRACE OF YOUR HUMAN EXISTENCE WITH YOUR VAMPIRE POWER.
THAT WILL BE YOUR GRADUATION EXAM.
PFT.
UNDERSTAND REN?
HUH?
WHERE'S MAAKA-KUN?

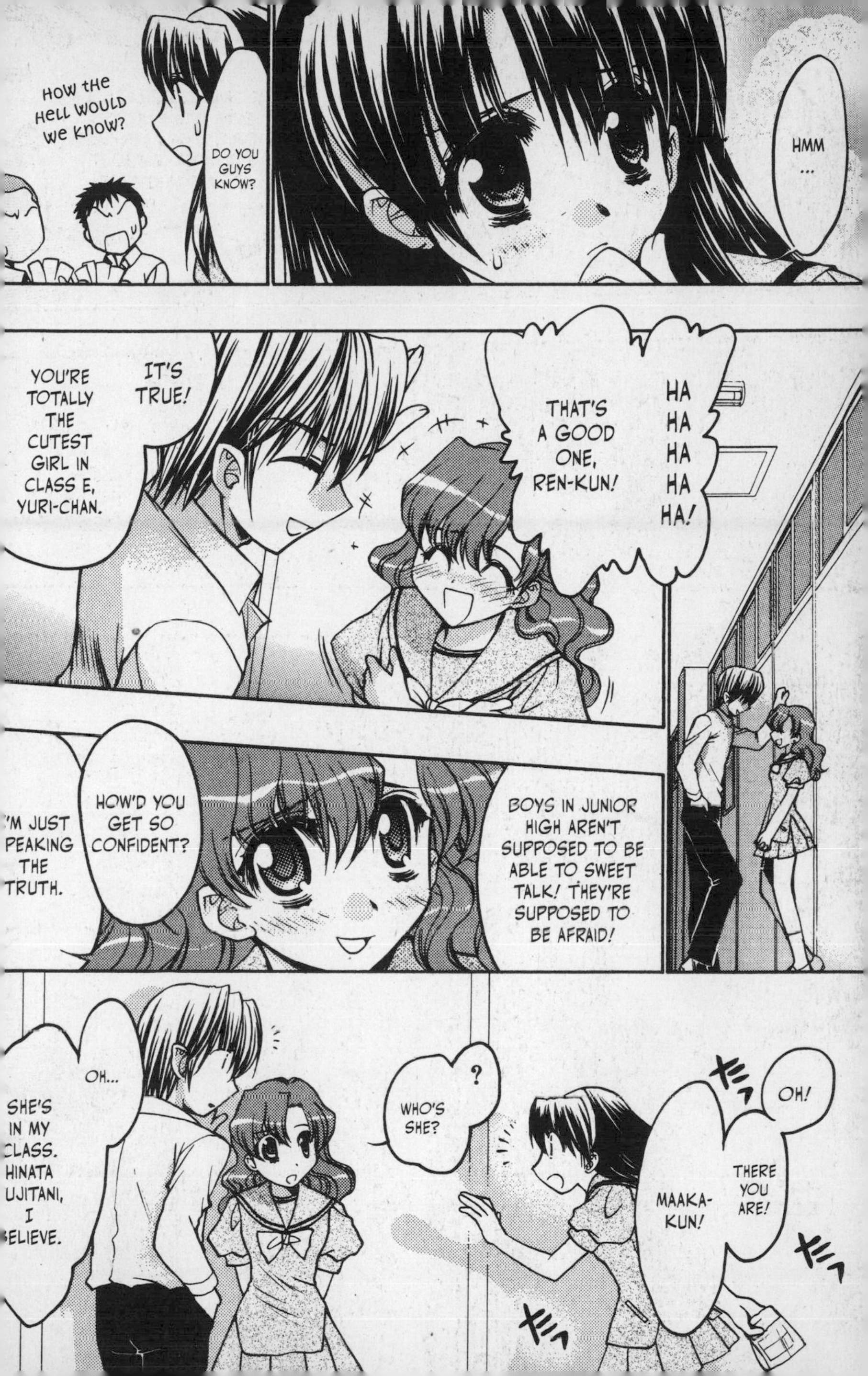
HMM ...
DO YOU GUYS KNOW?
How the hell would we know?
HA HA HA HA HA!
THAT'S A GOOD ONE, REN-KUN!
IT'S TRUE!
YOU'RE TOTALLY THE CUTEST GIRL IN CLASS E, YURI-CHAN.
BOYS IN JUNIOR HIGH AREN'T SUPPOSED TO BE ABLE TO SWEET TALK! THEY'RE SUPPOSED TO BE AFRAID!
HOW'D YOU GET SO CONFIDENT?
'M JUST PEAKING THE TRUTH.
OH!
THERE YOU ARE!
MAAKA-KUN!
?
WHO'S SHE?
OH...
SHE'S IN MY LASS. HINATA UJITANI, I ELIEVE.

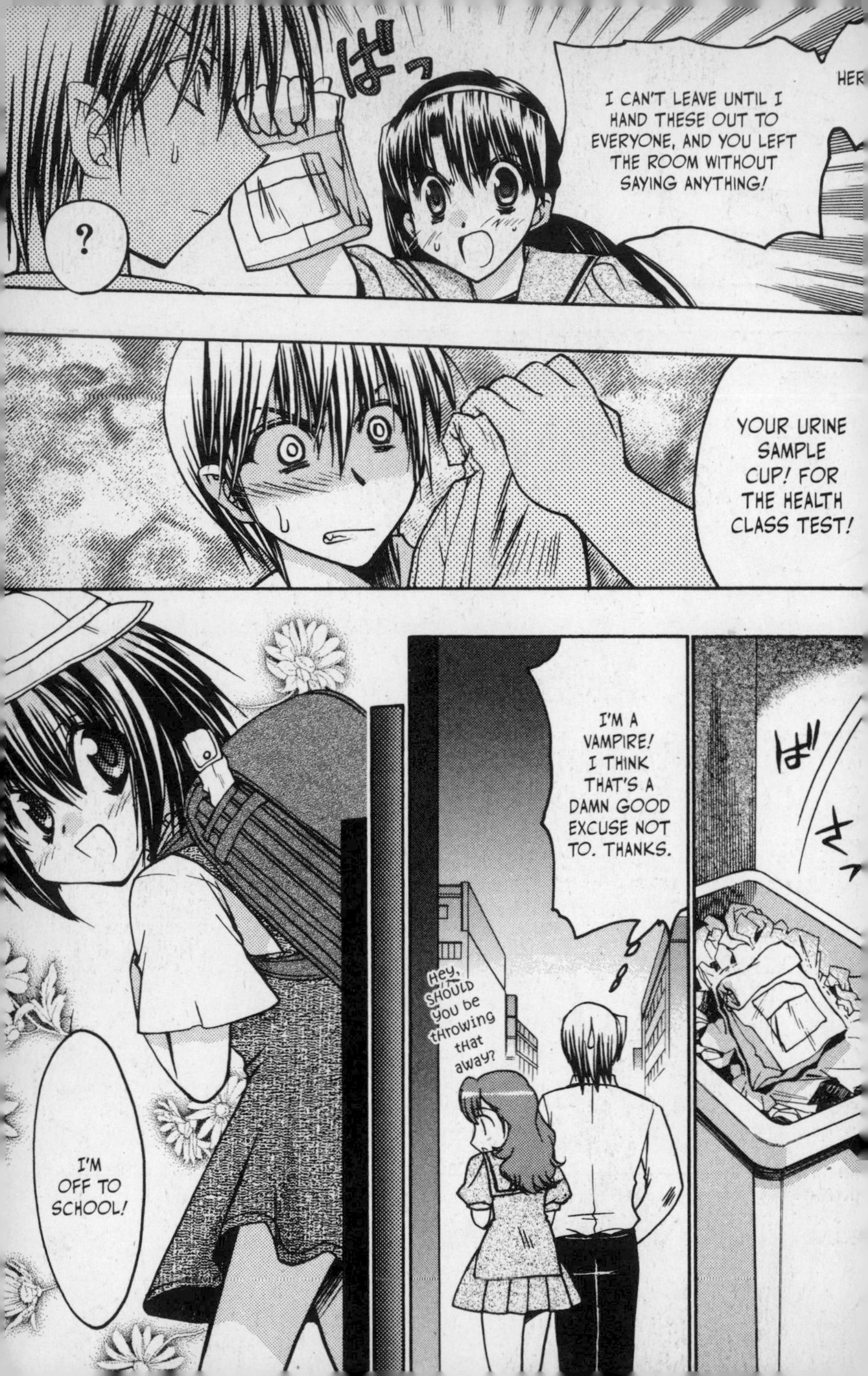
HER
I CAN'T LEAVE UNTIL I HAND THESE OUT TO EVERYONE, AND YOU LEFT THE ROOM WITHOUT SAYING ANYTHING!
ばっ
?
YOUR URINE SAMPLE CUP! FOR THE HEALTH CLASS TEST!
ばさっ
I'M A VAMPIRE! I THINK THAT'S A DAMN GOOD EXCUSE NOT TO. THANKS.
Hey, SHOULD you be throwing that away?
I'M OFF TO SCHOOL!

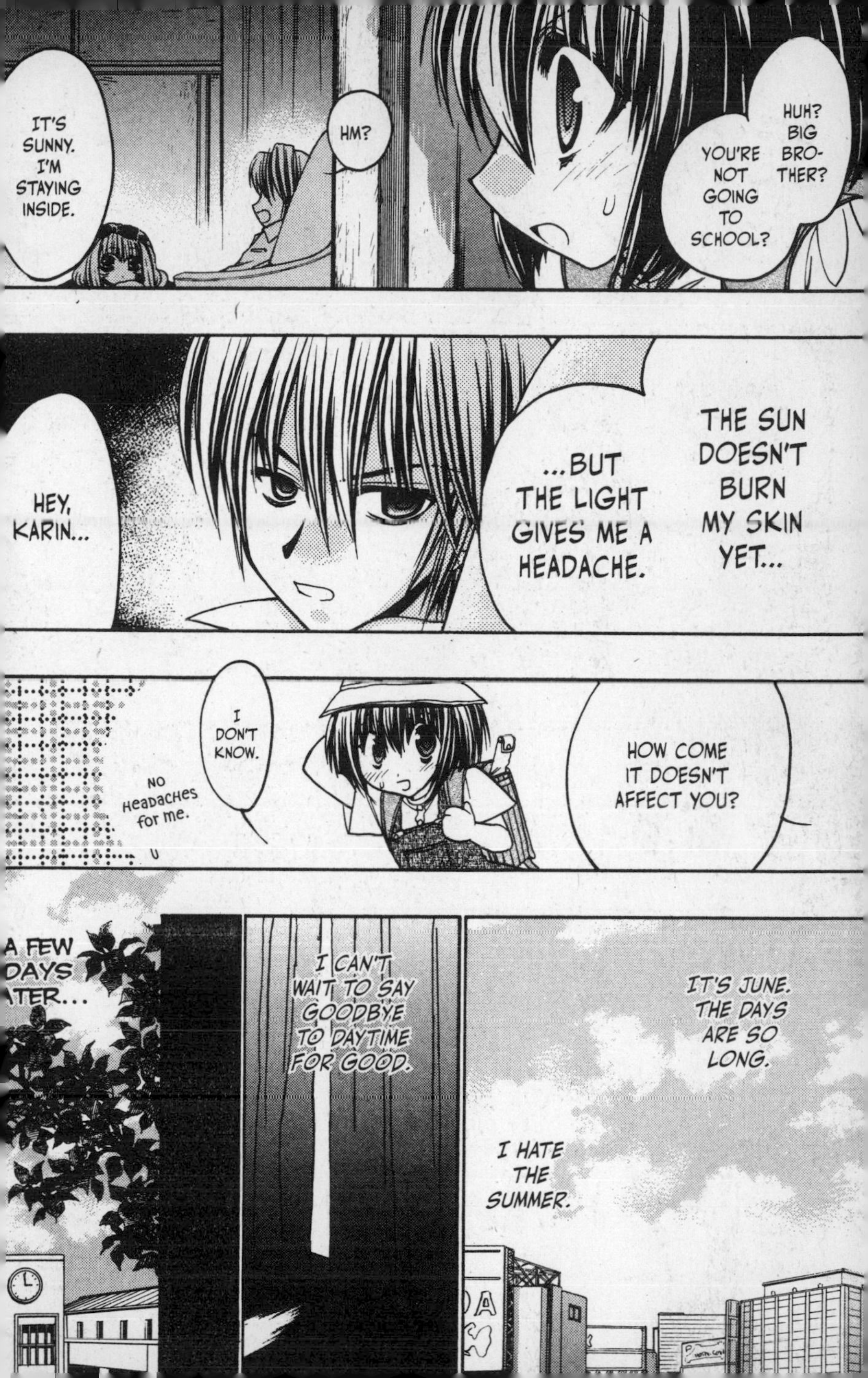
HUH? BIG BRO- THER?
YOU'RE NOT GOING TO SCHOOL?
HM?
IT'S SUNNY. I'M STAYING INSIDE.
THE SUN DOESN'T BURN MY SKIN YET...
...BUT THE LIGHT GIVES ME A HEADACHE.
HEY, KARIN...
HOW COME IT DOESN'T AFFECT YOU?
I DON'T KNOW.
No headaches for me.
IT'S JUNE. THE DAYS ARE SO LONG.
I HATE THE SUMMER.
I CAN'T WAIT TO SAY GOODBYE TO DAYTIME FOR GOOD.
A FEW DAYS TER...

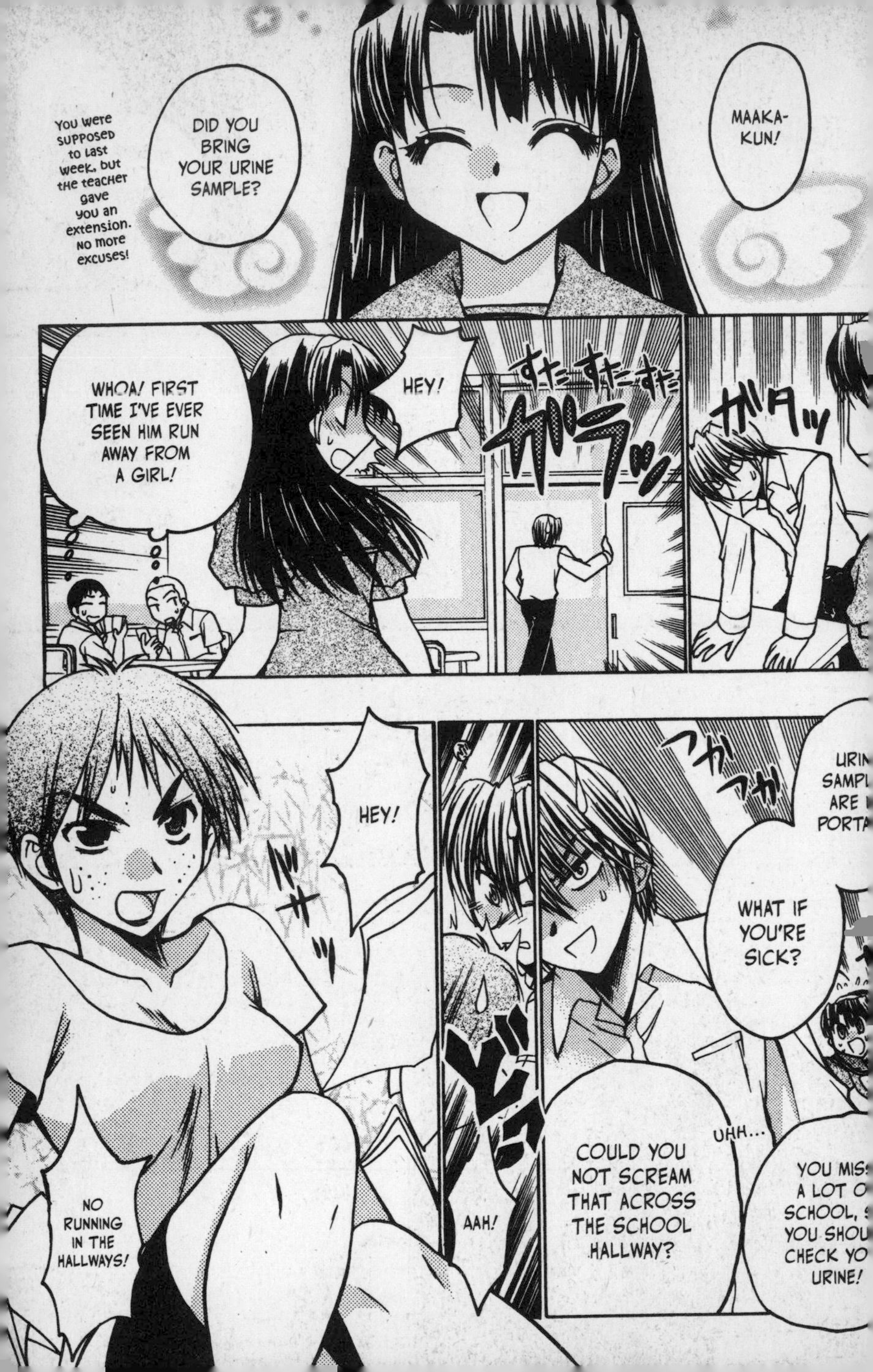
MAAKA-KUN!
DID YOU BRING YOUR URINE SAMPLE?
You were supposed to last week, but the teacher gave you an extension. No more excuses!
ガタッ
すたすたすた
ガラッ
HEY!
WHOA! FIRST TIME I'VE EVER SEEN HIM RUN AWAY FROM A GIRL!
URIN SAMPL ARE I PORTA
WHAT IF YOU'RE SICK?
YOU MISS A LOT O SCHOOL, S YOU SHOU CHECK YO URINE!
UHH...
COULD YOU NOT SCREAM THAT ACROSS THE SCHOOL HALLWAY?
AAH!
HEY!
NO RUNNING IN THE HALLWAYS!

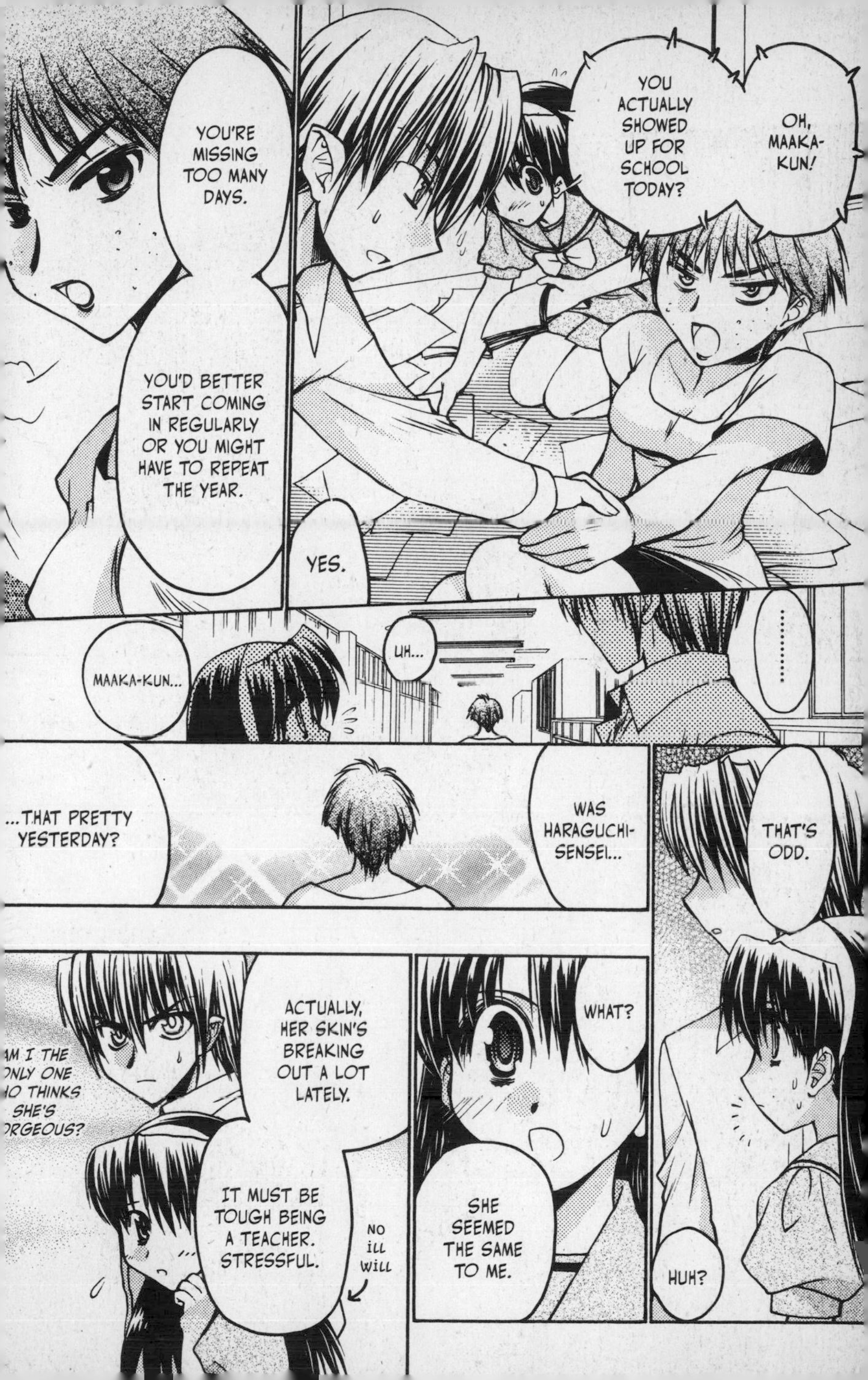
OH, MAAKA-KUN!
YOU ACTUALLY SHOWED UP FOR SCHOOL TODAY?
YES.
YOU'RE MISSING TOO MANY DAYS.
YOU'D BETTER START COMING IN REGULARLY OR YOU MIGHT HAVE TO REPEAT THE YEAR.
......
UH...
MAAKA-KUN...
THAT'S ODD.
WAS HARAGUCHI-SENSEI...
...THAT PRETTY YESTERDAY?
HUH?
WHAT?
SHE SEEMED THE SAME TO ME.
ACTUALLY, HER SKIN'S BREAKING OUT A LOT LATELY.
AM I THE ONLY ONE HO THINKS SHE'S ORGEOUS?
IT MUST BE TOUGH BEING A TEACHER. STRESSFUL.
NO ILL WILL

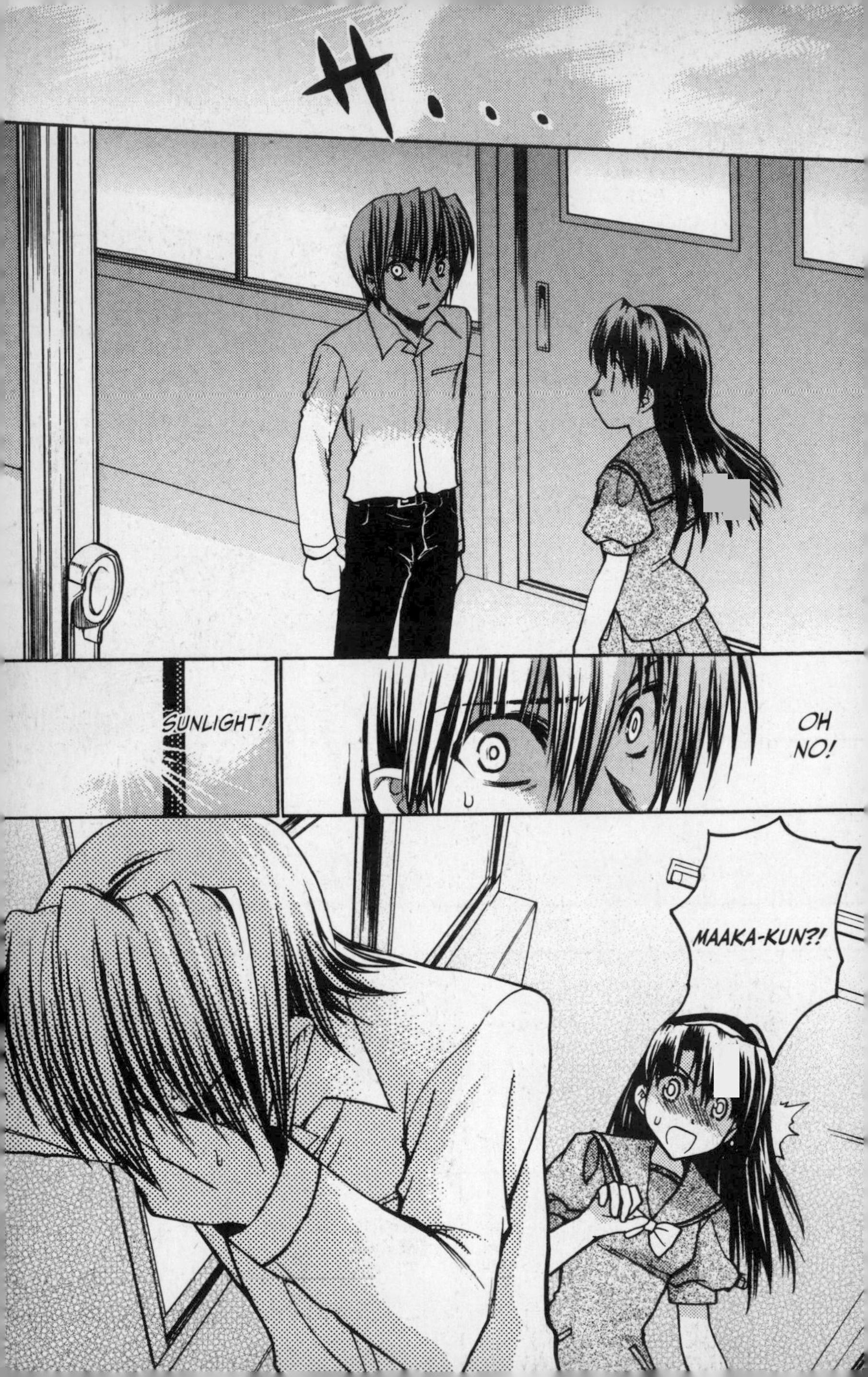
OH NO!
SUNLIGHT!
MAAKA-KUN?!

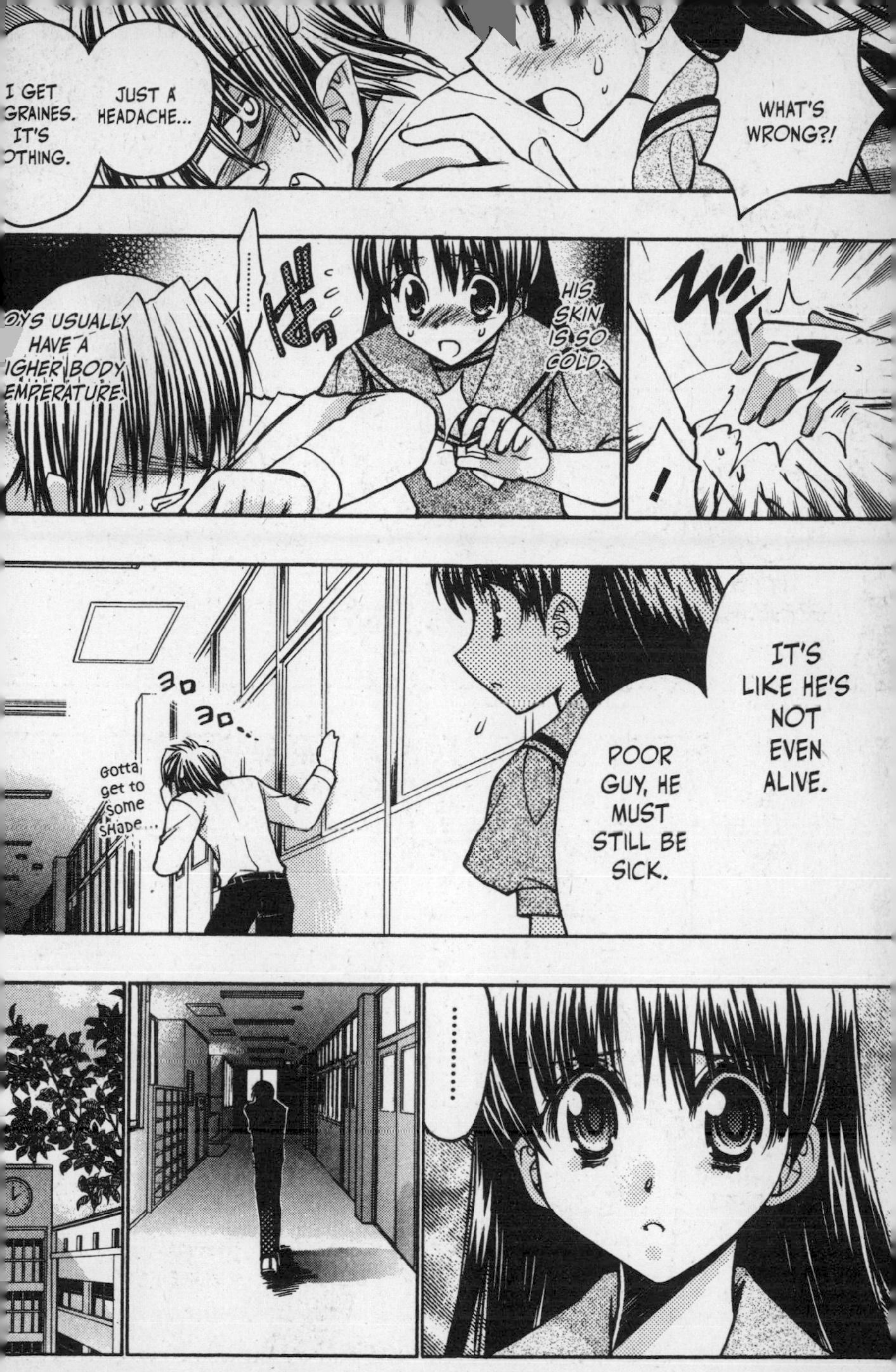
WHAT'S WRONG?!
JUST A HEADACHE...
I GET GRAINES. IT'S OTHING.
!
......
HIS SKIN IS SO COLD.
OYS USUALLY HAVE A IGHER BODY EMPERATURE.
IT'S LIKE HE'S NOT EVEN ALIVE.
POOR GUY, HE MUST STILL BE SICK.
ヨロ ヨロ...
Gotta get to some shade...
......

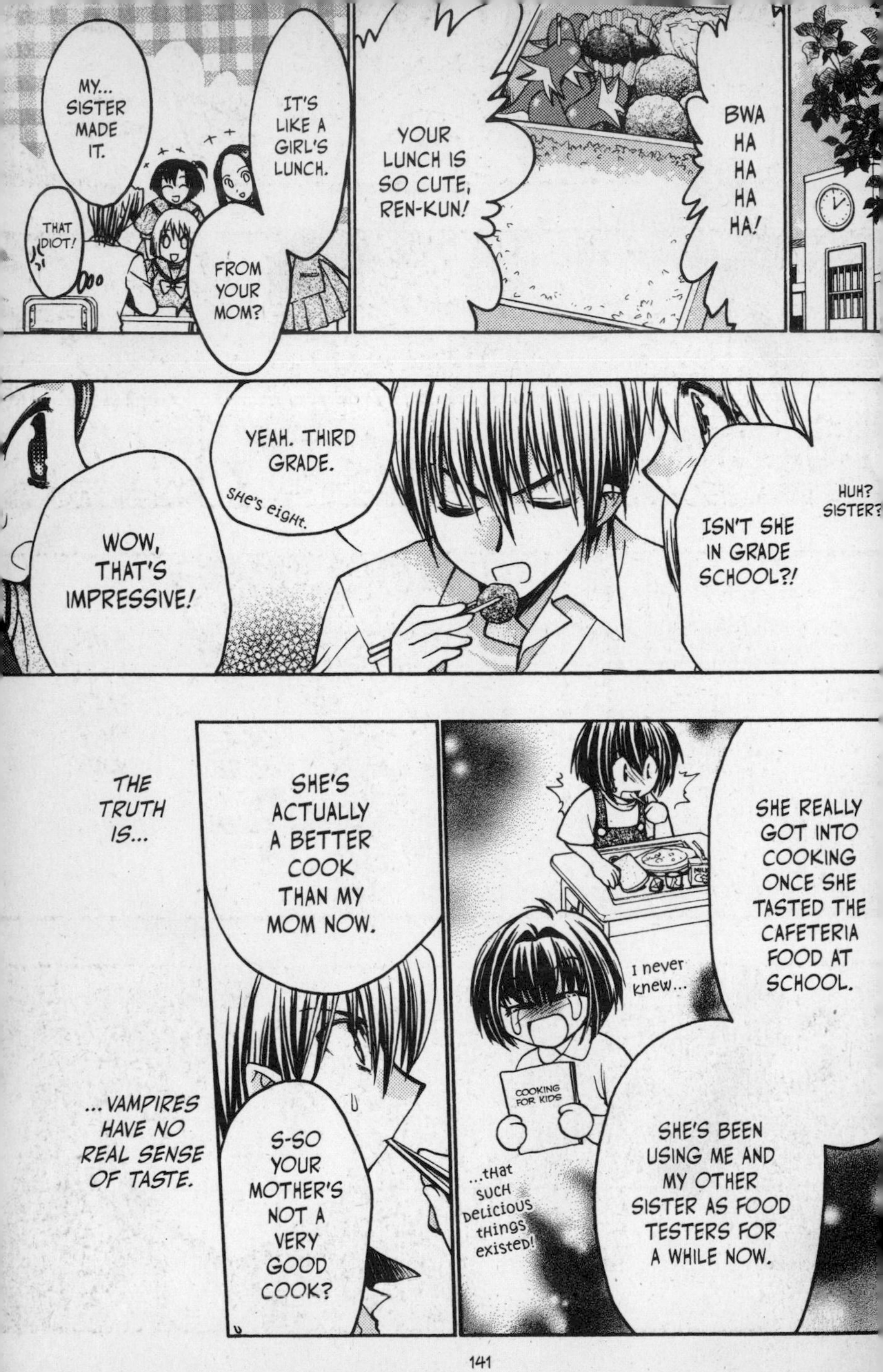
BWA HA HA HA HA!
YOUR LUNCH IS SO CUTE, REN-KUN!
IT'S LIKE A GIRL'S LUNCH.
MY... SISTER MADE IT.
FROM YOUR MOM?
THAT IDIOT!
HUH? SISTER?
ISN'T SHE IN GRADE SCHOOL?!
YEAH. THIRD GRADE.
SHE's eight.
WOW, THAT'S IMPRESSIVE!
SHE REALLY GOT INTO COOKING ONCE SHE TASTED THE CAFETERIA FOOD AT SCHOOL.
I never knew...
COOKING FOR KIDS
...that such delicious things existed!
SHE'S BEEN USING ME AND MY OTHER SISTER AS FOOD TESTERS FOR A WHILE NOW.
SHE'S ACTUALLY A BETTER COOK THAN MY MOM NOW.
S-SO YOUR MOTHER'S NOT A VERY GOOD COOK?
THE TRUTH IS...
...VAMPIRES HAVE NO REAL SENSE OF TASTE.

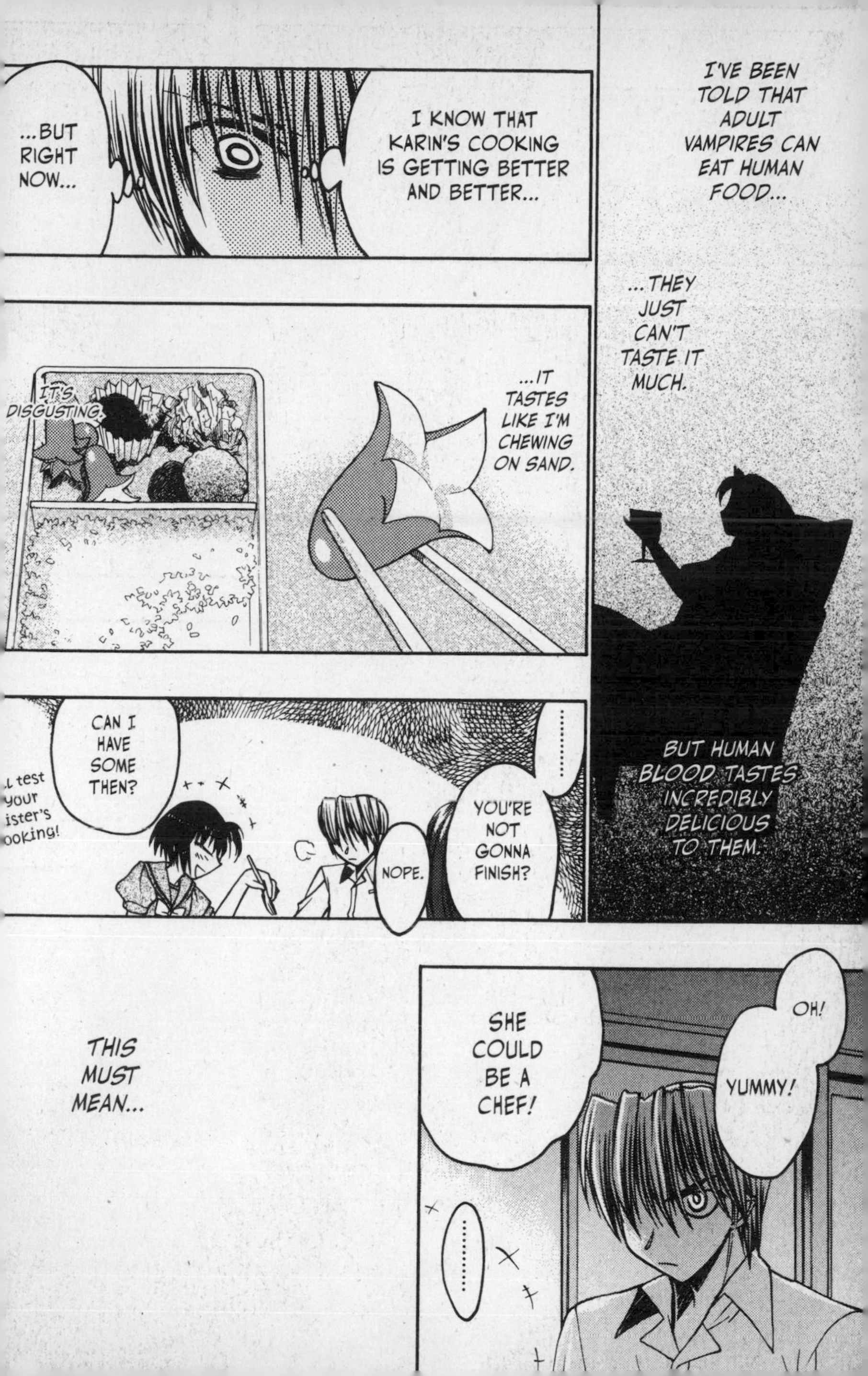
I'VE BEEN TOLD THAT ADULT VAMPIRES CAN EAT HUMAN FOOD...
...THEY JUST CAN'T TASTE IT MUCH.
BUT HUMAN BLOOD TASTES INCREDIBLY DELICIOUS TO THEM.
I KNOW THAT KARIN'S COOKING IS GETTING BETTER AND BETTER...
...BUT RIGHT NOW...
...IT TASTES LIKE I'M CHEWING ON SAND.
IT'S DISGUSTING.
......
YOU'RE NOT GONNA FINISH?
NOPE.
CAN I HAVE SOME THEN?
OH! YUMMY!
SHE COULD BE A CHEF!
......
THIS MUST MEAN...

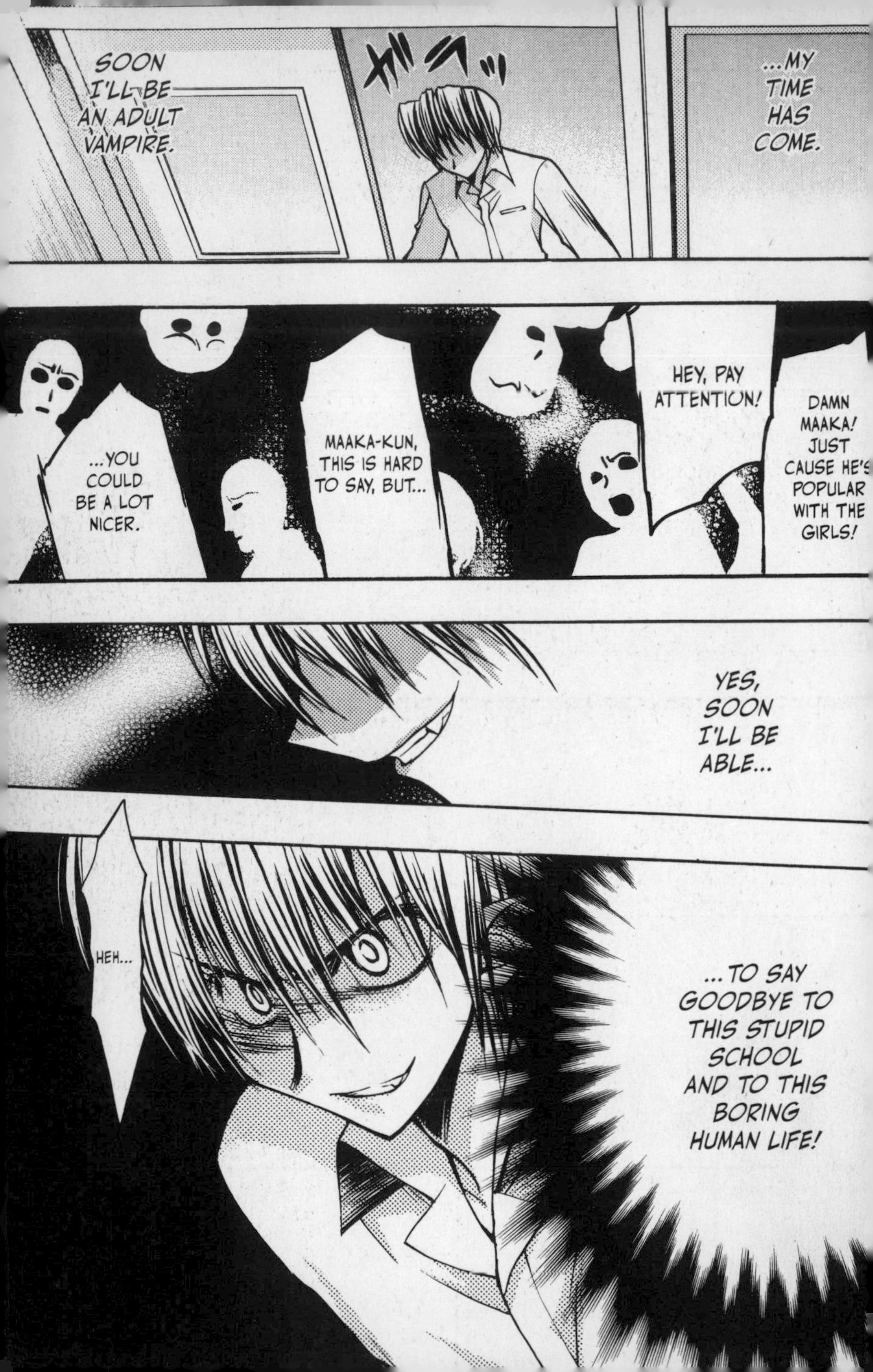
...MY TIME HAS COME.
SOON I'LL BE AN ADULT VAMPIRE.
DAMN MAAKA! JUST CAUSE HE'S POPULAR WITH THE GIRLS!
HEY, PAY ATTENTION!
MAAKA-KUN, THIS IS HARD TO SAY, BUT...
...YOU COULD BE A LOT NICER.
YES, SOON I'LL BE ABLE...
...TO SAY GOODBYE TO THIS STUPID SCHOOL AND TO THIS BORING HUMAN LIFE!
HEH...

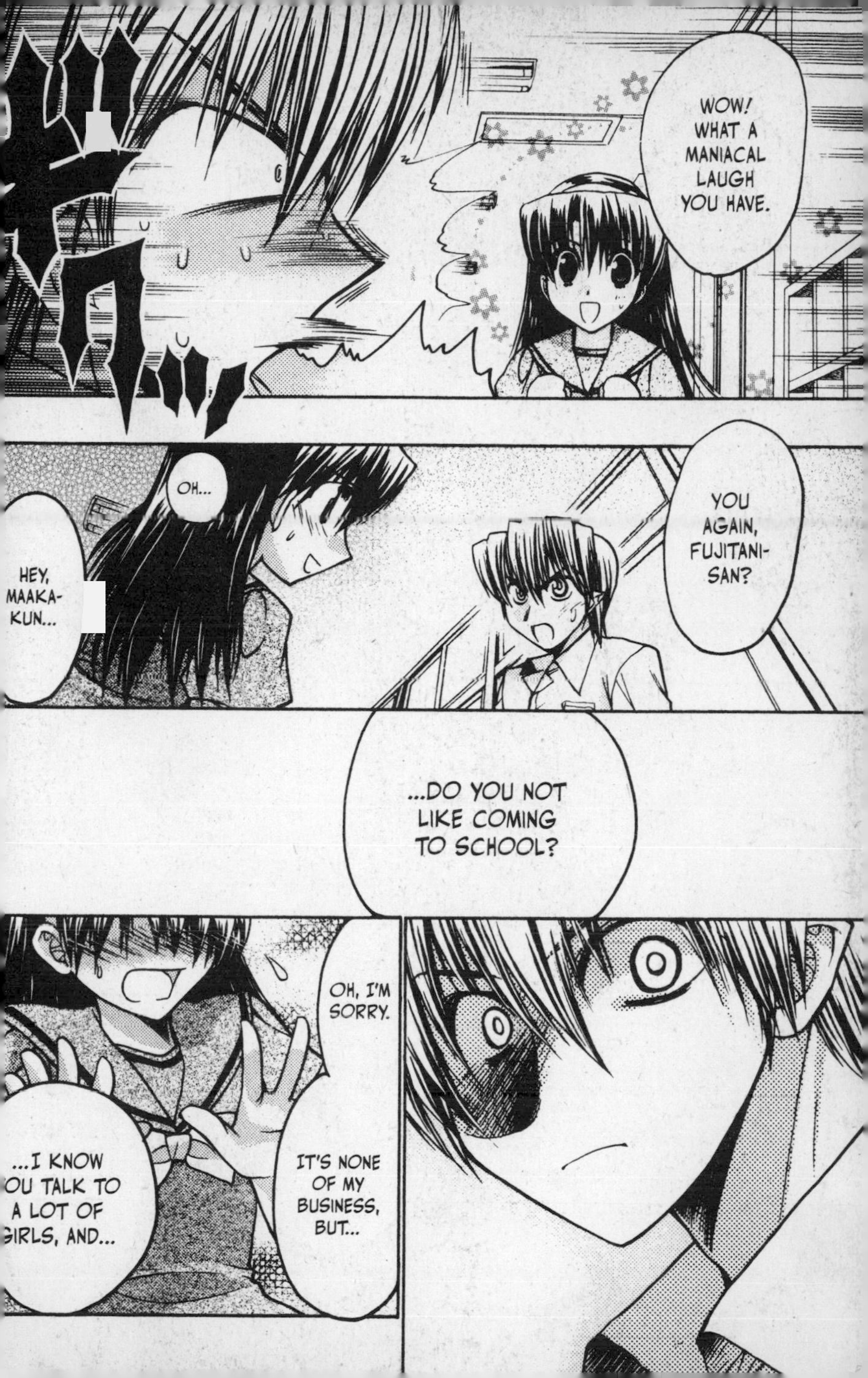
WOW! WHAT A MANIACAL LAUGH YOU HAVE.
YOU AGAIN, FUJITANI-SAN?
OH...
HEY, MAAKA-KUN...
...DO YOU NOT LIKE COMING TO SCHOOL?
OH, I'M SORRY.
IT'S NONE OF MY BUSINESS, BUT...
...I KNOW OU TALK TO A LOT OF GIRLS, AND...

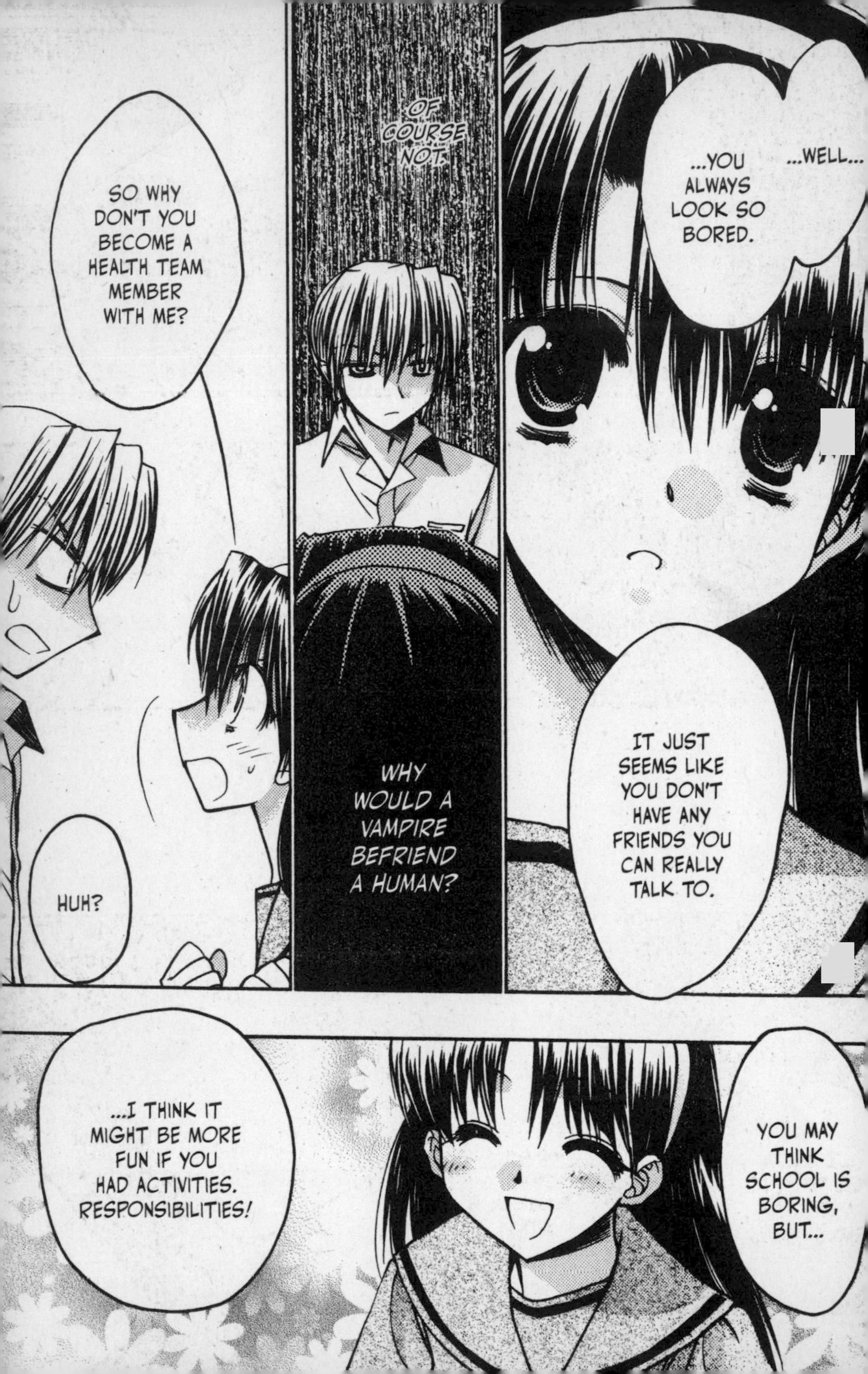
...WELL...
...YOU ALWAYS LOOK SO BORED.
IT JUST SEEMS LIKE YOU DON'T HAVE ANY FRIENDS YOU CAN REALLY TALK TO.
OF COURSE NOT.
WHY WOULD A VAMPIRE BEFRIEND A HUMAN?
SO WHY DON'T YOU BECOME A HEALTH TEAM MEMBER WITH ME?
HUH?
YOU MAY THINK SCHOOL IS BORING, BUT...
...I THINK IT MIGHT BE MORE FUN IF YOU HAD ACTIVITIES. RESPONSIBILITIES!

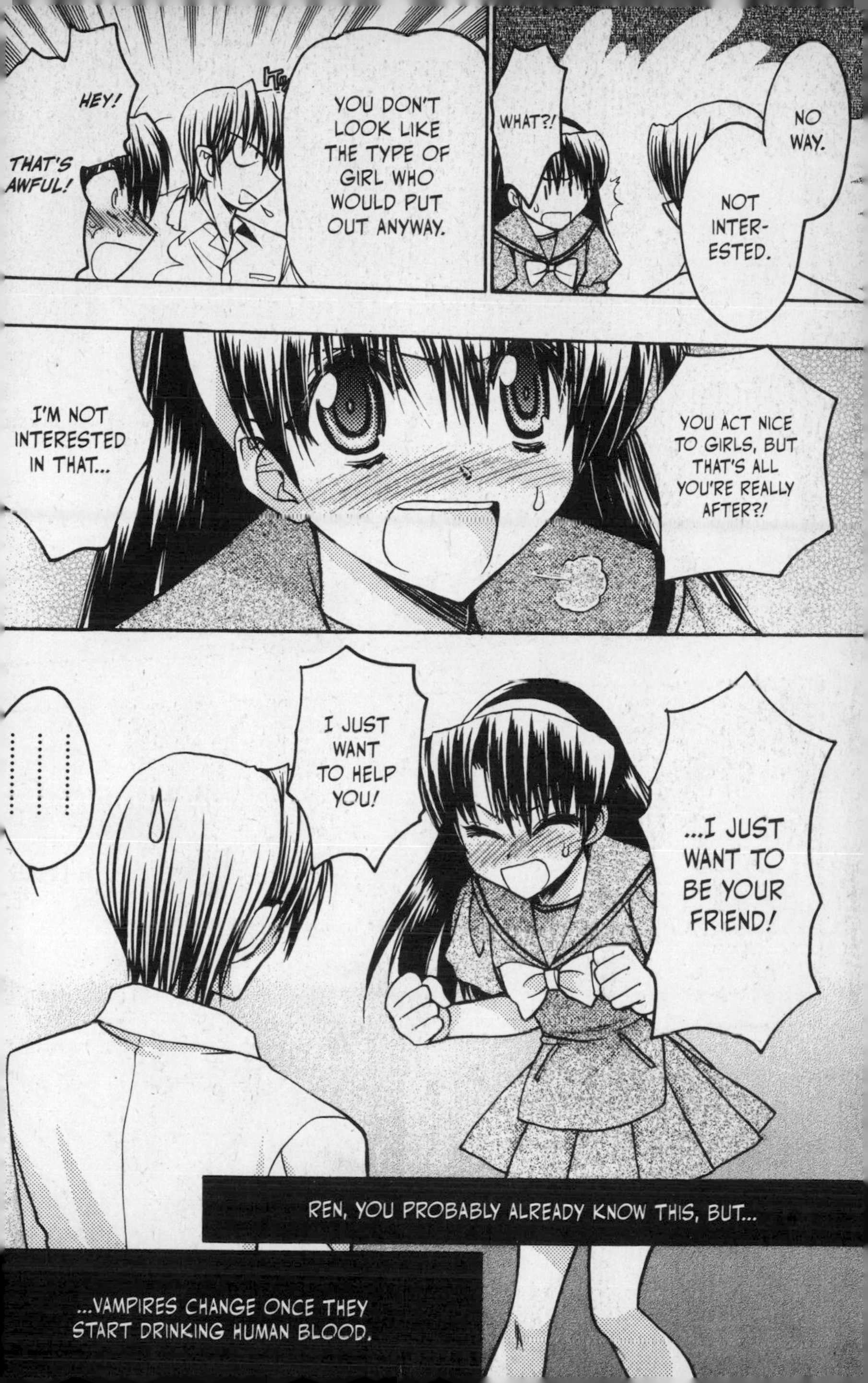
NO WAY.
NOT INTERESTED.
WHAT?!
YOU DON'T LOOK LIKE THE TYPE OF GIRL WHO WOULD PUT OUT ANYWAY.
HEY!
THAT'S AWFUL!
YOU ACT NICE TO GIRLS, BUT THAT'S ALL YOU'RE REALLY AFTER?!
I'M NOT INTERESTED IN THAT...
I JUST WANT TO HELP YOU!
...I JUST WANT TO BE YOUR FRIEND!
......
REN, YOU PROBABLY ALREADY KNOW THIS, BUT...
...VAMPIRES CHANGE ONCE THEY START DRINKING HUMAN BLOOD.

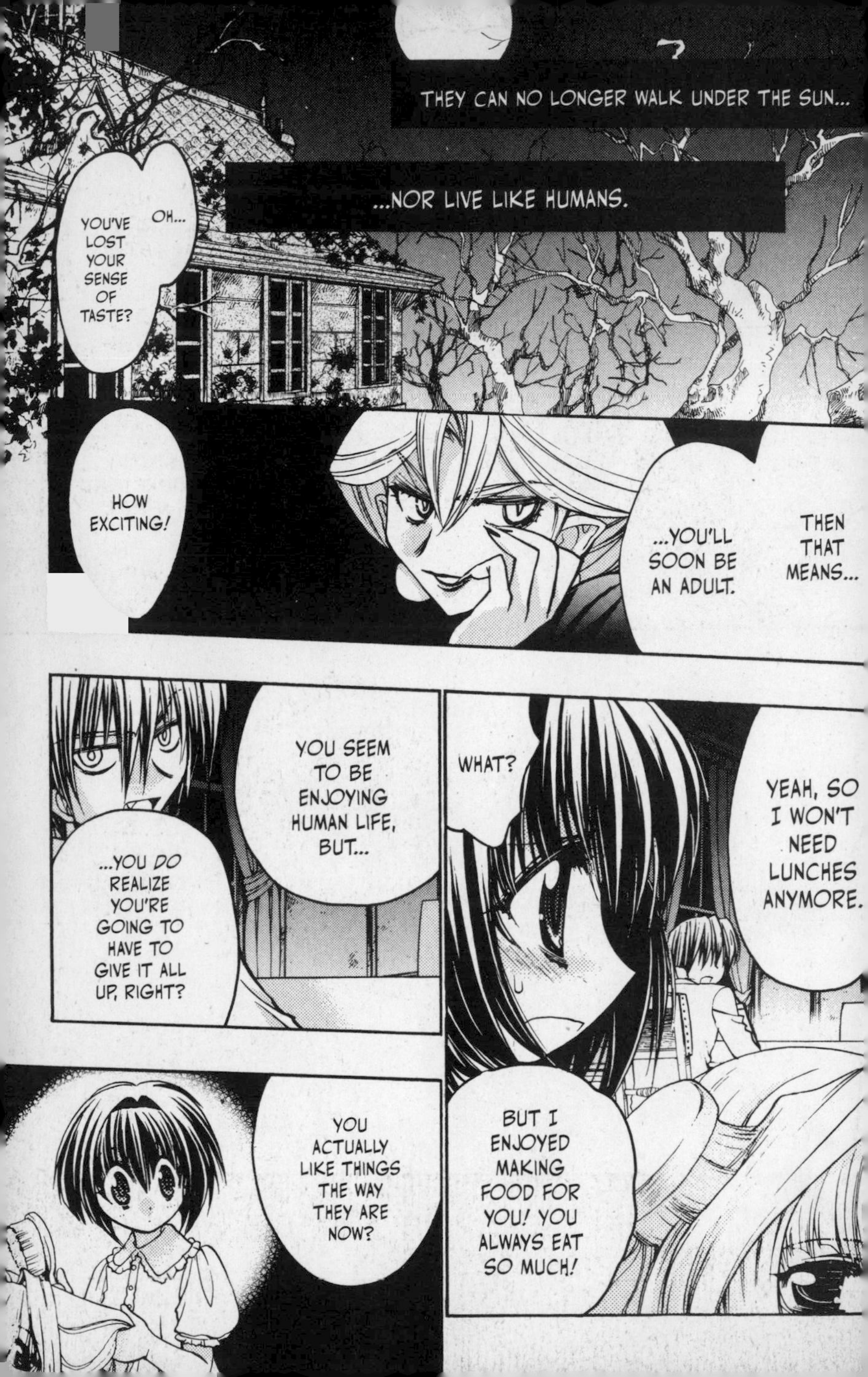
THEY CAN NO LONGER WALK UNDER THE SUN...
...NOR LIVE LIKE HUMANS.
OH... YOU'VE LOST YOUR SENSE OF TASTE?
THEN THAT MEANS...
...YOU'LL SOON BE AN ADULT.
HOW EXCITING!
YEAH, SO I WON'T NEED LUNCHES ANYMORE.
WHAT?
BUT I ENJOYED MAKING FOOD FOR YOU! YOU ALWAYS EAT SO MUCH!
YOU SEEM TO BE ENJOYING HUMAN LIFE, BUT...
...YOU DO REALIZE YOU'RE GOING TO HAVE TO GIVE IT ALL UP, RIGHT?
YOU ACTUALLY LIKE THINGS THE WAY THEY ARE NOW?

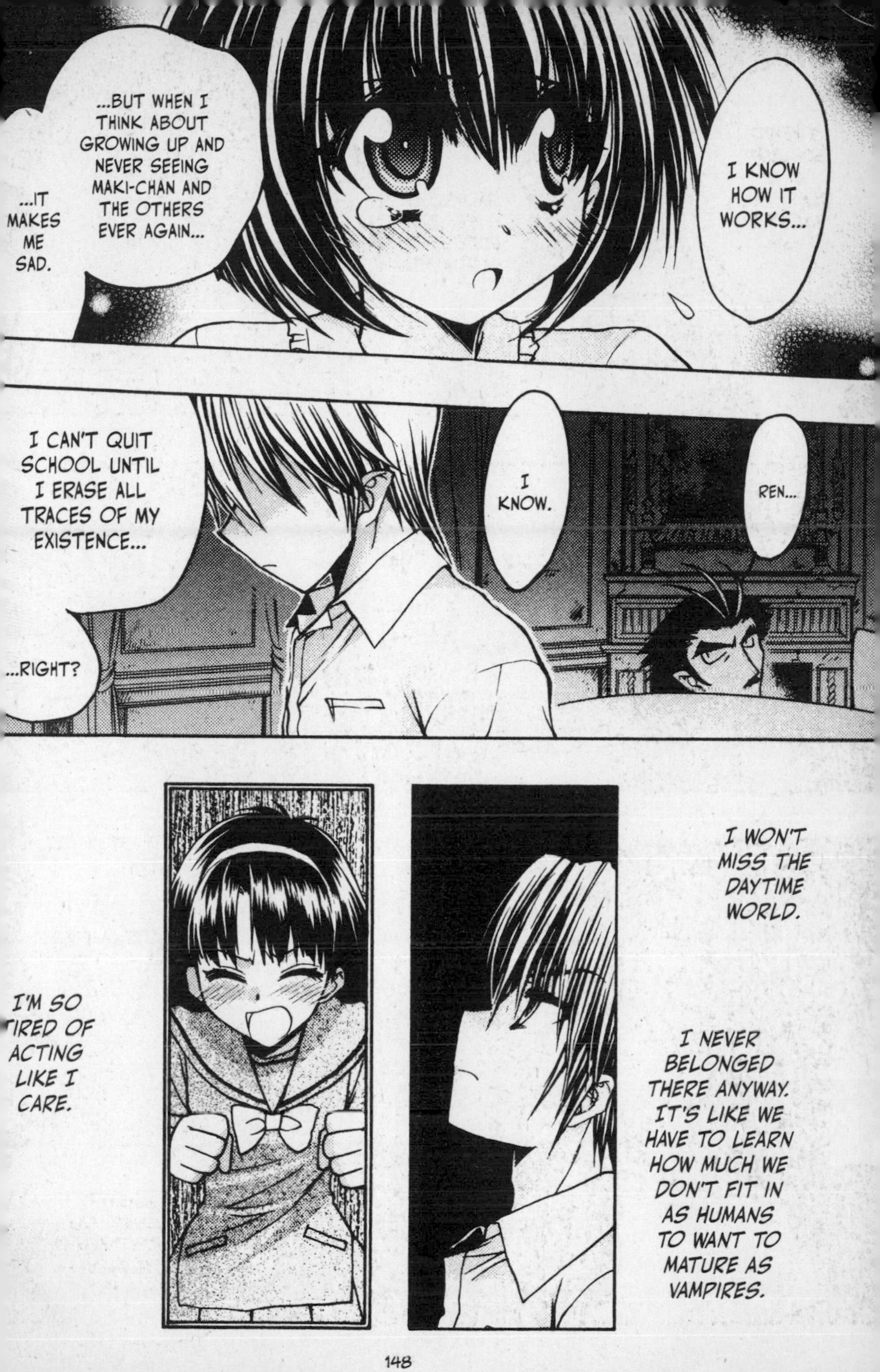
I KNOW HOW IT WORKS...
...BUT WHEN I THINK ABOUT GROWING UP AND NEVER SEEING MAKI-CHAN AND THE OTHERS EVER AGAIN...
...IT MAKES ME SAD.
REN...
I KNOW.
I CAN'T QUIT SCHOOL UNTIL I ERASE ALL TRACES OF MY EXISTENCE...
...RIGHT?
I WON'T MISS THE DAYTIME WORLD.
I NEVER BELONGED THERE ANYWAY. IT'S LIKE WE HAVE TO LEARN HOW MUCH WE DON'T FIT IN AS HUMANS TO WANT TO MATURE AS VAMPIRES.
I'M SO TIRED OF ACTING LIKE I CARE.

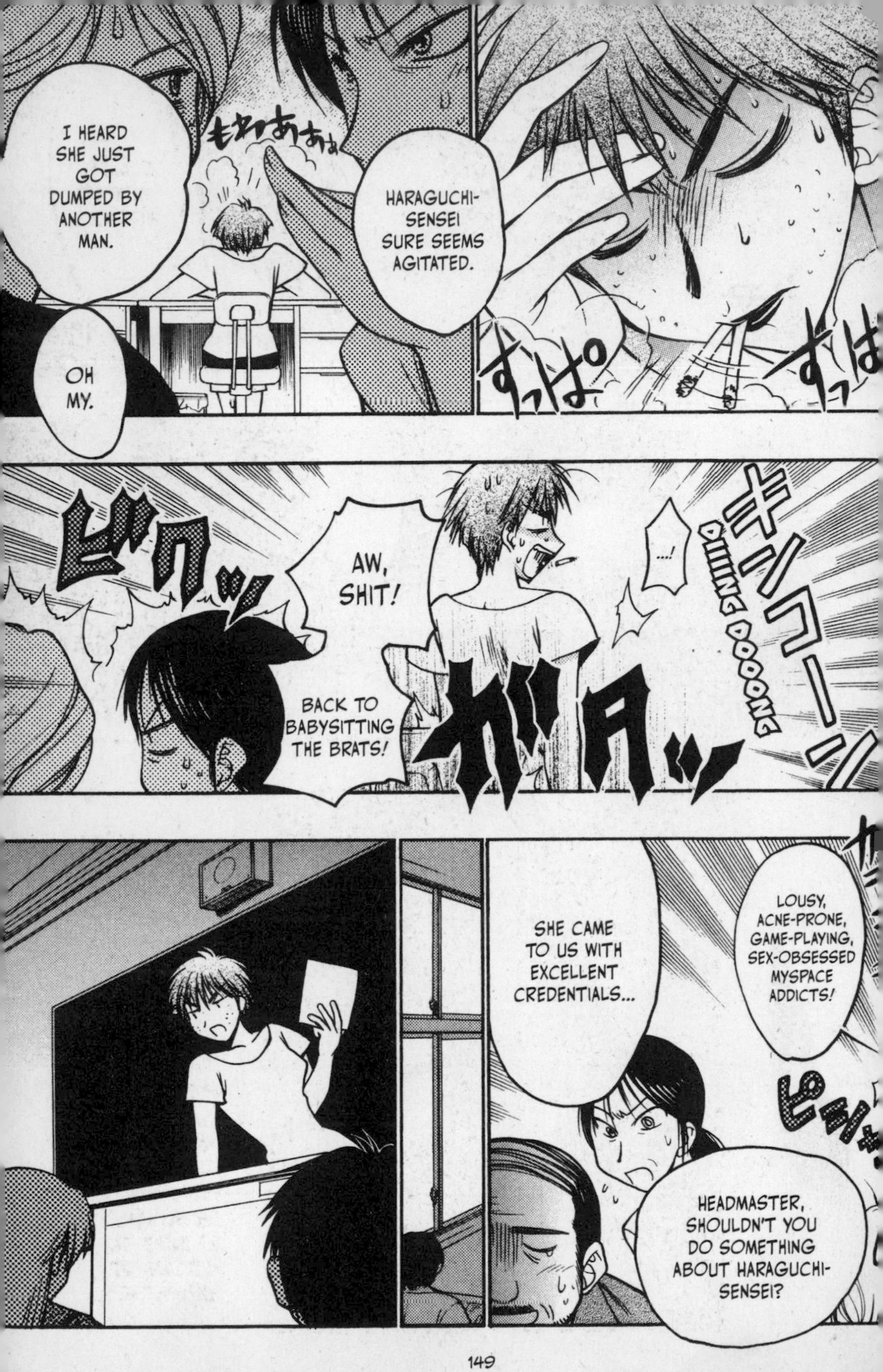
HARAGUCHI-SENSEI SURE SEEMS AGITATED.
I HEARD SHE JUST GOT DUMPED BY ANOTHER MAN.
OH MY.
...!
DIIIING DOOOONG
AW, SHIT!
BACK TO BABYSITTING THE BRATS!
LOUSY, ACNE-PRONE, GAME-PLAYING, SEX-OBSESSED MYSPACE ADDICTS!
SHE CAME TO US WITH EXCELLENT CREDENTIALS...
HEADMASTER, SHOULDN'T YOU DO SOMETHING ABOUT HARAGUCHI-SENSEI?

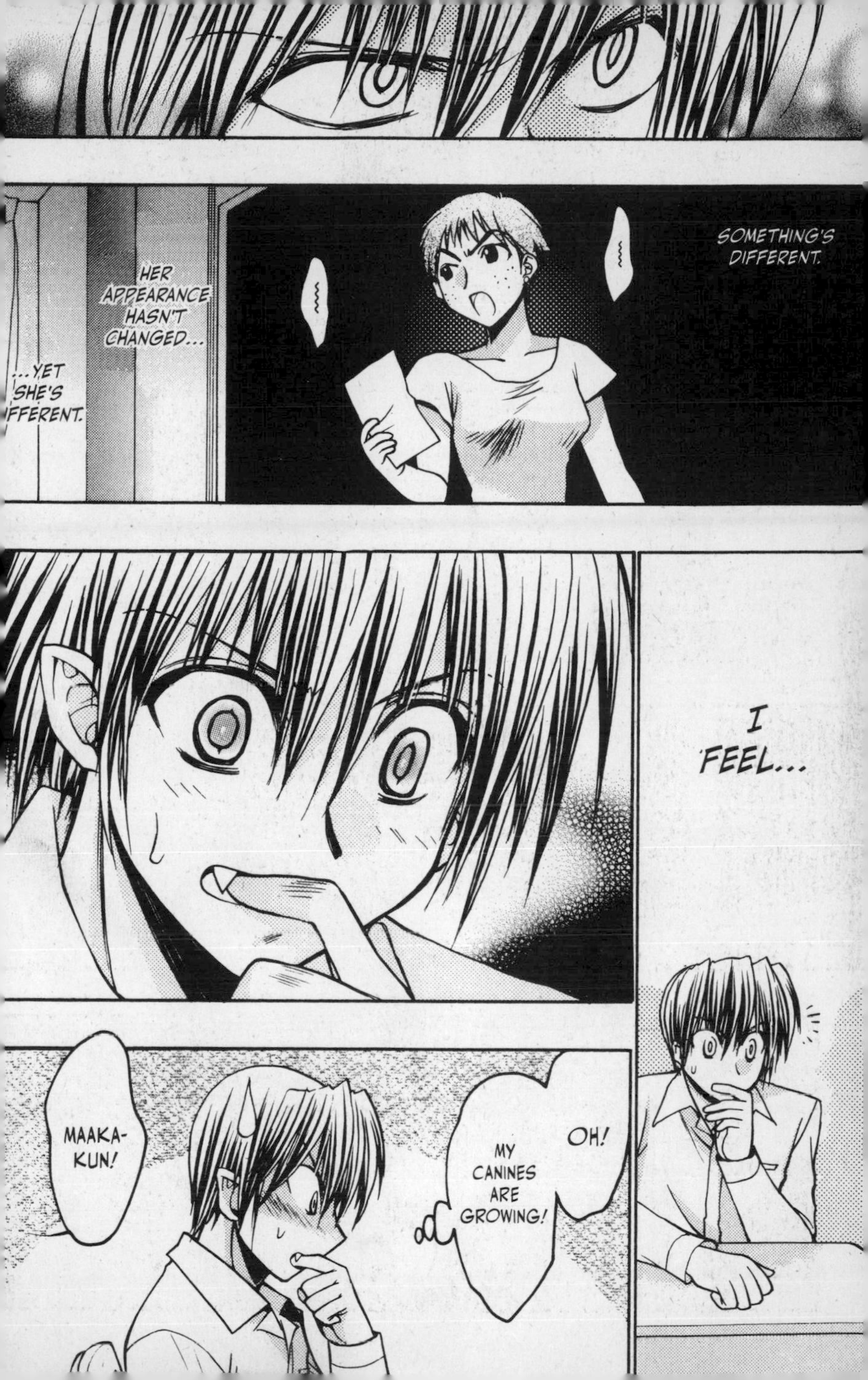
SOMETHING'S DIFFERENT.
HER APPEARANCE HASN'T CHANGED...
...YET SHE'S FFERENT.
I FEEL...
OH!
MY CANINES ARE GROWING!
MAAKA-KUN!

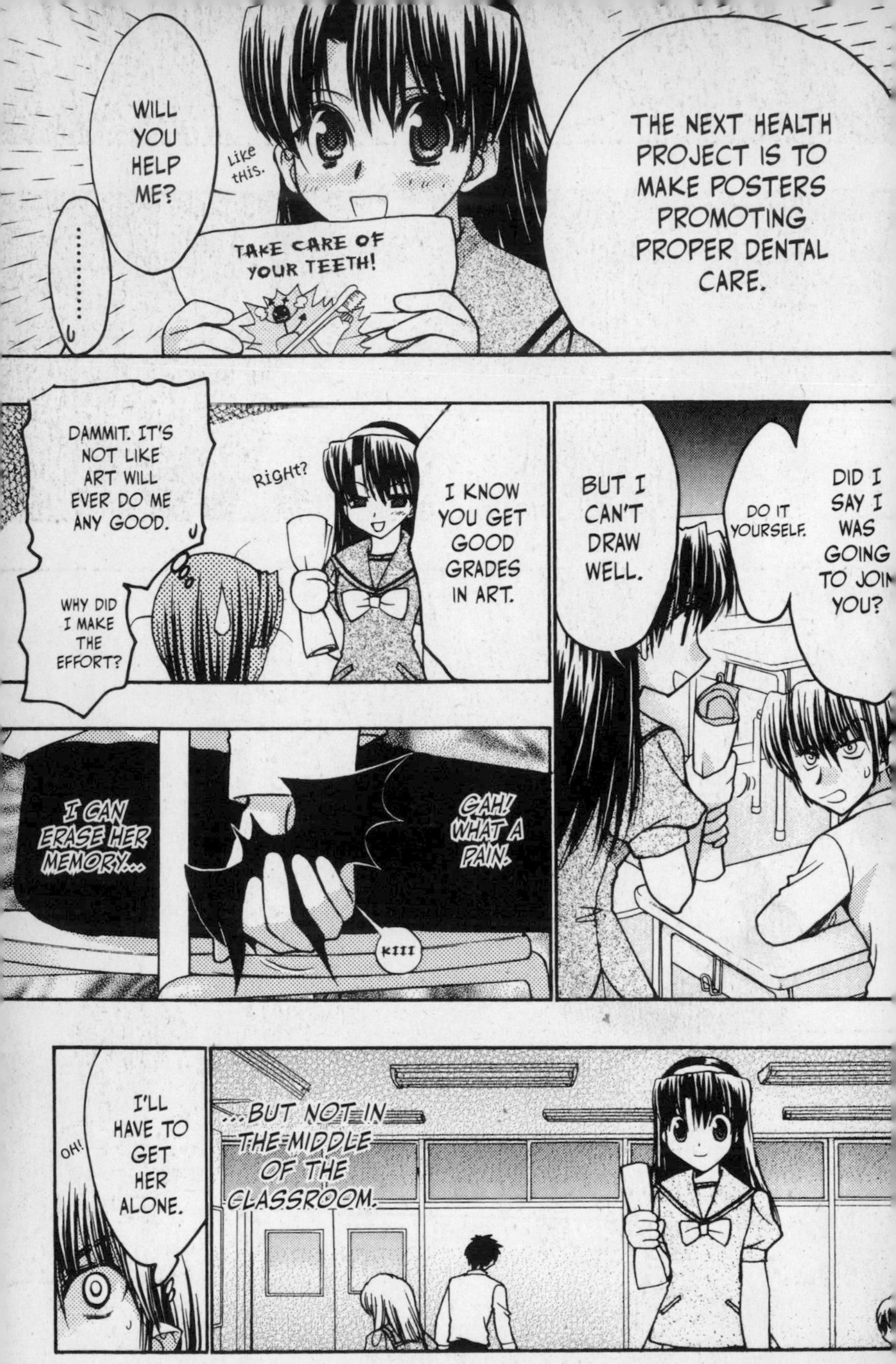

THE NEXT HEALTH PROJECT IS TO MAKE POSTERS PROMOTING PROPER DENTAL CARE.
WILL YOU HELP ME?
Like this.
TAKE CARE OF YOUR TEETH!
......
DID I SAY I WAS GOING TO JOIN YOU?
DO IT YOURSELF.
BUT I CAN'T DRAW WELL.
I KNOW YOU GET GOOD GRADES IN ART.
Right?
DAMMIT. IT'S NOT LIKE ART WILL EVER DO ME ANY GOOD.
WHY DID I MAKE THE EFFORT?
GAH! WHAT A PAIN.
KIII
I CAN ERASE HER MEMORY...
...BUT NOT IN THE MIDDLE OF THE CLASSROOM.
I'LL HAVE TO GET HER ALONE.
OH!

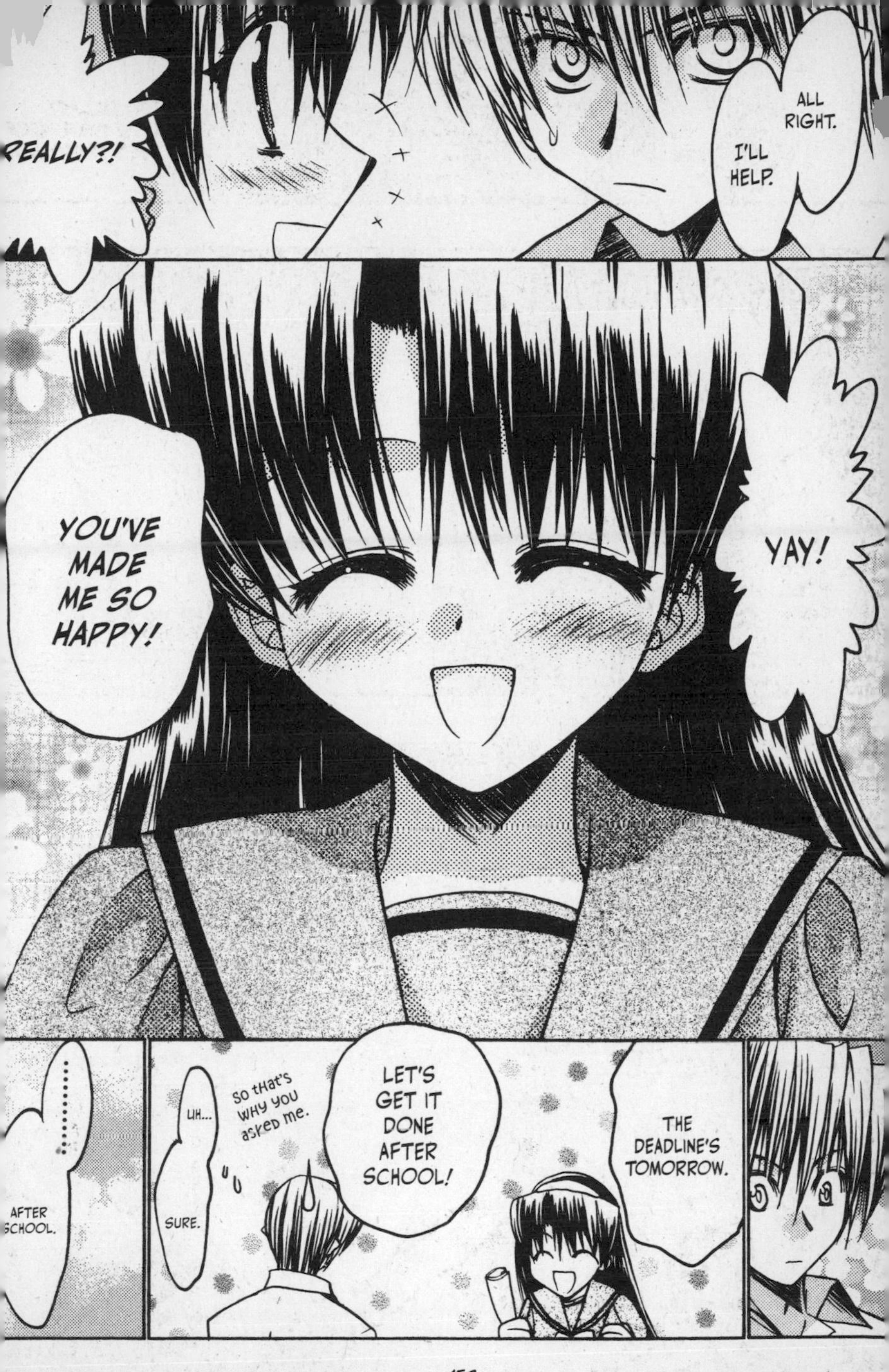
ALL RIGHT. I'LL HELP.
REALLY?!
YAY!
YOU'VE MADE ME SO HAPPY!
THE DEADLINE'S TOMORROW.
LET'S GET IT DONE AFTER SCHOOL!
So that's why you asked me.
UH... SURE.
......
AFTER SCHOOL.

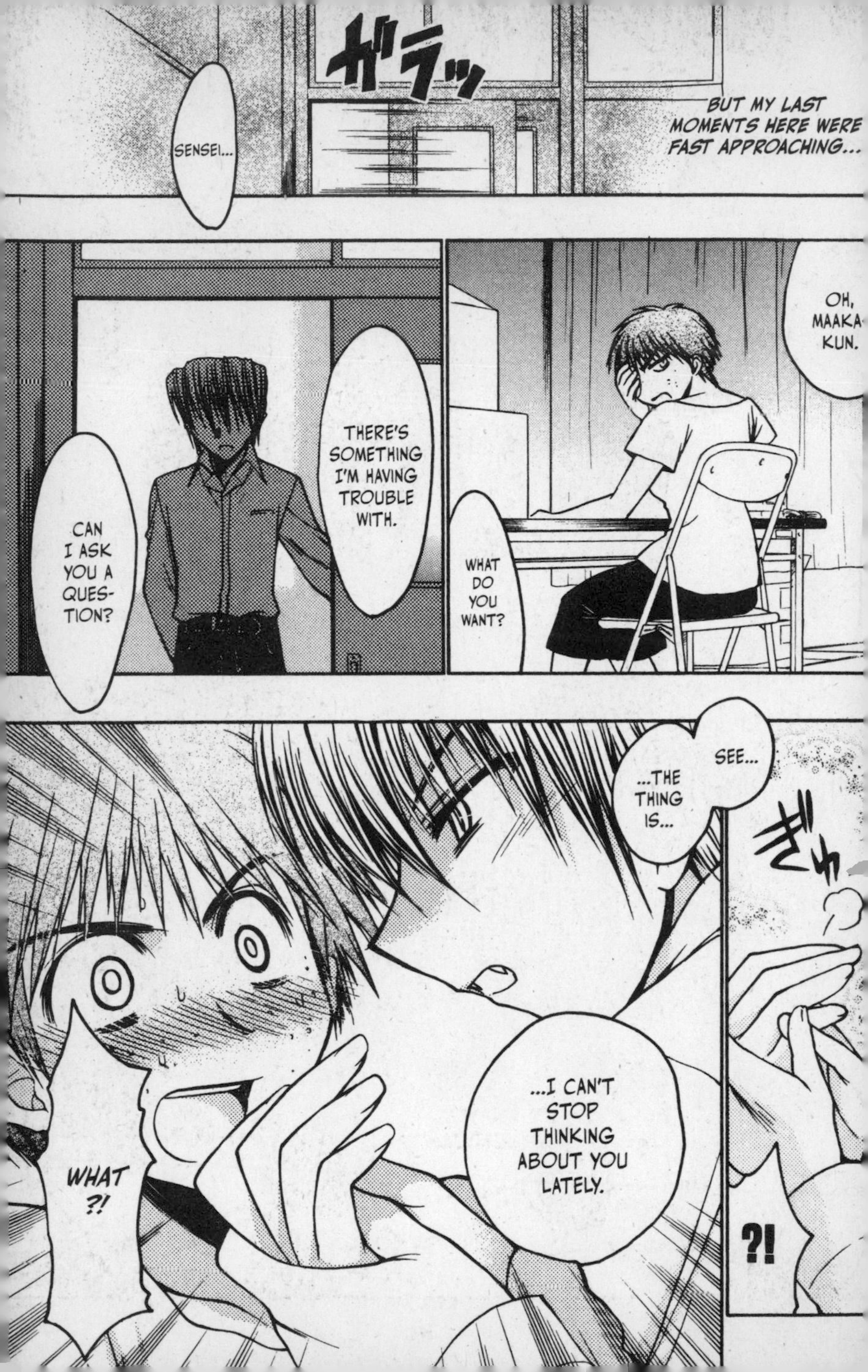
BUT MY LAST MOMENTS HERE WERE FAST APPROACHING...
ガラッ
SENSEI...
OH, MAAKA-KUN.
WHAT DO YOU WANT?
THERE'S SOMETHING I'M HAVING TROUBLE WITH.
CAN I ASK YOU A QUESTION?
ぎゅ
?!
SEE...
...THE THING IS...
...I CAN'T STOP THINKING ABOUT YOU LATELY.
WHAT ?!

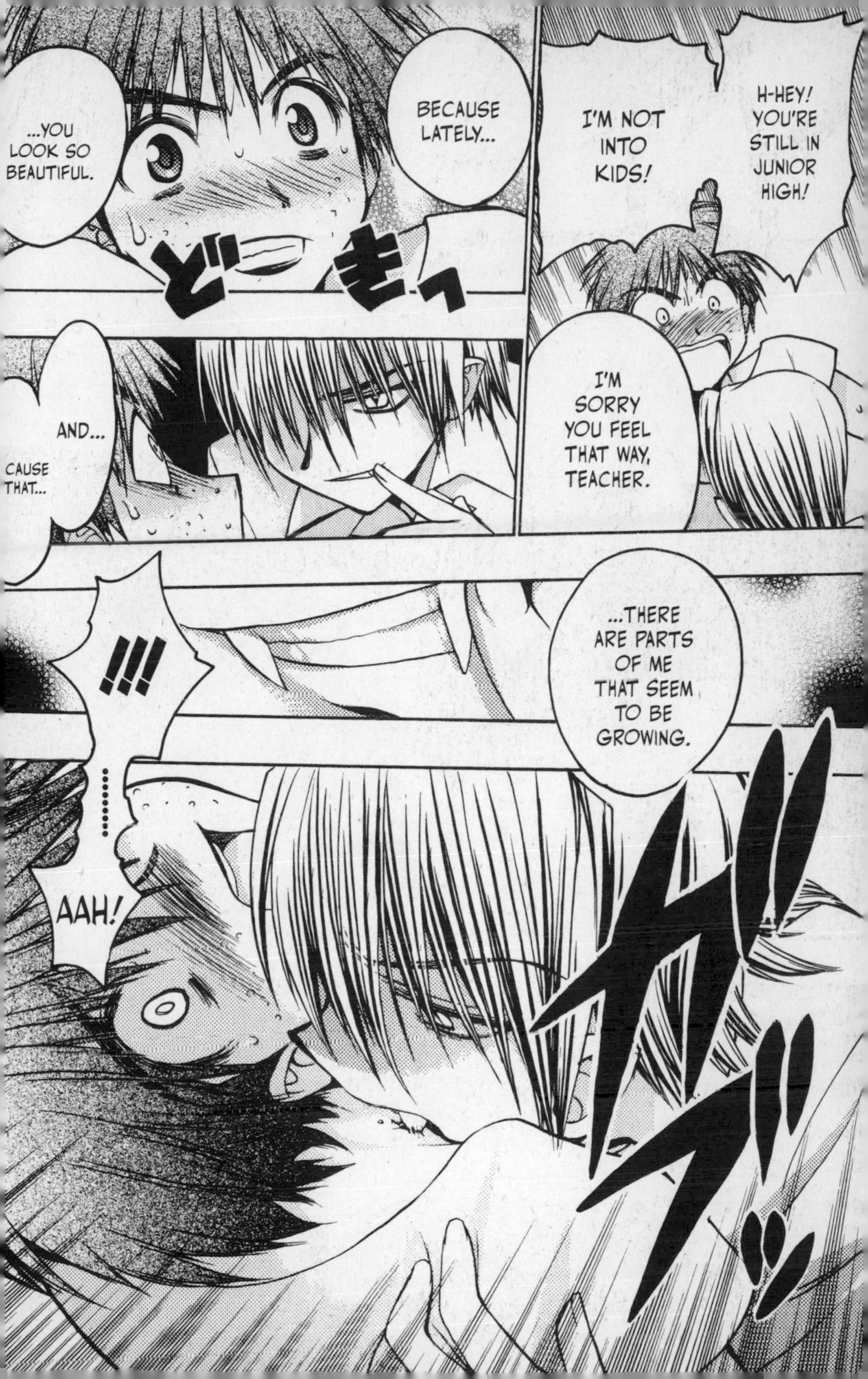
H-HEY! YOU'RE STILL IN JUNIOR HIGH!
I'M NOT INTO KIDS!
I'M SORRY YOU FEEL THAT WAY, TEACHER.
BECAUSE LATELY...
...YOU LOOK SO BEAUTIFUL.
どきっ
AND...
CAUSE THAT...
...THERE ARE PARTS OF ME THAT SEEM TO BE GROWING.
!!!
......
AAH!

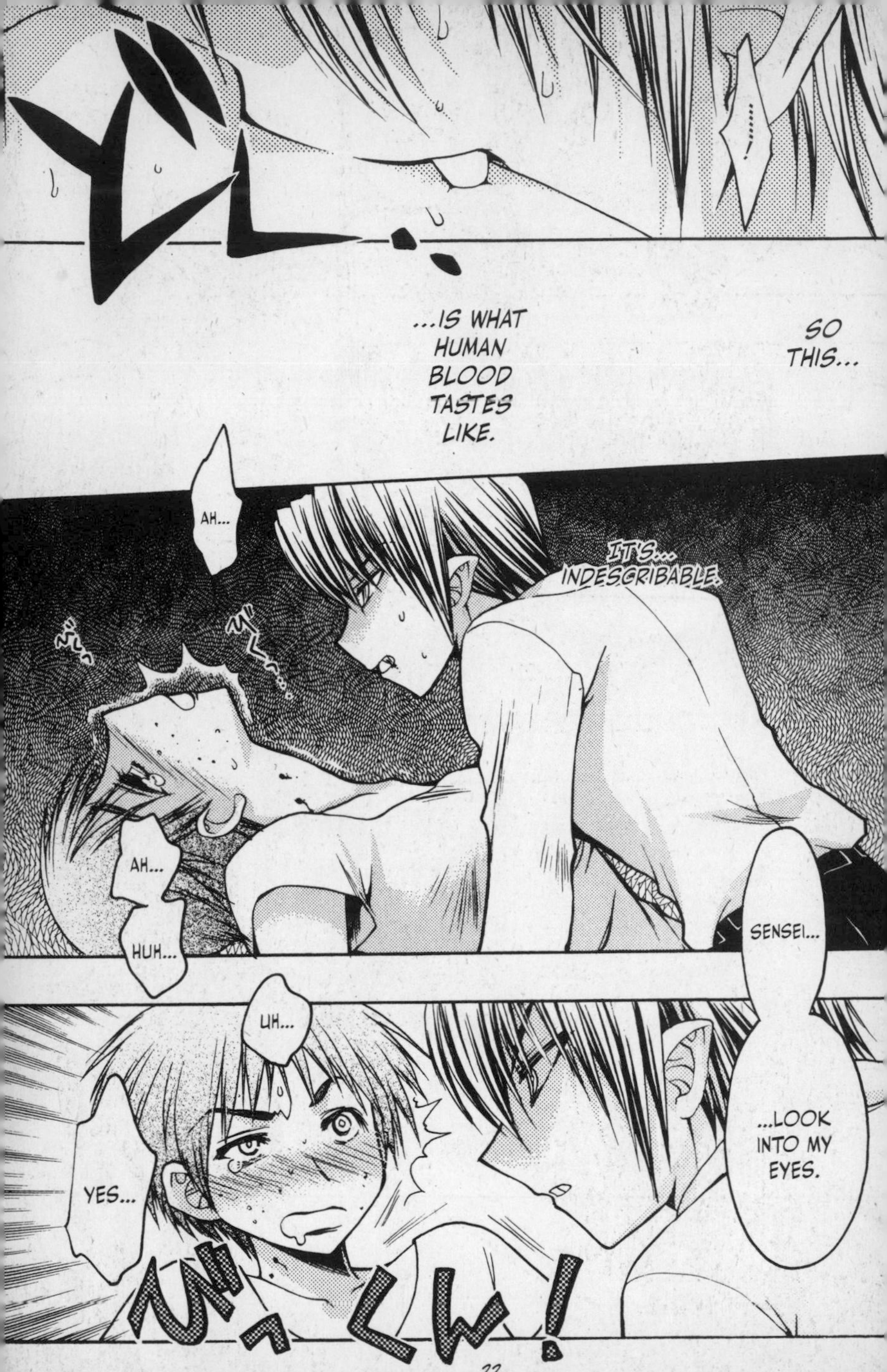
SO THIS...
...IS WHAT HUMAN BLOOD TASTES LIKE.
IT'S... INDESCRIBABLE.
AH...
AH...
HUH...
SENSEI...
...LOOK INTO MY EYES.
UH...
YES...

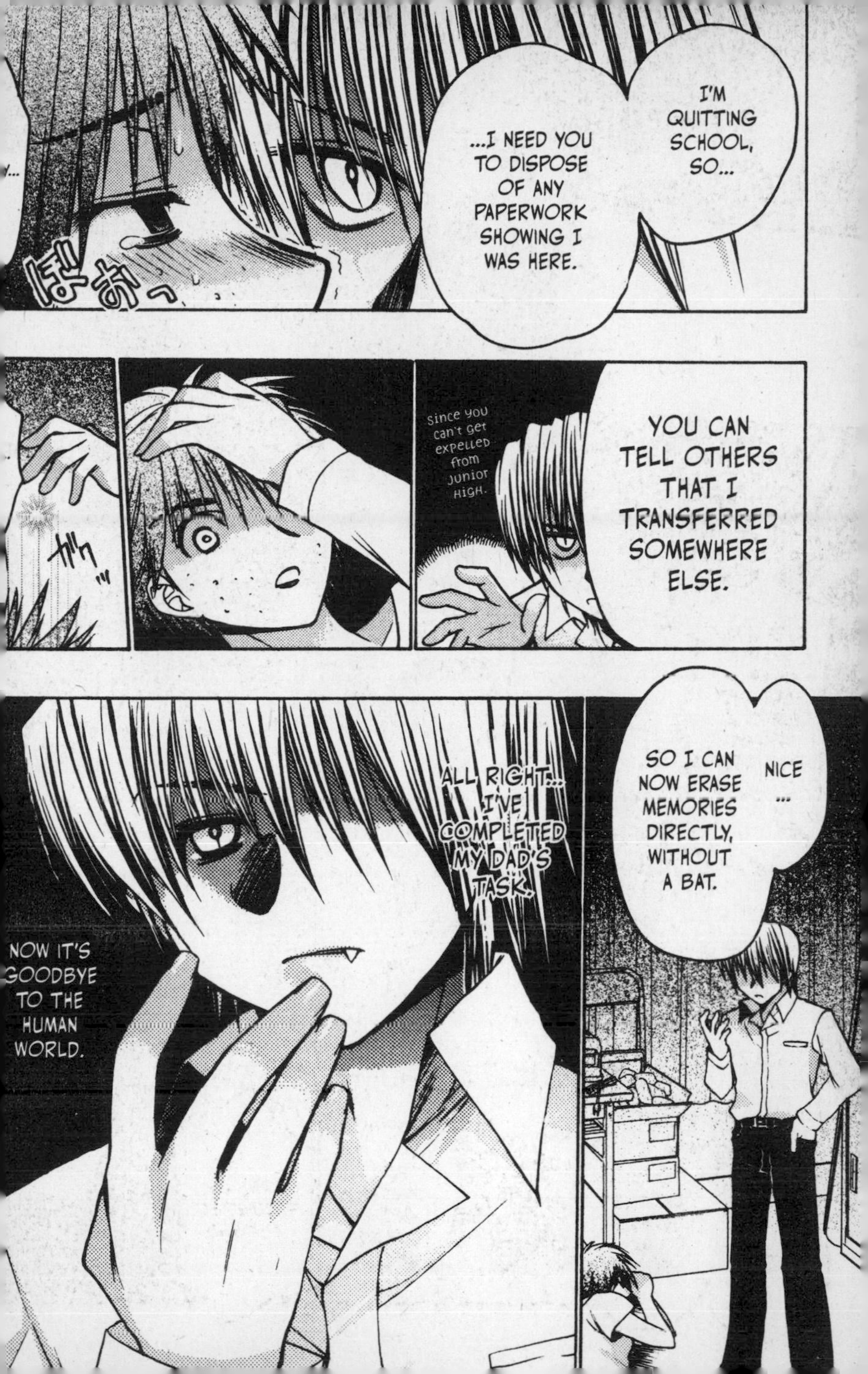
I'M QUITTING SCHOOL, SO...
...I NEED YOU TO DISPOSE OF ANY PAPERWORK SHOWING I WAS HERE.
YOU CAN TELL OTHERS THAT I TRANSFERRED SOMEWHERE ELSE.
Since you can't get expelled from junior high.
NICE ...
SO I CAN NOW ERASE MEMORIES DIRECTLY, WITHOUT A BAT.
ALL RIGHT... I'VE COMPLETED MY DAD'S TASK.
NOW IT'S GOODBYE TO THE HUMAN WORLD.

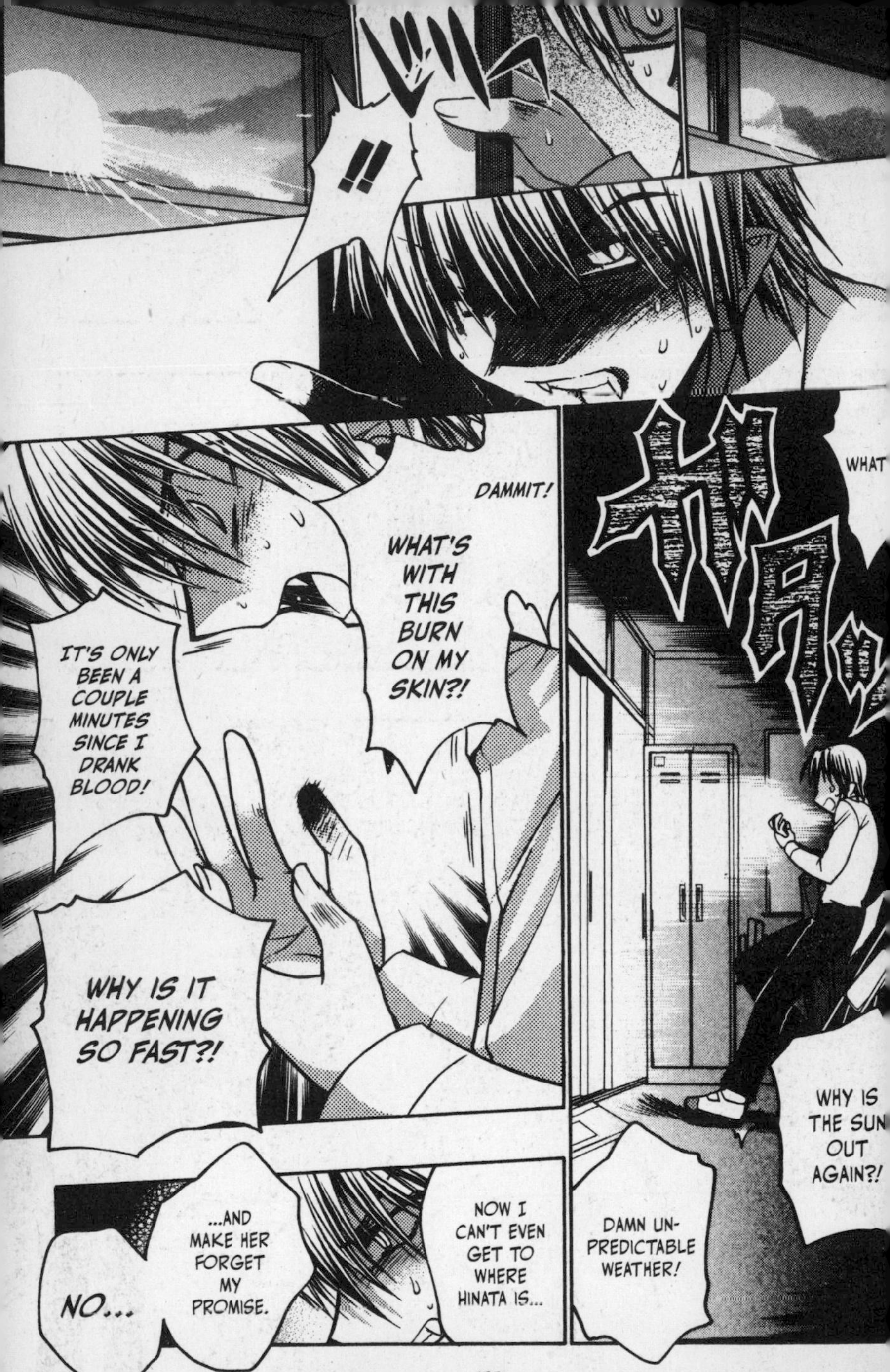
!!
WHAT
WHY IS THE SUN OUT AGAIN?!
DAMN UN-PREDICTABLE WEATHER!
DAMMIT!
WHAT'S WITH THIS BURN ON MY SKIN?!
IT'S ONLY BEEN A COUPLE MINUTES SINCE I DRANK BLOOD!
WHY IS IT HAPPENING SO FAST?!
NOW I CAN'T EVEN GET TO WHERE HINATA IS...
...AND MAKE HER FORGET MY PROMISE.
NO...

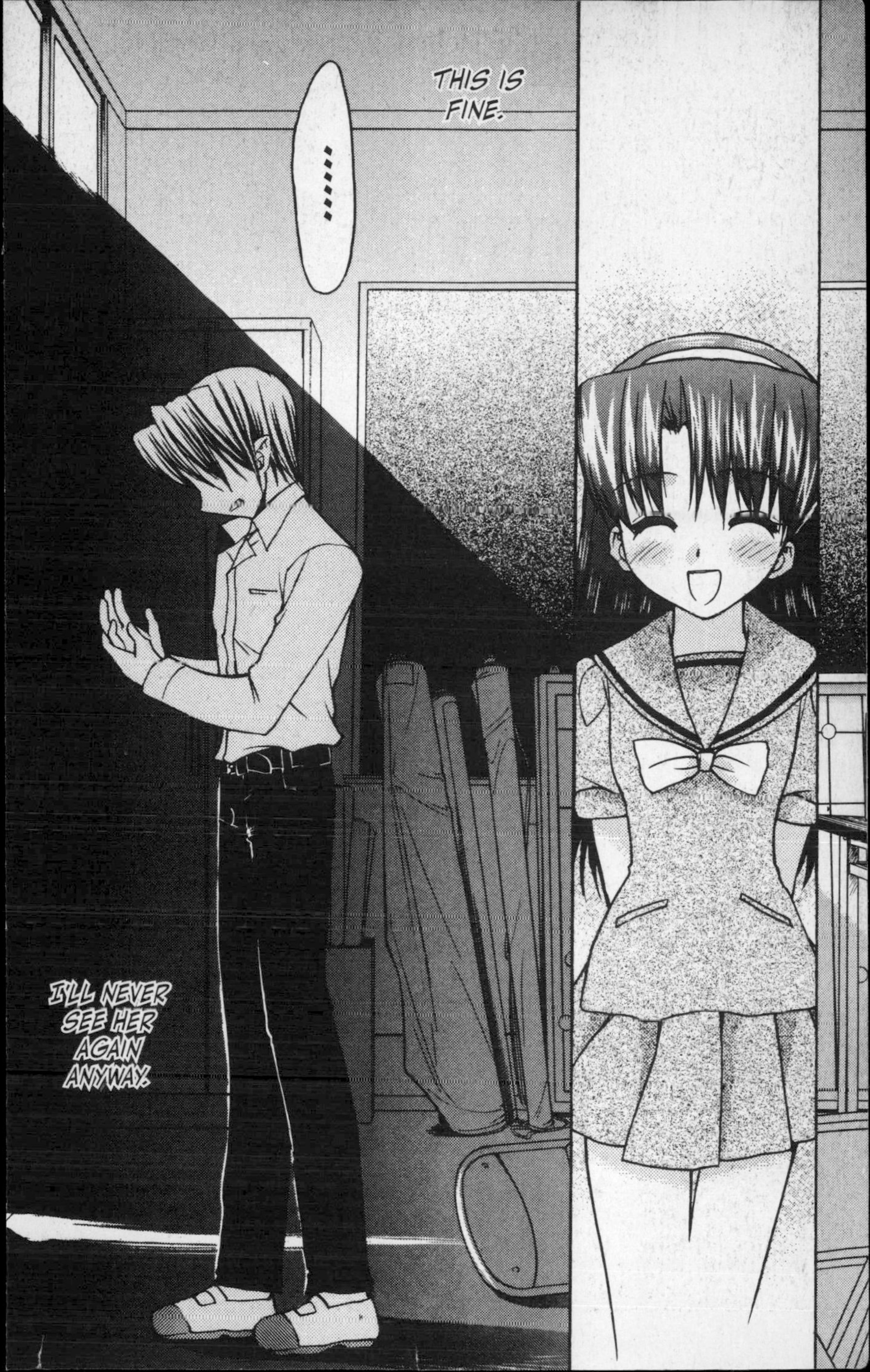
THIS IS FINE.
......
I'LL NEVER SEE HER AGAIN ANYWAY.

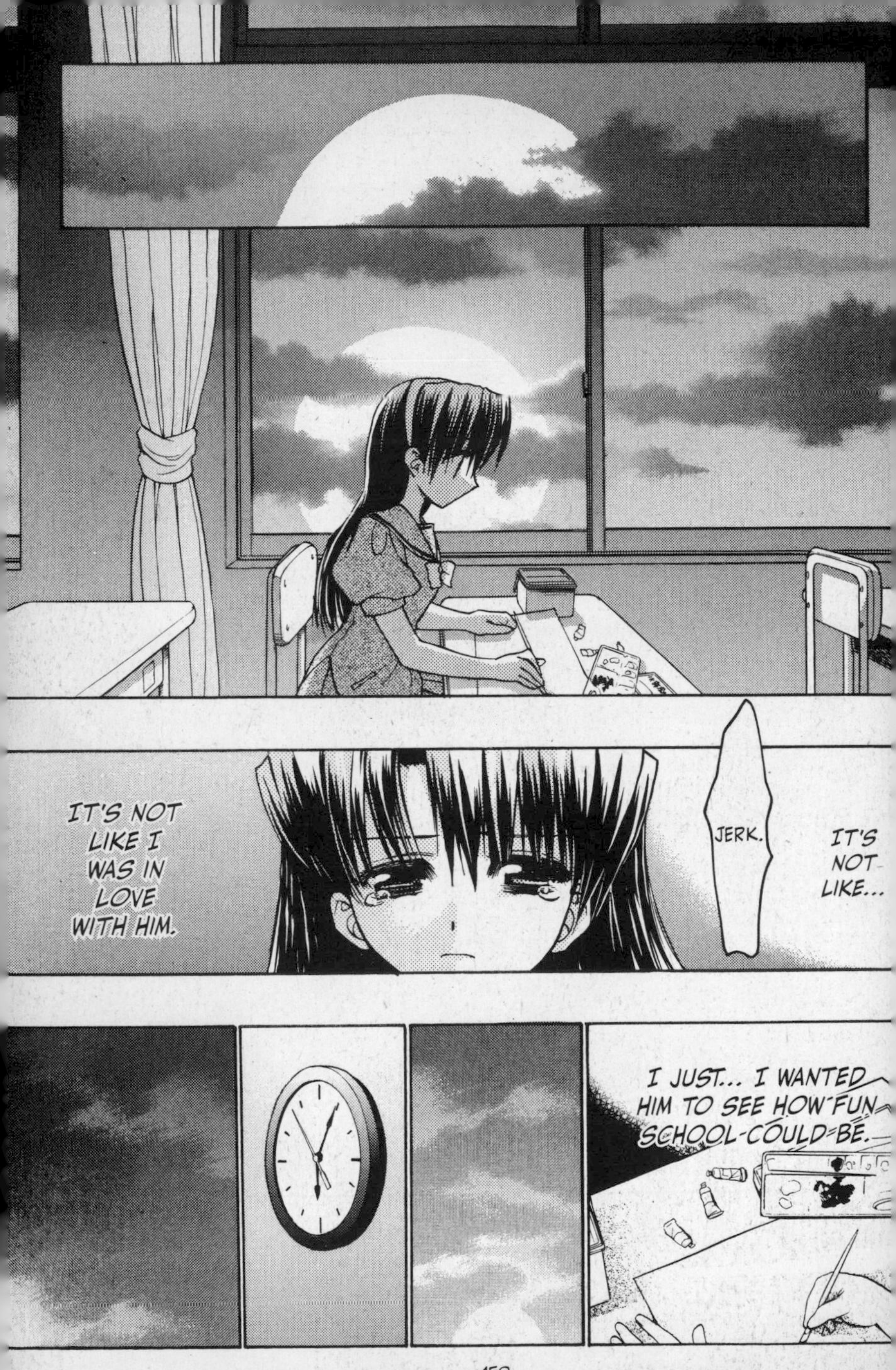
IT'S NOT LIKE...
JERK.
IT'S NOT LIKE I WAS IN LOVE WITH HIM.
I JUST... I WANTED HIM TO SEE HOW FUN SCHOOL COULD BE.

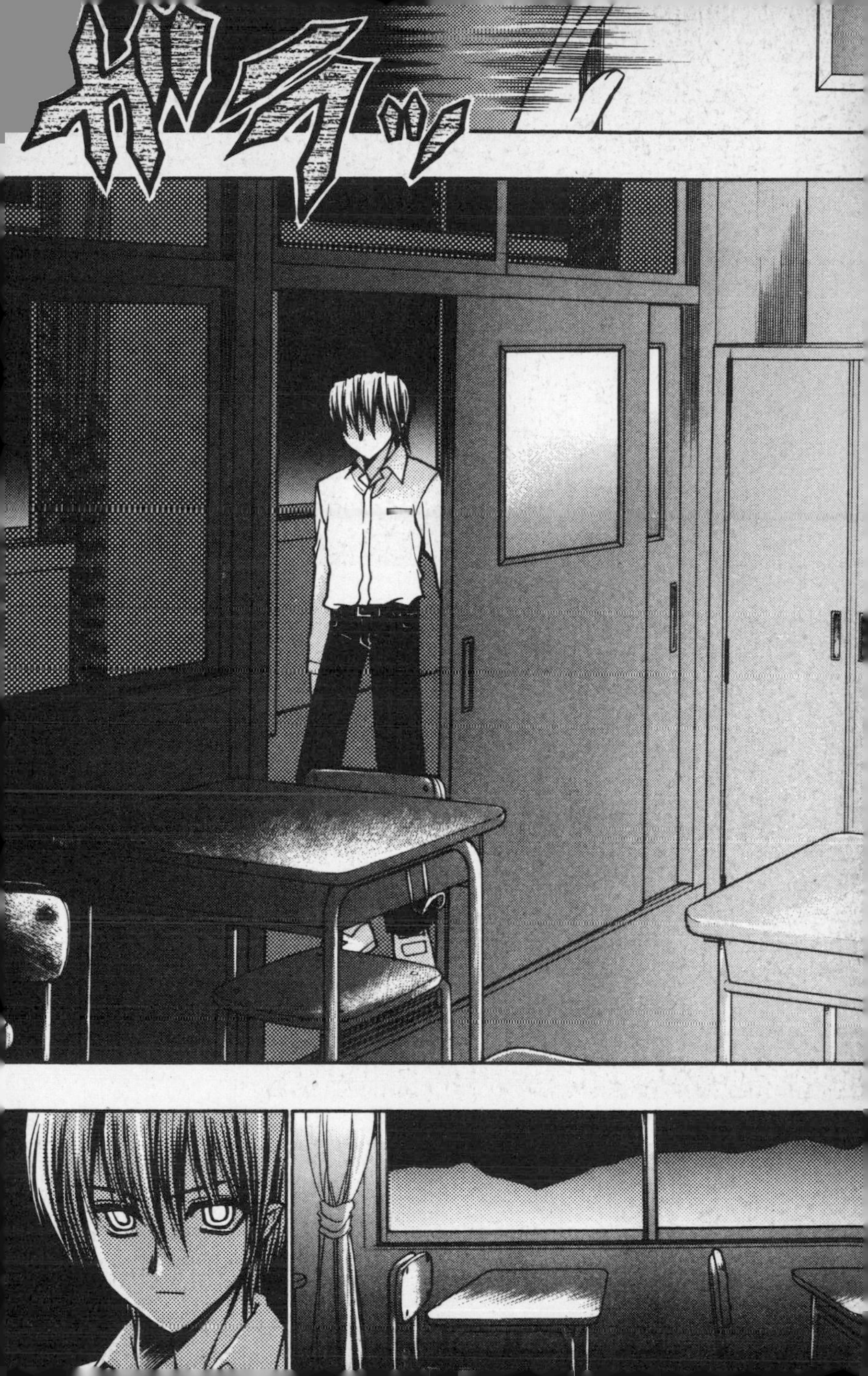

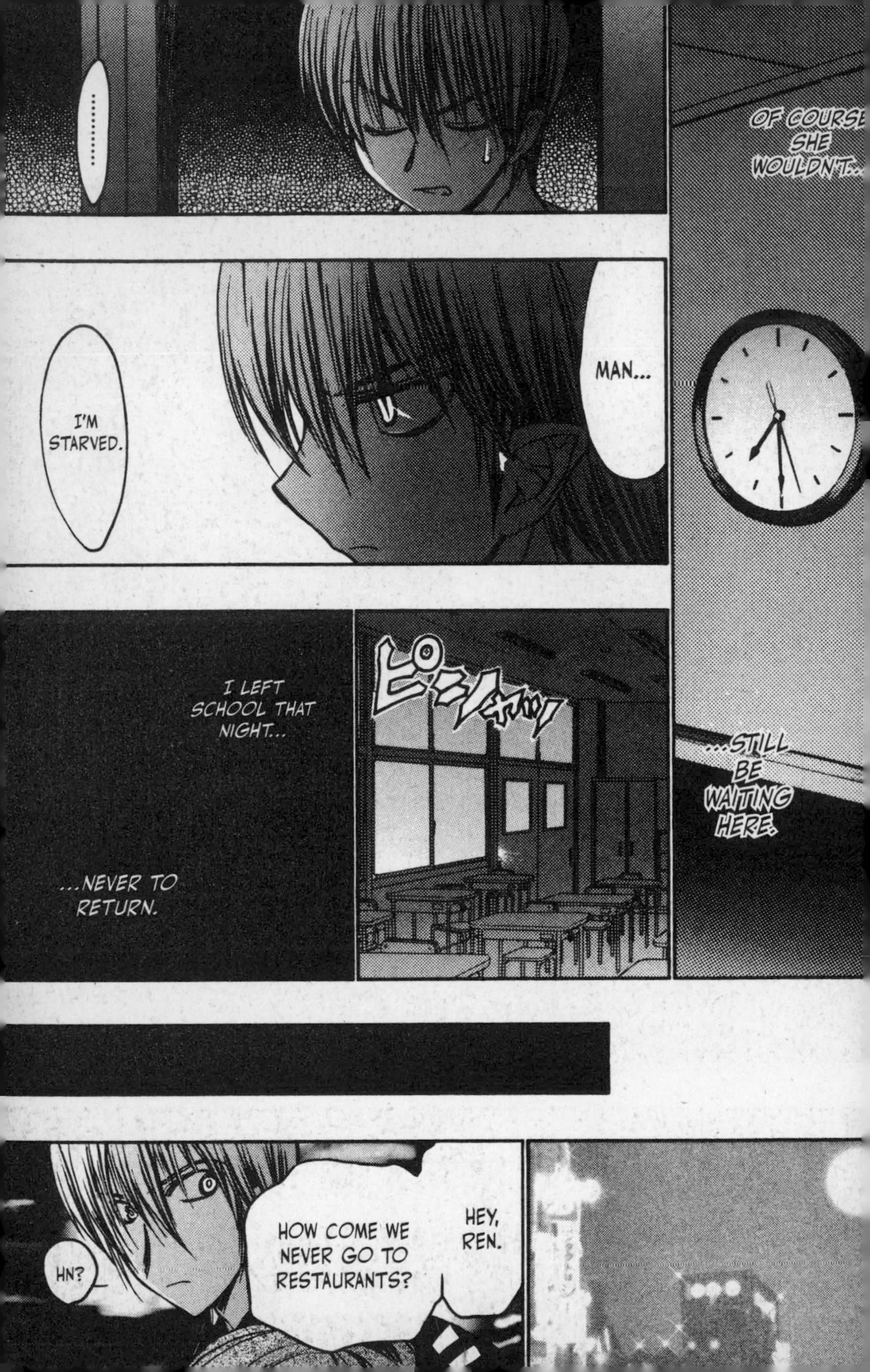
OF COURSE SHE WOULDN'T...
...STILL BE WAITING HERE.
......
MAN...
I'M STARVED.
I LEFT SCHOOL THAT NIGHT...
...NEVER TO RETURN.
HEY, REN.
HOW COME WE NEVER GO TO RESTAURANTS?
HN?

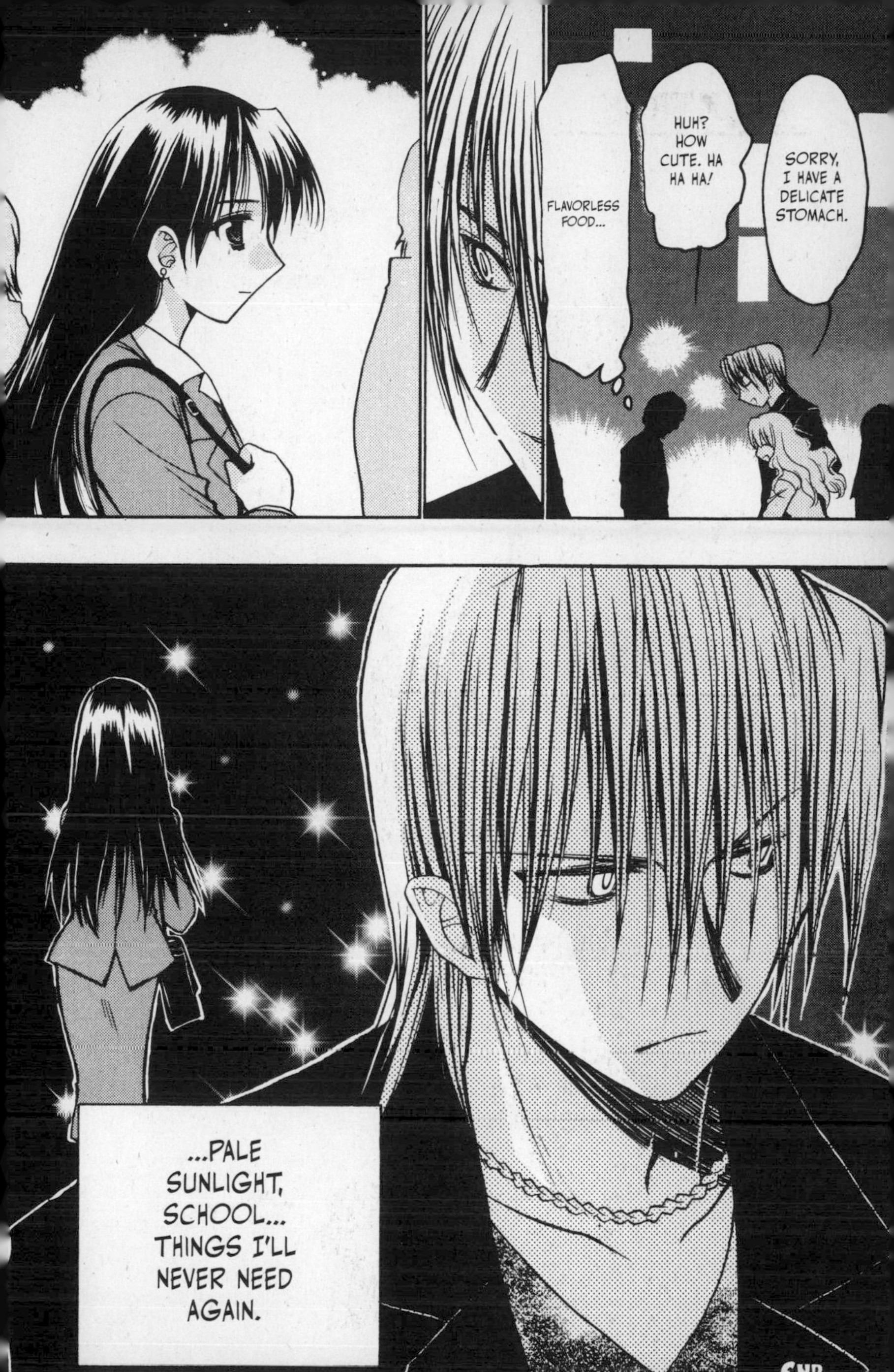
SORRY, I HAVE A DELICATE STOMACH.
HUH? HOW CUTE. HA HA HA!
FLAVORLESS FOOD...
...PALE SUNLIGHT, SCHOOL... THINGS I'LL NEVER NEED AGAIN.
END

# EXTRAS

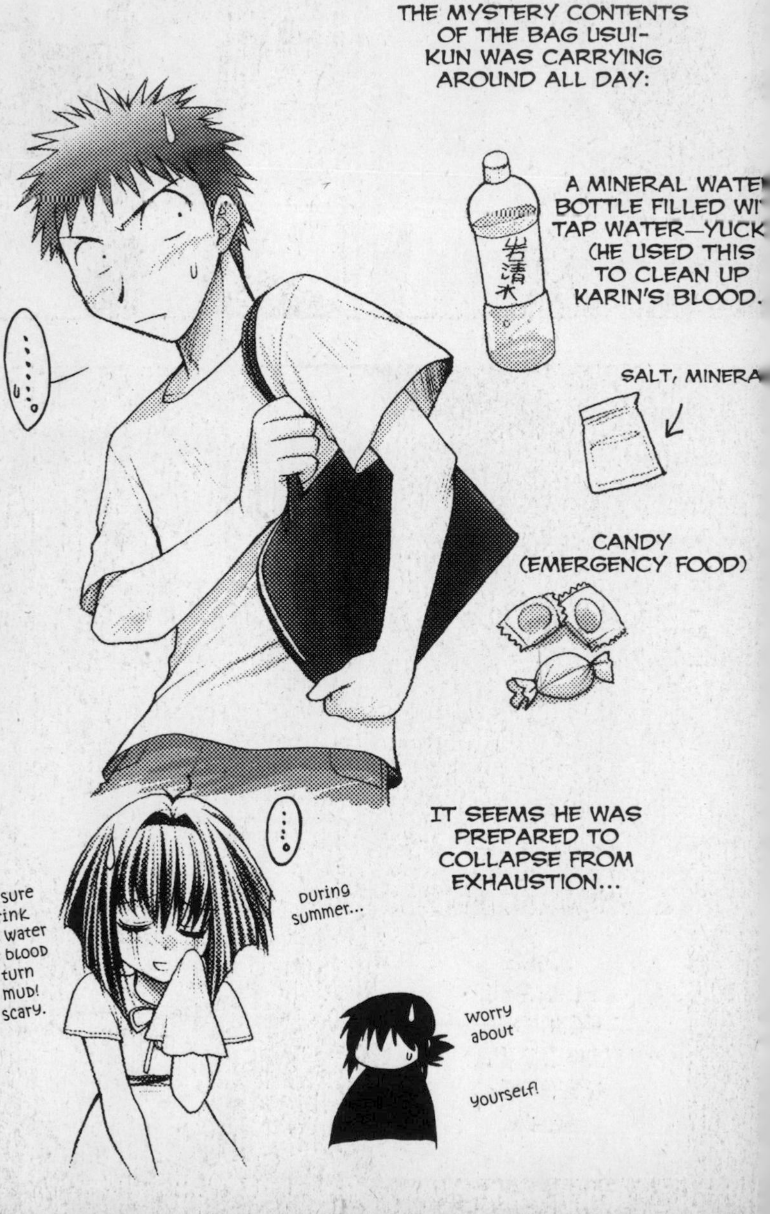
THE MYSTERY CONTENTS OF THE BAG USUI-KUN WAS CARRYING AROUND ALL DAY:
A MINERAL WATE
BOTTLE FILLED WI
TAP WATER—YUCK
(HE USED THIS TO CLEAN UP KARIN'S BLOOD.
岩清水
SALT, MINERA
CANDY (EMERGENCY FOOD)
......
IT SEEMS HE WAS PREPARED TO COLLAPSE FROM EXHAUSTION...
...
During summer...
...make sure you drink enough water or your blood will turn into mud! How scary.
Worry about
yourself!

## SUPER FAN

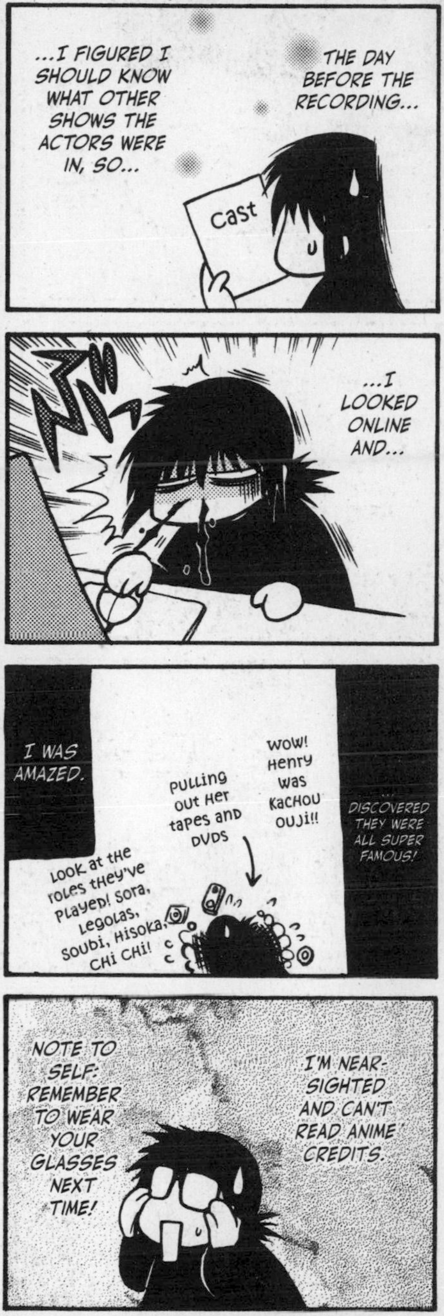
THE DAY BEFORE THE RECORDING...
...I FIGURED I SHOULD KNOW WHAT OTHER SHOWS THE ACTORS WERE IN, SO...
Cast
...I LOOKED ONLINE AND...
...DISCOVERED THEY WERE ALL SUPER FAMOUS!
WOW! Henry was KACHOU OUJI!!
Pulling out her tapes and DVDs
I WAS AMAZED.
Look at the roles they've played! Sora, Legolas, Soubi, Hisoka, Chi Chi!
I'M NEAR-SIGHTED AND CAN'T READ ANIME CREDITS.
NOTE TO SELF: REMEMBER TO WEAR YOUR GLASSES NEXT TIME!

The voices match the characters perfectly!

## CREEPY MATCH

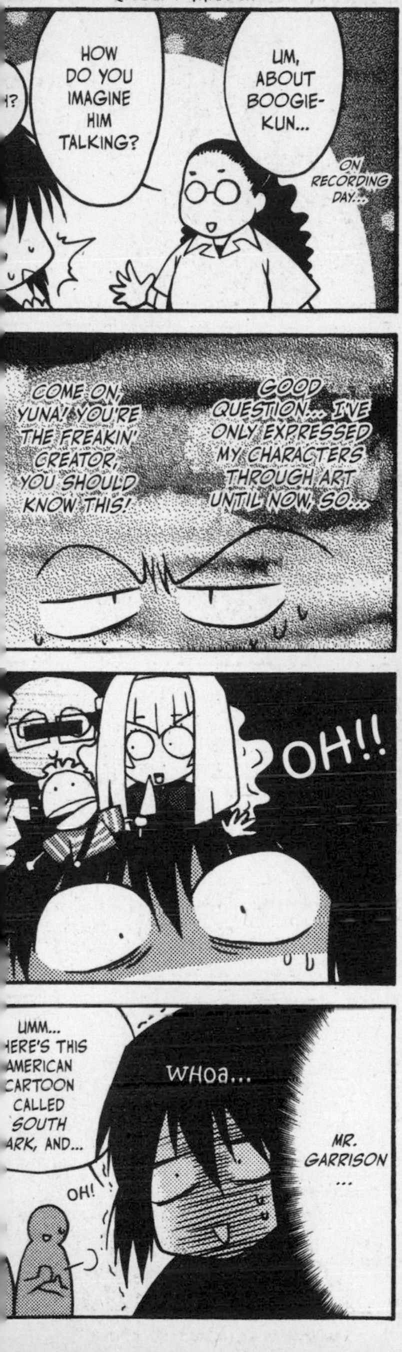
ON RECORDING DAY...
UM, ABOUT BOOGIE-KUN...
HOW DO YOU IMAGINE HIM TALKING?
GOOD QUESTION... I'VE ONLY EXPRESSED MY CHARACTERS THROUGH ART UNTIL NOW, SO...
COME ON, YUNA! YOU'RE THE FREAKIN' CREATOR, YOU SHOULD KNOW THIS!
OH!!
MR. GARRISON ...
WHOa...
UMM... HERE'S THIS AMERICAN CARTOON CALLED SOUTH ARK, AND...
OH!

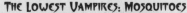

## Funny, but Unlikely

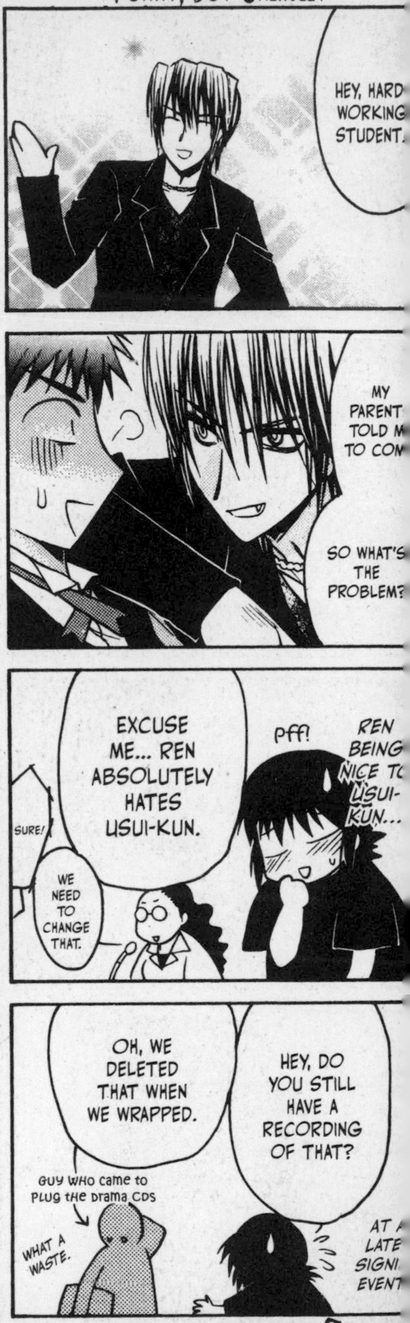
HEY, HARD WORKING STUDENT.
MY PARENT TOLD M TO COM
SO WHAT'S THE PROBLEM?
REN BEING NICE TC USUI-KUN...
Pff!
EXCUSE ME... REN ABSOLUTELY HATES USUI-KUN.
SURE!
WE NEED TO CHANGE THAT.
HEY, DO YOU STILL HAVE A RECORDING OF THAT?
AT LATE SIGNI EVENT
OH, WE DELETED THAT WHEN WE WRAPPED.
Guy who came to plug the drama CDs
WHAT A WASTE.

Wanted to listen to it in private.

## The Lowest Vampires: Mosquitoes

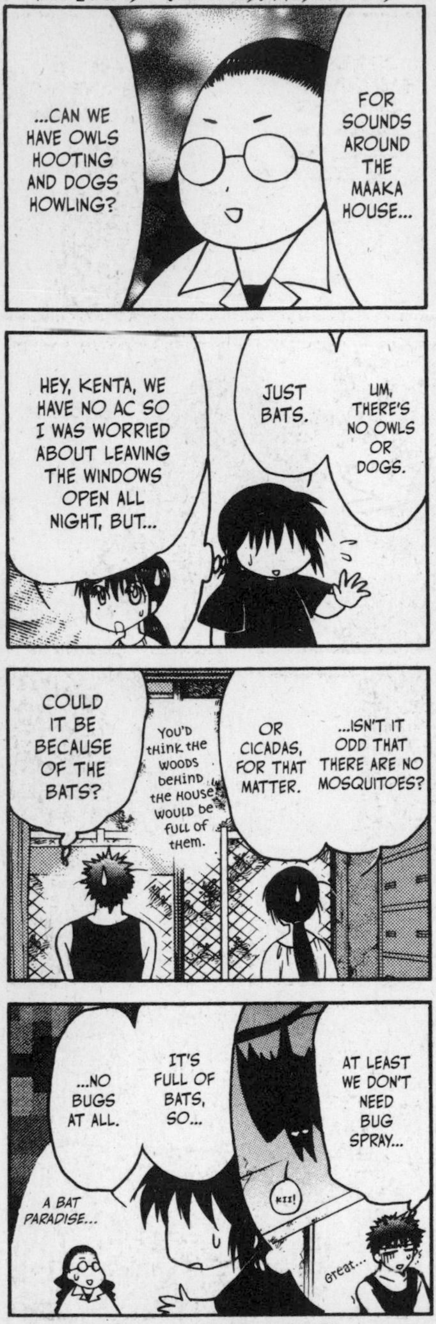
FOR SOUNDS AROUND THE MAAKA HOUSE...
...CAN WE HAVE OWLS HOOTING AND DOGS HOWLING?
UM, THERE'S NO OWLS OR DOGS.
JUST BATS.
HEY, KENTA, WE HAVE NO AC SO I WAS WORRIED ABOUT LEAVING THE WINDOWS OPEN ALL NIGHT, BUT...
...ISN'T IT ODD THAT THERE ARE NO MOSQUITOES?
OR CICADAS, FOR THAT MATTER.
You'd think the woods behind the house would be full of them.
COULD IT BE BECAUSE OF THE BATS?
AT LEAST WE DON'T NEED BUG SPRAY...
IT'S FULL OF BATS, SO...
...NO BUGS AT ALL.
KII!
Great...
A BAT PARADISE...

See you in Volume 5!

# IN OUR NEXT VOLUME...

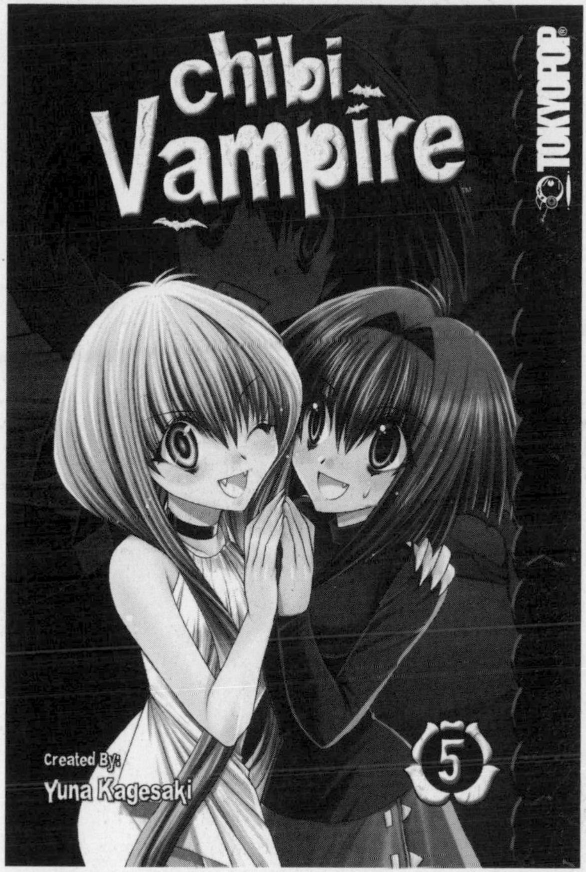
chibi Vampire
TM
TOKYOPOP
Created By:
Yuna Kagesaki
5

KARIN CONTINUES TO COME TO TERMS WITH HER FEELINGS FOR KENTA, BUT HER FLIRTING WILL HAVE TO BE PUT ON HOLD FOR NOW. KARIN'S GRANDMOTHER IS IN TOWN, AND THAT'S ENOUGH TO PUT HER ENTIRE FAMILY INTO A PANIC. ELDA MARKER IS NO SILVER-HAIRED, COOKIE-BAKING MATRIARCH. SHE'S A HOT AND HEAVY VAMPIRE VIXEN WITH A TASTE FOR BLOOD, BUT A DISTASTE FOR EVERYTHING ELSE HAVING TO DO WITH THE HUMAN RACE. SO HOW CAN KARIN POSSIBLY TELL HER ABOUT HER NEW HUMAN FRIEND? IT'S GOING TO BE ONE FREAKY FAMILY REUNION THAT YOU'RE NOT GOING TO WANT TO MISS!

# FOOD

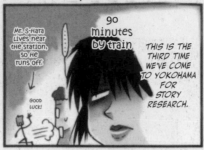

THIS IS THE THIRD TIME WE'VE COME TO YOKOHAMA FOR STORY RESEARCH.
90 minutes by train
Mr. S-Hara lives near the station, so he runs off.
GOOD LUCK!
THE GREAT YOKO-HAMA
WE IGNORE ALL SIGHTS AND RUN DOWN THE STAIRS.
THEY HAVE THE BEST STEAKS IN TOWN HERE!!
はあ はあ
KAGESAKI-SAN, DID WE COME HERE SO YOU COULD EAT?
Had to run to keep up with her.
CAN WE COME HERE FOR "RESEARCH" AGAIN NEXT MONTH?
ガタン ゴトトン
I SUP-POSE ...
THE TRAIN RIDE'S EXPEN-SIVE, TOO.

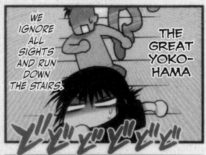

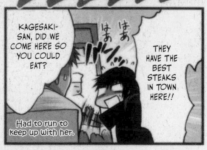

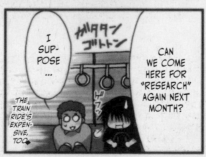

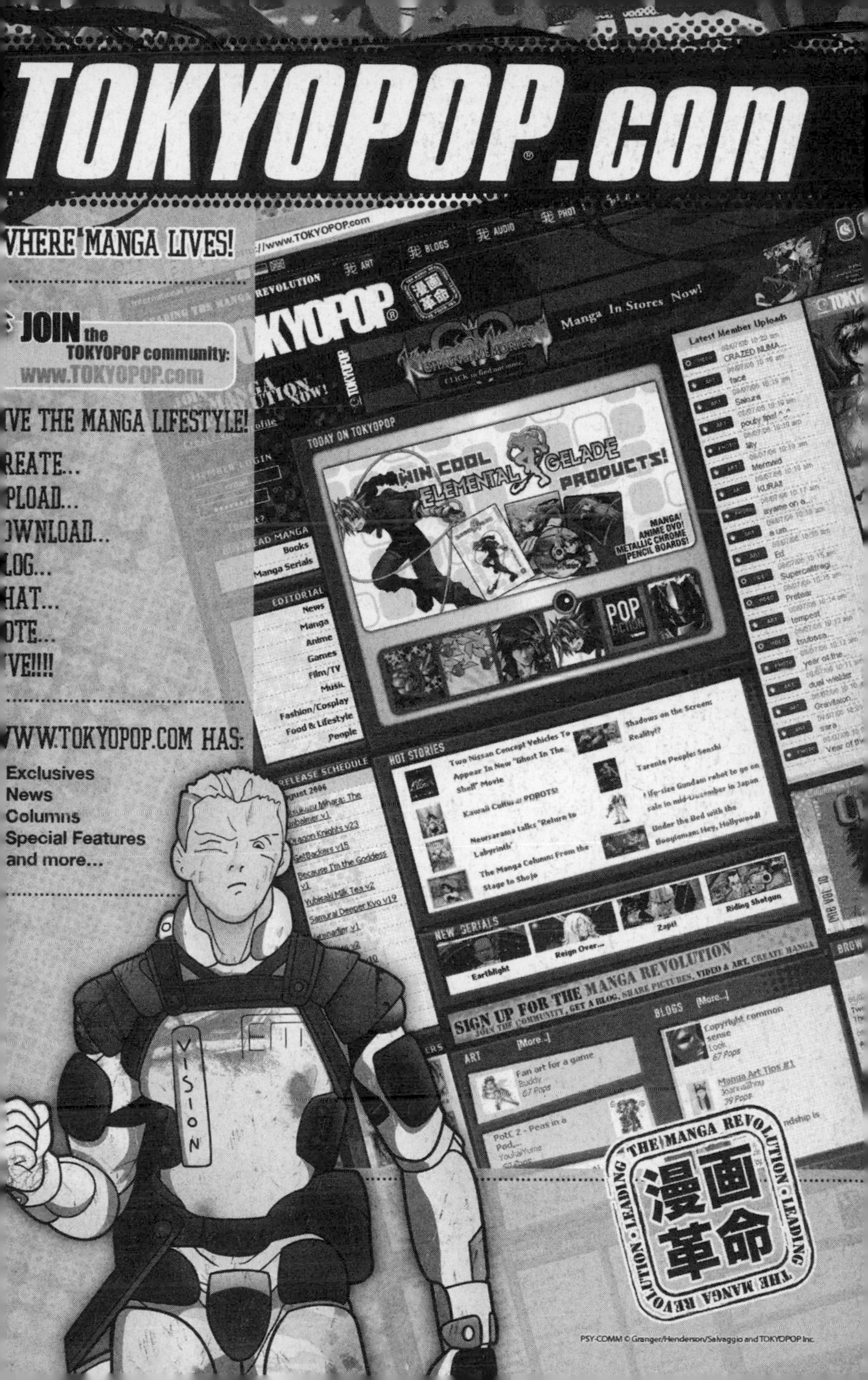

TOKYOPOP.com
VHERE MANGA LIVES!
JOIN the TOKYOPOP community:
www.TOKYOPOP.com
IVE THE MANGA LIFESTYLE!
REATE...
PLOAD...
OWNLOAD...
LOG...
HAT...
OTE...
IVE!!!!
VWW.TOKYOPOP.COM HAS:
Exclusives
News
Columns
Special Features
and more...
WIN COOL ELEMENTAL GELADE PRODUCTS!
MANGA! ANIME DVD! METALLIC CHROME PENCIL BOARDS!
Manga In Stores Now!
Latest Member Uploads
TODAY ON TOKYOPOP
HOT STORIES
NEW SERIALS
SIGN UP FOR THE MANGA REVOLUTION
THE MANGA REVOLUTION · LEADING · THE MANGA REVOLUTION · LEADING
漫画革命
PSY-COMM © Granger/Henderson/Salvaggio and TOKYOPOP Inc.

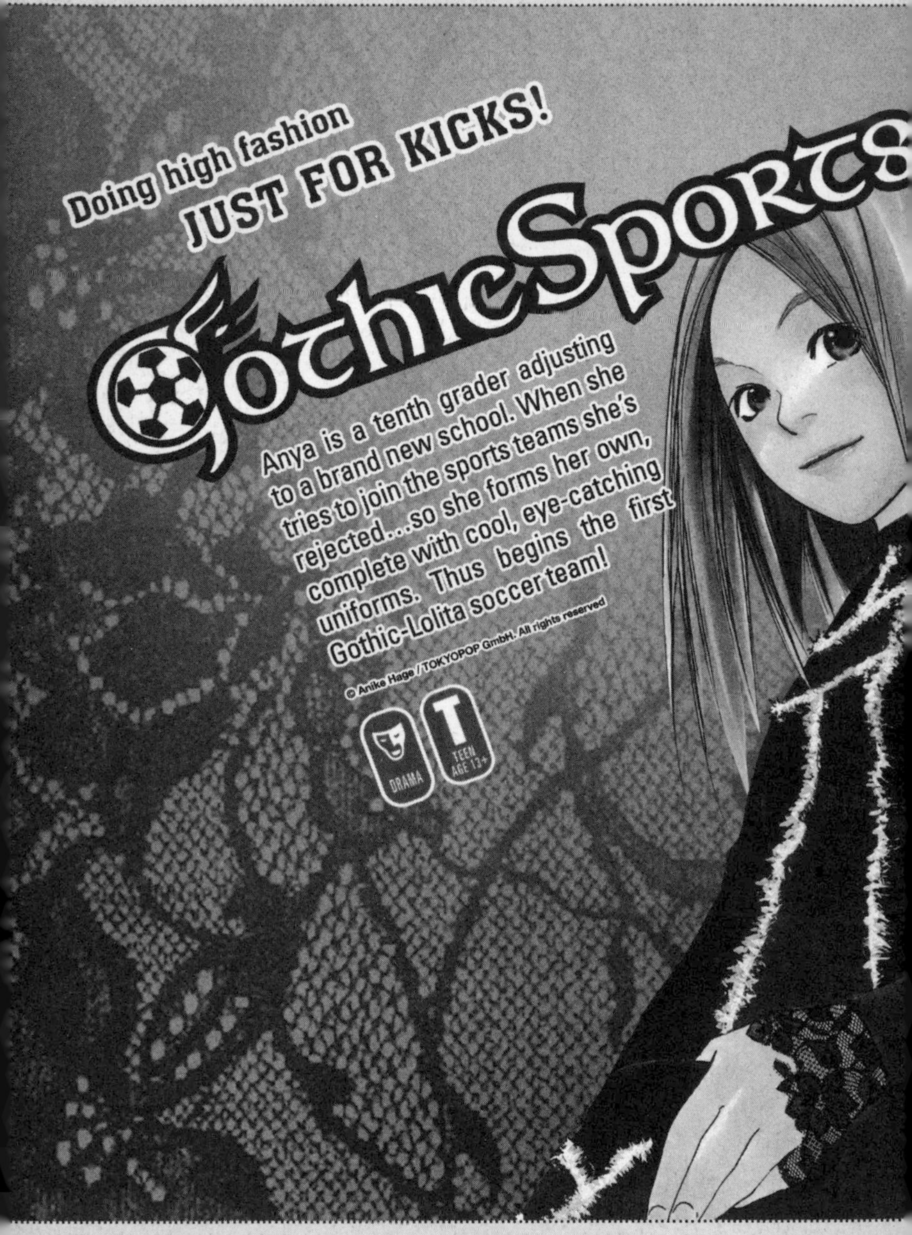
Doing high fashion
JUST FOR KICKS!
GothicSports
Anya is a tenth grader adjusting to a brand new school. When she tries to join the sports teams she's rejected...so she forms her own, complete with cool, eye-catching uniforms. Thus begins the first Gothic-Lolita soccer team!
© Anike Hage / TOKYOPOP GmbH. All rights reserved
DRAMA
T
TEEN AGE 13+

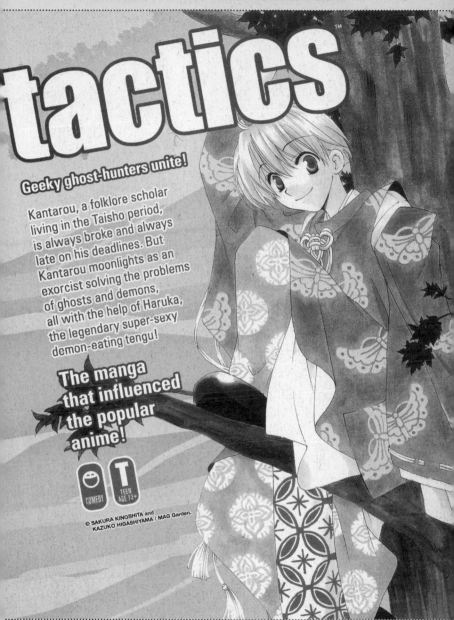

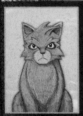

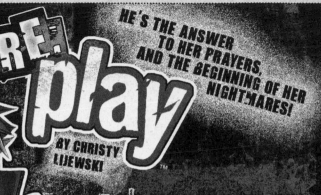

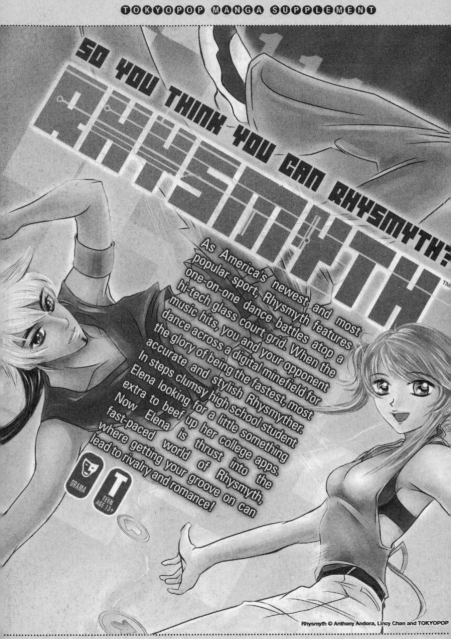

# SO YOU THINK YOU CAN RHYSMYTH?

## RHYSMYTH™

As America's newest and most popular sport, Rhysmyth features one-on-one dance battles atop a hi-tech glass court grid. When the music hits, you and your opponent dance across a digital minefield for the glory of being the fastest, most accurate and stylish Rhysmyther.

In steps clumsy high school student Elena looking for a little something extra to beef up her college apps. Now Elena is thrust into the fast-paced world of Rhysmyth, where getting your groove on can lead to rivalry and romance!

DRAMA

T
TEEN
AGE 13+

FOR MORE INFORMATION VISIT: WWW.TOKYOPOP.COM

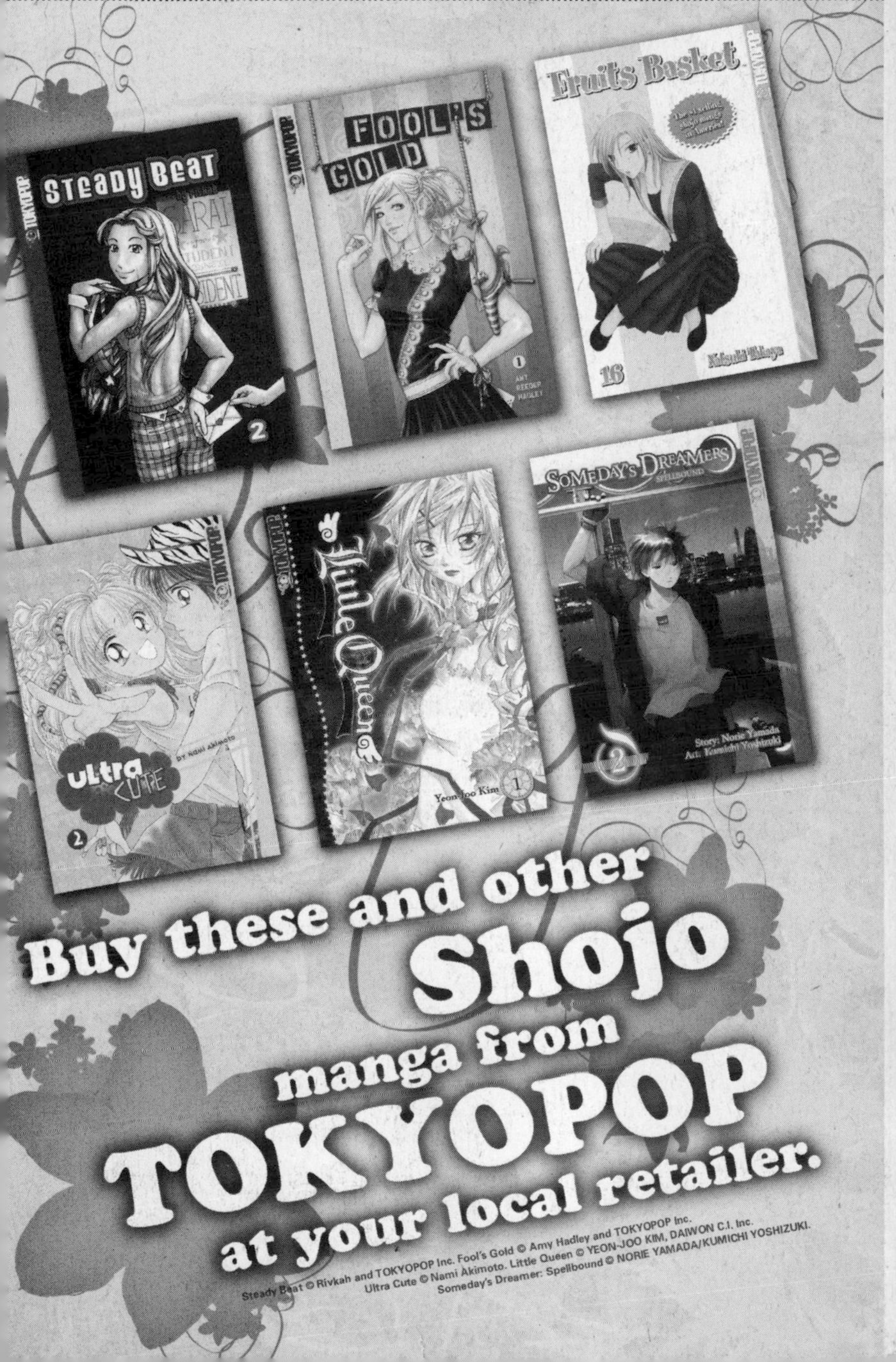
STEADY BEAT
2
FOOL'S GOLD
Fruits Basket
16
SOMEDAY'S DREAMERS
SPELLBOUND
ultra CUTE
Little Queen
Yeon-Joo Kim
Buy these and other
Shojo
manga from
TOKYOPOP
at your local retailer.
Steady Beat © Rivkah and TOKYOPOP Inc. Fool's Gold © Amy Hadley and TOKYOPOP Inc.
Ultra Cute © Nami Akimoto. Little Queen © YEON-JOO KIM, DAIWON C.I. Inc.
Someday's Dreamer: Spellbound © NORIE YAMADA/KUMICHI YOSHIZUKI.

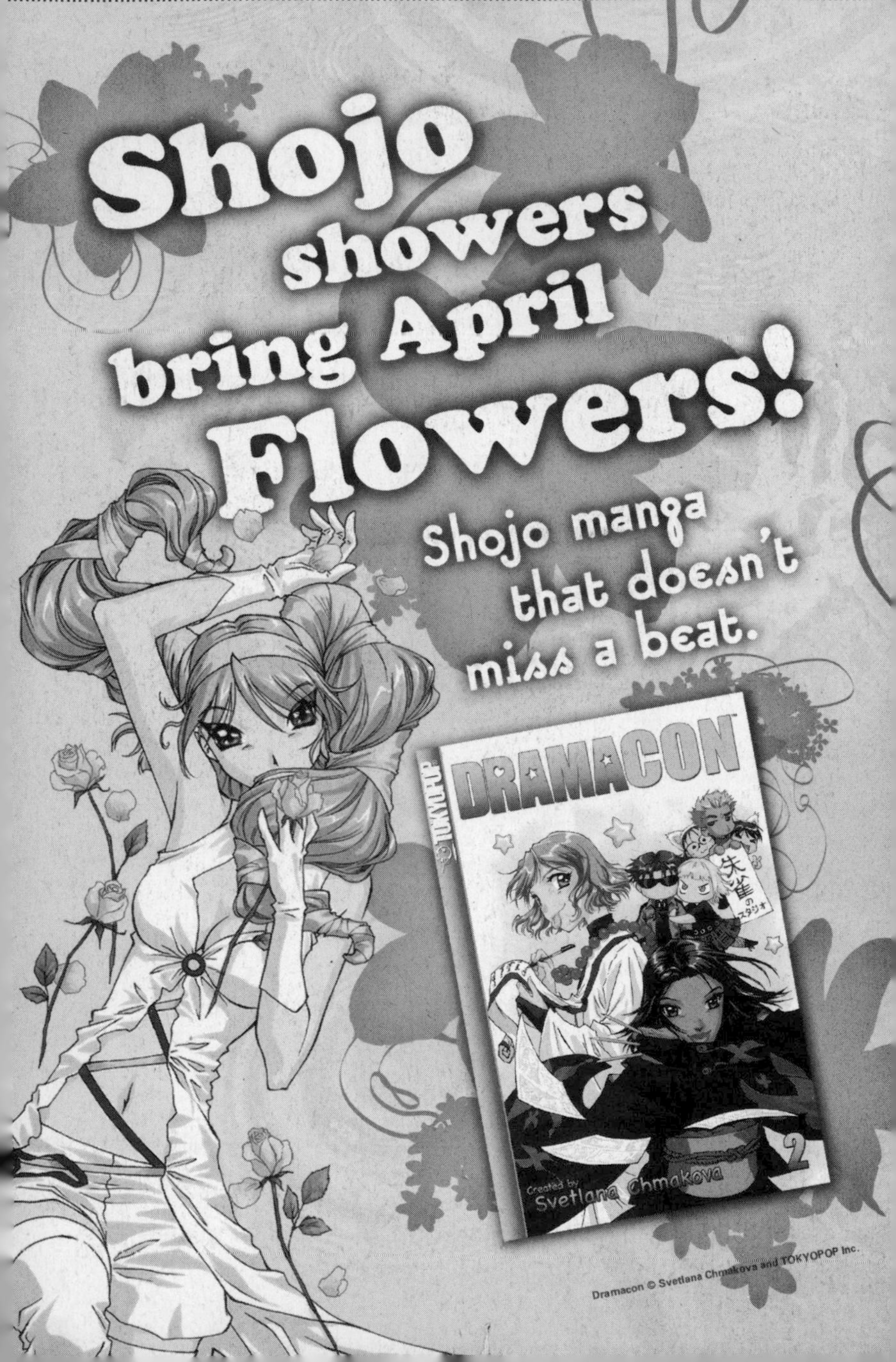
Shojo showers bring April Flowers!
Shojo manga that doesn't miss a beat.
DRAMACON
TOKYOPOP
Created by Svetlana Chmakova
2
Dramacon © Svetlana Chmakova and TOKYOPOP Inc.

# STOP!

## This is the back of the book.
## You wouldn't want to spoil a great ending!

This book is printed "manga-style," in the authentic Japanese right-to-left format. Since none of the artwork has been flipped or altered, readers get to experience the story just as the creator intended. You've been asking for it, so TOKYOPOP® delivered: authentic, hot-off-the-press, and far more fun!

# DIRECTIONS

If this is your first time reading manga-style, here's a quick guide to help you understand how it works.

It's easy… just start in the top right panel and follow the numbers. Have fun, and look for more 100% authentic manga from TOKYOPOP®!

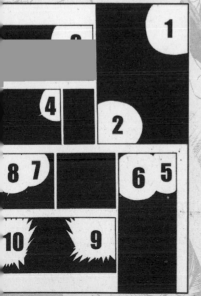

NOV 09

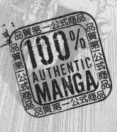

100%
AUTHENTIC
MANGA